DB125 You and your money

Personal Finance

Edited by Jerome De Henau and Jonquil Lowe

This publication forms part of the Open University module DB125 *You and your money*. Details of this and other Open University modules can be obtained from Student Recruitment, The Open University, PO Box 197, Milton Keynes MK7 6BJ, United Kingdom (tel. +44 (0)300 303 5303; email general-enquiries@open.ac.uk).

Alternatively, you may visit the Open University website at www.open.ac.uk where you can learn more about the wide range of modules and packs offered at all levels by The Open University.

The Open University, Walton Hall, Milton Keynes MK7 6AA

First published 2019

Edited and designed by The Open University.

Typeset by The Open University.

Printed in the United Kingdom by Bell and Bain Ltd, Glasgow

ISBN 978 1 4730 2498 4

1.1

Contents

Personal acknowledgements

Personal Finance is the result of a collaborative process, and invaluable contributions were made by a number of people. We are grateful to our external assessor Lindsey Appleyard, Research Fellow at Coventry University, and Sam Harborne, an OU student, for their helpful feedback during the writing of this book.

We are indebted to our amazing OU colleagues who have authored some of the chapters and tirelessly peer-reviewed them all: Alan Shipman, Hedley Stone and Rajiv Prabhakar. Invaluable feedback was also gratefully received from Martin Higginson. Our thanks to Hor Chan, too, for his contribution to the early drafts of some sections, and to the following previous OU authors who have generously allowed us to build on their earlier work: George Callaghan, Ian Fribbance, Martin Higginson and Sue Himmelweit.

We would also like to thank our curriculum managers, Nic Morris and Jo Hoskins, for their professional and enthusiastic project coordination; our patient and talented editors, Natasha Wiseman and Andrew Farrow; Gareth Hudson, who has provided frictionless project management, and Chris Hough and Katie Belcher for their superb design. And also, of course, our many OU colleagues working tirelessly behind the scenes, involved in copy-editing, proofreading, and providing media assistance, archive research, copyright clearance, and so much more. An extra thank-you goes to Nic Morris for her great cover photograph – a second career clearly beckons!

Jerome De Henau and Jonquil Lowe, 2018

Disclaimer

Contributors

George Callaghan, Senior Lecturer in Economics, The Open University

Jerome De Henau, Senior Lecturer in Economics,
The Open University

Ian Fribbance, Executive Dean, Faculty of Arts and Social Sciences,
The Open University

Martin Higginson, Senior Lecturer in Economics, The Open University

Susan Himmelweit, Emeritus Professor, The Open University

Jonquil Lowe, Senior Lecturer in Economics and Personal Finance,
The Open University

Rajiv Prabhakar, Senior Lecturer in Personal Finance,
The Open University

Alan Shipman, Lecturer in Economics, The Open University

Hedley Stone, Lecturer in Economics, The Open University

Preface

Wherever you live in the world, you need to manage your money well. In some countries, provision of state support if you fall ill, lose your job or retire has always been limited, or non-existent. In many others, including the UK, the comprehensive state welfare systems that were established in the previous century are being rolled back. As a result, you are increasingly expected to take care of your own financial well-being, in good times and in bad.

Personal Finance has been written as part of the learning material for the Open University module DB125 *You and your money*. It offers insight into managing your money and covers key issues, such as: where your income comes from and where it goes; the role of debt, saving and investing; housing; insurance; caring decisions; and saving for retirement.

This book includes an introduction to budgeting and the household balance sheet, which are powerful tools to aid managing your money. Throughout, there are activities to reinforce your understanding of the subjects covered, and to prompt you to reflect on how the ideas and techniques described relate to your own life. You'll also find a useful glossary of terms at the back.

But *Personal Finance* also drills deeper, seeking to explain how economic, social and political systems shape the way we all conduct our lives. It explores alternative systems and cultures, drawing on data and case studies from around the globe. To aid this exploration, you will be gently introduced to economic perspectives and some economic tools.

Therefore, this book has two aims: to help you manage your own personal finances better, which could improve your current and future financial well-being (enabling you to do the things you value); and to help you take the initial few steps into the subject of economics, explored through the context of how you use and manage your own money.

Whether you are reading *Personal Finance* as part of your formal studies at The Open University (or elsewhere) or from general interest, we are confident that it will enrich your understanding and analysis of the world, and enhance the financial decisions you make as part of your everyday life.

Chapter 1
Personal finance – setting the context

Alan Shipman and Hedley Stone

Contents

1 Introduction

Few of us have enough money for all the things we'd like to achieve in life. As most things have a price, people must continually decide what they most need, and how they can afford it. Moreover, money spent today won't be available tomorrow, whereas money put aside in a safe place allows more to be spent later on. Even the better-off must make choices over how to manage their money, and good money management is vital for the less well-off.

Financial constraints prevent most people from achieving all their goals immediately. If there isn't enough money available to simultaneously take a holiday next year, give to a charity, get married and buy a flat, we must decide what's most important. There needs to be a **trade-off** between using money and resources in some ways, rather than in others.

Trade-off
A sacrifice of something in order to have (more of) something else.

However, personal finance is not just a household affair. The decisions people make and the outcomes of those decisions are closely bound to the wider social, economic and political background against which our lives play out.

So we must manage our money, but we will seldom have complete control. This chapter starts your exploration of how to understand and make the most of this state of affairs by introducing you to four broad themes, which will be used throughout *Personal Finance*. These four themes are likely to affect you and your money wherever you are, and whatever stage in life you have reached.

- **The changing economic, political and social context**

  How changes in society, politics and the economy impact on the decisions made by individuals and households, and how their decisions affect the economy as a whole.

- **Individuals, households and other relationships**

  How an individual's financial decisions can be influenced by, and impact on, other members of the same household and wider communities, such as extended family, work, neighbourhood and other institutions.

- **Economics and the real world**

  An introduction to economic approaches and the extent to which they explain and aid financial decision-making.

- **The life course and financial planning**

  How financial products and other strategies enable households to allocate resources through time with the aim of achieving goals and building **financial resilience**.

Financial resilience
The ability to cope financially with life events or quickly return to the pre-event financial situation.

Sections 2 to 5 of this chapter outline each of these themes in turn, and how they relate to personal finance.

Box 1.1 What are 'households' and 'families'?

Throughout this book a 'household' is defined as: 'one person living alone or a group of people (not necessarily related) living at the same address who share cooking facilities and share a living room, sitting room, or dining area' (ONS, 2016, p. 2).

A 'family' is defined as: 'a married, civil partnered or cohabiting couple with or without children, or a lone parent, with at least one child, who live at the same address. Children may be dependent or non-dependent' (ONS, 2016, p. 2).

These were the definitions in use by the UK Office of National Statistics (ONS) when the data for this book were gathered.

Official definitions of households and families used in other countries are similar but not always exactly the same, despite attempts to unify statistical definitions worldwide. We have kept these variations in mind when comparing household statistics.

---

2 The changing economic, political and social context

The financial decisions households need to make, and the opportunities and constraints around those decisions, are inevitably affected by changes in the world around them. While the different types of change are endless, we have chosen to focus on the following key changes that now affect most people in most parts of the world:

- **demography**
- public policy
- financial service provision
- technology.

You will encounter others from time to time in this book, but these four make their presence felt throughout *Personal Finance*.

Demography
The structure of a country's population taking account of factors such as age, sex and ethnicity.

2.1 Demographic change

In most parts of the world, people are living longer and the average age of populations is rising. People living longer (increasing **longevity**) is generally good news, especially if accompanied by good health in later life. But increasing longevity means that most people must plan for a longer life, and manage their money over a greater length of time, including when they are no longer able or willing to work.

Longevity
The length of an individual's life (usually measured in years).

Longer lives also contribute to growth in countries' populations, when the rate at which people are dying falls below the rate at which they are being born. However, an increasing number of countries have also seen a fall in the rate at which people are being born, to the point at which their populations have stopped growing.

Declining birth rates are associated with a fall in **fertility rate**. When a country's fertility rate falls below 2, normally its population will fall in the long-term, unless people from other countries immigrate there.

Fertility rate
The average number of children (live births) per woman.

Table 1.1 Estimated fertility rates (children per woman), selected countries, 1950–2015

Country/region	1950–55	1970–75	1990–95	2010–15
Emerging countries, for example:	**6.06**	**5.40**	**3.36**	**2.65**
China	6.03	4.77	1.90	1.60
India	5.90	5.41	3.83	2.44
Brazil	6.10	4.68	2.72	1.78
South Africa	6.05	5.50	3.34	2.55
Kenya	7.48	7.99	5.65	4.10
Industrialised countries, for example:	**2.82**	**2.16**	**1.67**	**1.67**
Russia	2.85	2.03	1.54	1.70
US	3.31	2.03	2.03	1.88
Germany	2.13	1.71	1.30	1.43
France	2.75	2.30	1.71	1.98
Italy	2.36	2.32	1.27	1.43
UK	2.18	2.01	1.77	1.88
Japan	2.96	2.13	1.48	1.41

Source: UN (2017), Table A.22

Emerging countries (or economies)
Countries that are getting richer by emerging from economic isolation and/or newly industrialising (also called 'developing countries').

Industrialised countries (or economies)
Countries with relatively high incomes per inhabitant and mature industrial structures (also called 'developed countries').

Activity 1.1 Reading a table

Allow 15 minutes for this activity.

1   Look at Table 1.1 and describe any patterns you can see in the data it shows.

2   Think of some possible reasons for fertility rates appearing to be in decline. When thinking about the reasons, it might help to reflect on your own family situation, or recent generations of people you know.

Comment

1   According to Table 1.1, fertility rates have trended downwards almost everywhere. By 2010−15, fertility rates had dropped below 2 in some of the **emerging countries** of Asia (China) and Latin America (Brazil), as well as in North America and Europe. Fertility rates were higher in emerging countries than in more developed, **industrialised countries** to start with in the 1950s.

2   The second question cannot be answered by looking at the data in this table. A number of economic, social and political factors may have contributed to the fall in fertility rates. For example, some people may have chosen to have fewer children than their parents for

social reasons (e.g. smaller families allow more educational and work opportunities for women), and because it is expensive to raise children. Limiting family size has become easier as contraception enables some women to choose whether to have children and, if so, how many.

Some people may have been forced to have fewer children than their parents – as in China, which enforced a one-child policy on urban households between 1979 and 2016 (BBC, 2015). And in some countries, people's increased focus on work, and a greater proportion of younger people living alone, may have reduced the number of couples having children.

You have probably thought of other factors that have also contributed to falling fertility rates, in some or all of the places where it's happened.

The prospect of an ageing and declining population, caused by rising longevity and falling fertility rates, poses many challenges for countries' residents and governments. These include the question of how to pay pensions to a rising number of retired people, and provide the care they sometimes need in later life, when there are simultaneously fewer people of working age – whose taxes help pay for these, or who could provide care and financial support for their own older relatives.

You will look at some of these challenges in more detail in Chapters 8 and 9 of *Personal Finance*.

2.2 Public policy changes: shifting responsibilities

For much of the twentieth century, governments around the world tried to promote their citizens' economic and social well-being by taking over, or sharing, some of the problems they faced. Social policies shifted some responsibilities from individuals and their families on to government agencies, employers, and 'third sector' organisations, such as **friendly societies**, charities and trade unions. This mainly took the form of expanded **welfare state** arrangements, especially in Western and Eastern Europe.

In many countries, essential services such as schooling and social housing were increasingly provided by the state free of charge or with a **subsidy**, paid for out of general taxation. Tax proceeds also provided

Friendly societies
Membership organisations where, in return for regular small payments, members could claim financial support if unable to work due to, say, illness or old age. Some still exist today.

Welfare state
A system where the state funds or provides public services and redistributes income and wealth to provide social protection to its citizens.

Subsidy
Money paid to reduce the purchase price of a product or service.

basic benefits for people with too little income to support a minimum standard of living. Healthcare could also be financed out of general taxation – for example, the National Health Service (NHS) in the UK – or through government- or employer-subsidised insurance schemes. Financing was introduced for a range of other benefits (including old-age pensions, and income for people unable to work) through state-run social insurance schemes. These insure against risks (like unemployment or sickness) for which affordable private insurance is not readily available on the market. Social (or national) insurance works by everyone paying into the same scheme, so that money is there for those who become entitled to claim. If you have worked in the UK, you may have seen **National Insurance contributions** as an item on your pay slip.

National Insurance contributions
A UK tax paid by both workers and employers that forms the basis for entitlement to a range of state benefits, including a state pension.

However, in the past 50 years, there has been some reversal of this trend of state-provided or subsidised essential services. Policy has been changing in many countries, so that responsibilities shift from government back on to households. Some of the most generous welfare states have been scaled down by restricting some social benefits to those who most need them, and introducing charges for public services that used to be free.

There are many motivations for this policy shift. Governments argue that they can no longer afford such social protections or that most people are now sufficiently well-off not to need them anymore. But there are also arguments that welfare provision has harmful side-effects, for example making people too reliant on the state and discouraging them from working and supporting themselves.

Risk
Where the chance of something happening can be measured or estimated.

Box 1.2 'The great risk shift'

Scaling down the welfare state not only transfers financial responsibility back on to households, but also entails a transfer of **risk**. A risk is something that might happen to alter the outcome of an action or plan, with either negative or positive consequences. One way to measure someone's exposure to risk is to observe how much their situation is subject to rapid and erratic change over time. For example, someone whose income jumps around, receiving a lot of money in some weeks and very little in others, is likely to be more at risk financially than someone who can rely on the same sum of money coming in each week.

Economist Jacob Hacker examined changes in the risks faced by families in the US by measuring the variability of their incomes – how rapidly these changed in different years. He found a sharp increase in this measure of risk in the 1990s (Hacker, 2006). This reflected a reduction in the social benefits available to low-paid American families, greater insecurity of employment for many of those families and a move away from the sort of **progressive tax system** that can reduce income inequality by making the better-off pay more.

Political and social change are, according to Hacker, 'slowly eroding the confidence of middle-class Americans that they'd have stable jobs, generous benefits, and smooth upward mobility, and their children would enjoy greater economic security than they'd enjoyed' (Hacker 2006, p. 12).

Progressive tax system
A system of taxation that is characterised by an average tax rate that increases with taxable income. In other words, the higher a person's income, the greater the proportion taken away in tax.

The American welfare state is scattered with programmes such as food stamp schemes and tiny cash benefits

The scaling down of welfare states has often occurred without much public resistance, especially when accompanied by promises of lower taxation and rising economic prosperity. But in some countries, a combination of reduced social protection, low incomes and high unemployment has become a contributor to economic migration – people going abroad to find better-paid work.

Some countries traditionally allowed, or even welcomed, immigration, on the basis that this helped their economies to grow by preventing labour shortages and boosting tax revenue. This idea is confirmed by some economic studies, such as Dustmann and Frattini (2014) concerning the UK. The richer countries of Europe and North America were the biggest destinations for international migrants in the early twenty-first century (IOM, 2017) – many were migrants from within the same region, such as from one EU member state to another (Eurostat, 2017). But over time, policies have tended to become more restrictive, especially among countries with larger welfare states.

2.3 A changing financial services industry

Financial services
The part of the economy that delivers financial products, including banking and insurance.

Many countries, emerging as well as industrialised, have in the past 50 years experienced a growth of their **financial services** sector. This is the part of an economy that delivers financial products, including: current accounts, credit (loans), savings accounts, insurance policies, payment and money-transfer services, foreign exchange, private pensions, investment funds and financial advice.

Gross domestic product (GDP)
The monetary value of everything produced within a country, in a specified period (usually a year).

In some countries, such as the UK and the US, the financial sector forms a substantial part of the service economy and has become a major source of employment and **gross domestic product (GDP)**. For example, financial services comprised 6.6% of GDP in 2016 in the UK (having peaked at over 9% in 2009), and 7.3% in the US, (OECD, 2017). In comparison, manufacturing's share of UK GDP dropped to 10% in 2016 (EEF 2017), from over 25% in 1970 (by contrast, Germany's manufacturing share of GDP was much higher at 23% in 2016).

Financial sector deregulation and re-regulation

Financial sector growth has been partly a response to public policy changes. Governments inevitably increased the demand for 'retail' financial services (those sold to households) when they reduced their provision of social insurance and other welfare state assistance. At the same time, they made it easier for firms to supply various financial products and services by removing regulations that had previously restricted their availability. For example, until the 1970s most governments made it difficult for households to borrow money for anything except buying a home (with a mortgage) or durable goods (with hire purchase), or to move large sums of money internationally.

The subsequent **deregulation** was followed by rapid growth in the sale of financial services to households. Deregulation (also called liberalisation) was intended to give firms more freedom and incentive to offer a wider range of financial products to a larger number of people and open up the industry to competition between providers within and across national borders.

Financial sector deregulation was part of a wider global trend, from the 1970s onwards, as governments tried to reduce their role in the economy. Other moves in this direction – observed in Eastern Europe, China, India, Latin America (and other emerging countries), as well as the EU and US – included the privatisation of state-owned industries, and reductions in personal and corporate income tax, offset by efforts to reduce public spending.

However, deregulation has not been plain sailing and the twenty-first century has seen some re-regulation of financial services too. Tighter regulation has sought to avert damage to the economy caused by the financial sector taking on too much risk – such risk-taking had the damaging consequences of the **global financial crisis** in 2008. Regulation of financial businesses has also proved necessary to ensure that providers make certain essential products available to customers, and to tackle the **mis-selling** (see Box 1.3) of inappropriate products.

Deregulation
Removal of state regulation, usually aimed at promoting competition, innovation and new entry.

Global financial crisis
An event that started in the US mortgage market and rapidly brought the international banking sector to the brink of collapse, averted only by governments spending billions on 'bailing out' the banks.

Mis-selling
Selling a product or service that is unnecessary or inappropriate for the buyer, and/or not fully explained to them.

Third-party products
Items sold or distributed by one company but supplied by another (the third party).

Ombudsman scheme
An alternative to going to court, for resolving disputes between consumers and firms. Typically free for consumers to use.

Box 1.3 Mis-selling financial services

Mis-selling can involve inducing customers through misleading or absent information to buy a product that is inappropriate given their circumstances, or that they don't need. It may involve adding on a costly and unnecessary product without customers' knowledge or consent. Cases have arisen in many countries.

India

In 2017 the Reserve Bank of India (the country's central bank) made banks liable for the first time for mis-selling of **third-party products**, such as insurance policies and investment funds. Previously, customers who were mis-sold such products had to pursue their complaint with the third party, but can now complain to the bank concerned and, if necessary, the **ombudsman scheme** for the banking sector (*Economic Times*, 2017).

> ## US
>
> Navient, a major student loan provider, was accused in 2017 of extending high-cost loans for college courses that were never likely to generate the additional earnings for students that were needed for repayment. This resulted in government-led lawsuits against Navient (Cowley and Silver-Greenberg, 2017).
>
> ## UK
>
> In possibly the biggest mis-selling to date, UK banks and other lenders added costly payment protection insurance (PPI) to many of their loans without asking or telling their customers. They were eventually forced to set aside money to refund up to 34 million mis-sold PPI policies (Osborne, 2013). The estimated cost had risen to £40bn by 2016 (Treanor, 2016).
>
> ## Australia
>
> In an echo of the UK experience, in 2017 the Commonwealth Bank of Australia agreed to refund around A$10 million (US $7.7 million) to over 65,000 customers, to whom it had mis-sold consumer credit insurance (CCI) on credit card debts; and another A$586,000 to around 10,000 customers who had excessive CCI added to their home-loans (ASIC, 2017).

Reducing financial exclusion

Financial exclusion
Inability to obtain necessary products and services from financial providers in an appropriate form or at an affordable price.

Governments and regulators also try to make sure that essential financial products are not made unavailable or unaffordable for vulnerable households, a situation termed **financial exclusion**. An important example is ensuring access to a bank account, since this is not only essential for day-to-day transactions but is often also a 'gateway' to being able to apply for other financial products and services.

Basic bank account (BBA)
A bank account with reduced features.

For example, in the UK, because most households need a bank account for receiving wages and social benefits and making payments, regulators ensured that banks would make at least a **basic bank account** (BBA) available to anyone, an initiative later adopted by the European Union (EU) for all its citizens. A BBA allows the holder to deposit money, withdraw it (in a branch or through machines) and make payments. Unlike standard current accounts, it does not allow the holder to become overdrawn (spend more than is in their account), and is unlikely to pay any interest when the account has a positive balance. But BBAs typically avoid the fees and minimum-balance requirements that are often imposed on standard accounts.

Along with accounts run through the Post Office, BBAs helped to reduce the proportion of UK households without bank accounts from 20–25% in the late 1990s, to just a few per cent today (The Poverty Site, n.d.; Rowlingson and McKay, 2017).

2.4 Technological change

Banks have long been the place where most people's experience of financial services begins. They are usually highly visible on the high street and online, and are subject to regulations which make them one of the safest places to keep money. Even when many banks in Europe and North America were at risk of financial collapse in 2007–08, most of their customers were covered by **deposit insurance** that would have stopped them losing their money. Governments at that time also spent large sums of public money to prevent large banks and other retail financial institutions collapsing.

Deposit insurance
A compulsory scheme that refunds depositors (up to a maximum amount) if their bank becomes unable to return their money.

Traditional banking has, however, been greatly affected by technological change. This change is often encouraged by regulators seeking to make long-established banks improve their services and open their markets to new providers.

The early years of the twenty-first century witnessed a growth of new financial technology (fintech), some of which changed the way that banks work, and some enabling other companies to compete with them. Among these technological innovations were:

- **Open banking**, which has made it possible for bank customers to give firms, such as comparison services and retailers, direct access to their bank accounts, making it easier, for example, to compare rival banking services (based on the customer's actual account usage) and to pay for things without the need for plastic cards.

- **Online platforms** that have made 'crowd funding' and peer-to-peer (P2P) lending available as alternative ways for people to borrow money or invest their savings, rather than going to a bank or other traditional financial firm.

- **New ways of accessing banking services through a mobile phone**, which have widened their availability in areas without physical bank branches or fixed-line internet connections.

- **Contactless payments**, allowing account holders to pay small sums through the swipe or tap of a mobile phone or plastic card, eliminating the need for physical cash.

- **Mobile computer applications (apps)** that reduce consumers' costs, for example by monitoring their home electricity consumption or linking their car insurance to how far they travel.

- **Crypto-currencies** (Bitcoin and Ethereum were the early leaders), which aim to function as financial assets and a means of payment that are not directly authorised or controlled by central banks.

- **The 'blockchain'**, a technology pioneered by crypto-currencies, which creates multiple copies of the record of transactions, offering greater security (for example, from hacking and fraud) for money and asset transfers.

Technology changes: once state-of-the-art, the mobile phones of the 1990s soon became obsolete

These rapid changes in financial technology have occurred alongside many other technological changes, including the first steps towards artificial intelligence, driverless vehicles, industrial-scale solar energy and the remote delivery of skilled human services via robots (such as tele-surgery and rescues by drones).

Although past technological changes have created new jobs (which re-employ those who are replaced by machines, once they have acquired new skills), it is possible that the latest innovations will reduce people's employment opportunities on an unprecedented scale. For example, rapid progress in the development of driverless vehicles was already, in 2017, putting at risk the jobs of five million professional drivers (3% of the workforce) in the US (Greenhouse, 2017).

Activity 1.2 Technology and your finances

Allow 5 minutes for this activity.

Can you think of new technologies at home or work, and how they may affect your finances?

Comment

Becoming an expert in new technologies at work may help you to earn more but, if robots replace your job, you'll need a new way to earn your living. In our home life, new technology means that many things from cars to fridges are gathering data about how we use them, which may affect, for example, the cost of our car and home insurance.

2.5 Building financial capability to improve decision-making

The complexity of financial products and the dangers of mis-selling have led to calls for individuals and households to develop more **financial capability**. The exact meaning of financial capability is open to debate, and evolving as institutions and practices change, but there is a broad consensus across countries about its key components.

Financial capability
The knowledge, skills, attitudes and behaviours that mean people manage money well, both day-to-day and through significant life events, and can handle periods of financial difficulty.

In the US, the National Financial Capability Study (NFCS) focuses on four key components of financial capability (Finra, 2016):

- making ends meet
- planning ahead
- managing financial products
- financial knowledge and decision-making.

In the UK, six components of financial capability are favoured (Finney and Hayes, 2015):

- making ends meet
- planning ahead
- organised money management
- controlling spending
- staying informed
- choosing products.

Getting on top of your finances requires knowledge and planning

Greater financial capability can, along with appropriate regulation, help people to find the right financial services and avoid buying inappropriate ones. Advocates of financial capability argue that the more financially capable people become, the less risk they run of, for example, making purchases they regret, saving too little, or getting into too much debt.

One intention of this book, *Personal Finance*, is to help you expand your financial capability in all these areas. An aspect of this is understanding key financial concepts.

Activity 1.3 Are you equipped to handle your financial affairs?

Allow 15 minutes for this activity.

Part of being financially capable is having relevant financial knowledge so that you understand the impact of events on your money, and the potential implications of choices that you make.

The following questions, designed to test financial knowledge, are an extract from a survey constructed by the Organisation for Economic Cooperation and Development (OECD). The survey is used by many countries worldwide to measure and track the financial capability of their citizens.

1 Five brothers are going to be given a gift of $1000 in total to share between them. Now imagine that the brothers have to wait for one year to get their share of the $1000 and inflation stays at 2%. In one year's time will they be able to buy:

    (a) the same as $1000 today

    (b) the same as $980 today, or

    (c) the same as $1020 today?

2 You lend $25 to a friend one evening and he gives you $25 back the next day. How much interest has he paid on this loan?

3 Suppose you put $100 into a savings account with a guaranteed interest rate of 2% per year. You don't make any further payments into this account and you don't withdraw any money. How much would be in the account at the end of the first year, once the interest payment is made?

4 [Following on from Question 3 above], how much would be in the account at the end of five years? Would it be more than $110, exactly $110, or less than $110?

5   If someone offers you the chance to make a lot of money it is likely that there is also a chance that you will lose a lot of money. True or False?

6   High inflation means that the cost of living is increasing rapidly. True or False?

7   It is less likely that you will lose all of your money if you save it in more than one place. True or False?

Source: OECD (2017, Table 2, pp. 15–16)

Comment

The answers to Activity 1.3 are given at the end of this chapter.

When you have read all of *Personal Finance*, and completed the activities, you should be able to confidently answer all of these questions.

_____

3 Individuals, households and other relationships

The ways in which people manage their financial affairs depend on the kinds of households they live in. Even in a single-person household, where one person has sole responsibility for financial decisions, their decisions may be influenced by relationships to members of other households.

In a multi-person household, one person's financial decisions can affect others, and may be influenced by the preferences and needs of others. Decisions may be reached together, although the power to make the decisions – and so influence the outcomes – may not be equally distributed among the household members. An example of these tensions is around saving for retirement within families: a person doing unpaid work caring for the children often becomes reliant on the main earner to make pension decisions on behalf of the household; but this can lead to poor outcomes for the carer later on, in the event of death or divorce.

3.1 Changing household structure

Living arrangements in many parts of the world have been changing in recent decades, and these changes have financial implications. Table 1.1 in Section 2.1 of this chapter shows that, around the world, fertility rates have been declining, implying a falling average family size. But does this mean that households are also getting smaller on average? Or might there be other factors that are increasing the number of 'extended' families, offsetting any fall in average household size? For example, more elderly relatives moving back in to be cared for by their children.

The answers vary from country to country, but we can learn a lot by looking more closely at data for the UK, which is reasonably typical of long-established, high-income industrial countries. The composition of UK households in 1996 and 2017, as compiled by the Office for National Statistics (ONS) is shown in Table 1.2 (overleaf).

Table 1.2 Types of households in the UK, 1996 and 2017

	1996		2017	
Number of households (millions)	23.7		27.2	
Average household size (people)	2.42		2.39	
Type of household (% of all households)				
One-person households	27.8		28.3	
One-family households	68.4		67.6	
Couple		58.5		57.7
no children			27.4		27.7
dependent children			23.8		22.2
non-dependent children only			7.3		(7.8)
Lone parent		9.9		9.9
Two or more unrelated adults	3.1		2.9	
Multi-family households	0.7		(1.1)	
All households	100		100	

Source: calculated from ONS (2017), Tables 1 and 7

> Please note that the percentages in tables like Table 1.2 do not necessarily add up to exactly 100% due to rounding. For example, the main column for 2017 adds to 99.9% even though all types of household have been counted.
>
> Note, too, that for each year the main column of figures has been broken down in places into sub-categories. For example, in 1996, 58.5% of one-family households were couples and 9.9% were lone parents, which equals 68.4% one-family households in total.

Table 1.2 classifies UK households into four types: One-person, One-family, Two or more unrelated adults, and Multi-family. The distinction between the last three categories can be understood by thinking back over the definition of 'household' and 'family' given in Box 1.1 earlier in this chapter: unrelated adults in a household do not constitute a family as they are not related by kinship, marriage, civil partnership or cohabitation, while families living together, whether related or unrelated, can form a multi-family household.

Because one-family households are a large category (more than two-thirds of all households), Table 1.2 breaks them down into sub-categories:

- In the second column of each year, couples are distinguished from lone parents.

- In the third column of each year, couples are further broken down into those with no children, those with dependent children, and those with children who are not dependent.

Apart from the top two rows, which give actual numbers, the figures in Table 1.2 are percentages of total households. That's why the 'All household' row is 100 for both years. That's 100%, meaning that all households have been classified into one of the rows above. The other numbers in each column show the percentage of households falling into a particular category. So, for example, in 1996, 7.3% of UK households comprised couples with children who were all **non-dependent**.

The data in Table 1.2 show that the 'traditional' UK family, of a couple with children, was still the most common type of household in the early twenty-first century, and that the average number of people in a household had remained stable since the mid 1990s at around 2.4. But the patterns giving rise to this average had changed over that 20-year period.

Non-dependent children

Children (or a child) who have reached a specified minimum age, are not in full-time education, and have no known partner or children.

Activity 1.4   Changing households

Allow 5 minutes for this activity.

Use Table 1.2 to answer the following questions:

1   Which types of household rose as a percentage of the total (i.e. became more common) between 1996 and 2017?

2   Which types of household became less common?

Comment

The answers to Activity 1.4 are given at the end of this chapter.

Households vary within and between countries

3.2 Financial relationships within households

Living arrangements impact directly on many other areas of people's lives, including their finances – how they pay their way, meet their everyday needs, and plan for the future. Although the proportion of one-member households has in many places been rising, most people still live in a multi-person household. Relationships between members of the same household can be complex. They involve issues of power and responsibility, and these in turn have implications for caring for household members and sharing and controlling money between them.

Some households put all their money into one pot. In others, individuals in the household keep some of their own money to themselves. As mentioned at the start of this section, even a one-person household may still have financial relationships with others outside the household: perhaps parents, family, friends or partners that they don't live with. Households may be helping each other financially and sending money to relatives living elsewhere.

Households may also break up: perhaps as a result of separation, divorce or bereavement. The financial effects of such break-ups can be devastating. Death of a partner, relative or friend and divorce are two of the most distressing life events, emotionally and also financially.

Financial stress can be particularly high for lone parents who, while not sharing decisions with another adult, often have to make tough financial choices with limited resources in providing for their children. Figure 1.1 shows the percentage of families headed by single parents in different countries. It shows that the UK's growth in lone parenthood was mirrored in other high-income countries.

This is important because there is evidence (House of Lords, 2017) to suggest that lone parents are more likely to suffer financial exclusion (see Section 2.3 of this chapter) than couples with children.

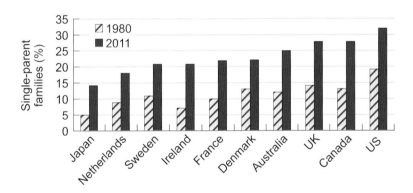

Figure 1.1 Percentage of families with children that are headed by single parents (selected countries) 1980 and 2011 (Chamie, 2016; OECD, 2017)

The proportion of lone-parent families remains much lower (below 10% in the early twenty-first century) in some large 'emerging' countries such as India, China, Indonesia and Turkey. But the large populations of these countries mean that, despite this low proportion, the actual number is high – they now account for most of the children living in lone-parent households worldwide (Chamie, 2016).

4 Economics and the real world

We constantly make simplifications to help us understand the world. You've already seen an example: social scientists divide households into a number of different types based on their composition. But not every household fits easily into those categories – for example, where members divide their time between two households or couples feel very much together even though they live apart because of work, or by choice.

In this section, we are going to look at two types of simplification – one that describes the economy, and the other used by us all as individuals every day. Both shape the way that economists look at the world.

4.1 Households in the economy

In Section 3 of this chapter, we looked at what happens inside households. However, households also play a key role in the wider economy. They are closely connected to two other sectors: government (also called the public sector), comprising central and local government, state agencies and state-owned corporations; and corporations, the sector made up of big businesses, including privately owned financial institutions and small/medium enterprises. The interdependence of these three sectors – where changes in one affect the others – must be taken into account when planning and managing your personal finances. The three sectors are linked together by flows of goods and services, and by flows of money.

The flow of income between sectors of the economy

Circular flow of income
A simple economic model illustrating the exchange of goods, services and money within the economy.

The flows of money between the household, corporate and government sectors are illustrated in Figure 1.2. The arrows show the direction the money travels, from one sector to another. This is one way of depicting what economists call the **circular flow of income**, because money that starts as expenditure by one sector flows as income to the others, and then back to the starting-point as the other sectors spend it.

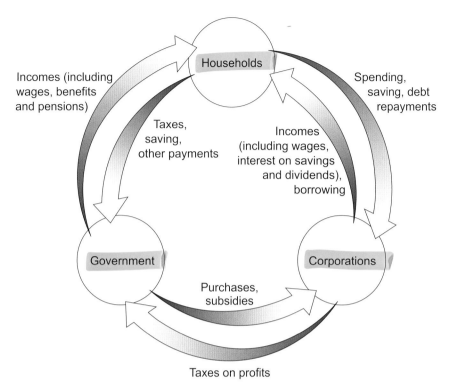

Figure 1.2 Money flows between sectors in the economy

These flows of money illustrate how the sectors are linked together in a continuous process over time. Each pair of money flows from Figure 1.2 is described below and overleaf, along with some examples.

Please note that Figure 1.2 represents what is called the 'domestic economy', ignoring international flows. Therefore, money sent or spent abroad, or spent on goods made abroad by any of the three sectors, and money received from abroad, is not shown.

Households and corporations

The money flow out of households into corporations comprises mainly our spending on goods and services, and savings with/payments to financial corporations. For instance, it includes spending on clothes, food and leisure activities, payments on rent, repayments of debt, paying bank charges, or buying shares and other financial products.

The money flow into households from corporations comprises mainly incomes and loans. For example, it includes income from employment and self-employment, interest on savings accounts, investment income and dividends, and private pensions. It also includes money borrowed using a credit card, and financial payouts, such as from an insurance claim. You will find out about each of these in later chapters.

Households and government

The money flow out of households into government comprises mainly taxes, some savings and some payments to the government. For instance, it includes taxes on income, local property tax (Council Tax in most of the UK), money saved in public banks or government savings schemes (e.g. National Savings & Investments (NS&I) products in the UK, such as premium bonds), and government bonds. It also includes payments for services such as rental payments for living in council properties.

The money flow into households from government includes benefits, tax credits and incomes. For example, retirement pensions and working-age social security benefits, and the income from employment of those working for the government, such as civil servants and firefighters.

Corporations and government

The money flow out of corporations into government comprises mainly taxes, for instance, corporation tax.

The money flow into corporations from the government includes spending on goods and services, and subsidies. For example, purchases of equipment for hospitals, schools and the armed services.

Activity 1.5 Households in the circular flow model

Allow 10 minutes for this activity.

Four of the six arrows in Figure 1.2 show the money flows into and out of households. Try to think of examples of monetary transactions in which you've been involved recently that match these four household money flows.

Comment

There are many different examples that you might have thought of here, such as:

- spending on food at the local supermarket – a money flow from households to corporations

- borrowing money on a credit card – a flow from corporations to households

- picking up state benefits or pension from the Post Office® – a flow from government to households

- income tax – a money flow from households to government.

Box 1.4 Money flows *within* sectors, as well as between them

In the household sector there are flows between members of the same household, flows between different households, and flows to small household-run businesses and to charities. (Charities are neither profit-making businesses nor government bodies. Much of their income is from households and many of the goods and services they provide (typically free) go to households. Therefore, by convention they are included as part of the household sector.)

Examples of flows (or transfers) within households include: 'pocket money to children', a 'housekeeping allowance' from one adult partner to another, and financial support for students or elderly members of the household.

Flows between different parts of the household sector include: households' payments for domestic services, such as childminding and cleaning, and charity donations.

The interdependence of these sectors in the economy means that changes in one can affect the others. For instance, if a large number of households decided to spend less of their income on high street shopping, this might reduce the profits of corporations. It would also reduce the amount of money the government receives through taxes on expenditure – such as value added tax (VAT). Changes in other sectors can, in turn, have an impact on the household sector. For example, if corporations made people unemployed in response to their falling profits, then some household budgets might be severely reduced, and government revenue would fall further because of lower income tax receipts.

Financial decisions are not taken in isolation from the economic context, and decisions by individual households to spend or save more can have a significant effect on the wider economy when added up.

Activity 1.6 Impact of households on the economy

Allow 10 minutes for this activity.

1   Can you think of any ways in which many households taking similar financial decisions might affect the economy?

2   How might such economic changes then have a knock-on effect on the personal financial decisions of households?

Comment

There are many examples you might have thought of, but here's the one we chose:

1   If many households decide to increase their spending because they are confident their income will rise in the future or has risen already, corporations might create more jobs and employ more people in order to produce the extra products that households are willing to buy.

2   This might result in corporations making more profits and some of it could translate into paying higher wages, making at least some households better off, so that they can spend or save more or pay off debts.

Box 1.5 How models can help us understand
the economy

The circular flow of income model shown in Figure 1.2 is an
example of an economic model. A model simplifies reality down to
the essentials, so that these are easier to think about. For example,
Figure 1.2 classifies banks and other financial firms, alongside
manufacturers and other non-financial firms, as 'corporations'.
That's why the flow of income from corporations to households
includes wages, interest on savings, and borrowing. In other
economic models, financial and non-financial firms may be treated
separately.

Models can be used to examine and understand complex interrelationships, identifying what is causing what, and even gauging
the strength of the connection if 'cause' and 'effect' can be
numerically measured. Although they can be extremely helpful in
assessing and acting in complicated situations, it must always be
remembered that models are simplified representations of the real
world – they leave out much of what goes on. Models can help us
to understand the economy, and how households can operate
within it, but they must always be tested against 'real world'
evidence to make sure that they have not excluded something
important or included something trivial, and that their simplifying
assumptions are justified.

4.2 Simplified decisions and the risk of bias

It's not just economists who simplify the real world – we all do it all
the time! However smart and well-educated we are, our ability to make
good decisions, including financial decisions, is limited by the
information we have, and the speed and accuracy with which we can
process it. Humans experience something called **bounded rationality**,
especially in 'interactive' situations where the available actions, and
their likely consequences, depend on what other people know and
choose to do. Before deciding anything, we often have to decide which
decisions are most important, and skip through the smaller ones
quickly in order to focus our attention on the bigger ones.

Bounded rationality
Capacity for reasoned
decision that is
constrained by lack of
time and the ability to
process information.

Some psychologists suggest there are two ways of thinking: a 'slow' approach is when people attempt to be rational, identifying all options and anticipating their likely results, in order to select the best; but the pace of life often requires a 'fast' approach, relying on incomplete or intuitive reasoning to reach a decision without much time and effort. According to Daniel Kahneman, who popularised this distinction (and won a Nobel Prize for Economics in 2002):

> [Fast thinking] operates automatically and quickly, with little or no effort and no sense of voluntary control.
>
> [Slow thinking] allocates attention to the effortful mental activities that demand it, including complex computations. The operations … are often associated with the subjective experience of agency, choice and concentration.
>
> (Kahneman, 2011, pp. 20–21)

Heuristics
Mental short cuts used to guide someone in the direction of probable solutions to a problem, while minimising mental effort.

Many people regard themselves as good intuitive decision-makers – and when the 'fast' approaches are pitted against the 'slow' ones, they tend to fare quite well. This has led some psychologists to argue that a quick intuitive decision will often do as well as a slow, laboriously reasoned one. They argue that humans have evolved to make intuitive decisions whose outcome gets close to the 'rational' outcome, within a fraction of the time and effort this would require. In particular, **heuristics** (rules-of-thumb decisions) can match (or even exceed) the results of those taken with much more thorough and time-consuming evaluation (Gigerenzer and Goldstein, 1996, p. 651). Others point to the sad fate of Buridan's Ass (named after the fourteenth-century philosopher Jean Buridan), which starved to death because it couldn't decide between two equally good sources of food.

According to the Gigerenzer-Goldstein view (which challenges Kahneman's), the 'fast' and 'slow' lanes often lead to the same place, so those in the fast lane get there first (or, in the donkey's case, avoid contemplative starvation).

However, the view that 'fast' decision processes can lead people astray has gained ground, not least because of many experiments that seem to suggest that people are prone to systematic misjudgements (or biases) when they make snap judgements. People's ability to make choices that are beneficial to them, whether using fast or slow judgements, can also be affected by their emotions – as some discover when they react to sadness or stress by 'comfort shopping', only later to regret how much they've spent.

Indecision between two equally good options led to the demise of Buridan's Ass

Psychologists have carried out numerous experiments to show that people, even experts in their field, would tend to make decisions that are biased by their quick judgements and **behavioural traits**. Box 1.6 (overleaf) illustrates why some behavioural traits can affect financial decisions. Can you think of any times when your own financial decisions have been affected by these traits?

Behavioural trait
Psychological features that influence the way an individual processes information and makes a decision, and that reflect their bounded rationality.

Box 1.6 Why behavioural traits affect financial decision-making

Delayed rewards

If we put time and effort into financial planning, it may take years to see the financial benefit. And if our choice means putting money aside, there's an immediate pain (of having less to spend) in exchange for a distant, uncertain gain. So making the right choices for the long-term – and not over-prioritising the present – can be very hard.

Infrequency

Many of our really big financial choices – like changing job, taking a training course, buying a house – aren't taken very often. So there's not much time to practise, but there is much scope to forget what we learned from one big financial choice to the next.

Complexity

There are many types of financial product, often with small differences in design which nevertheless make a very big difference to the way they perform, in different conditions or across varying spans of time. As options become more complex, the reliability of our decision-making deteriorates – and we become more inclined to make no choice, just letting things carry on as they are.

Unpredictability

Financial planning involves projecting ourselves into situations we don't really want to think about – such as what life will be like when we're very old and may need medical care, or what life might be like if we were suddenly unable to work. And even the future's pleasanter aspects can be very hard to predict – ten years ago, did you anticipate the pleasures you now get from your smart phone, your partner, or the things in your fridge?

Inertia

We tend to feel comfortable with (or uncomfortable about changing) our existing arrangements and routines, so we often stick with them even when it might be better to change.

Source: summarised from Thaler and Sunstein, 2009, Chapters 4–6

Companies (including financial institutions) often exploit these biases in their advertisements and marketing, in order to generate more sales:

- Insurers (when allowed to do so) have sometimes used scenes of carnage to sell accident policies, appealing to people's emotions and to our tendency to over-estimate the likelihood of a bad event if its consequences are extremely severe.

- Supermarkets make some goods seem like a bargain by putting them next to a much more expensive item.

- Firms exploit people's fear of missing out on a bargain when they announce that the discount on offer might soon be withdrawn.

- Shops can even exploit our difficulty with doing simple sums when under pressure: 'Buy one get one free' can seem like a better deal than '50% off', until we realise – sometimes after passing through the till – that it gives us the same unit price, and twice as much as we may actually need.

4.3 'Nudging' choices to improve financial decision-making

Given the way that behavioural traits often impair decision-making, some experts have advised governments against leaving people to take important financial decisions unaided. Their solution is to modify the 'architecture' of those decisions so that people are steered towards the choice that turns out to be best for them (when all the information is properly assessed).

Behavioural nudges of this type often turn decision-bias to an advantage. For example, governments that want people to enrol in a pension scheme, without making it compulsory, may make it one that people must opt out of rather than opt into. This approach, making membership of the scheme the **default option**, exploits the 'inertia bias' that leads people to stay put if they haven't time or motivation to move. Or a pension scheme's designers might put the favoured option first on a list of possible options, knowing that people often assume the best has been placed at the top of the list, even if they're actually listed in a random order.

'Nudging' has proved popular with policymakers, and won the economist who popularised it, Richard Thaler, a Nobel Prize in 2017. But its use remains controversial. Critics argue that financial decisions

Behavioural nudges
Indirect suggestions designed to change or influence a person's behaviour.

Default option
Situation or option someone is left in/ with, if they do not act to change it.

are often made unnecessarily complicated (perhaps deliberately) by competing providers and intermediaries, and that people would be able to make unbiased decisions (without being nudged) if governments required those products to be standardised or simplified to make them more open to comparison.

There is also the concern that because government advisors also take uncertain decisions, and can make mistakes, they may sometimes nudge people in a direction that doesn't turn out best for them. Moreover, different governments have different ideologies, so that a nudge favoured by one regime might not be supported by another. As you read through this book, you will think more about these questions.

5 The life course and financial planning

So far, we have set the scene for personal finance by looking at households, the changing context in which they live and work, and the way they interact with other sectors of the economy. We can now begin to consider the ways in which individuals and households can deal with the various challenges that arise with managing their money.

5.1 The life course

Some life events can be planned for: starting a family, taking a course, passing a driving test and reaching retirement age. But they rarely go entirely according to plan; and many other events – such as getting ill or losing a job – can take us by surprise. The 'life course' is a modern term for the age-old idea that people pass through stages in life that follow some sort of pattern, and are predictable to an extent. For many people, a typical pattern of the life course might start with youth, then adolescence, and young adulthood, perhaps going from being single to becoming part of a couple. Adulthood may then entail having dependent children who later on, in turn, become independent. The later part of the life course is usually marked by retirement.

The life course won't be the same for everyone, as some people won't form part of a couple or have children, while others will separate or divorce. Life courses can also change over time. For example, the later stage of 'retirement' did not feature in life courses during early European industrialisation in the nineteenth century, when typical longevity was little longer than the usual length of a working life. Retirement may disappear entirely from the life course of many who are in work today, if they are unable to put aside enough money for a retirement pension, and so are forced to work as long as they physically can. In many emerging countries retirement does not really exist either.

Each of the life-course stages has different financial implications for individuals and their households. Importantly, thinking about our life course encourages planning ahead for each of these different stages. For example, many people delay thinking about their provision for retirement because they don't want to think about growing older or death, but they often come to regret this later in life when they realise that they would have benefited from earlier planning.

Many people in India, lacking pensions, work into old age

Activity 1.7 Planning for your own life course

Allow 15 minutes for this activity.

1   Try jotting down what you think your personal and financial circumstances might be in five years' time. Then make a list of goals that you would like to achieve by then.

2   If you had performed a similar exercise five years ago, what would you have expected your current personal and financial situation to be? How close would it have been to what has actually happened to you?

3   Does your response to Question 2 affect what you think your circumstances might be in ten years' time?

Comment

One of the authors of this chapter found the concept of 'globally networked computers' amusing but irrelevant on first hearing about it in 1990, but they were working for an internet-based company by 1995. The past, while not always a reliable guide to the future, can be a good reminder of its unpredictability.

5.2 Financial planning through the life course

Although life is full of unusual events and experiences, anticipation of the typical features of the life course makes it possible to map out some of the things that everyone must think about, and plan ahead for, in relation to their personal finances.

As we have already touched on in this chapter, financial planning involves making decisions, in order to prepare an individual or household for future stages of life and possible future events. It also involves managing the present stage of life, both to achieve immediate goals and to free up the resources needed for planning ahead.

A tool to help decision-making

There is a decision-making tool widely used in many different contexts (such as business and career planning) that can be adapted for use in financial planning. The exact origin of the tool is unknown. It is nicknamed GROW, after the acronym formed by its keywords: Goals, Resources, Options and (this term varies, but commonly) What next?

In Figure 1.3 (overleaf), we have adapted this tool for financial planning decisions by adjusting the labels and adding a fifth stage – Evaluate and Review. So you could call our version a GROW-ER tool! This fifth stage emphasises that financial planning is an ongoing process that needs to adapt as circumstances change.

We have also added a reminder to the tool that financial planning is affected by changes in the wider social, political and economic context, and the collective decisions of households also impact on that context.

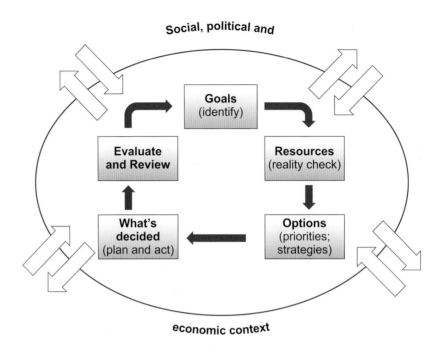

Figure 1.3 The GROW-ER financial planning tool (adapted from the GROW model)

Opportunity cost
The cost of having (or doing) something, measured in terms of the best alternative that could have been had (or done) instead.

Box 1.7 Stages of the GROW-ER financial planning tool

- **Goals**
  An individual or household needs to identify their aims and ambitions in the short-, medium- and long-term.

- **Resources**
  What income and other resources are available to meet those goals? Life is full of hard financial choices: spending more on one thing means having less to spend on other things. When doing (or buying) something involves giving up something else, the real cost is what would have been done (or bought) instead, but now can't be. This is called the **opportunity cost**. For example, if I could put some money into a top-rated savings account this month, but instead spend it on a lottery ticket that wins nothing, the money from the savings account that I missed out on is the opportunity cost of my spending decision. (At the start of the chapter we mentioned trade-offs between different decisions. Opportunity costs are used to measure trade-offs between these different goals.)

- **Options**
  If (as is likely) resources mean that not all goals can be met, goals must be put into some order of priority and/or scaled back, through agreement of what is most important and realistically achievable. This stage also includes identifying the strategies available to pursue prioritised goals. For example, if the priority is building up a deposit for buying a home, there are various strategies for saving money and various financial products that promise to protect and grow those savings. These must all be evaluated and compared.

- **What's decided**
  This involves selecting the most suitable option to form a definite plan and putting that plan into action. If several people (household members or others) are needed to make the plan work, responsibilities must be divided up between them.

- **Evaluate and Review**
  The plan must be regularly monitored to see how well it is performing, taking account of any changes in personal circumstances and the wider context, and any new options that become available. The plan may need to be revised – by running through the GROW process again – if the actions taken so far aren't meeting the goals, or if the goals and priorities have changed. That's why the financial planning process (Figure 1.3) is shown as circular.

Activity 1.8 Using the GROW-ER financial planning tool

Allow 10 minutes for this activity.

1   Take a look at the list of goals that you made for Question 1 of Activity 1.7. Have you listed the goals in any particular order?

2   Now list the goals again, in order of priority for you, given your circumstances and resources.

3   Are there any trade-offs you have to make between your goals? And has this exercise prompted you to rethink any of your goals?

Comment

There are an endless number of goals that you may have; also, different people will prioritise the same goals in different ways. However, as shown in Box 1.6, we all have a tendency to prioritise having something today rather than in the future (which is not necessarily good financial planning). One reason for using a financial planning tool is that it can prompt us to think about more distant, but important goals.

Risks and returns of financial decisions

Return
The actual or expected reward from saving or making an investment, which may comprise a flow of income and/or a profit or loss due to a change in the value of the investment.

There are actually rewards sometimes for not spending now in order to have more to spend later. If you are looking to build up a target amount for a future purchase or a pension, then just a few years' delay in starting to put the money aside can greatly increase the amount you have to put aside, to be sure of meeting the target. In addition, many financial products involve trade-offs of their own. For instance, there tends to be a trade-off between the **return** on investment and the risk it involves: the higher the expected return, the higher the risk attached.

Weighing up the risks and returns of financial decisions

Choosing the right financial product depends not only on how much risk – if any – can be afforded, but also how risk averse a person or household is. Risk aversion is the preference for a lower but more certain return, rather than a higher but less certain return, **other things being equal**.

Activity 1.9 Your attitude towards risk

Allow 10 minutes for this activity.

1   When it comes to your own personal finances, do you think you are risk averse, or a risk taker?

2   What changes in your circumstances might affect your answer to Question 1?

Comment

Some of the circumstances that might affect your attitude to risk include whether or not you have children, your age, and your economic circumstances.

Later chapters of *Personal Finance* (especially Chapter 5, Savings and investments, and Chapter 7, Insurance and life events) will invite you to think more about what kinds of risk you might want to take, your attitudes to risk, and how these might change at different stages of your life course.

Other things being equal

From the Latin *ceteris paribus*, this term is used by economists and others to indicate that while changing one factor, other factors remain unchanged.

6 Conclusion

In this chapter, you have started to consider how the financial decisions we make are much more complex than they may seem at first, being affected by factors such as the shifting economic context and the types of households we live in.

Given this complexity, Section 1 outlined four themes that will be used throughout *Personal Finance* to organise our thinking. Section 2 then described some of the main social and economic changes that have increased people's scope and need to manage their personal finances. In Section 3 we considered changes in households and ways of living, and the importance of looking at the interrelationships between individuals and their households. Section 4 introduced you to the idea of using a simple model as a way of making sense of often complex relationships. It also included a warning to beware of making assumptions that people will always act rationally and in their own best interests: we are all beset by behavioural traits. These traits can impair our judgement and enable providers to influence our decisions – a topic you'll return to in Chapter 3 when you will look at advertising and marketing. Section 5 described the importance of change over the life course, and introduced a financial planning tool that can help you to navigate through the changes.

Understanding this broader social and economic context (and the models and tools introduced in this chapter) will help you work through the rest of this book, and to develop an understanding of the role of personal finance in a consumer society, such as the UK. It will help to explain why financial capability has become an important issue for government, financial providers, financial regulators and consumer watchdogs. And above all, it should enable you to enhance your own financial capability, making the most of the money available to you, and using it to better achieve the things you value.

Answers to activities in Chapter 1

Answers to Activity 1.3

1   The correct answer is b) $980. This question tests whether you understand the impact of rising prices (inflation) on the buying power of your money. You'll learn about this in Chapter 2.

2   The correct answer is none. This question tests your understanding of the concept of interest. You'll learn about this in Chapters 4 and 5 which look at debt, savings and investments.

3   The correct answer is $102. This tests your ability to work out the amount of interest on savings.

4   The correct answer is more than $110. This is testing whether you are aware of 'compounding' (the way interest is earned on interest added to your original balance). You will study this in Chapters 4 and 5.

5   This is true. It's a fundamental rule of savings and investments, which you will look at in Chapter 5.

6   This answer is also true. This is testing your understanding of the term 'inflation'.

7   This answer is also true. It is a key way of protecting yourself against the risk of bad investment outcomes. You'll look at this more deeply in Chapter 5.

Answers to Activity 1.4

1   There was a small rise in the proportion of:

   o   one-person households (from 27.8% to 28.3%)
   o   multi-family households (from 0.7% to 1.1%).

2   There was a corresponding decline in the proportion of one-family households, from 68.4% to 67.6%. Within this category, there was a rise in the proportion of households with no children and those with non-dependent children, and a corresponding fall in the proportion with dependent children. The proportion of households comprising two or more unrelated adults declined slightly, from 3.1% in 1996 to 2.9% in 2017.

References

Australian Securities & Investments Commission (ASIC) (2017) *Commonwealth Bank to Refund over $10 Million for Mis-sold Consumer Credit Insurance*, press release, 17-268MR [Online]. Available at http://asic.gov.au/about-asic/media-centre/find-a-media-release/2017-releases/17-268mr-commonwealth-bank-to-refund-over-10-million-for-mis-sold-consumer-credit-insurance/ (Accessed 14 August 2017).

BBC (2015) 'Explainer: what was China's one-child policy?', *BBC News*, 29 October [Online]. Available at www.bbc.co.uk/news/world-asia-china-34667551 (Accessed 4 December 2017).

Chamie, J. (2016) '320 million children in single parent families', *Global Issues* [Online]. Available at www.globalissues.org/news/2016/10/15/22568 (Accessed 15 October 2017).

Cowley, S. and Silver-Greenberg, J. (2017) 'Loans "designed to fail": states say Navient preyed on students', *The New York Times*, 9 April [Online]. Available at www.nytimes.com/2017/04/09/business/dealbook/states-say-navient-preyed-on-students.html (Accessed 4 December 2017).

Dustmann, C. and Frattini, T. (2014) 'The fiscal effects of immigration to the UK', *The Economic Journal*, vol. 124, no. 580, pp. F593–643.

The Economic Times (2017) 'RBI makes Banks responsible for mis-selling third party products' [Online]. Available at https://economictimes.indiatimes.com/industry/banking/finance/banking/rbi-makes-banks-responsible-for-misselling-third-party-products/articleshow/59295959.cms (Accessed 4 December 2017).

Engineering Employers' Federation (EEF) (2017) *UK Manufacturing 2017/18, the Facts* [Online]. Available at www.eef.org.uk/campaigning/campaigns-and-issues/manufacturing-facts-and-figures (Accessed 4 December 2017).

Eurostat (2017) *Immigration in EU Member States*, 15 December [Online]. Available at http://ec.europa.eu/eurostat/en/web/products-eurostat-news/-/EDN-20171215-1 (Accessed 5 February 2018).

Financial Industry Regulatory Authority Foundation (Finra) (2016) *Financial Capability in the United States 2016*, July, New York [Online]. Available at www.usfinancialcapability.org/downloads/NFCS_2015_Report_Natl_Findings.pdf (Accessed 4 December 2017).

Finney, A. and Hayes, D. (2015) *Financial Capability in Great Britain, 2010 to 2012*, London, Office for National Statistics [Online]. Available at www.bristol.ac.uk/media-library/sites/geography/pfrc/pfrc1504-financial-capability-in-gb-2010-2012.pdf (Accessed 4 December 2017).

Gigerenzer, G. and Goldstein, D. (1996) 'Reasoning the fast and frugal way: models of bounded rationality', *Psychological Review*, vol. 103, no. 4, pp. 650–69.

Greenhouse, S. (2017) 'Driverless future?' *The American Prospect*, 21 March [Online]. Available at www.prospect.org/article/driverless-future (Accessed 4 December 2017).

Hacker, J. S. (2006) *The Great Risk Shift*, Oxford, Oxford University Press.

House of Lords (2017) *Tackling Financial Exclusion: A Country that Works for Everyone?*, HL paper 132 [Online], Available at https://publications. parliament.uk/pa/ld201617/ldselect/ldfinexcl/132/132.pdf (Accessed 15 June 2018).

International Organization for Migration (IOM) (2017) *Global Migration Trends Factsheet* [Online]. Available at gmdac.iom.int/global-migration-trends-factsheet (Accessed 4 December 2017).

Kahneman, D. (2011) *Thinking Fast and Slow*, London, Penguin.

Kahneman, D. and Tversky, A. (1979) 'Prospect theory: an analysis of decision under risk', *Econometrica*, vol. 47, no. 2, pp. 263–92.

Office for National Statistics (ONS) (2017) *Dataset: Families and households* [Online]. Available at www.ons.gov.uk/peoplepopulationandcommunity/ birthsdeathsandmarriages/families/datasets/ familiesandhouseholdsfamiliesandhouseholds (Accessed 29 March 2018).

Organisation for Economic Cooperation and Development (OECD) (2017) *G20/OECD INFE Report on adult financial literacy in G20 countries* [Online]. Available at http://www.oecd.org/daf/fin/financial-education/G20-OECD-INFE-report-adult-financial-literacy-in-G20-countries.pdf (Accessed 23 March 2018).

Osborne, H. (2013) 'PPI – facts and figures from the biggest mis-selling scandal of all time', *The Guardian*, 4 March [Online]. Available at www. theguardian.com/money/2013/mar/04/ppi-facts-figures-biggest-mis-selling-scandal (Accessed 4 December 2017).

The Poverty Site (n.d.) *United Kingdom: Without a Bank Account* [Online]. Available at www.poverty.org.uk/73/index.shtml (Accessed 4 December 2017).

Rowlingson, K. and McKay, S. (2017) *Financial Inclusion Annual Monitoring Report 2017* [Online]. Available at www.birmingham.ac.uk/Documents/news/ 15518-CHASM-Report-Stage-4.pdf (Accessed 4 December 2017).

Thaler, R. and Sunstein, C. (2009) *Nudge*, London, Penguin.

Treanor, J. (2016) 'Bill for PPI mis-selling scandal tops £40bn', *The Guardian*, 27 October [Online]. Available at www.theguardian.com/money/2016/oct/ 27/ppi-mis-selling-scandal-bill-tops-40bn-pounds (Accessed 4 December 2017).

United Nations (UN) (2017) *World Population Prospects: The 2017 Revision*, vol. 1, Comprehensive Tables ST/ESA/SER.A/400 [Online]. Available at https://esa.un.org/unpd/wpp/Publications/Files/WPP2017_Volume-I_Comprehensive-Tables.pdf (Accessed 28 March 2018).

To cite this chapter, use the following format in your reference list:

Shipman, A. and Stone, H. (2019) 'Personal finance – setting the context', in De Henau, J. and Lowe, J. (eds) *Personal Finance*, Milton Keynes, The Open University, pp. 7–54.

Chapter 2
Income

Jerome De Henau and George Callaghan

Contents

1 Introduction

> Every job from the heart is, ultimately, of equal value. The nurse injects the syringe; the writer slides the pen; the farmer ploughs the dirt; the comedian draws the laughter. Monetary income is the perfect deceiver of a man's true worth.
>
> (Jami, 2015, p. 102)

When thinking about our money, one of the first things we may like to know is from where and how we'll get any income, before considering how we could spend it or save it. Studying income is an important part of financial planning and **budgeting**. As the quotation above implies, high incomes may be a poor measure of a person's true worth and do not guarantee happiness, but having enough income to meet one's needs and life goals is the foundation of most financial planning.

Section 2 of this chapter starts by looking at what income is and how it is different from wealth. Section 3 then examines the social and economic background to income, such as how average levels of household income have changed over the years and the different sources of income. As paid employment is by far the largest income source for most people, Section 4 will explore the world of work and the salaries that different jobs pay. Section 5 looks at how income changes over the life course and the connection this has with household formation and financial planning. The final sections look at the impact of taxes and benefits, and how to begin drawing up a **cash flow statement** – one of the first practical financial planning tools you will come across in this book, which allows people to keep track of what is happening to their money.

Budgeting
The process of using a detailed plan of future income and expenditure to manage personal finances, and work towards achieving goals.

Cash flow statement
A record of income and spending over a certain past period of time.

2 Income, wealth and assets

To start, it is important to understand the difference between income and wealth.

- **Income** is a *flow* of money received over a period of time, such as a salary every month, weekly rent from a property, annual interest from savings, or a weekly cash benefit for children.

- **Wealth**, also called **assets**, is a *stock* of resources, valued at a given point in time, that have been accumulated over time or transferred between people (for example through inheritance). A house, a car, investments, personal possessions, a piece of the London 2012 Olympic cauldron or a sculpture by the famous artist Modigliani are all assets.

There are three main types of asset:

- **Financial assets** – for example, money in a savings account, shares or a pension fund. These often produce a stream of income (interest, dividends).

- **Physical assets** – for example, objects of art and jewellery, cars, land or property. Physical assets usually have to be sold to be transformed into cash, but property is one obvious exception because it can produce income – a rent – without being sold.

- **Intangible assets** – for example, pension rights, insurance, **human capital** or a company's brand. Copyrights of artistic and intellectual creation and patents for inventions are other examples of intangible assets.

Human capital is the value of your skills, experience and education that you can use to generate cash by selling your labour in exchange for earnings; in other words you can create employment income. Human capital is a peculiar form of asset akin to a financial asset, as the income it produces does not deplete the value of the asset. Indeed, selling labour can increase human capital, since it can rise in value as experience is gained. We will come back to this concept in the next sections.

Note that most assets are marketable (can be sold or bought on a market). However, some are not, such as money held in some types of pension, which may be specific to one person only.

Income
Money *flows* received over a specified period of time.

Wealth, or **assets**
The *stock* of everything that a person owns at a given point in time that has a monetary value (for example, property, investments and cash).

Human capital
The value of your skills, experience and education that allows you to sell a service as labour in exchange for earnings.

(a)

(b)

(c)

(d)

Assets can take a variety of forms. Diamonds (a) are assets (as are the copyrights of the James Bond movies and books). A house in Rio de Janeiro, Brazil (b), higher-education qualification (c), and shares or bonds on the financial markets (d), are also assets.

We can also distinguish **liquid assets** from those which are less liquid. Liquidity is the degree of ease or speed at which an asset can be converted into cash while keeping close to its estimated value. Cash in an instant-access account is extremely liquid by nature, while a house is much less so, as it takes time to sell. A work of art may be estimated at a high price but if no one wants to buy it – in other words, there's no market for it – it is quite illiquid. Shares are more difficult to categorise. They can usually be sold and bought quickly on financial markets, but if their value rises and falls rapidly all the time, it is not sensible to rely on being able to sell them in a hurry for a specific amount. Therefore it is usual for households to treat shares as illiquid assets. You'll explore more about markets for shares in Chapter 5.

Liquid assets
Those assets that can be quickly converted into a reliable, predictable sum of cash.

Activity 2.1 Income or asset?

Allow 5 minutes for this activity.

Identify each of the following items as either income or an asset, making a note of your answers:

1   Sam's regular pension of £200 per week.

2   £1200 in your bank account.

3   Alysia's right to claim a pension many years ahead, based on two years of membership in a pension scheme at work.

Comment

The answers to Activity 2.1 are given at the end of this chapter.

---

3 What sort of income?

In Chapter 1, you saw that income flows between different sectors – the state, corporations and households. In fact, the main source of income for most people of **working age** is paid employment: either earnings from a salary paid by a public- or private-sector employer, or from profits earned through self-employment activities. In developing countries, income from self-employment usually takes a larger share of total income than in developed countries, and cash transfers from the state (such as social security benefit payments) are still limited in many of these countries (ILO, 2015).

Working age
The age range within which people are assumed to be available for work.

3.1 Sources of income

Figure 2.1 (overleaf) shows the sources of income for households with adult working-age members in selected countries. (You will learn about income for pensioners in Chapter 8.) This is a bar chart, similar to the one you looked at in Figure 1.1 in Chapter 1. However, in this case, each bar shows total income (100%) for the average household in each country. The different sections of each bar show the proportion of income that comes from each source: 'Wages' refers to earnings from working for an employer (bottom section of each bar); 'Self' is income from self-employment (next section up); 'State' is for cash received from the state (such as unemployment benefits); and lastly 'Other' stands for any other sort of income, such as transfers between households, income from savings and lottery wins. The income shown here is gross household income – the income households receive before any deduction in the form of taxes is made.

Figure 2.1 demonstrates that in more affluent countries the vast majority of household income comes from paid employment, and in particular wages and salaries, rather than self-employment.

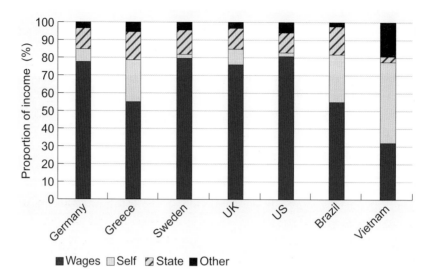

Figure 2.1 Proportion of income from different sources in selected countries for an average household with adult members of working age (adapted from ILO, 2015)

Activity 2.2 Differences in income

Allow 10 minutes for this activity.

What is the difference between income from employment in Greece and the US? Make a note of your answer.

Comment

The answer to Activity 2.2 is given at the end of this chapter.

The chart does not include income received from informal activities, which is less easy to measure in official statistics. In broad terms, informal employment is work undertaken for pay, but which is unregistered or hidden from the state, for tax and/or benefit purposes, and is sometimes also illegal. In the UK and other high-income countries, the size of the informal economy represents a smaller fraction of all economic activities, compared to a majority of developing countries, in which more than half of employment is informal, and accounts for as many as eight out of ten jobs in India (Elliott, 2013; ILO, 2013).

3.2 Distribution of income in the population

Sources of income also vary by level of income. For example, in most affluent countries, the poorest 10% of households receive more in the form of cash transfers from the state than other households, while those with the highest income (the richest 10% of households) receive relatively more income from investments and also from self-employment (ILO, 2015).

Assessing your own income often involves knowing where it sits in comparison with others'. Social scientists, in particular economists and statisticians, examine differences of income between households by comparing against the **mean** income, the **median** income, and the distance between the top **percentile** and the bottom percentile (or in the example above, between the '10% richest' or 'top 10%' of a distribution and the bottom 10% of a distribution). Box 2.1 explains these statistical concepts and how they are used in the context of examining income inequality.

Mean
The average of a set of values measured as the sum of all the observations divided by the number of observations.

Median
The average of a set of values measured as the middle value when the set is arranged in order.

Percentile
The value at any one of the points that divides a set of values into 100 equal parts when the set is arranged in order.

Box 2.1 Comparing incomes with mean, median and percentiles

Social scientists often want to measure the 'average' of a set of numbers, for example to compare it to another set. There are different ways of measuring that average:

- The mean provides a general measure of the size of the values involved. The mean is calculated by adding up all the values in a set of numbers and dividing that total by the number of values in the set.

- The median is the middle value of a set of numbers arranged in order (called an 'ordered set'). It divides the values into two equal parts. This indicates that half of the set will have values less than or equal to the median and half of the set will have values equal to or greater than the median. (If the set has an even number of values, the median is the mean of the two middle values.)

An example

The following set of data is the monthly income of ten different people. We have not used any particular currency, so you can think of them in pounds, dollars or any currency you prefer.

Person A: 1000; Person B: 4000; Person C: 1000; Person D: 3000; Person E: 2000; Person F: 2000; Person G: 22,000; Person H: 1000; Person I: 1000; Person J: 3000.

The mean of these incomes is 4000 (all incomes added together = 40,000 ÷ 10 = 4000).

To work out the median, the incomes must first be put in order, as shown in Figure 2.2. The median is 2000. That is because the fifth and sixth values are both 2000, so the mean of them is taken, which is (2000 + 2000) ÷ 2, which is 2000.

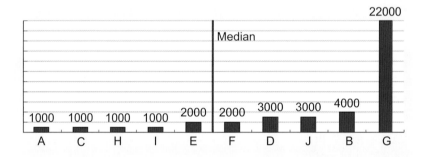

Figure 2.2 Finding the median with an even number of observations in the set

In the example, the two measures of average have produced very different results. This difference is important because incomes vary a great deal, and a small minority of people have extremely high incomes. But the mean can imply that most people's incomes are higher than is in fact the case. It may lead us to believe that most people's incomes are near this number: in fact, in all countries, the mean income is higher than most people's incomes because the extreme values (called 'outliers') – in this case Person G's very high income – skew the result.

In contrast, the median income is unaffected by extreme values. It might give more reliable information about the income most people get in situations like the example shown, where very few people (in this case just one person) have a very high income.

Percentiles

Percentiles are an extension of the median concept. A percentile is any of the 99 values that divide the ordered set into 100 equal parts, so that each part represents a 100th of the data. For example, the 10th percentile cuts off the lowest 10% of data, whereas the 90th percentile cuts off the lowest 90% of data (leaving the highest 10%). The median is the 50th percentile, because half of the ordered set will be below it and half above it.

Using this data, the income of the 10th percentile would be 1000. It is also the income of the 10% poorest group, since only one individual is represented here. If there were more than one individual, the income of the 10% poorest group would be the average of the incomes of those below the 10th percentile.

Activity 2.3 Measures of inequality

Allow 15 minutes for this activity.

Let's use the data set in Box 2.1 to derive measures of income inequality. Answer the following questions, making a note of your calculations and answers:

1 What is the 90th percentile? (Hint: use Figure 2.2 to work out where the 90th percentile falls.)

2 Divide your answer to Question 1 by the median (2000).

3 What is the 10th percentile?

4 Divide the median by your answer to Question 3.

5 Compare your answers to Questions 2 and 4. What do they tell you about the distribution of income between wealthy and poor people?

6 Divide your answer to Question 1 by your answer to Question 3. What does this tell you?

Comment

1 The 90th percentile falls between the ninth and tenth observations. Therefore, the 90th percentile is the mean of the top two values, which is (22,000 + 4000) ÷ 2 = 13,000.

2 The ratio of the 90th percentile to the median = 13,000 ÷ 2000 = 6.5.

3 The 10th percentile falls between the first and second observations. Therefore, it is the mean of the bottom two values, which is (1000 + 1000) = 1000.

4   The ratio of the median to the 10th percentile = 2000 ÷ 1000 = 2.

5   The ratio in Question 2 is much bigger than the ratio in Question 4. This tells you that the top 50% of this income distribution is more unequal than the bottom 50%, which actually is a usual feature of the income distributions in most countries. You can see this intuitively if you look back to Figure 2.2.

6   13,000 ÷ 1000 = 13. This tells you that the top 10% earn at least 13 times the bottom 10% of individuals in this set of incomes.

Income inequality is important to monitor because it has been shown that excessive inequalities have detrimental effects on many key social and economic outcomes (OECD, 2015). Wilkinson and Pickett (2009) also found an association between the level of income inequality in a country and:

- **social cohesion** – there is more crime in more unequal countries, an important element of economic stability, as well as social well-being of course

- **levels of trust** – there is less trust between people in more unequal countries, an important factor for sustainable economic and social relationships

- **indicators of individual well-being** – for example, there are more health problems reported on average in more unequal countries.

3.3 Income, living standards and the role of inflation

Standard of living
The material, mental, physical and social quality of life enjoyed by an individual or household, depending on factors such as income, housing conditions, the environment and public services such as health and education.

Knowing the level of our income in isolation, even in comparison with other people's, is not enough if we are to plan financially for our personal goals. We would like to know what we can achieve with our income, how it will affect the things we can buy now and in the future and perhaps the status it conveys. In other words, we want to know how our income affects our quality of life and well-being.

Income is generally a means to achieving a certain **standard of living**. Household income can approximate a measure of living standard but it would only capture the monetary part of someone's quality of life, what people can afford to buy. It is not a direct measure of someone's well-being, which depends on other factors such as physical and mental health and the quality of social relationships, as argued by the philosopher Martha Nussbaum and the Nobel-Prize economist Amartya Sen in many of their works (Nussbaum and Sen, 1993).

The Nobel-Prize-winning economist Amartya Sen is famous for arguing that measures of well-being and development extend beyond income and consumption

3.4 Inflation and living standards

To assess the value of income over time in terms of what we can buy, we need to take account of **inflation**, which is the general increase in the level of prices of goods and services over the years. If inflation is positive, the purchasing power of a given amount of money is gradually reduced. For example, the average price of a pint of milk in the UK in 1978 was 13p, compared to 45p in 2018 (ONS, 2018). This means that you would have needed 3.5 times (= 45 ÷ 13) as much cash in 2018 as in 1978 to buy the same item.

Inflation
A continual increase in the level of prices.

Measures of inflation reflect the change in price not of just one item, but of a basket of goods and services generally consumed by a population over a specified period. A common measure used in many countries to represent such a basket of goods is a consumer price index (CPI), a composite index that tracks the value of typical goods and services consumed in a country, usually each month.

Inflation means that buying the same item requires more income

For example, if 12 months ago the average price of a basket of goods in a country was 100 and increased by 5% when measured again today, the rate of inflation over the past 12 months is said to be 5% and the price of the basket would be 105 today.

The calculation is:

$$100 \times (1 + \text{inflation rate}) = 100 \times (1 + 5\%) = 100 \times 1.05 = 105$$

If the UK CPI is 105 compared to its previous reference measure of 100, this tells you that you would now need £105 to be able to buy the same things that you could buy a year ago with £100.

Activity 2.4 The impact of inflation on purchasing power

Allow 10 minutes for this activity.

Now let's take a look at the impact of inflation over two years. Make a note of your calculations and answers to the following questions.

If inflation over the next 12 months is predicted to be 3%:

1 How much would the CPI of 105 become in 12 months' time, compared to its value of 100, 12 months ago?

2 What does it mean for the increase in prices over two years?

Comment

1 By applying the same principle as for the previous calculation, in 12 months' time the CPI would be 105 × (1 + 3%) = 105 × 1.03 = 108.15. This means the CPI will be 8.15% higher in a year's time than it was a year ago (when it was 100).

2 Prices would have increased by 8.15% over the two-year period. The weekly shopping basket that cost a UK consumer £100 a year ago would cost £108.15 by the end of next year if the inflation forecast turns out to be right.

So, what does inflation do to the value of our money? At this stage it is important to introduce the concepts of **real value** and **nominal value** to describe the purchasing power of a person's income. The nominal value is the monetary or cash value as it stands in each period. If your monthly income was 1000 a year ago and was still 1000 next year, its nominal value wouldn't change.

However, carrying on with our previous example, with prices having increased by 8.15% over that two-year period, the measure of the purchasing power of that income – called the real value – would be less than 1000. It would in fact be 925 (which is 8.15% lower than the 1000 you started with two years ago). Real values can only be calculated with respect to a specified reference year: in this case we have chosen 12 months ago as our reference date.

Real incomes can be used to measure how standards of living have changed over a period of time. Since the late 1970s the price of milk may have more than trebled (in fact, a 246% increase) in the UK and prices overall may have been close to a five-fold increase (a 383% overall inflation between 1978 and 2018), but mean nominal incomes have actually risen nine times over that period (ONS, 2017a). Therefore, accounting for inflation, real incomes have still nearly doubled. This means that average (material) standards of living in the UK nearly doubled over that period.

However, households don't get to keep all their money – some is taken away in taxes – and what lifestyle it buys depends also on how many people the income has to support.

Real value
The nominal value adjusted for inflation to reflect the purchasing power of an item.

Nominal value
The monetary or cash value of an item as it stands.

So a more accurate measure of a household's standard of living is its real 'equivalised disposable income':

Disposable income
Also called 'net income'. Income after income tax and social security contributions have been deducted from gross income.

- **Disposable income** means that it is the income after direct taxes such as income tax and **social security contributions** have been deducted; sometimes it is referred to as 'net income'.

- **Equivalised household income** is a measure that takes account of the size of the household, as households of different sizes have different needs. Typically, larger households need a higher income than smaller households in order to afford a similar living standard for its members, as there are more mouths to feed. (You'll find more on this notion in Chapter 3, Section 5.1.)

Social security contributions
Regular (mostly compulsory) payments made by people of working age to a social fund, used to provide them with certain cash benefits in case of accidental or planned loss of income (unemployment, illness, retirement).

On the basis of real disposable equivalised income, over recent decades inequalities have increased in many developed countries. Although the average living standard has almost doubled over that period, it has been mainly driven by large increases at the top end of the distribution of incomes, rather than at the bottom end (OECD, 2011). Taking the UK as an example, Figure 2.3 shows the evolution in real terms of the average income for all households and also for the poorest 10% (the group with income below the 10th percentile) and the richest 10% of households (the group with income above the 90th percentile) between 1977 and 2015–16. This pattern of income inequality is very similar in the US, too (Stiglitz, 2012).

Equivalised household income
A household's actual (usually disposable) income adjusted to take account of household size and composition, to enable comparison of different households' (material) standards of living.

Box 2.2 Reading a line chart

So far in this book, you have looked at data presented as a bar chart. Figure 2.3 is different: it shows a line chart. Line charts are especially useful for showing trends where you have a series of figures over many time periods (called 'time series data'). The horizontal axis in Figure 2.3 shows time, while the vertical axis gives the value of each plot. Each plot is in effect a dot on the chart and the dots have been joined together to form a continuous line.

Figure 2.3 shows the lines for four different series of data so that you can compare the trends and changes in them.

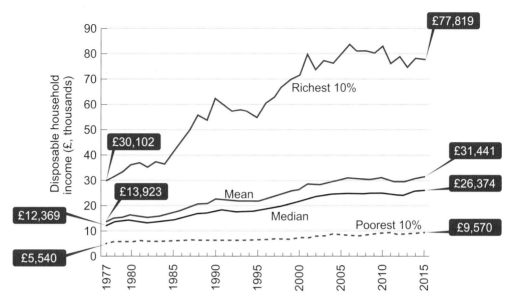

Figure 2.3 Changes in average real equivalised disposable household income in the UK for different income groups 1977–2015/16 (2015/16 prices) (adapted from ONS, 2017a)

Activity 2.5 Changes in real income

Allow 15 minutes for this activity.

In Figure 2.3, what sort of patterns can you see when comparing the progression of the real incomes of the poorest 10% and the richest 10% of households, and with respect to average incomes? Note down your answers.

Comment

While, according to Figure 2.3, median living standards and those of the bottom 10% of the income distribution did indeed nearly double since 1977, they increased faster in the richest group, widening income inequalities as a result. In 2015 the richest 10% of households had an average disposable income eight times as high as that of the poorest 10%, compared to roughly five times as high in 1977. Most of the increase in inequality occurred in the second part of the 1980s and again in the second part of the 1990s. Income inequality then reduced in the aftermath of the financial crisis of 2007–08. The crisis hit the investment incomes among the richest 10%, while at the same time the UK tax-and-benefit system acted to stabilise the income of the poorest households. However, it is worth noting that the average real disposable income across all the income groups was only slightly higher in 2015 than a decade before, signalling one of the longest periods of real income stagnation for the UK population in modern times.

At-risk-of monetary poverty rate
Measure of the risk of falling into poverty when having too low an income. It is the proportion of households with an income below a threshold (called the poverty line), usually 60% of the median income of the population.

Income inequality can also be measured by looking at the **at-risk-of monetary poverty rate**, a measure of relative low income that calculates the proportion of individuals living in households with income below a certain threshold relative to the mid-range of incomes. This threshold (called the 'poverty line') is usually 60% of median household equivalised disposable income. In many countries children are more likely to live in households with relatively low income compared to childless adults of working age. This is especially the case for children in lone-parent households (EIGE, 2016).

Most developed countries have experienced increasing income inequalities since the early 1980s. The main factors behind this are changes in the labour market and industrial transformations in the economy, affecting gross income, as well as changes in tax and benefit policies, affecting disposable income (Cingano, 2014). The next sections explore these phenomena in more detail, starting with the labour market.

4 Wages and employment

As employment is the main source of income in most developed countries, let us spend some time understanding how wages, salaries and other income from paid employment are determined and differ between people across time and countries.

4.1 Paid employment and the labour market

In standard economic theory, a **labour market** is the arena in which employers (who need labour) come together with employees (who supply their labour in exchange for pay). It is where employers and employees, either individually or collectively (via trade unions and/or professional organisations), negotiate their working conditions, their objectives and performance requirements and, of course, pay. One strand of economic theory, called **classical economics**, stipulates that employers' typical aim is to maximise the profits of their companies, while employees' aim is to maximise the earnings they can get, reflecting their skills and effort (their human capital). Studies have shown that workers indeed rank good pay as very important, but they also highly value job security and an interesting job that matches their skills and abilities (Mayfield and Mayfield, 2014).

In the 1980s, policymakers such as Margaret Thatcher in the UK and Ronald Reagan in the US, influenced by the works of economists such as Friedrich von Hayek and Milton Friedman, adopted a view that what mattered was to prioritise employers' freedom to hire and fire, and set their employees' wages at a level consistent with commercial goals of making profits. Popular support for this policy was encouraged through a narrative that trade union power undermines economic strength, an argument contested by many (for example, Stiglitz, 2012). In the UK, Thatcher (1984) even characterised unions as a threat to democracy, dubbing them the 'enemy within'.

This attack on trade unions was closely aligned with the policies of deregulation and privatisation, described in Chapter 1, and a loosening of other labour protection laws. The result was a decline in the institutional power and membership of the unions. Although they often remained the body responsible for negotiating employees' wages and conditions, their bargaining position was weakened. This is one of the factors behind the rise in wage inequalities in many developed

Labour market
The arena in which employers (who need labour) come together with employees (who supply their labour in exchange for pay) to decide on activities to perform (working hours and tasks) and rewards (pay).

Classical economics
A school of economic thought developed in the late eighteenth to nineteenth centuries.

countries throughout the 1980s and 1990s (OECD, 2011). Such changes resulted in increasing differences between workers in their pay, pay progression, security of employment and access to workplace benefits, such as good pensions and paid leave.

It was argued that more flexible contracts would help more people enter the labour market, thereby reducing the unemployment rate. There is some evidence to support this (OECD, 2011). However, the impact on different groups is uneven. Evidence for European countries has shown that looser employment legislation was not associated with lower unemployment for younger people or increased chances of their getting permanent jobs on the expiry of a fixed-term contract (Gebel and Giesecke, 2016).

The majority of jobs in the UK and elsewhere are still relatively secure, permanent contracts for full-time hours, with access to some workplace benefits. However there has been a growing number of jobs, often part-time and/or temporary, that offer less protection and pay.

A salient example is zero-hour contracts in the UK: contracts that do not guarantee a minimum number of hours of paid work, making working time and income unpredictable. According to some research (Marsh, 2017), zero-hours contracts have a negative impact on people's health, including their stress levels.

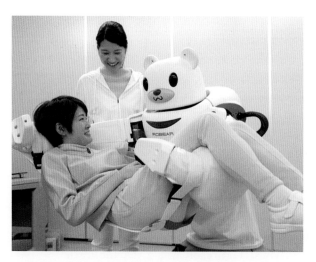

A Japan-made robot that can lift elderly people or hospital patients off their bed into a wheelchair

Technological innovation is another important driver of change. Recent technological changes have not only transformed manufacturing jobs, owing to increased reliance on machines, they have also accelerated automation of many medium-skilled jobs in services and manufacturing that require routine processes, a prime target for computerisation (Autor et al., 2003). Even low-paid jobs that require direct contact with clients (such as care staff and waiting staff) are also increasingly prone to automation. Robots that provide social care to elderly people are being introduced in Japan, for example, to combat a shortage of skilled care workers (Lewis, 2017). High-skilled jobs that require creativity, cognitive skills and specialisation could use technology to complement workers' skills; their wages could therefore increase more rapidly, although some of this group, too, may face job insecurity owing to the increasing risk of automation (Eurostat, 2017).

Another major change over the last 60 years in all developed countries has been the massive increase in women's employment. In the UK women made up 29% of the paid workforce in 1900 (Lindsay, 2003), which means about one woman in three of working age was in paid employment. By 1955 their employment rate increased to 46%, and was close to 71% in 2017. Men's employment was very high in the first half of the twentieth century, at about 90%, then started to fall from the 1970s onwards in most developed countries. It was close to 80% in the UK at the end of 2017 (ONS, 2017b), in large part due to longer years spent in full-time study and better social protection for disabled people. The rise in female employment was driven by greater access to education, industrial and technological change, which led to a shift from heavy manufacturing to services, and an increase in part-time employment, especially in continental Europe.

Table 2.1 Male and female employment and share of part-time employment 1986–2016 (UK, Italy)

	UK				Italy			
	1986	**1996**	**2006**	**2016**	**1986**	**1996**	**2006**	**2016**
Total employment (thousands)								
Men	14,135	14,480	15,636	16,842	13,635	12,727	13,463	12,853
Women	10,255	11,801	13,405	14,786	6,665	7,037	8,926	9,388
All	24,390	26,281	29,041	31,628	20,300	19,764	22,388	22,241
% part-time								
Men	3	7	9	11	2	3	4	8
Women	44	44	42	41	9	13	26	33
All	21	24	24	25	5	6	13	19

Source: Eurostat (2017)

Activity 2.6 Trends in employment – UK and Italy

Allow 15 minutes for this activity.

Looking at Table 2.1 above, compare the trends in total employment and part-time employment between men and women in the UK and Italy. Make a note of your answers.

Comment

The answers to Activity 2.6 are given at the end of this chapter.

4.2 How much are people paid?

If you are an employee, the level of your wage or salary is determined by a series of desirable personal characteristics and qualities (including skills and qualifications, that is your human capital), as well as the environment in which you work (type of activity, regulatory framework, cultural norms). Some are more under your control than others.

Educational attainment

Usually, the higher a person's educational attainment the higher their pay. For example, academic, professional and vocational qualifications develop transferable skills (such as critical thinking and problem-solving) that are useful and valued in many different jobs. However, for some jobs, specific skills will also be required. The field of qualification can matter as much, if not more, than the length of study and level attained. For example, a qualified plumber may not have much luck securing a job as conductor of an orchestra.

Experience

In general, the greater experience a person has in a field, the higher paid job they can attain. Experience is measured by years of paid activity that a worker has carried out in the same job, company, or industry. What matters is the type of skills that were developed and the extent to which these are specific to a job. For example, a graphic designer's skills will not necessarily come in useful if they want to change their career after 20 years to practice law. They will need significant retraining and will start with no experience of being a lawyer – hence their pay in their new career could be at junior level. However, other skills from their years of working, such as experience of dealing with clients and working to deadlines, are deemed transferable and might give them an advantage over other, younger and inexperienced, junior lawyers.

Activity 2.7 Your human capital

Allow 10 minutes for this activity.

Thinking about your own skill set, education and experience, which do you think would be easily transferable to another job in the same industry? Which would not be useful as they are too specific to a particular role? And which would be almost universal for any type of job? Note down your answers for future reference.

Comment

You might have thought of some generic skills as transferable, such as communicating, computing, reasoning, presenting arguments and problem-solving. Other more specific skills will depend on your job or specialism (e.g. laying tiles on a roof, knowing all the law of the land, playing hockey).

People may have career breaks, because of periods of unemployment, unpaid caring work, or economic inactivity for other reasons (such as studying or illness). The length of the break will, depending on its nature, likely reduce a person's years of experience. This can pause the building of their skills and even result in losing skills if regular practice or updating are required. For many highly qualified women, interrupting their career to raise their children can be more damaging than for less qualified women, as you will explore in Chapter 9. Part of the differential in pay between men and women of otherwise equal qualifications is explained by the higher propensity of women leaving the labour market to have and raise children.

Job characteristics

Contextual factors also play an important role in explaining wage levels. The skills needed for a job will be more or less rewarded depending on how much in demand they are. The business activity carried out will require more or less labour and skills, and as a result the level of responsibility, complexity of the task, rarity of the skill, and attractiveness of the product or service sold on the market will determine the capacity of the business to increase wages. An IT developer who works for a commercially successful video game company may be paid more than an IT developer with the same skills and experience who is working on the same type of product, but whose company is a struggling 'travel app' start-up in a highly competitive environment.

This last point is important because the economic strength and competitiveness of the sector in which the work is being done will greatly determine the possibility for employees to obtain higher wages, depending on their mobility. Two contradictory effects are at play. In buoyant industries with local competitors, employees may be able to bargain wages up within their company as they can threaten to go to a competitor offering more. Employers may also want to raise wages to attract the best candidates and remain competitive. However, if the competition is fierce but employees are not so mobile, companies may reduce or limit wage increases in order to cut costs and remain in business.

The impact of competition from cheap labour in other countries, such as China, especially in the manufacturing sector (e.g. textile and machinery), may also push or hold down wages to avoid job losses. By the same token, if employers need a specific skill that is rare locally, they will tend to raise the wages to attract more candidates; for example, incentivising workers to move town or even country. In all countries, migrant work has always been an important resource in different sectors, where local skills could not be found or the working-age population was too small. Migration within Europe and especially within the US played a significant role in boosting these countries' economies after the Second World War (Zimmerman, 2016).

Collective bargaining and legislation

The existence of a labour market means that employees and employers will negotiate the price (wage) at which the employees' human capital is hired. As discussed, trade unions have a role in securing employees' working conditions (including their pay). Legislation and regulation can give a framework for such negotiations to occur. For example, governments often require employers to pay at least a minimum wage and to provide basic employees' rights, for example for pension, sick pay and paid holiday, and may regulate overtime and atypical working hours. Companies can then decide whether to offer additional benefits to their employees on top of the legal rights.

The factors combined

Again using the UK as an example, Table 2.2 (overleaf) shows that highly qualified occupations, such as professionals, are much better paid than less qualified occupations, such as clerks and elementary occupations. There are, however, variations within the former group; for example, medical professionals achieve higher earnings than business professionals, reflecting the more complex skills needed to do these jobs, especially the greater responsibilities and risks associated with them. They therefore pay higher wages to attract and retain employees.

Table 2.2 Median annual gross earnings of UK employees by gender and selected occupation, 2017

	Average (median) annual gross pay (£)			Women among employees (%)
	All	**Men**	**Women**	
Chief executives and senior officials	86,332	92,820	70,000	28
Medical practitioners	61,245	83,744	48,313	45
Production managers and directors	44,588	45,771	35,346	18
Police officers	40,616	41,931	37,876	28
Business, research and administrative professionals	38,748	42,801	34,477	39
Secondary education teaching professionals	35,763	38,887	32,835	63
Nurses	27,316	30,544	26,745	86
Managers and directors in retail and wholesale	26,000	29,944	21,365	43
Skilled trades occupations	25,252	26,415	15,516	11
Process, plant and machine operatives	23,256	24,248	16,480	12
Culture, media and sports occupations	23,000	25,098	18,797	41
Bank and post office clerks	19,969	22,528	18,468	70
Refuse and salvage occupations	19,390	19,495	15,968	<1
Secretarial and related occupations	15,138	16,544	14,998	92
Care workers and home carers	13,703	16,198	13,206	83
Sales assistants and retail cashiers	10,468	13,935	9,299	66
Cleaners and domestics	7,203	10,138	6,677	77
All employees	**23,474**	**28,810**	**18,224**	**50**

Source: adapted from Annual Survey of Hours and Earnings (ONS, 2017c)

Table 2.2 also shows differences in annual earnings between men and women. In some cases, this reflects the large prevalence of part-time employment in female-dominated occupations (e.g. sales assistants or cleaners). But it also reflects differences in hourly pay that are influenced by a series of factors, which are determined by gender social norms (such as gaps in years of experience, differences in promotions, or outright discrimination). The extent to which this difference occurs will depend on the company, industry and occupation.

Typically, there is a larger difference for higher managerial occupations, where pay is more often determined individually. At mid and lower levels of earnings (lower-skill occupations), some collective bargaining coverage by trade unions (more prevalent in manufacturing and public services than in finance and retail, for example) and the existence of a legal minimum wage help reduce inequalities (Schäfer and Gottschall, 2015; O'Reilly et al., 2015).

5 Income profiles and the life course

Understanding how income may change over a lifetime is an essential part of financial capability, enabling individuals and households to build robust financial plans. You've seen that earnings tend to be influenced by life events, for example with career breaks to raise children or periods of unemployment. Being aware of these possibilities is a prerequisite for taking steps now to plan ahead to make them more affordable or reduce their financial damage. Individual income profiles over the working life will vary greatly between different individuals. Nevertheless, there are some typical patterns that many households should plan for.

Still taking the UK as an example (but many high-income countries are similar), Figure 2.4 shows annual earnings at different ages for men in different parts of the earnings distribution. The dotted line represents the 10th percentile, showing the earnings profile of the 10% of lowest male earners. It could be thought of as typical of the profile of earnings over the life course of a man with lower skills, peaking early in life and then remaining essentially flat. The solid line represents the 80th percentile, in other words the threshold for the top 20% of male earners. It can be thought of as similar to the lifetime profile of a highly educated professional with earnings that are not just higher but peak much later in life.

By contrast, women can expect a much different profile, similar in trend but different in magnitude. Figure 2.5 shows that the earnings of higher-earning women peak much earlier and at about only two-thirds of the peak for higher-earning men. The main reason is that women more often than men reduce their working hours to look after their family when they have one. Low-earning women see their income from employment plateau even earlier.

However, care should be taken in using these diagrams. The data give a snapshot of UK men and women of all ages at a point in time. They do not track how particular individuals' earnings change as they age. This means the charts do not capture the way that individuals may, for example, start in life as low-earners but move into higher-earning percentiles as they gain qualifications and experience.

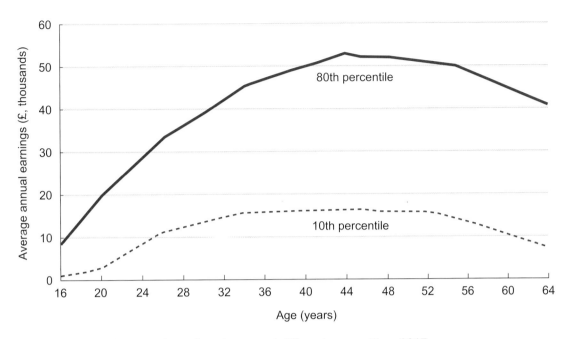

Figure 2.4 UK male annual earnings by age at different percentiles, 2017 (created using data from ONS, 2017c)

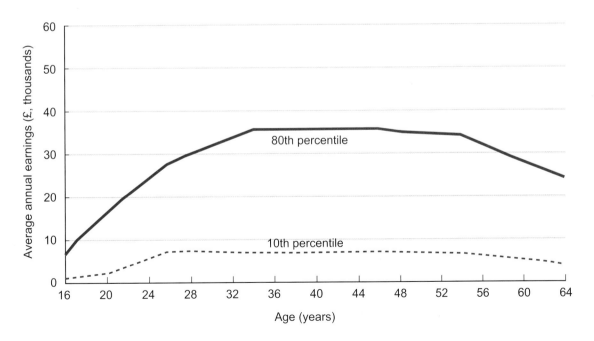

Figure 2.5 UK female annual earnings by age at different percentiles, 2017 (created using data from ONS, 2017c)

Also, many individuals live in different households over their life course. As some move into partnership, they may share some or all their income with their partner, and divide paid and unpaid work between them, especially with the arrival of children. Chapter 9 will come back to these issues and look at the long-term consequences of giving up earnings in the short term and the risks to individual financial independence in case of relationship breakdown.

Activity 2.8 Your income profile

Allow 10 minutes for this activity.

Thinking about your own household (or just you if you are a one-person household), try sketching and making notes about your own individual or household income profile for the past and the future. What pattern or shape is it likely to take in the future? How might this impact on your financial goals?

Comment

Your profile may be a bit bumpier, especially if you are self-employed or on temporary contracts, or if you have reduced your working hours to take care of relatives. However, it is true that gaining skills and qualifications may help achieve higher earnings over time.

6 Income tax and social protection

Taxation is neither good nor bad in itself. Everything depends on how taxes are collected and what they are used for.

(Piketty, 2015, p. 612)

So far, we have been looking at **original income**, which comes mostly from employment, although it may also come from other sources, such as savings. However, as Figure 2.6 shows, on top of original income the government may add cash benefit payments, resulting in what is called **gross income**. From gross income certain amounts are deducted (**direct taxes**, such as income tax and social security contributions) that result in disposable income or 'net income'.

Original income
Also sometimes called 'market income'. Income from employment, savings and investment prior to any government intervention.

Gross income
Original income from employment and investments plus cash transfers (benefits) from the state, but before any deduction in the form of income tax and social security contributions.

Direct taxes
Taxes on income or profits payable by the person or organisation receiving them (in contrast to indirect taxes, which apply to spending).

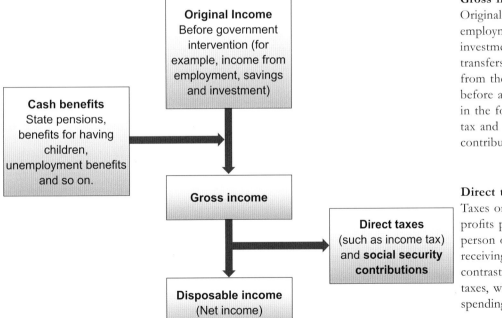

Figure 2.6 Stages of earnings and income

Activity 2.9 Benefits and taxes in the circular flow of income

Allow 5 minutes for this activity.

How might you represent the stages shown in Figure 2.6 as flows between sectors in the circular flow of income diagram that you studied in Chapter 1 (Figure 1.2 in Section 4.1)? Make notes of your answer, for example by sketching out Figure 1.2 and labelling the flows.

Comment

The answer to Activity 2.9 is given at the end of this chapter.

Exploring taxes and benefits is important to personal finance for two reasons:

- First, it enables accurate calculation of the amount of income that is available to spend or save. It would be difficult to budget and plan ahead without knowing this. (Budgeting will be discussed in Chapter 3.)

- Second, it provides understanding of how taxes and benefits redistribute income between richer and poorer people. They could be viewed as a burden on personal choice but they pay for protection and services that benefit us and others. They reduce the number of things we have to provide for ourselves, such as roads and schools. They can ensure we live in a society that is less unequal and more cohesive, and make us feel more secure if we trust that there is state support available in the event of an unexpected dip in our own finances or if we are unable to earn a decent living. They represent the compromise between individual interests and the interest of everyone as members of a society.

Figure 2.7 shows how total tax revenue to the governments of a number of affluent countries is split between different types of taxes (as at 2014). Some of these taxes are personal and related to individual income and gains, some are applied to corporations' profits or activities, and some are charged on the use of income such as expenditure on goods and services, usually attracting sales tax or value added tax (VAT). In these countries, the proportion of tax revenue made up by personal income tax and social security contributions (by employer and employee) is above 50%, except in the UK. Note that the US relies more on personal income tax than its European counterparts. Section 6.1 of this chapter explores taxation of personal income from employment.

In many countries, social security contributions are paid by both employees and employers. Historically, these payments formed the basis for paying social security benefits related to unemployment, illness and retirement in many countries, such as the UK, Germany and Italy. Note that the proportion of government revenue from social security contributions is lower in the UK than in Germany and Italy, for example. Northern European countries tend to amalgamate tax revenues from all sources to pay for social protection and public services. In Section 6.2, I will look at different types of social security benefits.

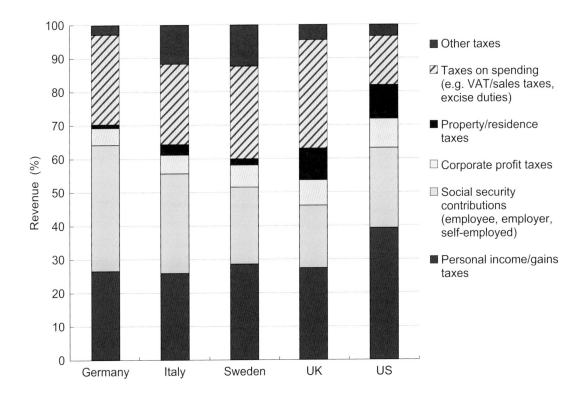

Figure 2.7 Sources of total government revenue in different countries, 2014 (created using data from OECD, 2017)

6.1 Personal income tax

Most income tax systems are characterised by five main features:

1 **Taxable income**, which is the part of gross income, including income that is not in cash (such as workplace benefits), that is liable for tax (for example regular earnings and bonuses, company car). Not all income is taxable; for example, gifts from a friend, some interest from savings, and lottery wins.

2 **Deductions** for specific circumstances or needs: this might include, for example, tax relief for childcare expenses, pension contributions and gifts to charity.

3 **Unit of assessment**, which is whether tax applies to the income of each individual or the joint income of some or all couples.

4 **How the tax is levied**. This might be at source, such as the UK's **Pay As You Earn (PAYE)** system for employees, or at the end of a period, after the person liable to pay the tax has declared all their income.

5 **Tax schedule**, which is the range of tax rates applied to bands of taxable income.

Although historically the 'unit of assessment' was total household income, individual taxation is now the norm in most developed countries. This means that individual incomes of household members are taxed separately. In the US, Spain, France and Germany (partially), household-based taxation still prevails, sometimes with special rules to account for children.

Most income-tax systems around the world operate with a tax schedule whose effects are said to operate on a 'progressive' tax schedule. A progressive tax system is one that taxes people with higher incomes proportionally more heavily. This means that the **average tax rate** on an income of say 50,000 is higher than the average tax rate on an income of 25,000.

One simple way to make taxation progressive is to allow for a chunk of income to be 'exempt' from tax, or taxed at 0%. In the UK it is called a personal allowance (PA).

For example, let's consider a simple tax system, where everyone is taxed at 20% on any income above a PA of 10,000.

Pay As You Earn (PAYE)
A system that a UK employer or a pension provider uses to deduct income tax and National Insurance contributions before they pay the wages of employees or the pension of the beneficiaries.

Average tax rate
Amount of tax due divided by taxable income, expressed as a percentage.

As this is a progressive system, the average rate of tax on higher incomes will be higher than on lower incomes. For example, the tax on an income of 25,000 is calculated as follows:

- Deduct 10,000 from 25,000.

- This leaves 15,000 to be taxed at 20%.

- 20% of 15,000 is 3000, so 3000 is the tax due on an income of 25,000. This gives an average tax rate of $3000 \div 25,000 \times 100 = 12\%$.

Activity 2.10 Calculating and comparing the average rate of tax

Allow 10 minutes for this activity.

Now try working out and comparing average tax rates for an individual and a household, making a note of your calculations as you go.

Using the above example of a simple tax system with a PA of 10,000 and a tax rate of 20%:

1 Calculate the tax due and the average tax rate for an individual with an income of 50,000 and check whether the tax system is progressive.

2 Calculate the tax due and average tax rate for a household with two adults each earning 25,000, assuming the unit of assessment is the individual. Compare with your answer to Question 1.

Comment

The answers to Activity 2.10 are given at the end of this chapter.

Let's look at how that works out across a range of incomes. You can see in Figure 2.8 (a) that in our example of a very simple tax system (PA of 10,000, tax rate 20%), the average tax rate increases gradually as income rises and gets closer to the 20% tax rate, and that the PA becomes a smaller proportion of taxable income. The 20% tax rate is an example of what is called the **marginal tax rate**; that is, the rate at which the last pound is taxed (i.e. any additional pound will be taxed at 20%).

Marginal tax rate
Percentage of tax due on the last (highest or top) unit of income (e.g. last pound or euro).

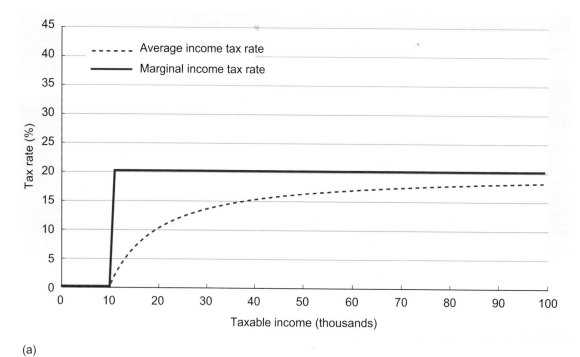

(a)

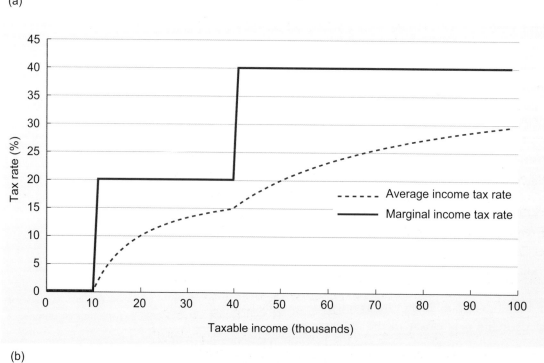

(b)

Figure 2.8 Examples of progressive tax systems

Many countries have made the system more progressive than this example by adding more tax (higher) rates to the tax schedule, for example taxing higher earners more highly after their income reaches a certain point. In chart (b) in Figure 2.8, you can see how this causes the average tax rate to rise more steeply at higher incomes than under the simpler system in chart (a). However, even then someone not far above the start of the '40% income band', say earning about 45,000, has an average tax rate of 17%, only 2 percentage points higher than under the simple system.

The other important feature of income tax systems is the nature and extent of deductions. Many countries accept that some income received should not be taxed. It can be the result of trying to influence someone's behaviour by rewarding them for doing the 'socially correct' thing. For example, contributing to a pension is deducted from the taxable earnings in many countries to encourage saving for retirement (more on this in Chapter 8). Other common tax deductions designed to influence behaviour are donations to charity or investing in growing companies. Childcare expenditure may also attract some tax relief in some countries in order to encourage parents to remain in paid employment (more on this in Chapter 9).

6.2 Social security benefits

Most developed countries' tax and benefit systems redistribute income between people – usually from the rich to the poor or from childless people to families with children – and over time, for example, by enabling people to build up an entitlement to receive future pension. Over their life course most people will both pay tax and receive some benefits. The availability of state benefits is important as part of the way of coping with unexpected events, which will be examined in Chapter 7.

Social protection can be delivered in cash – for example, to replace income lost due to unemployment or illness, or to cover additional needs due to, say, having children or a disability. (I will focus on cash benefits in this chapter.) It can also be 'in kind', meaning the provision of services, such as subsidised education, healthcare, and social care. The value of these services is an important (though often overlooked) component of a person's income, as these services would otherwise have to be paid for or foregone.

In most affluent countries with a well-developed system of social security, cash benefits are typically granted to the groups listed under 'Who for?' in Table 2.3.

Table 2.3 Main features and scope of social-security systems

Who for?[1]	Duration	Type of benefit	Entitlement	How much?	Who pays?
People on a low income	Either temporary or long-term	Mostly income replacement; partly help with costs	Usually means-tested	Often flat-rate[2]	Usually the state
Parents to help with cost of children	Temporary (during parental leave from work)	Income replacement	Universal[3], contributory or means-tested	Income-related or flat-rate	The state, employers or both
	Long-term (child benefits and childcare subsidies)	Help with costs	Often universal, may be means-tested	Often flat-rate	The state, employers or both
Unemployed	Usually temporary	Income replacement	Contributory or means-tested	Income-related or flat-rate	The state
Sick or injured	Usually temporary	Income replacement	Contributory or means-tested	Income-related or flat-rate	The state, employers or both
Disabled	Long-term	Help with costs	Universal	Often flat-rate	The state

1. A person may fall into more than one group at the same time – for example, the disabled often have a low income.

2. 'Flat-rate' means the same amount of cash benefit is given to everyone with the same circumstances, regardless of income. However, additional benefit payments may be provided, depending on circumstances and need (for example, extra cash for disabled children).

3. 'Universal' means everyone accepted as being in the 'Who for?' group may get the benefit, regardless of their income and without needing a record of contributions.

Looking at Table 2.3, you can probably see that long-term benefits are more likely to be flat-rate, means-tested and paid for by the state. This reflects the fact that these benefits are expensive and that often the people who receive them are less likely to be in work, and so attached to an employer. However, where there is an employer – as in the case of many parents – there is scope for the state to pass some or all of the cost to employers.

For example, the state may require employers to pay a minimum amount of sick pay or paid maternity leave, but might provide help with those costs for small employers.

(a)　(b)

(c)　(d)

Government revenue can pay for public services, such as healthcare and long-term care (a), childcare (b), education (c) and public transport (d)

Another important difference is whether the benefit is replacing lost income or covering additional needs (due to disability or the presence of children). The same person can receive both forms of benefits; for example a parent may receive benefits to replace income lost due to time off work following the birth of a child and child benefits to help with child costs. The same goes for those who can no longer work, sometimes permanently, because of an injury, illness, or disability: they may receive benefits to replace lost income and also to cover additional costs, such as needing help with day-to-day activities or adaptations to their home.

Some income-replacement benefits will be proportional to the income lost, while others will take the form of a flat-rate payment. For example, in many countries unemployment benefit is paid as a proportion of the lost income – generally within limits, for a short period of time and linked to social security contributions – after which it may become flat-rate. Income-related benefits favour higher earners, while flat-rate benefits are proportionately more generous to low earners.

You can also see in Table 2.3 that there are three main ways in which a person may be entitled to receive cash benefits: universal, contributory or means-tested.

- Under universal systems, the benefit is the same regardless of the claimant's situation. An example for many decades was child benefits in the UK and Scandinavian countries, where the amount received was the same regardless of parental income and without any need to pay contributions (but could vary by age and size of family).

- Contributory benefits usually refer to a form of social insurance, where a person becomes entitled to income replacement, for example in case of unemployment or retirement, through building up a record of paying social security contributions.

Means-tested
Payments that are made only to those who are assessed to have a certain level of income or less, and in some cases a certain level of assets or less.

- **Means-tested** benefits have spread across countries, especially for transfers that aim to help avoid people falling into extreme financial poverty. Some unemployment benefit is also means-tested in the UK. Even child benefit was transformed in the UK, when in 2013 it became taxed away for higher-income parents. Other common forms of means-tested benefits include benefits for low-income families with children, and those paid to boost low wages of workers.

Means-tested cash benefits have increasingly been used in many countries to control public spending, while at the same time targeting the support at those most in need. However setting the adequate level of support is a difficult exercise in balancing competing objectives, including simplicity of administration. If set too low or available to too narrow a group of beneficiaries, benefits won't be effective in reducing poverty; if too high or too wide, the benefits system may end up being too costly and vilified by a majority of taxpayers.

Moreover, if the level of support is set too high, recipients might not feel the need to work as they can rely on benefits, creating a disincentive to work. This can thus conflict with other government goals such as increasing employment, thus increasing tax revenue necessary to pay for the benefits.

On the other hand, if the means-testing is too harsh, that is if the benefit is clawed back too rapidly as an individual's other income rises, this might discourage people from looking for employment altogether or from working additional hours (another disincentive to work).

When looking for jobs or at increasing earnings, people want to strike a balance between the gains from working relative to not working, and additional costs of working relative to not working (such as transport, childcare, and of course income tax). This is known in economics as an 'opportunity cost', a concept you met in Chapter 1, Section 5.2.

Strong disincentives caused by the benefit structure are called an **unemployment trap**. This is where people have little or no incentive to move into work because of the extent to which their other sources of income (cash benefits) would be clawed back. A **poverty trap** can then occur if, on top of that, the benefit is too low to lift the person out of poverty, but too high compared to what alternatives such as paid employment offer.

Unemployment trap
A situation in which people looking for jobs cannot find any that pay better income than that they get when unemployed.

Poverty trap
A situation in which workless people cannot find a job that pays decent enough income, while the income that they receive from the state remains too low to escape the risk of poverty.

7 Cash flow statement: the income side

Hopefully you've been convinced that a knowledge of the tax and benefits system, especially for the country you live in, is essential in order to be able to calculate net income accurately and so plan your finances effectively. A powerful tool in financial planning is the cash flow statement. Thinking back to the income profiles you looked at in Section 5 of this chapter, a cash flow statement is like taking a slice through the income profile over a short period of time, such as a year, month or week. It enables you to look in detail at the flow of money coming into a household over that period and where it goes when it is spent. This is the first step in taking control of your finances. In this section, we'll look at inflows – that is, income. The spending side of the cash flow statement – outflows – is covered in Chapter 3.

There are different issues to be considered in recording the income side of a cash flow statement, as explained below.

Disposable (net) income – The statement should record the flows of income actually received. For most people, this will represent their net (disposable) income, their take-home pay. For example, in the UK, employees' salary or pay will normally already have had income tax deducted (via PAYE), as well as National Insurance contributions and pension contributions. But some people will receive some income paid gross, such as self-employment earnings or investment returns. In this case, the gross income should be recorded in the cash flow statement, but it must be remembered that there may be tax still due on this income at the end of the tax year. These tax payments should either be subtracted from income or may be recorded as an expense.

All sources of income – You should also include all the different sources of income, using the categorisations from Figure 2.1 – including income from paid employment, self-employment, savings and investments, pensions and social security benefits. Any additional income is recorded under the 'other' category.

Frequency of income – Think about how frequently different types of income are received. For instance, a household may receive a combination of weekly benefits and monthly pay. If the cash flow statement is drawn at monthly intervals, then all flows of income occurring during that period need to be recorded and added up in the statement.

Individual or household – The cash flow statement can be drawn up at the level of the household or individual. Which is chosen will depend on household composition, but to get an accurate figure of total household income it is necessary to include all income earners.

Activity 2.11 Creating a cash flow statement – income

Allow 10 minutes for this activity, though you may need to ask people for information and come back to it.

Copy and complete the income part of the cash flow statement in Table 2.4 for your own household, or for just yourself. If you are in a multi-person household, the normal assumption would be that the income of other household members would be recorded. However, if this is not possible, simply complete this using your own income.

Table 2.4 Your household cash flow statement (income side), previous month

Components of income	Person 1	Person 2	Person 3	Total household income for each category
Wages and salaries				
Self-employment				
Savings and investment				
Pension				
Social security benefits				
Other income				
Total income				

Comment

You can check the internal consistency of the table by ensuring that the overall total in the bottom right of the table equals the sum of column and row totals. Keeping a record of your finances is helpful as a starting point for budgeting, as will be discussed in detail in Chapter 3.

Note that recording income is different from constructing an average cash flow statement that takes account of receipts that do not recur every month (for example, an end-of-year bonus or a tax refund). However, an average cash flow statement can be very useful as a tool for checking whether a household is living within its means overall and as a basis for starting to plan ahead. To create an average cash flow statement, the most common technique is to record all income over a year in order to calculate an annual income first and then convert it into an equivalent monthly amount. Rather than recording every item of income month by month or week by week, you could instead work from the frequencies of different types of income. For example, you would multiply a weekly income by 52 and then divide by 12 to get the monthly equivalent.

8 Conclusion

This chapter has focused on various aspects of income, such as its different sources, including paid employment and state benefits. It has also helped to develop the four themes of *Personal Finance*. For example, Sections 3, 4 and 5 explained how the changing social and economic context impacts upon paid employment, the most important component of household income. In addition, the interrelationship between individuals and households and how income changes over the life course were examined in Section 5. Section 6 returned to the economic context, explaining the tax and benefits system, and applied this knowledge to the individual. Finally, Section 7 introduced the cash flow statement, a crucial first step in financial planning. The economic, political and social contexts are hugely relevant when looking at the different factors that influence the determination of wages, as well as how people's opportunity costs of working versus not working are affected by changes in government tax and benefit policies.

Taking these aspects together, this chapter represents some important early steps in building financial capability. Having established where income comes from, the following chapters explore how it can be spent, supplemented by borrowing, or saved and invested. Chapter 3 starts this process by looking at expenditure.

Answers to activities in Chapter 2

Answers to Activity 2.1

1   This is income, a regular flow of money each week.

2   This is an asset. In this case it is financial (and you may be able to earn interest on it), and liquid (it is easily converted into cash).

3   This is an asset. In this case, it is intangible, and is normally non-marketable. It is usually illiquid until the owner is above a specified age.

Answer to Activity 2.2

In Greece, households on average receive 55% of their total income in the form of wages and salaries, compared to 81% in the US. About a quarter of average income in Greece is received from paid self-employment activities, a much larger share of income than in all the other more affluent countries in the figure but lower than the proportion in Brazil or Vietnam.

Answers to Activity 2.6

• There was a faster increase in total employment for women than men in both countries. This increase was twice as large in the UK: a 44% increase for women, versus 19% for men; whereas in Italy, the change for women was similar, at 41%, but was negative for men.

• Part-time employment is much more prevalent among women in the UK than Italy, but has increased sharply in Italy over the period shown. Part-time employment for men, while much lower than for women, has increased in both the UK and Italy, the latter especially in the aftermath of the 2007–08 economic crisis.

Answer to Activity 2.9

In terms of the money flows between households, government and corporate sectors described in Chapter 1, Figure 1.2, income tax and social security contributions (called National Insurance contributions in the UK) are examples of money flowing from the household to government sector, while benefit payments flow in the opposite direction.

Answers to Activity 2.10

1   The tax due on 50,000 can be calculated as follows:

    o   Deduct the first 10,000 from 50,000.
    o   This leaves 40,000 to be taxed at 20%.
    o   20% of 40,000 is 8000, which is the tax due. Thus the average tax rate is $8000 \div 50,000 \times 100 = 16\%$.

    Since 16% is higher than the 12% average tax rate on income of 25,000, the tax schedule is indeed progressive.

2   As you saw earlier, tax on 25,000 would be 3000. So, in this household of two adults each earning 25,000, total household tax would be 6000. This is less than the 8000 tax paid by the individual in Question 1. Thus, under a progressive tax schedule with the individual as the unit of account, a household with only one earner pays more tax than a household with the same taxable income, but spread across two (or more) earners.

References

Autor, D. H., Levy, F. and Murnane, R. (2003) 'The skill content of recent technological change: an empirical exploration', *Quarterly Journal of Economics*, vol. 118, no. 4, pp. 1279–333.

Cingano, F. (2014) 'Trends in income inequality and its impact on economic growth', *OECD Social, Employment and Migration Working Papers*, no. 163 [Online], OECD Publishing, Paris. Available at http://dx.doi.org/10.1787/5jxrjncwxv6j-en (Accessed 7 March 2018).

Elliott, L. (2013) 'UK shadow economy worth £150bn', *The Guardian*, 4 June [Online]. Available at www.theguardian.com/business/2013/jun/04/uk-shadow-economy (Accessed 14 April 2017).

European Institute for Gender Equality (EIGE) (2016) *Poverty, Gender and Lone Parents in the EU*, 19 September [Online]. Available at http://eige.europa.eu/rdc/eige-publications/poverty-gender-and-lone-parents-eu (Accessed 12 July 2017).

Eurostat (2017) *Online database*. Available at http://ec.europa.eu/eurostat/data/database (Accessed 20 October 2017).

Gebel, M. and Giesecke, J. (2016) 'Does deregulation help? The impact of employment protection reforms on youths' unemployment and temporary employment risks in Europe', *European Sociological Review*, vol. 32, no. 4, pp. 486–500 [Online]. DOI: https://doi.org/10.1093/esr/jcw022 (Accessed 7 March 2018).

International Labour Office (ILO) (2013) *Women and Men in the Informal Economy: A Statistical Picture*, 2nd edn [Online], ILO, Geneva. Available at www.ilo.org/wcmsp5/groups/public/—dgreports/—stat/documents/publication/wcms_234413.pdf (Accessed 14 April 2017).

International Labour Office (ILO) (2015) *Global Wage Report 2014/15* [Online], ILO, Geneva. Available at www.ilo.org/global/research/global-reports/global-wage-report/2014/lang—en/index.htm (Accessed 14 April 2017).

Jami, C. (2015) *Killosophy*, Criss Jami, CreateSpace Independent Publishing Platform.

Lewis, L. (2017) 'Can robots make up for Japan's care home shortfall?', *Financial Times*, 18 October [Online]. Available at www.ft.com/content/418ffd08-9e10-11e7-8b50-0b9f565a23e1 (Accessed 24 October 2017).

Lindsay, C. (2003) 'A century of labour market changes: 1900 to 2000', Office for National Statistics, *Labour Market Trends*, special feature, March.

Marsh, S. (2017) 'Zero-hours contracts affect young people's health, study finds', *The Guardian*, 5 July [Online]. Available at www.theguardian.com/uk-news/2017/jul/05/zero-hours-contracts-affect-young-peoples-health-study-finds (Accessed 19 July 2017).

Mayfield, M. and Mayfield, J. (2014) 'What workers want: a global perspective', *Competitiveness Review*, vol. 24, no. 4, pp. 332–46 [Online]. DOI: https://doi.org/10.1108/CR-01-2013-0006 (Accessed 7 March 2018).

Nussbaum, M. and Sen, A. (eds) (1993) *The Quality of Life*, Oxford, Oxford University Press.

Office for National Statistics (ONS) (2018) *Time Series: RPI Ave Price – Milk: Pasteurised, Per Pint* [Online], dataset. Available at https://www.ons.gov.uk/economy/inflationandpriceindices/timeseries/cznt/mm23 (Accessed 28 March 2018).

Office for National Statistics (ONS) (2017a) *The Effect of Taxes and Benefits on Household Income* [Online], dataset for financial year ending 2016. Available at www.ons.gov.uk/peoplepopulationandcommunity/personalandhouseholdfinances/incomeandwealth/datasets/theeffectsoftaxesandbenefitsonhouseholdincomefinancialyearending2014 (Accessed 20 May 2017).

Office for National Statistics (ONS) (2017b) *A02 SA: Employment, Unemployment and Economic Inactivity for People Aged 16 and Over and Aged from 16 to 64 (Seasonally Adjusted)* [Online], dataset. Available at www.ons.gov.uk/employmentandlabourmarket/peopleinwork/employmentandemployeetypes/datasets/employmentunemploymentandeconomicinactivityforpeopleaged16andoveranda-gedfrom16to64seasonallyadjusteda02sa (Accessed 20 November 2017).

Office for National Statistics (ONS) (2017c) *Annual Survey of Hours and Earnings*, 2017 provisional results [Online]. Available at www.ons.gov.uk/employmentandlabourmarket/peopleinwork/earningsandworkinghours/bulletins/annualsurveyofhoursandearnings/2017provisionaland2016revisedresults/relateddata (Accessed 20 November 2017).

O'Reilly, J., Smith, M., Deakin, S. and Burchell, B. (2015) 'Equal pay as a moving target: international perspectives on forty-years of addressing the gender pay gap', *Cambridge Journal of Economics*, vol. 39, no. 2, pp. 299–317 [Online]. DOI: https://doi.org/10.1093/cje/bev010 (Accessed 24 July 2017).

Organisation for Economic Co-operation and Development (OECD) (2011) *Divided We Stand: Why Inequality Keeps Rising* [Online]. Available at www.oecd.org/els/soc/dividedwestandwhyinequalitykeepsrising.htm (Accessed 7 March 2018).

Organisation for Economic Co-operation and Development (OECD) (2015) *In It Together: Why Less Inequality Benefits All* [Online]. Available at www.oecd.org/els/in-it-together-why-less-inequality-benefits-all-9789264235120-en.htm) (Accessed 24 July 2017).

Organisation for Economic Co-operation and Development (OECD) (2017) *OECD Tax Database* [Online]. Available at www.oecd.org/tax/tax-policy/tax-database.htm (Accessed 20 July 2017).

Piketty, T. (2015) *Capital in the Twenty-First Century*, Cambridge, MA, Harvard University Press.

Schäfer, A. and Gottschall, K. (2015) 'From wage regulation to wage gap: how wage-setting institutions and structures shape the gender wage gap across three industries in 24 European countries and Germany', *Cambridge Journal of Economics*, vol. 39, no. 2, pp. 467–96.

Shaikh, N. (2004) 'Amartya Sen: a more human theory of development', *Asia Society* [Online]. Available at https://asiasociety.org/amartya-sen-more-human-theory-development (Accessed 15 February 2018).

Stiglitz, J. (2012) *The Price of Inequality*, New York, WW Norton.

Thatcher, M. (1984) *Notes for 1922 Committee* [Online]. Available at www.margaretthatcher.org/document/136215 (Accessed 3 December 2017).

Wilkinson, R. and Pickett, K. (2009) *The Spirit Level: Why Equality is Better for Everyone*, London, Penguin Books.

Zimmerman, K. (2016) 'Refugee and migrant labor market integration: Europe in need of a new policy agenda', paper presented at the *EUI Conference on the Integration of Migrants and Refugees*, Florence, 29–30 September 2016.

To cite this chapter, use the following format in your reference list:

De Henau, J. and Callaghan, G. (2019) 'Income', in De Henau, J. and Lowe, J. (eds) *Personal Finance*, Milton Keynes, The Open University, pp. 55–106.

Chapter 3
Expenditure

Jonquil Lowe and Martin Higginson

Contents

1 Introduction

In Chapter 2 you saw how income can come from many sources. Broadly speaking, there are two ways in which disposable income may be used: you can spend it or save it. This chapter looks at spending (otherwise known as expenditure). Later chapters will look at what happens to income that is not spent.

Choices about spending are crucial to achieve financial security and goals. If an individual or household spends more than their income, this will lead to debt; whereas spending less allows people to save or pay off previously accumulated debts. In this chapter, you will also consider what determines individual and household expenditure.

In today's society there are many opportunities to spend money: goods and services can be bought online, in shops, from catalogues, via the TV, and from big out-of-town retail parks and centres that provide immersive shopping experiences.

Advertising and the ease of internet shopping continually tempt people to spend money – whether it's money they already have, or money they can borrow. Some spending may be on the essentials of life such as food and accommodation. But the reasons for spending go far beyond such practical and functional uses. Increasingly, wherever you are in the world, twenty-first century living involves being part of a **consumer society**; spending money has become a leisure activity in its own right for a growing part of the population (while at the same time, others still struggle to put food on the table).

Consumer society
A society in which people place a high value on possessions and are continually encouraged to buy more.

Opinions others make about us are often based on what we buy and the possessions we own. So spending can also be a means of signalling who we are; it forms an integral part of how we relate to one another.

In Sections 2 and 3 of this chapter, we'll explore some of the economic and social influences that affect the way households and individuals spend money. This broader discussion provides an important context for Section 4, which introduces budgeting. This is a way of improving household finances by planning spending in relation to income, and it is the bedrock of being able to achieve financial goals. Budgeting is explained first with reference to a one-person household, before discussing the more complex issues about the management and control of finances that arise in multi-person households, including those with children (Section 5).

2 Economic influences on spending

In this section, you'll consider how household expenditure is influenced by economic factors, such as income, price level and relative prices of different goods and services. But first let's look at how the spending decisions you make when combined with those of everyone else in the country you live in – together called **household consumption** – are important to the economy as a whole.

2.1 Household consumption and the economy

The circular flow of income diagram that you looked at in Chapter 1 highlighted the way in which consumers' actions have an impact on other sectors of the economy, in particular government and corporations. Apart from paying taxes, the biggest way that consumers influence the economy is through their spending decisions: how much to spend and on what. When the spending of all households is added together, household consumption is usually the largest part of a country's gross domestic product (GDP), and so is very important as a driver of economic growth (i.e. the growth of a country's GDP).

Household consumption
A term used by economists to describe total spending on goods and services by all the households living in a particular country or economy (as distinct from spending by an individual household).

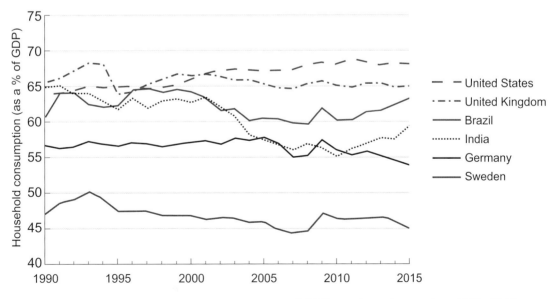

Figure 3.1 Household consumption as a percentage of GDP – selected countries, 1990–2015 (data from United Nations, 2017)

Activity 3.1 Patterns in household consumption

Allow 10 minutes for this activity.

Looking at Figure 3.1, which two features in the data stand out to you?

Comment

The two features that stand out for us are:

- In most countries, household consumption has been a fairly stable proportion of GDP over the 25-year period shown – you can see this because the lines are mostly fairly straight and level, varying by 5 percentage points or less over the whole period. The main exception is India, where the percentage fell from a high of 65% in the early 1990s, to a low of 55% in 2010 before climbing back to 59%.

- The level of household consumption as a proportion of GDP varies greatly between some of the countries.

The variation in the proportion of consumption in GDP across countries could be due to differences in the level of government spending in each country (one of the major contextual changes that you looked at in Chapter 1). For example, Figure 3.1 shows that household consumption is a relatively low percentage of GDP in Sweden, and government spending there is around a quarter of GDP (United Nations, 2017). By contrast, household consumption is a much higher proportion of GDP in the US, where government spending is only around one-seventh of GDP (United Nations, 2017).

This seems to highlight the trade-off you read about in Chapter 1: in countries where the state provides less financial support, households must take on more responsibility for looking after their own financial well-being, which often implies higher household spending.

We can check this theory further by looking at the breakdown of consumption between different types of spending in Figure 3.2.

Figure 3.2 is a standard bar chart, but this time turned on its side to make it easier to read the bar labels. Figure 3.2 shows a striking difference between the spending in Sweden and the US: 22% of US household consumption goes on health (medical products, outpatient services and hospital services paid directly by households), compared with just 4% in Sweden. Americans also spend more (9% of household consumption) on social protection, insurance and financial services, compared with 6% in Sweden. This, again, tends to support our theory that private spending on these sorts of items is higher in countries where state spending on public services and the welfare state is less.

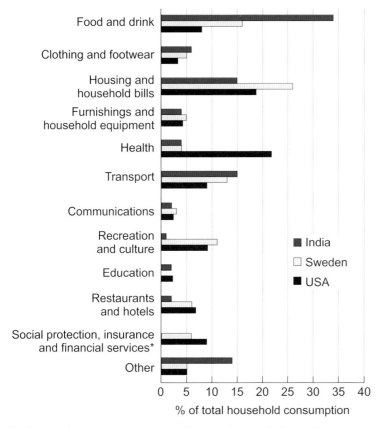

*No 'Social protection, insurance and financial services' data available for India.

Figure 3.2 Breakdown of household consumption by type of spending (data from OECD, 2017)

Figure 3.2 also shows that a higher proportion of household consumption in India (34%) goes on food and drink than in Sweden (16%) or the US (8%). This is typical for less wealthy countries, as is the lower spending on recreation and culture, and restaurants and hotels.

The other major difference shown is the high proportion of household consumption in Sweden that relates to housing and bills. Figure 3.2 tells us nothing about the reason for this, so we would need to look for explanations elsewhere. For example, one reason might be price differences. Indeed, in 2016, the price of domestic electricity in Sweden was 39% higher than in the US (Department for Business, Energy and Industrial Strategy, 2017).

2.2 Household spending and income

The patterns shown in Figure 3.2 for all households in wealthier and poorer countries are likely to be similar to those that appear when we look at individual households.

In general, we might expect people to consume more as their income rises. However, a household's level of income doesn't just affect how much it spends overall, it also affects the types of goods and services that it buys. With more money available:

- A smaller proportion of total spending is needed for necessities like food. Households may switch to more expensive foods but any rise in the amount spent on food is likely to be smaller than the rise in income.

- Spending on leisure goods and services (for example, eating out and visits to the cinema) – which may previously have been unaffordable luxuries – tends to rise.

- Household spending on some other goods, such as tobacco, tends to decrease. This is because people's tastes also change as their income increases so that, for instance, they may opt for healthier lifestyles and therefore buy fewer things that are harmful to health.

2.3 Household spending and the price level

You saw in Chapter 2 that inflation reduces purchasing power: the same income buys less if general prices rise. However, if earnings, benefits, pensions and other incomes also rise, households will not necessarily have to reduce the amount they spend.

Where income does not keep pace with rising prices, there can be conflicting effects. On the one hand:

- households might cut their spending, especially on non-essential items

- households might switch to cheaper substitutes – for example, shopping at discount stores instead of premium supermarkets.

On the other hand:

- when luxuries become unaffordable, households might increase their consumption of smaller, affordable treats – this is sometimes called the 'lipstick effect' because allegedly it traces back to the **Great Depression** of the 1930s when, despite high unemployment and fortunes being lost, sales of cosmetics rose
- if prices are expected to carry on rising, households might decide to bring forward major purchases on the basis that they'll have to pay more if they delay.

Conversely to the final point above, during periods when the general price level is falling (**deflation**), as was the case in Japan during much of the first decade of the twenty-first century (OECD, 2018), consumers might postpone spending in the expectation that they can buy goods and services more cheaply if they wait.

Great Depression
A period of falling or stagnant economic activity and high unemployment in the US and many other countries during the 1930s.

Deflation
A continual decrease in the general level of prices.

2.4 Household spending and relative prices

Variations in the price of different goods and services relative to each other can be an important driver of changes in the pattern of consumption. When the prices of some goods and services fall (or increase less quickly), people may buy more of these and less of the now relatively more expensive items. For example, if the prices of imported goods fall in the UK, people might switch to buying more oranges and bananas, rather than home-grown apples. When electronic goods, such as TVs and mobile phones, first came on to the market, they tended to be expensive. But, as prices came down, more people bought them, and many households decided to own several, rather than just one TV or mobile phone.

However, people do not necessarily buy more of something when its price falls. Take petrol: if the price drops, rather than make more car journeys because they can buy more petrol, households might choose to spend the money they've saved on other things such as leisure goods.

3 Social influences on consumption

Our spending decisions are sometimes influenced by less conscious considerations than simply the price of something, or how much money we have to spend. Social pressures can shape our spending decisions, too, and make us susceptible to the marketing messages of firms. This section looks at some of the theories about these social influences.

As you read this section, reflect on your spending behaviour and that of other people. Do the theories covered (at least in part) explain the spending decisions you and others make?

3.1 Consumption as status and identity

One of the reasons people seem to have to keep spending is because there is more to spending and consuming than simply satisfying needs. The concept of **social status** can provide a way to understand this. The sociologist Max Weber (1948 [1924]) saw a person's social status as their position in society, based on the level of authority and/or prestige that they hold in the eyes of others.

Social status
A position within society, or the honour or prestige that a particular individual or group is accorded by other members of society.

Like income, status is unevenly distributed, and while it is common that people with higher incomes have higher levels of status, this is not always the case. For example, in many societies ministers of religion, with modest incomes, can carry high levels of status; in the UK, the status of teachers and plumbers may not reflect their respective incomes. But in a world where jobs are no longer for life, Bauman (1999) argues that consumption has taken over from work as our source of status and also identity. As Bauman puts it, in a consumer society:

> the roads to self-identity, to a place in society, to life lived in a form recognisable as that of meaningful living, all require daily visits to the market place ... One needs to be a consumer first, before one can think of becoming anything particular.

> (Bauman, 1999, p. 26)

Max Weber (1864–1920), this photo taken in 1918

Bauman also suggests that consumption is not about creating a single identity for life (this may have been the case in the past, in relation to the job someone did). As trends and fashions shift, so the identity we adopt, and the consumption patterns that signal that identity, also change. This can create constant pressure on household and individual finances, as we try to keep up with those trends.

3.2 Displays of status

You may be familiar with the idea of the **status symbol** as a way of publicly displaying status to others. In traditional societies (non-consumer societies), status is symbolically displayed through body marks (such as tattoos or make-up), clothing, crowns, jewels and other objects, which are often passed down through generations. In a consumer society, the goods that people buy may have useful properties, but they can also act as status symbols. Buying a particularly sought-after type of mobile phone or car not only enables us to stay connected and on the move; it's also an act of **symbolic consumption**.

Symbolic consumption suggests that people are concerned about what others think of them, and that the opinions we hold about other people are based partly on what they consume and the material things they own. It gives a powerful motivation for spending.

Status symbol
Something that indicates the social standing of its owner. Usually a mark of high or superior standing.

Symbolic consumption
Consuming products or lifestyles for the social meanings attached to them, and for others to see.

To explore these ideas further, let's consider the work of two influential writers: first, Thorstein Veblen, and then Pierre Bourdieu. Both offer ideas that connect *why* we spend to the concept of status; they can help us reflect on why we, and other people, spend money in certain ways.

Veblen (1925) was writing a century ago, but his views still resonate today. He saw much spending as a way of displaying an individual's wealth. Rather than being bought simply for their function, some expensive and luxurious products are bought so that others can see how 'well off' the purchaser is. People who say things such as, 'Andrew must be loaded because he drives a Ferrari' are expressing Veblen's point: people will infer from Andrew's purchase of an expensive car that he is wealthy. If others react that way, then purchasing the Ferrari was a successful way for Andrew to acquire the status that is accorded when a person is perceived to be wealthy.

Conspicuous consumption
The ostentatious display of wealth in order to gain recognition by others of one's assumed or actual high status.

According to Veblen, people want to be seen as wealthy in a society in which being wealthy confers high status. Consumption has therefore taken on a symbolic role: the symbol of wealth is the Ferrari that Andrew drives; its price tag confers status.

Veblen would call Andrew's purchase of the Ferrari **conspicuous consumption**.

Veblen's own views of conspicuous consumption were scathing: he deplored the ways in which the 'leisure class' – the top 1% of the early twentieth century – lived a life of waste and ostentation, flaunting their symbols of conspicuous consumption (Abercrombie et al., 2000). Whether you share Veblen's views or not, his analysis can help explain why people buy clothes with 'designer labels' and other such obviously expensive goods. While it may be easier for people who are well off to indulge in this conspicuous consumption, a possible consequence for those on lower incomes, or with few assets, is the temptation to borrow money – and perhaps go into debt – to buy more expensive goods and services, in order to be seen as having a higher social status.

3.3 Signs of belonging

A somewhat different view of the aims of symbolic consumption is taken by Bourdieu (1977), who has written extensively on how consumption is used as a way of distinguishing people by **social class**. What defines social class is argued at length among academics, with factors such as income, occupation, education, cultural habits and power all being considered. Although a complex idea, for our purposes the significant thing about social class is that it divides the population into different social groups. People may make some effort to demonstrate which social class they belong to, and to distinguish themselves from members of other classes.

Social class
An informal ranking of people in a society based on their income, occupation, education and other factors.

For Bourdieu (1977), consumption and our tastes are influenced by experiences in childhood, family and schooling, but most crucially by social class. He talks of individuals unconsciously embodying the past history, culture, tastes and habits of their class, and reinforcing these through their own beliefs and actions. Historically, he argues, people were born into a particular class (lord of the manor, farmhand, and so on), but in modern society an important way of signalling class is through what we buy.

Clearly, income is important in deciding what you can buy; those in higher social classes can, in general, afford more expensive or more varied items. Yet Bourdieu also explains how tastes are important in differentiating people. According to Bourdieu, while individuals have some freedom in their purchasing decisions, their social class restricts the way in which they carry out these decisions by influencing their actual tastes. How one spends money not only becomes an ongoing struggle to maintain differences between social classes, including by buying things they might not like at first, it actually becomes the result of a taste that has been shaped by the very belonging (or aspiration to belong) to a specific social class.

Bourdieu's ideas can be extended beyond social class to understand how consumption can be used to signal belonging to any social group, be that punk, goth, hipster, environmentalist, intellectual or the many other group identities that wax and wane over time.

Activity 3.2 Social theories of consumption

Allow 5 minutes for this activity.

1   Do you think that Veblen's idea of conspicuous consumption explains the spending behaviour of people you know? Does it explain your own behaviour?

2   Do you think Bourdieu's idea of spending, to distinguish oneself from other social classes, is more useful than Veblen's idea of conspicuous consumption?

Comment

It's always easier to classify other people's consumption as conspicuous, than to recognise symbolic reasons for our own spending. We usually think that we make our spending decisions based on the material properties of the things we buy: whether we like the shape of a particular sofa or want a high-tech digital camera to take better photos. That's where Bourdieu's (1977) theory is particularly interesting and useful. It is saying that our taste – our liking for a sofa of that particular shape or our wish to produce high-quality photos – is produced by living in a particular social class. Therefore, simply following our tastes when we go shopping has the result of distinguishing ourselves from people in different social classes. We simultaneously buy what we want and engage in symbolic consumption.

3.4 Changing with the times

You can see from the comment section of Activity 3.2 that the idea of symbolic consumption isn't so much about individual wants, but a reflection of the type of society we live in. In common with other aspects of society, the status symbols change over time. For example, consider the fashion brand Burberry (see Figure 3.3 (a) and (b)): once a status symbol of the rich, over time you were as likely to see working-class tourists wearing the Burberry check as people from higher classes. Conversely, the working class often influence the middle and upper classes, in trends related to music or other aspects of fashion.

Moreover, symbolic consumption no longer necessarily means consuming more 'things'. Bellezza et al. (2017) suggest that 'busyness' at work, which they refer to as conspicuous consumption of time, is a status symbol to be aspired to in the US, contrasting with Veblen's conclusions that living a life of leisure was the ultimate display of wealth at that time.

(a)   (b)

Figure 3.3 Symbols of consumption can change over time

For those who seek status, there seems also to be a shift towards consumption that reflects cultural standing, rather than ownership of material things. Currid-Halkett (2017) finds that the spending patterns of the wealthiest have moved towards education, organic food and practising yoga, choices that she calls 'inconspicuous consumption'. Eckhardt et al. (2014) also use the term 'inconspicuous consumption', but in a slightly different way. They suggest wealthy consumers are shifting towards distinguishing themselves through more subtle, less obvious branding – such as smaller logos on clothing – making the signals identifiable, but only to the cognoscenti (those people 'in the know').

3.5 Marketing and advertising

Recognising the importance of symbolic consumption does not imply that most things that are bought are actually useless: most products have a function for us to consider buying them in the first place. For example, we want a vacuum cleaner to suck up dust, or we want a car to take us from A to B – and some advertisements do just focus on the quality or abundance of features that a product offers.

However, in contrast, many adverts seem to be offering something far more than the product in question. In Figure 3.4 (a) the item being advertised (a car) is not even shown. Instead, this advert uses symbolism, suggesting freedom and a sense that drivers of this car are rather trendy city-dwellers.

The advertisement for tomato sauce (Figure 3.4 (b)) also uses symbolism to appeal to consumers who might be expected to favour a high content of naturally grown tomatoes, rather than a mix of ingredients and flavouring typically found in such manufactured products.

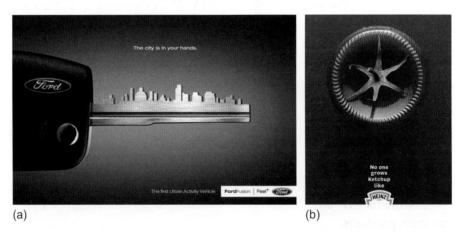

(a)   (b)

Figure 3.4   Advertising makes use of symbolism to generate sales

Marketing departments have long recognised that products and brands have these symbolic characteristics: advertising often uses symbolic images to sell products. Naomi Klein (2000), writing about brands and their role in a modern society, describes her view of what marketing departments are thinking about when they use symbolic images:

They dream ... about their brands' deep inner meanings – the way they capture the spirit of individuality, athleticism, wilderness or community ... Savvy ad agencies have all moved away from the idea of flogging a product made by someone else, and come to think of themselves instead as brand factories, hammering out what is true value: the idea, the lifestyle, the attitude.

(Klein, 2000, pp. 195–6)

It can be hard to escape the feeling that marketers are targeting us relentlessly. Online, adverts often pop up, tailored to your browsing history; tick boxes ask if your details can be passed on; stores offer loyalty cards to gather data about your shopping habits and then target you with personalised deals. Even TV commercials shift to anti-ageing creams and incontinence products as populations and TV audiences get older. The average age of BBC viewers is now above 60, as younger audiences turn to online content (Geddes, 2018).

A traditional marketing technique is to 'segment' (split) the population into different **socio-demographic groups**. Sophisticated databases identify where different categories of people are likely to live, and what media (print, TV, online, and so on) they are likely to use, so marketing messages can be placed carefully in the right locations/via the right media, to target products at specific types of people.

Socio-demographic groups
Categories in which individuals may be placed, based on a range of social, demographic and economic factors, such as age, gender, family type, income, occupation and ethnicity.

This helps to explain why adverts differ between national newspapers, and why junk mail in different areas of the same town may be selling different products. New techniques for targeting potential consumers arrived with the growth of the internet: marketing departments can now use information about us (which they buy or collect themselves through our internet browsing and use of social media) to produce advertisements that are increasingly individualised, to encourage us to buy their products.

Activity 3.3 Individualised marketing

Allow 5 minutes for this activity.

If you use social media, have you noticed adverts that pop up, which seem to be personalised to you, reflecting the things you like or buy regularly? Have you ever considered how that personalisation happens?

Comment

When you use social media, you typically give away a lot of information about yourself that the social media platform can sell to advertisers. This goes beyond the socio-demographic information – such as age, where you live, occupation, and so on – used in traditional marketing techniques.

Social media platforms also gather data about your interests, views and behaviours, based on, for example, pages you've 'liked', apps you've used, your purchasing history, and more. This information can help companies pinpoint the people most likely to buy their products, and decide who it is worth targeting with their marketing.

Consumer sovereignty
An assumption that consumers have the power to dictate the types, quality and quantity of the goods and services provided in a market place.

One view about marketing is that it provides information for consumers to help them make informed choices on how to satisfy their needs. This view suggests that products are made to suit consumers' *existing* needs, and marketing is used merely as a facilitating influence to alert the consumer about the suitability of the product. Products are carefully considered by potential buyers, alongside the price and how much money is available, and then an informed decision is made. This view of products responding to needs represents the idea of **consumer sovereignty** in the economy.

A rather different view is that marketing creates 'wants' or 'perceived needs' that were not previously there. This argument places more emphasis on the power of producers and sellers to use marketing as a way of manipulating emotions and persuading people to spend money, rather than on the power of the consumer. As you learned in Chapter 1, our behavioural biases make us susceptible to these tactics.

The US economist J. K. Galbraith (1958) argued that marketing is a necessary part of a system in which, rather than producers making things that consumers have decided they want, marketing makes consumers want the things that producers make. Galbraith likened this to a doctor running people over in order to ensure a steady stream of patients!

4 Budgeting

You have seen that there is much more to spending than conscious decisions about satisfying needs. For most people, unconscious social influences and marketing add to the pressure to consume. This makes it easy for households to spend beyond their means, even if they have a good income. On top of that, most households also need to save and invest for the future.

The process of budgeting can help to reconcile these competing pressures through actively controlling and planning household income and expenditure. It is an important technique to learn, to help you manage your own personal finances.

4.1 The budgeting process

Budgeting is a way of managing your finances, and it is most effective when carried out on a regular basis. A budget looks forward, in order to estimate income and expenditure over a future time period.

A budget will assist you in managing your finances in three ways:

- helping to control and correct excessive current spending

- checking that anticipated future spending can be met without having to borrow

- enabling planning to meet goals.

> In this section, we're going to explain how to draw up a budget manually because it's important to understand how it works. However, there are many online apps that automate much of the work, even taking transactions data direct from bank and credit card accounts.

The first step in the budgeting process could be described as a 'reality check'. It begins with the cash flow statement. The aim, initially, is to record all your current sources of disposable income (which you did in Chapter 2), and then every item of current expenditure.

Much of the income and spending data you need for your cash flow statement can be gleaned from your bank and credit card statements. But if you also make some purchases in cash, to obtain a full picture of how your money is used, it may be worth keeping a spending diary for a few weeks.

Activity 3.4 Keeping a spending diary

Allow 10 minutes every day for this activity.

Do you know exactly what you spend your money on? Many people don't. Try keeping a spending diary for a month in which you list all of your spending (cash and card) under various headings (which make sense for you), such as: workday lunches and coffees, miscellaneous groceries, pocket money for the children, and so on.

As you are recording your spending, think about what causes you to part with your money, and how important these different types of spending are to you.

Comment

Many people find that keeping a spending diary is an enlightening experience. It can be surprising just how much money in total vanishes on small but frequent purchases. Understanding where your money goes is an important part of developing good budgeting skills and habits.

It's helpful to classify expenditure under different headings (as you did in your diary) on the cash flow statement, too. The level of detail to include, and how broad the expenditure headings are, is up to you. Nevertheless, it is important to have some different headings if the budget is to be useful when thinking later about making changes.

To bring this to life, let's use the example of Shivani, who works for an insurance company and lives alone. The second column in Shivani's cash flow statement and budget (Table 3.1, page 132) gives details of Shivani's cash flow, recording her current income and current spending.

Not all income is regular – for example, a person might work overtime some weeks or months; the frequency of wages might be different from the frequency of any state benefits; and income may be especially variable for someone who is self-employed. This is even more relevant for expenditure, where you might pay, for example, your rent monthly, fuel bills quarterly, food shopping weekly, and holidays once or twice a year. Therefore, to add these to an average cash flow statement, all these types of income and spending need to be converted into the average amount spent on them for the chosen time period. This might be a week or a month: for Shivani, we have used a month, but the process is the same whatever time period is chosen.

We have not included units of currency in Table 3.1 (overleaf). If you live in the UK, you can think of the figures as pounds, as dollars if you live in the US, and so on. The process of budgeting is the same whatever currency you use.

The frequency of each cash flow can either be described (as shown in the second column of Table 3.1) as '1,600 per month' and '500 a year', or you could more formally set out 12 columns, one for each month (or 52 if you want to work weekly), showing when each item of income and spending falls. This is the better approach, if income and spending are particularly irregular, for two reasons:

1   it will be easier to work out the annual total, and so the monthly or weekly average

2   you will more easily see if there are particular months or weeks when you need to plan ahead to meet heavy expenses.

But such a large number of columns is easier to display in a spreadsheet than on the page of a printed book, so to save space Table 3.1 simply explains what the frequency of each cash flow is.

Box 3.1 Getting the cash flow sums right

To calculate monthly income or spending, you first need to multiply weekly amounts by 52, multiply quarterly amounts by four, and so on, to arrive at the annual amount. Then divide the annual amount by 12 (since there are 12 months in a year).

Don't be tempted to multiply weekly amounts by four to get a monthly equivalent – most months are longer than four weeks (28 days), so this shortcut would lead you to underestimate average monthly spending.

The calculations for adjustments to Shivani's monthly income and spending are shown in the third column of Table 3.1.

Table 3.1 Shivani's cash flow statement and budget

	Cash flow	Adjustment to monthly amounts	Average monthly cash flow	Budget
Disposable income				
Salary	1,600 a month		1,600	1,600
Christmas bonus	2,000 a year	2,000 ÷ 12 = 166.66	167	167
Total income			**1,767**	**1,767**
Expenditure				
Rent	800 a month		800	800
Property tax (e.g. Council Tax in England)	1,000 a year	1,000 ÷ 12 = 83.33	83	83
Household bills (water, electricity and gas)		20 + 32 = 52	52	45
Water	120 half yearly	120 × 2 ÷ 12 = 20	20	
Electricity and gas	Last 4 quarters: 70, 65, 105 and 140	380 (70 + 65 + 105 + 140) ÷ 12 = 31.66	32	
Home insurance	140 a year	140 ÷ 12 = 11.66	12	12
Other household (e.g. cleaning items)	40 a month		40	40
Food and non-alcoholic drinks	35 a week	35 × 52 ÷ 12 = 151.66	152	152
Alcohol and tobacco	0 a week		0	0
Communications (phone, internet etc.)	60 a month		60	45
Clothing and footwear	600 a year	600 ÷ 12 = 50	50	50
Personal care (toiletries etc.)	5 a week	5 × 52 ÷ 12 = 21.66	22	22

Table 3.1 Shivani's cash flow statement and budget (continued)

	Cash flow	Adjustment to monthly amounts	Average monthly cash flow	Budget
Health (e.g. medicines, dentist)	60 a year	60 ÷ 12 = 5	5	5
Transport (car loan, car insurance, bus and rail fares)		100 + 80 + 22 = 202	202	202
Car loan	100 a month			
Car insurance	80 a month			
Bus and rail fares	5 a week	5 × 52 ÷ 12 = 21.66		
Going out, lunches, coffees	65 a week	65 × 52 ÷ 12 = 281.66	282	150
Holidays	1,000 a year	1,000 ÷ 12 = 83.33	83	50
Gifts, charity donations	500 a year	500 ÷ 12 = 41.66	42	42
Loan repayments	30 a month		30	30
Total spending			**1,915**	**1,728**
Surplus (+) / deficit (−)			**−148**	**+39**

Shivani's average monthly cash flow is shown in the fourth column of Table 3.1. This is the reality check of her current income and spending each month. And subtracting her total spending from her total income indicates whether her current spending is sustainable, and whether there is any surplus income that can be used for meeting her goals.

Shivani has been overspending (as shown in Table 3.1 by the alarming deficit of 148 a month, on average). This means she will be running down any savings or building up debts, and this is not sustainable in the long run.

Therefore, Shivani's immediate goal is to get her spending under control. Her plan for doing this is shown by her budget figures in the last column of Table 3.1.

Activity 3.5 Budgeting for a surplus

Allow 10 minutes for this activity.

1   By comparing Shivani's budget in the last column of Table 3.1 with her currently average monthly income and spending, can you see where Shivani plans to make expenditure cuts to turn her current deficit into a surplus?

2   Suggest the sort of changes that she might make in her lifestyle to achieve these cuts.

Comment

1   Table 3.1 shows that Shivani will get her spending back on track by cutting down the amount she spends on going out, holidays, household bills and communication.

2   To achieve these cuts in spending, she may be planning to take packed lunches and her own coffee to work, and take cheaper holidays for a while. She might cut her energy and communication bills by shopping around for cheaper providers. This budget, provided she sticks to it, will leave her with a surplus of 39 each month.

4.2 Patterns of spending

In deciding where to make spending cuts, Shivani (in her budget shown in Table 3.1) needed to identify what constituted essential spending and what was non-essential.

Essential spending must be made to avoid bad outcomes, such as losing one's home, having household services cut off, being prosecuted, having too little to eat, or being unable to get to work. This makes paying rent and household bills, taxes, food and transport essential spending. There may be some leeway to reduce the amount spent on these items by shifting to cheaper alternatives, but they cannot be cut out altogether.

"FROM LIVING BEYOND OUR MEANS, WE'VE GONE TO LIVING BEYOND OUR WILDEST EXPECTATIONS!"

What is viewed as non-essential spending is more of a grey area. It will, to some extent, be influenced by the sort of social pressures that we looked at in Section 3 of this chapter. These social influences, also known as **social norms**, change over time. For example, in the mid to late 1990s, only a minority of UK households owned mobile phones and had access to the internet – yet most people now spend on these items and, in some countries like the UK, are increasingly expected to conduct transactions with government and other financial transactions digitally. So, are mobile phones and internet access now considered to be essential items to have? Many people would argue that to participate fully in contemporary society, having these items is a new social norm. Although not essential for physical survival, not having these items can make it harder to function day to day – for example, having to travel to the bank if you can't use online banking, and having to find publicly available internet services to claim state benefits or shop around for insurance.

Social norms
Informal understandings and rules that govern the appropriate behaviour of members of a society or a group.

If communicating and shopping online become the norm, and replace the face-to-face interactions that used to provide us all with daily human contact, being shut out from these technologies could also contribute to further social exclusion.

Returning to Shivani, the biggest planned cuts to her spending (Table 3.1) are on non-essential items, such as going out and holidays.

But she also plans to make some savings on essential items by shopping around for better deals.

Price discrimination
Charging different people or groups a different price for the same, or similar, goods or services.

Box 3.2 Tips to help make ends meet

There are many ways to save money. Here are a few of the more common ideas from personal finance experts, which might help you manage your finances.

- Shop around regularly for utilities, such as gas, electricity and internet, and when car and home insurances come up for renewal. Providers commonly charge existing customers more than new customers (a practice called **price discrimination**), so loyalty does not necessarily get rewarded.

- Use online price comparison websites to find the best deals, but make sure to check the quality of the deals, as well as the price.

- Paying monthly by direct debit may save money on some household bills. But some other bills, such as car and home insurance, may cost more if you pay monthly, rather than annually (because you are treated as if you are borrowing part of the annual payment).

- Keep an eye on subscriptions such as gym membership, magazines and news sites. Are you using them enough to warrant the cost? Could you save by switching to pay as you go?

- Think about whether a branded item is really value for money. Are you being swayed by symbolic reasons (see Section 3 of this chapter).

- Cut down on eating out and takeaway meals and beverages, e.g. by taking packed lunches to work and entertaining at home.

- Buy fresh fruit and vegetables in season. Check whether a local market is cheaper than the supermarket.

- Turn off lights, don't leave stand-by buttons on and turn down the thermostat one degree to save large amounts on energy bills – and help the environment.

- Use shopping lists to guard yourself against impulse buying.

Despite the availability of price-comparison services and online apps that automate shopping around, many people pay over the odds for the goods and services they buy. Reasons we've already mentioned include the problem of finding the best deals if you are digitally excluded, and paying higher prices for brands if they are seen as a status symbol. Yet another reason is if consumers think that a higher price equates to higher quality. The price of a product is often used as a mental shortcut to assess quality: as you have seen in Chapter 1, such mental shortcuts are called heuristics – that is rules of thumbs used to help assess situations when there is limited information available. A link between price and quality may sometimes be accurate, but not always; or at least the differences in price may not reflect differences in quality, especially when buying more expensive branded items. Consumers use a variety of other, accurate or inaccurate, mental shortcuts when spending (as illustrated in Activity 3.6).

Activity 3.6 Heuristics and spending

Allow 10 minutes for this activity.

Below is a list of some common heuristics used by consumers. Think about what each is suggesting you do, and who wants you to believe the heuristic.

- Generic products are just brands sold under a different label, at a lower price.

- When in doubt, a national brand is always a safe bet.

- Larger stores offer lower prices than smaller stores.

- Small shops give you better service than large stores.

- Stores that have just opened usually have attractive prices.

- Higher prices indicate higher quality.

- Larger sized containers are cheaper per unit than smaller sized ones.

- When buying heavily advertised goods, you are paying for the label not quality.

- If manufacturers invest a lot in advertising they must believe that their product will sell well.

- More recent products are likely to incorporate newer and better technology.

- It's best to look for well-established products, which have been tested by the market for some time.

(adapted from Solomon et al., 2002, p. 255)

Comment

Some of these heuristics are suggesting that you should buy from large stores; some from small stores. Some are signifying that you should search out bargains; others that it's not worth doing so. Some suggest that buying named brands is assurance of quality; others that they are a waste of money. In each case, there are some particular groups, producers or retailers, who would like you to believe in what is being said so that you spend your money on their products, rather than on those of their competitors: the heuristic itself can become part of the marketing strategy.

In budgeting, then, it's important to remember that price is not an automatic guide to quality. Good budgeting doesn't necessarily mean always looking for the lowest price: you need to consider functionality, durability and design, too.

A higher price may also be paid for ethical reasons, such as choosing a product that is environmentally friendly or organically grown, or to avoid goods and services produced using exceptionally low-wage labour in the developing world. These are all aspects of the quality of the products being purchased.

4.3 Budgeting and the life course

In this chapter, you've seen that the amount and pattern of spending by households is influenced by a complex mix of factors, such as income, prices, preferences, identity, social status, access to technology, behavioural biases and marketing pressure. The other major influence on spending is life stage, since circumstances and priorities change as individuals move through life.

In Chapter 2 you looked at actual data showing income levels by age. We have used this data as a basis for Figure 3.5, which shows the income profile for an individual – let's call him Dan. We have also added Dan's expenditure to this cash flow diagram. All figures are in real terms.

Of course, every individual's experience of income and spending over their life course is different. In Figure 3.5, we've assumed Dan goes to university and sees his earnings rise throughout his working life, falling back as he retires. Other people will have a different experience – for example, with earnings peaking much earlier in life, or interruptions during periods of caring or being unable to work. You will explore many of these differences later in *Personal Finance*.

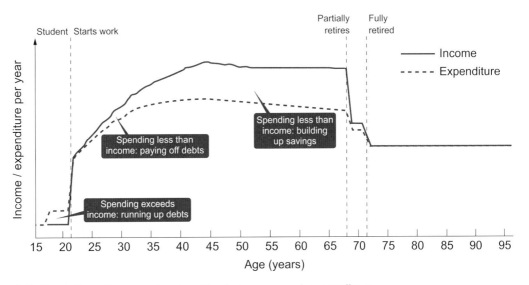

Figure 3.5 Cash flow diagram showing Dan's income and expenditure

Similarly, the pattern of spending shown in Figure 3.5 will not be the same for everyone. Dan starts his early life with debts (for example, student loans), spends less than his income in order to pay off those debts and starts saving (especially for retirement). He is able to carry on spending in retirement using pension income that his past savings provide.

Activity 3.7 Your cash flow over the life course

Allow 20 minutes for this activity.

Try drawing a cash flow diagram that shows the pattern of *your own* income and spending over your life so far.

Then (on the same diagram) try projecting your income and spending into the future, according to how you think they will develop over the rest of your lifetime.

Comment

The horizontal axis of your diagram should represent your age. The vertical axis should represent the value of your income and spending, but you don't need to mark on any particular values along a scale. A cash flow diagram can be a simplified representation of your income and spending. What's important is the relationship of spending to income and any big changes.

Anticipating how income and expenditure may change over the life course is a key part of the financial capability skill of planning ahead. Cash flow diagrams can help to identify stress points and vulnerabilities, and to explore the potential impact of financial actions you take now. Budgeting may itself be one of those actions, if it gets spending under control and avoids debt problems building up. Budgeting is also a tool for freeing up the resources needed for other types of planning ahead.

5 Managing money in multi-person households

With the example of Shivani, Section 4 of this chapter showed how budgeting can help a one-person household to manage its money. Table 1.2 in Chapter 1 shows that most people in the UK do not live alone – they live in multi-person households, perhaps as part of a couple, with or without children, or as a lone parent – and the same is true the world over.

This section examines some of the financial issues that arise when living with others. In particular, it considers how being part of a couple can have implications for budgeting, and looks at some of the budgetary implications of having children.

5.1 Economies of scale in consumption

There are ways in which living with others is cheaper than living alone, and this can help the household budget. Many purchases are collectively consumed in households: the housing and heating costs of a couple living together are likely to be less than twice those of one person living on their own, and that also might be true (to a lesser extent) of their food expenditure. Such savings result from what are called **economies of scale in consumption**; that is, the savings in the cost of something per person that arise when costs are spread across more people, because the total cost of the product rises less than proportionately to the number of people consuming it.

For a large household, items such as housing, heating and food generally cost less per person than for a smaller household. Another example would be car ownership: if a couple share a car they each have to pay less overall than if they both owned a car, because they save on the fixed costs of car purchase, road tax, parking permits, and so on.

Economies of scale in consumption
A decrease in the cost per person of maintaining a given (material) standard of living, as the size of a household increases.

Economies of scale in consumption arise for three main reasons (Nelson, 1988).

- Some goods and services have what is known as a **public good** element. A 'pure' household public good is one that, even though one person consumes it, is still available for anyone else in the household to consume at the same time. Heating a room is much like that – even though it could be heated for one person, the rest of the household can still make use of its warmth. In practice, few things are pure public goods because there may be some disadvantages in sharing (though not enough to negate all the benefits). For instance, sharing a car can have logistical problems if both people need it for different purposes at the same time.

Public good
A good or service that can be consumed simultaneously by different people, and from which each person can benefit, and cannot be excluded.

- Bulk-buying: many things are cheaper per unit if bought in larger sizes. Indeed, pensioners and people living alone often complain that many of the things they need are expensive because they have to buy them in small amounts. A quick look at a supermarket shelf soon shows this.

- Efficient use of the goods and services that a household buys: for example, the time and energy costs of cooking for an extra person are often very small, so by eating meals together (especially if everyone eats the same food) households can save money.

A quick look at supermarket shelves illustrates economies of scale through bulk-buying

Equivalence scales

We can obtain some guidance about the size of a household's economies of scale by using a **household equivalence scale**. These scales are used to calculate the effects on (material) standards of living in households of different sizes.

The 'OECD modified equivalence scale', explained in Box 3.3, is the scale most frequently used by governments in developed countries, both in official statistics and in calculating the relative levels of benefits for households of different size.

As you will recall from Chapter 2, it is common to think of household income as a rough indicator of the standard of living that a household might have, but standard of living also depends on how many people that income has to support.

Applying an equivalence scale (like that described in Box 3.3 overleaf) to actual income takes into account how much extra money a larger household would need to maintain the same standard of living as a single person on the same actual income. It captures the fact that larger households need more income to achieve the same standard of living, but not proportionately to the number of people. For example, a couple needs more, but not twice as much, as a single person to attain the same standard of living.

> **Household equivalence scale**
> An adjustment to the incomes of households of different size and composition, so that their (material) standards of living can be compared.

Activity 3.8 Comparing standards of living

Allow 15 minutes for this activity.

Imagine two work colleagues, John and Julie. They have the same job and each earns 30,000 a year. John lives on his own, while Julie is married to Anna, who does not have any income of her own.

1   Using the information in Table 3.2 and the method described in Box 3.3 (overleaf), what is the equivalence scale for Julie and Anna?

2   What is Julie and Anna's equivalised income?

3   Which household has the highest standard of living: John, or Julie and Anna?

Comment

The answers to Activity 3.8 are given at the end of this chapter.

Box 3.3 Household equivalence scales

To adjust a household's income to allow for its size and composition, official income statistics use the OECD modified equivalence scale. In this scale, a single adult with no dependent children is taken as the benchmark with an equivalence scale of 1. The equivalence scales for other types of household can be calculated by adding together the implied contributions of each household member (the 'contribution factor' shown in Table 3.2).

Table 3.2 OECD modified equivalence scale

Household member	Contribution factor
First adult (single person or head of household)	1.0
Each subsequent adult, or child aged 14 or over	0.5
Each child aged 13 or under	0.3

Source: OECD (2013)

For instance, Household A consists of a couple with one child aged 3. Using the OECD scale, the head of Household A would contribute 1.0, the spouse 0.5, and the child 0.3, giving a total equivalence scale of 1.8. This means that Household A would need an income 80% (0.8) higher than the income of a childless single person (who has an equivalence scale of 1, as shown in Table 3.2), to attain the same standard of living.

To calculate an equivalised household income, a household's actual (unequivalised) income needs to be divided by its total equivalence scale. So if Household A had an actual income of 36,000, its equivalised income would be 36,000 ÷ 1.8 = 20,000.

In other words, Household A has the same standard of living as a single person with an actual income of 20,000, even though it has an actual income of 36,000 (80% higher than the single person's income).

5.2 The impact of children on budgeting and financial planning

Even before we are born, money is spent on our behalf as parents and relatives buy cribs, buggies, toys and what seems like an endless list of items that babies are seen to need. The arrival of a baby into a household will inevitably alter the pattern, and often the total amount, of its expenditure – and it may affect the household income, as well. We can use the tools discussed in this chapter to explore these effects.

Figure 3.6 (overleaf) uses a cash flow diagram to illustrate the potential impact of having a child. You will look at these effects in much greater detail in Chapter 9, but the key points to note here are that:

- there may be a spike in spending around the time the baby is born

- spending is likely to remain higher throughout the whole period of the child's growing up

- income might fall if one or both parents reduce the amount they work, in order to care for the child (or alternatively, there might be a rise in spending if childcare needs to be paid for, to avoid a drop in income)

- there may be some new income from the state in the form of family benefits (in recognition that children are future workers who will one day contribute to the whole of society)

- the fall in income and rise in spending are likely to squeeze saving, so that eventual retirement income may be lower than it would have been.

Figure 3.6 highlights that having children may create stress points in a household's cash flow. Because of this, budgeting is highly relevant in situations such as planning and having a family. Recall the three purposes of budgeting described at the start of Section 4.1 of this chapter: controlling day-to-day spending; making sure there is enough income available for bills due; and planning for future goals.

Since income may fall and spending will rise, it is inevitable that having children will affect a household's standard of living. Using the equivalence scale introduced in Box 3.3 is a way of estimating that impact, and understanding how much extra income would be required if the household's standard of living is to be maintained at its 'before children' level.

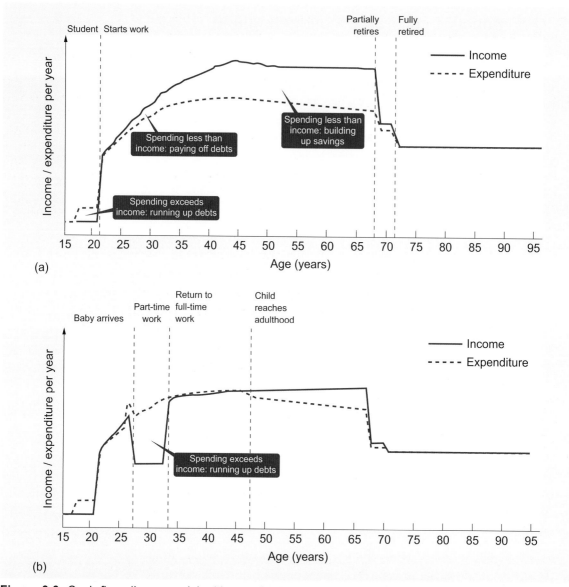

Figure 3.6 Cash flow diagrams: (a) without a family; (b) impact of having a baby

Activity 3.9 Children and a household's standard of living

Allow 15 minutes for this activity.

1   Using the equivalence scale (Table 3.2) and the method described in Box 3.3, work out by what percentage a single person would need to increase their income to maintain their 'before children' standard of living, if they have one child. Assume this household has no previous savings to draw on to meet its expenses.

2   How might the birth of the child affect the standard of living of the people in the household?

Comment

The answers to Activity 3.9 are given at the end of this chapter.

5.3 Couples and managing money

Couples and extended families that live together face important financial decisions about how to manage their money and expenses. The use of the words 'their money' immediately raises an important question that can influence this decision. That is, whose money is it when you are thinking of the household finances? For a couple living together, is it jointly shared and perceived to be equally accessible to both partners? Or does each person have their own individual money, and the couple comes to an agreement about how to pay bills and living expenses? The answer depends in part on the system of money management that a couple adopts, itself often influenced by social norms.

Box 3.4 Systems of managing household finances

Jan Pahl (2000) suggests there are four main systems couples use to manage their money.

The 'whole wage system'

Where one partner is given overall day-to-day management of the household finances. In a household where one partner (A) earns more and is the main 'bread winner', a first variant is for the other partner (B) to manage the money for the household, with partner A handing over their wages to partner B. In a second variant of the system, partner A retains control of their wages, and any money

---

partner B earns is handed over to A. Traditionally, these patterns have been more common in opposite-sex couples, where the man is the sole earner, or the woman earns relatively little compared with the man.

A system of 'housekeeping allowance'

Where the person who earns all, or most, of the income provides an allowance for spending for household purposes, and keeps the remainder. As in the whole wage system, this is more commonly found among households where earnings are relatively unequal.

The 'pooling system'

Where both partners share any income, usually in a joint account. Both partners manage the finances.

A system of 'independent management'

Where the partners keep their incomes separate, and make arrangements about how to split the household expenditure. This relies on both partners having an income, and is most frequently found when one or both partners have been in previous marriages or previous long-term relationships. Younger couples, before they have children, also tend to manage money more independently.

The choice a couple make about how they manage money is influenced by a variety of factors. The attitude towards who the money belongs to is an important aspect, but there are other factors. These include:

- who is deemed to have the most skills in managing money

- previous experience of other relationships

- attitudes towards gender roles

- how their parents manage money

- attitudes towards a relationship

- who earns more.

Pahl (2000) argues that there is a difference between the management of money and the control of it. While the management of money is a task that has to be carried out, and can be a burden, control over spending is a form of power and influence in the household. She found that, in many cases, women have less freedom over how money is spent in multi-person households: a woman is less likely than a man to feel that the money she manages is hers to spend on herself.

Burgoyne (2004) found that whatever system of money was adopted, and whoever managed it, the person who earned more of it seemed to retain more control. Burgoyne argues that the person with the main income decides how much allowance to give the other partner, thus retaining a degree of control over how it is spent.

The system of pooling income (see Box 3.4) may be thought of as being the fairest arrangement, because it gives freedom to both partners to spend money. However, in such a system, the budget becomes more difficult for either partner to manage since each partner has access to all income. One solution is to adopt the 'jam jar' (also called 'envelope') system, where money in different bank or building society accounts is allocated to different purposes – for example, having agreed individual accounts for personal spending. Interestingly though, both Pahl (2000) and Burgoyne (2004) found that even with this arrangement, women tend to feel less free in spending than their male partner: where the male income was higher, it was as if the source of the money exerted power over spending decisions. The source of money – that is, who has brought it into the household – has a psychological label of 'power' attached to it.

The ability to manage and budget money successfully in a way that both partners feel is equitable is not easy. Disagreements over money are a common reason for arguments between partners. Nevertheless, planning a budget and agreeing a system of money management can help to avoid tensions.

6 Conclusion

We have covered a lot of material about expenditure and budgeting in this chapter. In Sections 2 and 3, we looked at economic and social influences on spending, including symbolic consumption and the impact of marketing. These are all important components of the changing social and economic context, one of the four themes of *Personal Finance*.

The discussion of economic and social influences on expenditure is particularly relevant because it helps to underpin thinking about budgeting, by encouraging a greater reflection on why people spend money.

Section 4 of this chapter demonstrated how budgeting is a crucial component of financial planning (another *Personal Finance* theme), because it helps households to plan and adjust income and expenditure, in order to work towards desired goals. This reminds us that budgeting is an ongoing process, and it is important to revisit that process as the life course unfolds.

The chapter has also explored the interrelationship between individuals and households. Most households are made up of more than one person, and as we saw in Section 5, when people live together there may be financial advantages through economies of scale. But these advantages may not be equally shared, and couples, especially when they have children, need to think about how best to manage their money.

Answers to activities in Chapter 3

Answers to Activity 3.8

1   The scale for Julie is 1.0 and for Anna 0.5. These are added together to find their household equivalence scale of 1.5.

2   Julie and Anna's income is 30,000. Dividing this by the equivalence scale of 1.5 gives them an equivalised income of 20,000.

3   John's equivalised income is 30,000 (actual income of 30,000 divided by his equivalence scale of 1.0). This is higher than Julie and Anna's equivalised income of 20,000, so John has the highest standard of living.

Answers to Activity 3.9

1   The equivalence scale for a single person is 1. With one baby, the household's equivalence scale rises by the baby's contribution factor of 0.3 to 1.3. This means that the household needs an income multiplied by the ratio between the two equivalence scales. That is: 1.3 (household equivalence scale after the baby's birth) ÷ 1 (household equivalence scale before the birth) = 1.3.

And multiplying the new equivalence scale by 100, shows the percentage increase in income is: (1.3 ÷ 1) × 100 = 30%.

So the household needs 30% more income in order to maintain their pre-child standard of living.

2   If income increases by 30%, the household standard of living can be maintained at the pre-baby level, though that does not necessarily mean the standard of living of every person in the household will be unchanged: the parent is likely to have to cut back some areas of spending, such as going out, and may choose to spend proportionately more of the household income on the child.

If income is unchanged, falls, or rises by less than 30%, the household's material standard of living will fall. Of course, money is not everything, and many parents would argue that their quality of life has been improved by having children, so sacrificing expenditure on themselves is more than compensated for.

References

Abercrombie, N., Warde, A. and Deem, R. (2000) *Contemporary British Society*, Malden, MA, Polity Press.

Bauman, Z. (1999) *Work, Consumerism and the New Poor*, Buckingham, Open University Press.

Bellezza, S., Paharia, N. and Keinan, A. (2017) 'Conspicuous consumption of time: when busyness and lack of leisure time become a status symbol', *Journal of Consumer Research*, vol. 44, pp. 118–38 [Online]. Available at www0.gsb. columbia.edu/mygsb/faculty/research/pubfiles/19293/Conspicuous% 20Consumption%20of%20Time.pdf (Accessed 25 November 2017).

Bourdieu, P. (1977) *Outline of Theory and Practice*, Cambridge, Cambridge University Press.

Burgoyne, C. (2004) 'Hearts and purse strings: money in heterosexual marriage', *Feminism and Psychology*, vol. 14, no. 1, pp. 165–72.

Currid-Halkett, E. (2017) *The Sum of Small Things: A Theory of the Aspirational Class*, Princeton, NJ, Princeton University Press.

Department for Business, Energy and Industrial Strategy (2017) *International Domestic Energy Prices* [Online]. Available at www.gov.uk/government/ statistical-data-sets/international-domestic-energy-prices (Accessed 25 November 2017).

Eckhardt, G. M., Belk, R. W. and Wilson, J. A. J. (2014) 'The rise of inconspicuous consumption', *Journal of Marketing Management*, vol. 31, no. 7–8, pp. 807–26 [Online]. Available at www.tandfonline.com/doi/abs/ 10.1080/0267257X.2014.989890 (Accessed 25 November 2017).

Galbraith, J. K. (1958) *The Affluent Society*, Harmondsworth, Penguin.

Geddes, D. (2017) 'BBC viewers have average age of 60 as young default to Netflix', *The Times*, 29 March [Online]. Available at www.thetimes.co.uk/ article/bbc-viewers-have-average-age-of-60-as-young-default-to-netflix-7jg0skcdd (Accessed 28 February 2018).

Klein, N. (2000) *No Logo: Taking Aim at the Brand Bullies*, London, Flamingo.

Nelson, J. (1988) 'Household economies of scale in consumption: theory and evidence', *Econometrica*, vol. 56, no. 6 (November), pp. 1301–14.

Organisation for Economic Cooperation and Development (OECD) (2013) *What are Equivalence Scales?* [Online]. Available at www.oecd.org/eco/ growth/OECD-Note-EquivalenceScales.pdf (Accessed 20 August 2017).

Organisation for Economic Cooperation and Development (OECD) (2017) '5. Final consumption expenditure of households', *OECD. Stat* [Online]. Available at https://stats.oecd.org/Index.aspx?DataSetCode=SNA_TABLE5# (Accessed 24 November 2017).

Organisation for Economic Cooperation and Development (OECD) (2018) 'Consumer prices', *OECD.Stat* [Online]. Available at http://stats.oecd.org/viewhtml.aspx?datasetcode=MEI_PRICES&lang=en# (Accessed 12 January 2018).

Pahl, J. (2000) 'Couples and their money: patterns of accounting and accountability in the domestic economy', *Accounting, Auditing & Accountability Journal*, vol. 13, no. 4, pp. 502–17.

Solomon, M. R., Barmossy, G. and Askegaard, S. (2002) *Consumer Behaviour: A European Perspective*, 2nd edn, Harlow, Financial Times/Prentice-Hall.

United Nations (2017) *National Accounts Main Aggregates Database* [Online]. Available at https://unstats.un.org/unsd/snaama/dnlList.asp (Accessed 24 November 2017).

Veblen, T. (1925) *The Theory of the Leisure Class: An Economic Study of Institutions*, London, Allen and Unwin.

Weber, M. (1948 [1924]) 'Class, status and party', in Gerth, H. H. and Wright Mills, C. (eds and trans.) *Essays from Max Weber*, London, Routledge & Kegan Paul.

To cite this chapter, use the following format in your reference list:

Lowe, J. and Higginson, M. (2019) 'Expenditure', in De Henau, J. and Lowe, J. (eds) *Personal Finance*, Milton Keynes, The Open University, pp. 107–151.

Chapter 4
Borrowing and debt

Alan Shipman

Contents

1 Introduction

If a person or household spends more than the income they receive in a given period, and does not have savings or other liquid assets to draw on, the extra funds must be borrowed.

In this chapter, I'm going to look at the main reasons why people borrow money (Section 2) and the basics of borrowing, including what determines the amount of **interest** charged (Section 3). I then move on in Section 4 to look at the most common types of debt.

In Chapter 2, you saw how inflation reduces the buying power of money. This applies not just to the flow of income, but also to stock of debt a person has – which you may be surprised to realise is good for borrowers. Section 5 explores this important relationship between debts and inflation. In Section 6, I develop the idea of the household balance sheet and how this can be used to assess the financial health and riskiness of a household's situation. Then, in Section 7, I examine the relationship between cash flow and debts in the balance sheet.

Interest
The charge a borrower pays for the use of someone else's money; also the reward a saver gets for allowing their money to be used by someone else.

2 Why people borrow

Debt can be used to finance a range of purchases, from houses and cars to household goods and computers

'Debt' is an emotive word, but having debts is not always bad. Taking on debt may be part of a financial plan – for example, to finance big purchases that are not easily bought out of current income, or money already saved. The use of debt enables people to make these types of purchase early in life, as soon as these items are needed, before people have had a chance to earn or save much. So people often borrow in the early stages of their life course, expecting to repay their debt out of the income they subsequently earn. Some of these large loan-financed expenditures can be regarded as investments: spending that generates extra income in future, some of which may be used to repay the loan.

Activity 4.1 Borrowing for investment

Allow 5 minutes for this activity.

Think of some examples where borrowing may be considered to be an investment. Briefly consider how each of these examples adds to future income, making a note of your answer.

Comment

You might have thought, for example, that having a car would enable someone to earn more by travelling further to a better-paid job, or to take a job that requires people to have their own vehicle.

As you saw in Chapter 2, a university degree can be considered an investment in human capital that may open up opportunities for higher-paying jobs or promotions. Owning a home may add directly to income if part of it is rented out, and may increase disposable income by lowering accommodation costs if the total cost of ownership (including any mortgage repayment) is less than the cost of renting an equivalent property.

Borrowing also enables people to keep buying the things they need, at times when their income is temporarily too low to pay for them. This **consumption smoothing** can ensure that a household doesn't have to go without essentials, or miss out on regular payments for things like subscriptions and insurance. Borrowing may be the best way to smooth consumption – if, for example, it isn't easy to draw immediately on savings. Provided there is a sound plan for repayment, borrowing opens up more opportunities than would be available if everything had to be paid for 'up front'.

Consumption smoothing
Keeping expenditure relatively constant when there are variations in income, typically by use of borrowing, savings and/or insurance.

However, debt can also be run up unintentionally. For example, if I don't pay my rent on time, I fall into arrears. In effect, I am borrowing from my landlord. Similarly, if I have metered gas and do not pay my bill on time, I run up an unauthorised debt to the energy supplier. If my income will not stretch to buying food and other essentials, I might plug the gap by borrowing, even if I'm unsure of how I'll repay.

These types of debt are rarely part of a financial plan, and can occur on a large scale when incomes are low or households are going through hard times. Even borrowing that was planned can become a problem if circumstances unexpectedly change.

Debt plays an inescapable part in many households' finances during the life course, and usually a constructive one. But it requires careful management, as it can become a source of serious hardship if it starts to cost too much or the means to repay it are lost.

3 Borrowing and lending: the basics

Borrowing involves taking a loan from a bank or other lender. It results in debt – money owed to the lender – which must be paid back over time. When someone takes a loan, the amount they borrow is called the **principal** (also called the 'capital'). In addition to paying back the principal, lenders usually charge interest, adding a percentage to the outstanding debt. This compensates them for parting with their money for a time, and for the risk that some of what they lend might not be paid back.

Principal
Also called 'capital'. The original amount of debt taken out; also the sum put into savings or an investment.

Before looking at the most common types of household borrowing (in Section 4), it's useful to note some broad distinctions that experts make when talking about debt. I'll also consider the factors that influence the cost of borrowing.

3.1 Categories of debt

Secured and unsecured debt

Lenders can reduce the risk of not getting their money back by 'securing' the debt against an asset owned by the borrower. This means that if the borrower fails to make the agreed repayments the lender can force the sale of the asset and get repaid from the sale proceeds. Because this lowers the lender's risk, the interest rate on **secured debt** is usually lower than that for **unsecured debt**, which is not backed by any asset.

Secured debt
Type of borrowing, backed by an asset, such as a home, which the lender may seize if the debt is not repaid.

Activity 4.2 Secured or unsecured?

Allow 5 minutes for this activity.

If you have any debts at present, think about whether they are secured. If so, which asset is providing the security? If you are not in any debt, think of a loan you might need to take out in future.

Unsecured debt
Type of borrowing not backed by any asset.

Comment

An example of a secured loan is a **mortgage** (which you'll look at in Chapter 6 on 'Housing'), which is secured against the property it's used to buy. Some other loans that a household takes on, including those used to run a small business, may also be secured against a family's home.

Mortgage
A loan secured against property or land.

Other examples, which you'll look at in Section 4, are loans secured against cars, jewellery and other valuables. When buying household furniture and electrical items, credit may in effect be secured against the item you are buying.

Fixed-rate and variable-rate debt

On some debts, lenders charge a fixed rate of interest, meaning that the same interest rate applies throughout the whole term of the loan. Other debts may have a variable interest rate – this means the lender is allowed to adjust the rate upwards or downwards.

3.2 The cost of borrowing

When someone borrows money, they are expected to repay the principal plus interest on an agreed future date, and/or through a series of instalments. The way the interest is worked out can have a big impact on the total cost of borrowing.

Simple and compound interest

There are two different types of interest: simple and compound.

Simple interest is worked out by applying the interest rate to the principal. For example, suppose £10,000 is borrowed for a **term** of two years at a simple interest rate of 5%, charged at the end of each year. In this case £500 of interest (0.05 × £10,000) will be charged at the end of the first year, and £500 at the end of the second year.

In practice, simple interest is rare when borrowing money; compound interest is far more common. With compound interest, the interest is added to the principal. This increases the amount of outstanding debt, resulting in a higher interest charge next time.

Let's take the case of Tony, who – needing an extra £500 for the coming week – borrows it from a lender who charges daily interest of 2%. Table 4.1 shows what happens to Tony's debt over the course of the week, with compound interest.

Term
The period of time over which a debt is to be repaid; also the period of time over which money is saved or invested.

Table 4.1 Tony discovers compound interest

	Day 1	Day 2	Day 3	Day 4	Day 5	Day 6	Day 7
Outstanding debt (£)	500.00	510.00	520.20	530.60	541.21	552.03	563.07
2% per day interest charged (£)	10.00	10.20	10.40	10.61	10.82	11.04	11.26

Compounding
The process by which interest is added to the original amount borrowed or saved, increasing the outstanding balance and so causing the next sum of interest to be higher.

Reducing-balance loan (also called a repayment loan)
A loan whereby each regular repayment pays the interest and part of the principal. This reduces the amount owed and interest for each period is calculated on that reduced amount.

Interest-only loan
A loan whereby each regular payment pays the interest but the principal is left to be paid off in a single lump sum at the end of the term.

In Table 4.1, Tony starts by borrowing £500 on Day 1. The interest charged for Day 1 is added to the outstanding debt, so by the start of Day 2, Tony owes £510. Because the lender charges compound interest, the interest charge for Day 2 is 10% of the new balance: that is £510, not £500, as it would be with simple interest. This means the amount of interest charged on Day 2 is higher than on Day 1: £10.20, rather than £10.00. This process continues throughout the week. By the end of the week, Tony's daily interest charge is over £1 more than it was at the beginning and the amount he must pay back has grown to £563.07.

This example shows how **compounding** can make a debt grow rapidly. In practice, most lenders require interest, and often some of the principal, too, to be repaid during the term of the loan, which prevents the compounding effect from expanding the outstanding balance. The most common exception is for loans over very short periods.

Reducing-balance loans

With many types of borrowing, regular monthly payments are calculated so that they will pay off both the principal and interest in full by the end of the term. These are called **reducing-balance loans** (or repayment loans). They can be contrasted with **interest-only loans**, which charge interest throughout the term but leave repayment of the principal to the end.

Table 4.2 gives the example of £10,000 borrowed over one year at an interest rate of 5% a year and with monthly repayments. It shows a common way that lenders apply the interest and repayments. The loan is repaid in 12 equal instalments paid at the end of each month, each consisting of part of the principal along with the interest. Let's look at this in detail.

Table 4.2 Example of a reducing-balance loan

Month	Balance at start of month (£)	Interest charged on balance (£)	Fixed monthly repayment (£)	Balance at end of month (£)	Principal paid off this month (£)
1	10,000.00	40.74	855.57	9,185.18	814.82
2	9,185.18	37.42	855.57	8,367.03	818.14
3	8,367.03	34.09	855.57	7,545.55	821.48
4	7,545.55	30.74	855.57	6,720.73	824.82
5	6,720.73	27.38	855.57	5,892.54	828.18
6	5,892.54	24.01	855.57	5,060.98	831.56
7	5,060.98	20.62	855.57	4,226.04	834.95
8	4,226.04	17.22	855.57	3,387.69	838.35
9	3,387.69	13.80	855.57	2,545.93	841.76
10	2,545.93	10.37	855.57	1,700.73	845.19
11	1,700.73	6.93	855.57	852.09	848.64
12	852.09	3.47	855.57	£0.00	852.09
Totals		**266.79**	**10,266.79**		**10,000.00**

The 5% a year interest rate is converted to a monthly rate, which is 0.407%, or 0.00407 as a decimal. (You can get close to this by dividing 5% by 12, but the exact calculation is a little more complex.) Table 4.2 shows that, in the first month, interest is $0.00407 \times £10,000 = £40.74$. The lender has set a fixed monthly repayment of £855.57 which covers the £40.74 of interest and also pays off £814.82 of the principal. By the end of the first month, adding the interest and subtracting the repayment means the balance has fallen to £9,185.18.

Interest in the second month is charged on this new balance, and so is a bit lower than in the first month: at £37.42, rather than £40.74. Since the monthly repayment is fixed, this means a slightly bigger chunk of the principal is paid off: £818.14.

This process continues. You can see that each month the outstanding balance and interest charge both fall and the amount of principal paid off increases. By the end of the term, the principal plus interest have been paid off in full (with the balance at the end of month 12 equal to £0.00). Adding up the 12 monthly repayments, you can see that £10,266.79 has been paid in total, which exactly pays back the £10,000 principal plus £266.79 in interest.

This reducing-balance approach is the norm for loans where you borrow at a fixed interest rate for a set term and have to make regular repayments.

The same approach is also typically used to work out the regular repayments for a fixed-term loan that has a variable interest rate, but the repayments then have to be recalculated each time the interest rate changes. The aim is to ensure that, provided all the agreed payments are made, the debt falls to zero by the end of the term.

Activity 4.3 Effect of a reducing balance

Allow 10 minutes for this activity.

1   A lender asks for £10,000 principal along with 5% interest to be repaid in a single lump sum at the end of one year, instead of requiring monthly repayments. How much interest would the borrower have to pay?

2   Why is the total interest paid under the reducing-balance arrangement (shown in Table 4.2) different from the interest you worked out in your answer to Question 1?

Comment

The answers to Activity 4.3 are given at the end of this chapter.

Comparing costs of different loans: annual percentage rate (APR)

Although our examples so far have shown interest as the only charge that is made on a loan or other **credit**, there are often additional costs. For example, these might include:

Credit
An arrangement to receive cash, goods or services now and to pay for them in the future.

- **Compulsory charges that must be paid as part of a particular loan or credit deal**, such as an arrangement fee, administration fees for processing payments, and the cost of a particular insurance contract, if this is a condition of the deal.

- **Contingent fees that only some customers pay**, such as early repayment charges, where a customer pays off a loan before the end of its original term, or a charge for missing a payment.

- **Non-compulsory charges**, for example, fees paid direct to a broker who helped arrange the loan, and the cost of insurance that the customer chooses to take out.

As a result of extra charges such as these, the 'headline' interest rate advertised by lenders may not always tell the full story about the total cost of borrowing. For this reason, financial regulators often require lenders to provide a standardised measure of cost which takes into account the amount and timing of any compulsory charges, as well as interest. The standard measure is expressed as an annual rate to make it easy for borrowers to compare the cost of one loan with another. In the UK and elsewhere in Europe, this standardised rate is called the **annual percentage rate** (APR). The APR does not include contingent and non-compulsory charges.

3.3 Individual interest rates and credit scoring

Almost all countries have a central bank, which acts alongside the government to keep the economy stable. In the UK, the central bank is called the Bank of England; in the Eurozone, the European Central Bank (ECB); and the US has a group of central banks, collectively called the Federal Reserve System. The central bank acts as a banker to all other banks in the economy, including the online and high street banks where most individuals and households keep their money.

The central bank requires these banks to deposit some of their money with it and also lends funds to the banks overnight, if they are short of cash at the end of the day's operations. Since the banks must pay interest on any money they borrow, they require at least this rate of interest when they lend to anyone else. So this central bank interest rate (called Bank Rate in the UK) becomes the 'base rate' for other lenders. It provides a benchmark for the rate that banks charge individuals and households when they borrow.

The interest rate that lenders charge borrowers is almost always higher than base rate, for three main reasons:

- lenders try to keep their interest rates above the rate of inflation (more on this in Section 5)

- they may adjust interest rates for business reasons, for example increasing rates to earn more profit (though they might also offer reduced initial rates to attract new customers)

- higher interest rates reflect the risk of borrowers being unable to repay.

Annual percentage rate (APR)
A summary figure for comparing the cost of different debt products which reflects interest and other compulsory charges, as well as when and the frequency with which they are paid.

Different types of borrower pose different levels of risk. Someone with a high income from a steady job is likely to be considered a less risky borrower than someone on a low or unpredictable income. So lenders try to assess the **creditworthiness** of loan applicants and charge different people different rates to reflect this.

The most detailed form of assessment involves assigning each individual a **credit score**, based on information such as their income, age, employment status, spending patterns, past credit history, and whether they own a home. In most developed countries this process is outsourced by lenders to, or supplemented by, a **credit reference agency**, an organisation that specialises in compiling debt-relevant data about individuals. Their sources of such information may now extend to elements of **Big Data**, such as the number and type of connections a person makes using social media and where they shop online (King, 2014). Lower risk is associated with a better credit score and more favourable interest rates. This was captured in the definition of a bank, made famous by US comedian Bob Hope: 'a place that will lend you money if you can prove you don't need it'.

3.4 Alternatives to interest

Lending money to earn interest is viewed as unacceptable in some societies, both historically and today. The main ethical objection is that a lender's right to charge interest forces borrowers to take on most of the risk. They are required to repay the principal and interest whether the loan improves or worsens their fortunes. A different approach aims to share risk more evenly between borrowers and lenders.

Islamic financial institutions have developed a variety of loans compliant with sharia (religious law), intended to allocate risks more fairly and make credit more widely available than in systems where borrowers are charged interest. These include:

- **asset-based or lease-based finance** – the lender buys the asset that a borrower wants to purchase, then sells it to them in instalments, or allows them to pay for it gradually in a rent-to-own arrangement (see Section 4.2)

- **mutual funding (sukuk)** – borrower and lender finance a purchase or other project jointly, sharing any profit or loss (Abedifar et al., 2015).

Creditworthiness
A borrower's capacity to repay a loan or other credit.

Credit score
A rating based on financial information about an individual used to assess their creditworthiness, which affects how much they can borrow and on what terms.

Credit reference agency
A business that specialises in gathering and selling to lenders data used to assess individuals' creditworthiness on the basis of their circumstances and past borrowing record.

Big Data
Very large sets of data, often sourced from online interactions and transactions, on which statistical analysis can reveal previously unmeasured associations, patterns, trends or behaviours.

4 Types of borrowing

Households have many different needs, and so various types of borrowing have been developed to meet them. Banks are a common source of loans, but many are offered by other financial institutions, including mutual savings societies (see Box 4.1).

Box 4.1 Mutual savings schemes

Community schemes in which people pool some of their savings, creating a mutual fund from which others can borrow, is a very old idea, pre-dating the rise of modern financial institutions. Two particularly long-lasting forms are:

- **Rotating savings and credit associations (ROSCAs)** involve a group of people, known to each other, who meet regularly and pay a set amount into a pot which is then paid out to one member. Members take it in turns to receive the pot and use it however they wish.

- **Credit unions** take regular deposits from, and make loans to, a group of people who are connected in some way – for example, living in the same area, working for the same employer or belonging to the same place of worship.

Unlike modern banks, mutual associations try to encourage (and sometimes depend on) social ties between borrowers and savers, ensuring that people save when they can, only borrow when they need to, and are committed to keeping up their repayments. This often allows them to keep borrowers' interest costs relatively low.

This section reviews the commonest types of borrowing (except for home mortgages, which are discussed in Chapter 6). Household borrowing can be mainly subdivided into:

- **'mainstream credit'** – the types of loan that anyone with a reasonable credit score can access

- **'high-cost credit'** – mostly used by people who cannot get mainstream credit, and are forced to find alternatives which may have much higher interest rates and other charges.

There are also a few other types of borrowing that fall outside those categories. Figure 4.1 shows how common types of loan (further explained below) fall into these main categories.

Loan café menu

Mainstream credit	High-cost credit	Other borrowing
Personal loan (secured)	Pawnshop	Family and friends
Hire purchase	Rent-to-own	Student loan
Car loan	Overdraft (unauthorised)	
Personal loan (unsecured)	Payday loan	
Credit card		
Store card		
Overdraft (authorised)		
Catalogue credit		

Figure 4.1 Main types of borrowing. Within each column, types of borrowing are listed from those likely to have a lower APR (top of column) to those likely to have a higher APR (bottom of column).

4.1 Mainstream credit

Overdrafts

For those with a bank **current account** that permits it, one of the easiest ways to borrow money for a short period is to run up an overdraft. This means spending more from the account than is currently in it, so that the balance goes negative. Some current accounts have a built-in free overdraft. Even if there is no free overdraft amount, or the customer wants to borrow more than that amount, an overdraft can be a relatively cheap and flexible way to borrow. However, to ensure this, the customer needs to get their bank to agree in advance to the overdraft (called an 'authorised overdraft'). If the overdraft is not authorised in this way, interest charges are much higher and there are usually additional charges.

Current account
A bank account that allows money to be deposited and paid out immediately by cash, card or electronically.

Personal loans

Personal loans allow larger sums to be borrowed for longer periods than are normally available via an overdraft. They can be arranged at branches of a bank or other lender, by phone or online. Personal loans usually have an interest rate fixed for the term. They are reducing-balance loans (like the example in Table 4.2), so have fixed monthly repayments that ensure the whole loan and interest are paid off by the end of the term. Commonly, personal loans are unsecured. However, some lenders offer personal loans secured against the borrower's home.

Credit cards

Credit cards enable their holders to make purchases for which the card issuer pays in the first instance. The issuer then reclaims the cost from the card holder via a monthly bill. Subject to a minimum payment, the card holder chooses how much to pay back each month, so this is a very flexible way to borrow. Those who pay off the bill in full can get interest-free credit (usually for four to six weeks) between the date of each purchase and paying the bill. Otherwise, interest is charged on the balance owed.

Credit card interest rates are often relatively high, because this form of borrowing is unsecured and the card issuer has little control over the purchases made or the amount repaid. Issuers guard against excessive spending by setting a 'credit limit' on the total debt that a card holder can run up on the card.

However, these limits are often generous, as issuers make much of their profit from the interest charged on balances that are not paid off in full each month.

A flexible way to borrow

Box 4.2 Paying with plastic

There are different types of plastic payment card that often look very similar but work in different ways. In general, only credit cards are a form of borrowing. Debit cards let a person spend the money they have in their bank account, so this does not involve borrowing unless an expenditure moves the account into overdraft.

Another variation is the charge card. This lets the holder make purchases that the card issuer pays for initially but, unlike credit cards, the card holder must pay off the balance in full each month. There are also various types of prepayment card, which must be topped up before they are used. These cease to work once the prepaid amount is used up, so cannot run the user into debt.

Hire purchase and other retailer credit

Many retailers allow items to be bought on credit, with customers taking delivery immediately and settling their bill later. These forms of credit work in a variety of ways:

- **Hire purchase** – one of the first forms of household borrowing to be widely available, this has commonly been used to buy furniture and electrical goods. The retailer may take a fraction of the price immediately (as a deposit) and the rest is paid in instalments. The credit is secured against the item being purchased, with the buyer in effect hiring the item initially and completely owning it only when the final instalment has been paid.

- **Unsecured loan** – this is a personal loan arranged by the retailer (who typically earns commission from the lender). It's likely to be more expensive than hire purchase because the loan is unsecured, but the customer owns the goods from the outset.

- **Store card** – this usually works like a credit card but can be used for purchases only in a particular shop or group of shops.

- **Catalogue credit (also called mail order)** – this allows customers to chose items from a catalogue (traditionally printed, now often on a website), with purchases arriving by post. Payment is through regular instalments which are usually made up of the purchase price plus interest, though some catalogues offer interest-free purchases if repayment is made within a short time (up to a year). Even when catalogue prices are lower than shop prices, buying on credit can lead to more being paid because of interest and other added costs.

Car loans

Hire purchase has been widely used for purchasing cars, but since the 1990s another form of finance has become even more popular in some countries. Under a 'personal contract plan' (PCP), a buyer pays a deposit (down payment) followed by a series of (usually monthly) instalments. However, these are lower than they would be under a conventional hire-purchase agreement because they do not add up to the car's full purchase price. They pay only for the estimated drop in resale price of the car over the period of the PCP. At the end of the period (typically three years from new), the buyer chooses between paying off the balance in a final 'balloon' payment (usually much larger than the preceding instalments), or giving the car back for the dealer to resell.

There are various ways to finance a car purchase

4.2 High-cost credit

Rent-to-own

Rent-to-own (RTO) contracts are a way of buying household goods. They charge more than traditional hire purchase contracts because RTO providers target households that typically cannot get mainstream credit. One US customer described it this way:

> Rental places are in the business of letting poor people have nice things for more than retail. The rental is simple; it's just making twelve easy payments of $99.99 for something that might actually cost closer to $1000 if you paid it all at once. You are renting to own, so there's no risk; you just pay them when the bill's due, and when you're done, you own some furniture. In the meantime, you have some furniture, which is handier than the saving-up thing because sometimes you actually need a bed. Plus furniture rental places are pretty decent about you missing a week or two if you're having a rough patch, provided you generally pay on time and it doesn't happen too often. They get more interest that way.
>
> (Tirado, 2014, p. 137)

RTO retailers have, however, been criticised for charging high interest rates. In 2016 the Financial Inclusion Centre (a London-based think tank) found RTO agreements charging interest rates of up to 99.9% APR. They often further inflated the price by adding follow-up services and warranties that buyers might not need. It gave the example of a washing machine priced at £349.97 (including delivery) in an ordinary store for which BrightHouse (then the UK's largest RTO shop chain) charged £471 if paid for immediately, £936 if bought on weekly repayments over three years at 69% APR, or £1056.12 for customers required to add on product insurance (Evans and Allison, 2016).

Payday loans

Households that have run out of ready cash before their next payday arrives, and don't have any savings to draw from or friends and family who can help, often turn to a 'payday lender'. These specialise in making small unsecured loans to cover short periods, say 30 days. Although this may sound like an extreme situation, it is one that many people encounter at some stage in their life course. A 2013 poll by *Which?* (the UK Consumers' Association) estimated that 4% of households in the UK (around one million people) had had to make use of payday loans (Merrick, 2013). Interest is typically charged daily but compounded, with the capital and interest being paid off in a single lump sum at the end of the term. The APRs are often very high.

Box 4.3 Regulating payday loans

Payday lenders justify very high APRs by pointing to the high risk of lending instantly to people who have run out of money between paydays, also pointing out that, in cash terms, the amount of interest paid remains small provided the loan is repaid on time. However, if customers roll over the loan for a further period or repay it by taking out another loan, compounding means the interest charged escalates. The increasing number of people resorting to such loans, and the speed at which their debts can grow if not repaid quickly, has led many governments to put restrictions on payday lending.

For example, in 2014 the UK introduced new rules which limited the interest rates that payday lenders can charge (to 0.8% per day), and capped the total interest that can be charged at the sum originally borrowed (for example, if £100 were borrowed, the most

---

that the borrower would have to pay back with interest would be £200). These restrictions caused a number of payday loan providers to reduce their scale of lending or leave the UK market altogether. The curbs helped some households get cheaper payday loans, and rescued others from loans that had become a runaway expense. However, economists subsequently detected a rise in the use of other sources of short-term credit, such as unauthorised overdrafts, credit cards and RTO contracts (Hardy, 2018; FCA, 2019). Some of these were found to be charging APRs that were higher than the payday lenders' maximum.

Pawnshops and pawnbrokers

Although homes and cars are usually the only assets on which households can raise a secured loan, there is in many countries another traditional source: 'pawning' valuable possessions, such as jewellery or expensive clothes. These are used as security for a loan from a pawnbroker, who takes charge of the item and can sell it if the loan is not repaid. Pawning has a very long history – the world's oldest bank, Monte dei Paschi di Siena, started life in 1472 as a pawnbroker 'expressly instituted to give aid to the more underprivileged classes of the population during a time of particular hardship' (Monte dei Paschi di Siena, 2017). It is a widespread form of credit in many emerging economies, and experienced a new phase of growth in high-income countries in the early 2000s, especially among 23–35 year-olds who wanted extra money in the years after leaving full-time education (Rebell, 2016).

Three gold balls: a traditional pawnbroker's sign

4.3 Other borrowing

Student loans

While still seeking to provide school places free of charge, many governments have introduced loan systems for students who want to continue into higher education. The economic reasoning is that students expect to benefit from the education through higher earnings, so should pay the cost themselves, rather than being subsidised by taxpayers, many of whom do not get the chance to attend university.

Despite these justifications, student loans remain controversial. Critics argue that a highly educated workforce may benefit the economy as a whole, not just the individuals who receive the education. The higher incomes often enjoyed by holders of degrees (the widely observed 'graduate earnings premium') means that they already on average pay more income tax than most non-graduates over a lifetime. The associated debt may mean that studying inhibits, rather than enhances, life chances. For example, in the US, after a steady rise in mean university fees (to around $37,000 per year in 2016), the New York Federal Reserve found that 45% of people in their early twenties were still living with their parents, and calculated that overhanging student debt accounted for 35% of a sharp fall in home ownership rates for this age group (Conlin, 2017).

Some governments have sought to avoid this problem by:

- continuing to pay upfront for university education and recovering the cost through a 'graduate tax' on those who obtain degrees

- designing student-loan systems that come closer to a graduate tax by requiring repayments only when income exceeds a set threshold.

These approaches remain open to the criticism that graduates may end up paying back more in tax than just the fees they were charged, and more than non-graduates receiving the same income.

Friends and family

In many situations, people who need extra money turn first to other family members or friends. Friends and family often demand little or no interest, and may be flexible about when the money can be repaid. The scale of such private borrowing is hard to gauge, as neither side has the obligation or inclination to report it. A survey in the UK found 13% of people faced with an unexpected urgent bill of £200 would turn to friends or family, compared with 7% who would use commercial credit (Rowlingson and McKay, 2017). But another UK survey reported that loans from family and friends 'form only a very small proportion of all loans' (ONS, 2017, p. 21). Not everyone has extended-family funds they can draw on, and some avoid turning to people they know for financial help through embarrassment or fear that it will damage their friendship.

Activity 4.4 Which debt product?

Allow 5 minutes for this activity.

Philip, who has a secure job, wants to buy new sound equipment that costs £2000. He hopes to spread the cost over a couple of years. Suggest which type of borrowing might be suitable.

Comment

Having a secure job suggests Philip will have access to mainstream credit. A suitable option might be to take on an unsecured personal loan over a two-year term. You might have suggested that he use his credit card – this would probably be more expensive than the loan over two years, but would give him the flexibility to vary his repayments if he needed to.

Philip wants some new sound equipment

5 Debts and inflation

Like all other aspects of personal finance, debt is affected by inflation. This is the rise in the general price level (represented by an index of individual prices) over a period, usually a year, expressed as a percentage change. In Chapter 2 on income, which introduced consumer-price inflation (Section 3.4), you learned about the difference between nominal value (the monetary or cash value in any period) and real value (the buying power of that money once inflation has been taken into account).

Inflation is often presented as a bad thing: it erodes living standards if prices rise faster than wages and salaries, and complicates future planning if the inflation rate is hard to forecast. But, because inflation erodes the value of money, it needn't be bad for everyone. Inflation generally benefits people with debts, and penalises those who have lent money, especially if incomes are rising, as well as prices.

5.1 Why inflation may be good for debtors

Inflation may benefit people with outstanding debts in two ways: through the effect on the principal, and through the effect on the interest they are charged.

The principal (the capital sum originally borrowed) is a fixed amount in nominal terms. However, this amount gets steadily smaller in real terms if there is inflation. For example, suppose I borrow £1000 to be repaid in ten years' time. If prices double (rise by 100%) over the ten years, the real value of the £1000 will halve to just £500. The amount I shall be paying back in real terms is £1000 divided by (1 + 100%) or (1 + 1). If my income has risen over this time, the principal will also have become progressively smaller in real terms relative to the income out of which it is repaid.

If the borrowing was taken out at a variable interest rate, the lender is likely to increase the rate to compensate for inflation. However, many loans are taken out at an interest rate that is fixed for all or part of the term, and inflation will erode the real value of repayments during this fixed period. Think back to the reducing-balance loan demonstrated in Table 4.2. Interest adds a certain percentage to outstanding debt each time period. However, inflation erodes the real value of the amount added. If the inflation rate matches or exceeds the interest rate, the cost of borrowing may disappear altogether in real terms.

5.2 The real interest rate

We can examine the effects of inflation on borrowing in more detail by considering a one-year loan with a 10% interest rate. If there is no inflation, this is the **real interest rate** on the loan, as well as the nominal rate. But what if the inflation is 10%? At the end of the first year, the borrower must pay interest equivalent to 10% of the principal. But over the year, the value of money has been eroded by 10%. So, in real terms, the interest charge has disappeared. The precise calculation is a little more complex, but provided the rates involved are not too high, nor the term too long, a good approximation of the real interest rate can be obtained from this calculation:

Real interest rate
An interest rate adjusted for inflation – lower than the nominal interest rate if prices are rising.

Real interest rate = Nominal interest rate − Inflation rate

If the inflation rate goes above the interest rate, the real interest rate becomes negative. Borrowers are effectively being paid for taking out their loans, instead of paying for them.

Activity 4.5 Real interest payments

Allow 20 minutes for this activity.

Read the scenario below and answer the questions that follow.

Ten years ago, Mark took out a ten-year interest-only loan of £10,000 at a fixed interest rate of 10% a year. At the time, he earned £20,000 a year. In the last ten years, prices have risen by 5% a year (a total increase of 63% over the ten-year period). Mark's earnings have roughly kept pace with inflation, rising to £33,000 today.

1   In pounds, how much interest does Mark pay each year? Is this a nominal or real value?

2   Today, is the real value of Mark's interest payments lower or higher than ten years ago?

3   What is the real annual interest rate that Mark is paying?

Comment

The answers to Activity 4.5 are given at the end of this chapter.

5.3 Real interest rates in practice

Taking the US as an example, Figure 4.2 shows how inflation rates and nominal interest rates have varied over time. Inflation is measured here by the consumer price index (CPI), and nominal interest rates by the rate on long-term lending to the US government, considered to be a low-risk and therefore inexpensive form of debt.

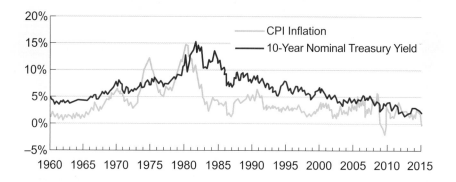

Figure 4.2 Inflation rates and interest rates in the US, 1960–2015 (Bernanke, 2015)

Activity 4.6 Interest rates in the US

Allow 5 minutes for this activity.

Does Figure 4.2 show that real interest rates were sometimes negative in the US during the period 1960 to 2015?

Comment

The real interest rate will be negative when inflation is higher than the nominal interest rate. Therefore, in Figure 4.2, you are looking for any periods when the line tracing the CPI is above the line for the interest rate. The figure does show that real interest rates were sometimes negative: during the periods 1974–76 and 1979–81, and several times since the global financial crisis of 2008.

---

6 Liabilities, assets and balance sheets

In accounting terms, debt is called a **liability**, meaning something that is owed to someone else, and must at some stage be paid back. To stay in a sound financial condition, a borrower must normally have assets at least equal to their liabilities. This ensures that, if necessary, the assets can be sold to pay off debts. (You may want to look back to Section 2 of Chapter 2 on 'Income' for a reminder of what counts as an asset.)

A household's **balance sheet**, which compares the value of its assets and liabilities, can be used alongside a cash flow statement and budget to get an overall picture of a person's or household's financial health.

Liability
An amount of money owed at a particular point in time.

Balance sheet
A record at a particular point in time of what a household (or business) owns or has use of, and what it owes.

6.1 The household balance sheet and net worth

The balance sheet shows how a household's assets (what it owns) compare with its liabilities (what it owes). The liabilities comprise all debts, whether owed to commercial or other lenders. The assets comprise everything that could potentially be converted into money to pay off debts. These include financial savings and any other money owed to the household, plus certain items, such as a home, that generally hold their value. However, some items that could be assets are not usually included in the balance sheet, because they cannot be turned into money right away. These include the value of the right to receive an income at some future date (for example, a state pension) and the value of a person's human capital.

Table 4.3 shows some typical items that might be found on a household balance sheet, and a useful way of setting this out. In this case the household's assets include:

- **financial assets** (money, shares and other financial investments) – which will be described in detail in Chapter 5

- **property** (the home) – examined in detail in Chapter 6

- **other physical assets** (for example, collectable items such as coins, stamps, antiques and works of art).

This household's liabilities include various unsecured loans, as well as a mortgage.

Table 4.3 Typical items on a household balance sheet

ASSETS	LIABILITIES
Liquid assets	**Short-term liabilities**
Cash	Unpaid bills
Current account balance	Credit card and store card debts
Savings account balances	Overdrafts
Debts owed to the household, repayable within one year	Loans repayable within one year
	Other money owed and repayable within one year
Total liquid assets	**Total short-term liabilities**
Other assets	**Other liabilities**
Home	Mortgage, outstanding balance
Other property (e.g. second home, buy-to-let home)	Other long-term loans secured against the home
Investment funds	Other loans not repayable within one year
Shares	Hire purchase agreements, outstanding balance
Government and corporate bonds	Other liabilities
Collectables	
Debts owed to the household and not repayable within one year	
Other financial assets	
Total other assets	**Total other liabilities**
TOTAL ASSETS	TOTAL LIABILITIES
	NET WORTH
	(Total assets minus total liabilities)

The asset side of the balance sheet (conventionally placed on the left) makes a distinction between 'liquid' and 'other' assets. Liquid assets are those that can be quickly converted into cash close to their value. This corresponds to the distinction made on the liability side (on the right) between 'short-term' and 'other' liabilities. I'll explain the reasons for separating and comparing these parts of the balance sheet in the next section, but there are a couple of points to note here:

- **Investments** – If you're already familiar with investments, such as shares, you may be surprised that they are not counted as liquid assets – after all, they can often be sold quickly on a stock market. However, as discussed in Section 2 of Chapter 2, where the value of an asset is volatile, selling quickly might mean getting less cash than expected, so it makes sense to treat these assets as illiquid.

- **Credit and store cards** – You may be wondering why these are classified as short-term liabilities when they are flexible and the debt could be rolled over indefinitely, provided the minimum payments are made each month. This is because credit and store cards are quite an expensive form of debt most suitable for short-term borrowing.

Subtracting the household's total liabilities from its assets gives a measure of the household's **net worth**, shown in the last line of Table 4.3. Net worth (or net wealth) is the amount of money the household would be left with if all its debts were paid off by liquidating its assets.

Net worth
The difference between total assets and total liabilities.

Activity 4.7 A balance sheet of your own

Allow 20 minutes for this activity.

Using the format of Table 4.3, try drawing up a balance sheet for yourself or your own household, including the separate classification of short-term and longer-term assets and liabilities. Where you have to estimate the value of an asset, think of a sensible way to do this – such as using the price of a similar item that's recently been on sale.

Comment

You may have been tempted to include your income as an asset and your spending as a liability. This is not correct. As you learned in Chapter 2, Section 2, these are *flows* (sums of money you receive or spend over a period of time), not *stocks* (the value of something at a point in time). They are closely related – for example, your income may briefly swell your current account balance (an asset) before flowing out to pay your bills and other spending. But only income that is unspent (left in your current account from month to month, or transferred to another form of saving) creates an asset.

6.2 Liquidity and solvency

Positive net worth is a good sign for a household's overall financial health; very well-off people like to be described as 'high-net-worth individuals'. But even if net worth is high, two types of financial problem can sometimes occur.

Liquidity problems

Liquidity
The ability to turn assets into ready money to finance immediate debt repayments and other expenditure.

Some assets (like an owner-occupied home) are difficult to sell, so are not very useful for settling debts that must be repaid right away. To be resilient against shocks to income (like job loss), a household with short-term debts must make sure these are matched by assets that can be turned into cash quickly. A household may become unable to keep repaying its debts because of a **liquidity** problem, if it hasn't enough easily saleable (liquid) assets to set against its short-term liabilities.

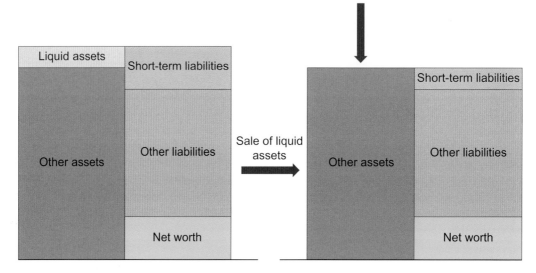

Figure 4.3 A liquidity problem when short-term liabilities exceed liquid assets

Figure 4.3 shows how a household can get into liquidity difficulties with debt, even if it has plenty of assets and positive net worth. Suppose this household had been successfully meeting its credit card bills out of income, but the main earner is suddenly made redundant. It still has credit card debts that fall due at the end of the month. The problem in this case is that short-term liabilities (the credit card debts) are not fully matched by liquid assets (such as money in savings accounts). When the liquid assets are fully used up, there is still a proportion of short-term debt that can't be repaid, even though the household's net worth remains positive.

There are a variety of options the household might consider to pay off this short-term debt:

- As the main earner has lost their job, this household might look like a poor credit risk. But assuming its long-term assets include a home, it may be able to get a loan secured against that. Because the loan is secured and is likely to be repayable over a long period, the interest rate should be lower than that payable for using the credit cards. Though if the household doesn't keep up the repayments on its new loan, it could now lose its home.

- Selling some of the longer-term assets to release cash.

- Cutting back spending, so that part of the household income each month can gradually pay off the remaining card debts.

- Claiming on any insurance policy that promises to pay out in the event of sudden income loss. (You will learn more about this and other types of insurance in Chapter 7.)

Solvency problems

A household may have a **solvency** problem if its liabilities are greater than its assets. This might happen if:

- it takes on more debt than it can really afford

- due to missed repayments, interest is compounded, thereby causing the outstanding debt balance to grow.

A fall in the value of some of the household's assets (such as a home or investments) can also leave them worth less than liabilities, causing a solvency problem. If there is a widespread fall in property or stock-market prices, household balance sheets that were previously healthy may suddenly worsen, with net worth becoming negative.

Solvency
The ability to repay all debts, typically shown by assets exceeding liabilities.

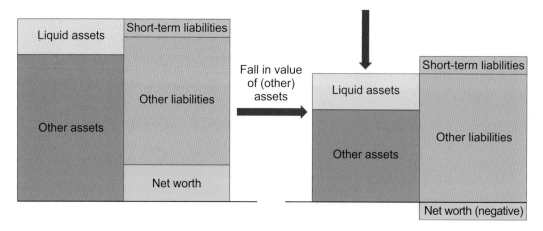

Figure 4.4 A solvency problem when asset values fall below liabilities

Figure 4.4 shows how a household can get into solvency difficulties when there's a sudden fall in the value of total assets, pushing their total value below total liabilities. The previous positive net worth is wiped out, and the household is technically insolvent, with negative net worth (shown by going below the line that represents zero assets). Notice that a solvency problem can occur even when there is no liquidity problem – even though technically insolvent, this household has liquid assets that are well above its short-term liabilities.

The household might only be 'technically' insolvent if its liabilities are long-term and there is a good chance of asset values rising again before the long-term debts need to be paid off. But technical insolvency should be a warning to the household, and it can turn into genuine insolvency if the time has come to pay off the debt.

6.3 Current asset ratio and leverage

Once a balance sheet is drawn up, in the format shown in Table 4.3, it's possible to do some simple calculations to help gauge the strength of the household's financial situation. This will indicate whether or not it is at risk of developing liquidity and solvency problems.

Current asset ratio
Total liquid assets as a proportion of short-term liabilities, giving an indication of liquidity.

The **current asset ratio** is an important indicator of the liquidity position, or the scope for paying off short-term debts out of readily-available assets. It is calculated as:

Current asset ratio = Total liquid assets ÷ Total short-term liabilities

The higher this ratio, the better is the household's liquidity situation. If the current asset ratio is less than 1 (that is, short-term liabilities exceed short-term assets), the household already has a liquidity problem if it cannot extend its short-term liabilities and has to pay them off. While there is no strict rule, personal finance experts generally recommend that a good target to aim for is a current asset ratio of 3 or 4.

Leverage gives a measure of overall indebtedness, expressing total liabilities as a proportion of total assets:

Leverage (%) = (Total liabilities ÷ Total assets) × 100

Leverage is sometimes also called 'gearing', although gearing can also denote other ratios (such as net worth to total assets). Leverage above 100% indicates that a household is already technically insolvent. Low leverage may indicate a comfortable solvency situation, but that doesn't mean that keeping it low is always a household's most rewarding financial strategy in the long term. Relatively high leverage can be beneficial for a household if it borrows to buy assets which then rise in value, but this strategy also carries risks if the assets don't perform as expected. This will be further examined in the context of purchasing a house in Chapter 6.

Leverage
The act of borrowing to buy an asset. Also a measure of the total liabilities as a percentage of total assets, giving an indication of solvency.

6.4 Affordability of household debt

The current asset ratio and leverage indicate the ease with which existing debts can be paid off out of assets in a crisis. They may be thought of as indicators of a household's financial resilience to shocks, such as job loss or a rise in interest rates.

Another aspect to resilience is being certain that household debt is affordable. To look at that, we need to use the cash flow statement and budget to assess the ongoing costs of meeting the repayments.

One widely used measure of affordability is the **debt-to-income (DTI) ratio**. This shows the household's regular debt repayments as a proportion of its gross income in the same period:

DTI ratio = Debt repayments due in a period ÷ Gross income over the period

Debt-to-income (DTI) ratio
The proportion of gross income that is absorbed by debt repayments.

Although debt repayments are actually made out of disposable income, the DTI ratio (based on gross income) is easy to calculate. It acts as an indicator of how easily the household is likely to be able to keep up its debt repayments, alongside all its other necessary spending.

There are no exact rules, but experts generally agree that a healthy DTI ratio should be no more than about 30%, and a ratio much above 40% is a cause for concern.

The DTI ratio is not just useful for individual households: governments also use ratios such as this to track the indebtedness of the household sector, because this can have a major impact on the economy as a whole. The global financial crisis that broke in 2008 arose, in part, because of households taking out mortgages (especially in the US) that became unaffordable when interest rates on the loans rose but house prices fell. Ten years later, concerns about household debt started to re-emerge in fast-growing middle-income economies like China, as well as in Europe and the US. This time, concern extended not just to mortgages but also to unsecured debts, such as car loans and borrowing on credit cards (Bank of England, 2016). A sharp rise in interest rates on debts, raising the proportion of borrowers' income taken up by debt repayment, could reduce household expenditure, which is generally the biggest component of national expenditure and GDP. This can trigger an economic slowdown, or even recession, which lowers the household sector's income and worsens its debt problems.

7 Debt and the life course

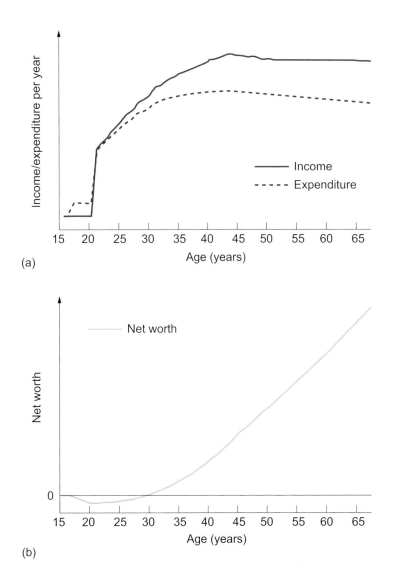

Figure 4.5 Example of cash flow and resulting changes in net worth

In Chapter 3 you explored the household's cash flow statement, which shows its current flows of income and expenditure over a period (such as a month or year), and how drawing up a budget can help to plan these flows in the future. The drawing up of the balance sheet is an important complement to setting out a budget, since it records the stocks of assets and liabilities that result from decisions to spend and save. If a household spends more than it receives in income during any year, its balance sheet the following year will show a decline in assets (as savings are run down) and/or a rise in liabilities (due to borrowing to finance the deficit). If the household spends less than it receives in income, its balance sheet at the end of the year will show a rise in assets, or a reduction in liabilities if debt is repaid.

Just as the cash flow can be illustrated in a chart, so can past and future changes in the balance sheet. Figure 4.5 (on the previous page) reproduces the cash flow diagram for Dan from Figure 3.5 in Chapter 3; and it adds a second chart that broadly maps what happens to Dan's net worth as he moves through his life course up to the point at which he retires.

As shown in the upper chart in Figure 4.5, Dan spends more than his income while he is studying in early adult life. This means he is running up debts, causing him to have a negative net worth, which is shown in the lower chart. Once Dan starts a job, his income exceeds his spending and he uses the surplus to repay his debts. As a result, his net worth climbs back to zero. Dan then keeps on saving in the years that follow, and his net worth builds up. Dan will draw on his savings to provide himself with income in his retirement years and so his net worth will fall as the savings are used up, as discussed in Chapter 8.

Activity 4.8 Your net worth over the life course

Allow 15 minutes for this activity.

In Activity 3.7, you drew a cash flow diagram, showing the pattern of your income and spending over your life so far, and projected into the future. Now try adding a diagram that shows how your net worth changes as a result of those flows of income and expenditure.

Comment

Your diagrams will look something like those in Figure 4.5, but reflecting your own particular patterns of income, spending and net worth. What's important is that if your expenditure exceeds your income, your net worth will be falling; and when you are spending less than your income, or paying-off debt, your net worth is rising.

Figure 4.5 uses a simple model designed to demonstrate the relationship between cash flow and net worth over the life course. As you've already learned in this chapter, net worth may also change because of other factors, such as variations in the value of assets. More sophisticated modelling takes other factors into account.

8 Conclusion

This chapter has investigated the role of debt in personal and household financial management as a way to finance large purchases that would otherwise not be possible – or long delayed in taking place – and as a way to keep expenditure steady when income fluctuates. I have explained how the cost of debt can be calculated, and why this varies according to the length and type of loan and the borrower's circumstances.

This chapter also introduced the household balance sheet, showing how this complements the cash flow statement and budget in showing a household's financial health or resilience. These are of concern not just for individual households but also for governments because of the way the household sector affects the other sectors of an economy. Finally, the chapter looked at the way a person's or household's balance sheet situation can vary through the life course, driven by decisions about income and expenditure.

Debt has a positive role to play in many aspects of financial planning and the inability to borrow may be an important aspect of financial exclusion. Borrowing too much can also lead to financial difficulty and stress. Households' widespread and increasing use of debt in many countries raises the importance of our next topic: the process of putting money aside and saving as a way to repay or avoid incurring debt, and to open up greater opportunities for achieving life goals.

Answers to activities in Chapter 4

Answers to Activity 4.3

1 Charging 5% on £10,000 at the end of the year would mean an interest charge of £500 (0.05 × £10,000).

2 Although the same initial sum of £10,000 is borrowed, total interest on the reducing-balance loan is lower (£266.79) than interest on the loan in Question 1 (£500). This is because, in Question 1, £10,000 is borrowed for the full year: in other words, the average amount owed during the year is always £10,000. By contrast, with the reducing-balance loan, part of the principal is being paid back each month. This means only £852.09 of the loan (the amount outstanding at the start of month 12) is borrowed for the whole year: £1700.73 of the loan is borrowed for 11 months; £2545.93 for 10 months, and so on. The full £10,000 is borrowed only for one month. Taking the year as a whole, the average amount owed is around £5400 (the amount outstanding halfway through the year, between months 6 and 7). Since the average sum borrowed is lower, the total interest charged is also lower.

Answers to Activity 4.5

1 Mark pays 10% × £10,000 = £1000 interest each year. This is a nominal value – it's the cash sum he pays each year.

2 If prices have risen by 63% over the last ten years, the real value of the interest payments today is lower. One way of thinking about this is that ten years ago, Mark had to give up £1000 of goods and services in order to pay the interest on this loan, which was 5% of his pay (£1000/£20,000). Today, he has to give up fewer goods and services in order to pay the interest: only 3% of his pay (£1000/£33,000).

3 You can use the simplified formula in Section 5.2 of this chapter to work out that the annual interest rate is 10% − 5% = 5% a year. Interest is adding 10% a year to the cost of the loan, but in real terms, inflation is reducing the cost by 5% a year.

References

Abedifar, P., Ebrahim, S., Molyneux, P. and Tarazi, A. (2015) 'Islamic banking and finance: recent empirical literature and directions for future research', *Journal of Economic Surveys*, vol. 29, no. 4, pp. 637–70.

Bank of England (2016) *UK Household indebtedness* [Online]. Available at www.bankofengland.co.uk/publications/Documents/.../fsr16nov5.ppt, Chart A.27 (Accessed 4 May 2017).

Bernanke, B. (2015) *Why Are Interest Rates So Low?*, Brookings Institution, 30 March [Online]. Available at www.brookings.edu/blog/ben-bernanke/2015/03/30/why-are-interest-rates-so-low/ (Accessed 15 February 2018).

Conlin, M. (2017) 'Rising student debt locking out US millennials from home ownership: Fed', *Reuters*, 13 July [Online]. Available at www.reuters.com/article/us-usa-studentloans/rising-student-debt-locking-out-u-s-millennials-from-home-ownership-fed-idUSKBN19Y2K2 (Accessed 15 February 2018).

Evans, G. and Allison, C. (2016) *Better and Brighter? Responsible Rent to Own Alternatives – Summary Report*, March [Online], London, The Financial Inclusion Centre. Available at www.inclusioncentre.co.uk/wordpress29/wp-content/uploads/2016/03/Better-and-Brighter-Responsible-RTO-Alternatives-Summary-150316.pdf (Accessed 15 February 2018).

Financial Conduct Authority (FCA) (2019) 'Consumer credit – high-cost short-term credit lending data', 21 January [Online]. Available at www.fca.org.uk/data/consumer-credit-high-cost-short-term-credit-lending-data-jan-2019 (Accessed 5 June 2019).

Hardy, Gwennan (2018) *Doorway to Debt: Protecting Consumers in the Home Credit Market*, March [Online], Citizens Advice. Available at www.citizensadvice.org.uk/about-us/policy/policy-research-topics/debt-and-money-policy-research/doorway-to-debt/ (Accessed 5 June 2019).

King, J. (2014) 'IMF World Bank: Credit scoring – friends, followers and settling scores', *The Banker*, October, pp. 184–8.

Merrick, J. (2013) 'Special report: the dark side of credit – a million new payday loans every month', *The Independent*, 29 June [Online]. Available at www.independent.co.uk/money/loans-credit/special-report-the-dark-side-of-credit-a-million-new-payday-loans-every-month-8680018.html (Accessed 26 January 2018).

Monte dei Paschi di Siena (2017) *History* [Online]. Available at http://english.mps.it/aboutus/about-the-group/history/pages/default.aspx (Accessed 15 February 2018).

Office for National Statistics (ONS) (2017) *Household Debt Inequalities* [Online]. Available at www.ons.gov.uk/peoplepopulationandcommunity/ personalandhouseholdfinances/debt/articles/householddebtinequalities/2016-04-04 (Accessed 24 January 2018).

Rebell, B. (2016) 'Why are millennials tapping payday loans and pawn shops?', *Reuters*, 7 January [Online]. Available at www.reuters.com/article/us-column-rebell-pawn-idUSKBN0UL0FP20160107# (Accessed 15 February 2018).

Rowlingson, K. and McKay, S. (2017) *Financial Inclusion Annual Monitoring Report 2017* [Online], University of Birmingham. Available at www. birmingham.ac.uk/Documents/news/15518-CHASM-Report-Stage-4.pdf (Accessed 24 January 2017).

Tirado, L. (2014) *Hand to Mouth: Living in Bootstrap America*, New York, Random House.

To cite this chapter, use the following format in your reference list:

Shipman, A. (2019) 'Borrowing and debt', in De Henau, J. and Lowe, J. (eds) *Personal Finance*, Milton Keynes, The Open University, pp. 153–195.

Chapter 5
Savings and investments

Hedley Stone

Contents

1 Introduction

Annual income twenty pounds, annual expenditure nineteen pounds nineteen and six, result happiness. Annual income twenty pounds, annual expenditure twenty pounds ought and six, result misery.

(Mr Micawber in *David Copperfield*)

(Dickens, 1850, p. 150)

Charles Dickens wrote this over 150 years ago, so a bit of updating is needed: today, for some people, 'twenty pounds' looks more like an hourly wage than an annual income. We also need to replace 'nineteen and six' with 'ninety-seven-and-a-half pence', and 'ought' with 'nothing'. But despite this, though he was writing about Britain, what Dickens had to say about income and expenditure is just as relevant today.

I'll start this chapter by defining some terms you are going to come across: first, let's distinguish between 'saving' and 'savings'.

Saving is the act of accumulating a *flow* of money over a particular time period – such as putting money into a building society account.

Savings (note the plural) are the current value of the accumulated sum of previous saving – the financial assets a household has acquired through saving, measured at a particular point in time.

If I already have £100 in a building society account, that £100 is my savings, but if I put an additional £25 a month into the account, I am saving £25 a month. After another two months, my savings will have increased to £150 (plus any interest earned).

This chapter explores the options available to households that have some spare income. In this introduction, and in Sections 2 and 3, I use the terms 'saving' and 'savings' to encompass putting money into 'savings products', such as deposit accounts, and also 'investment products', which comprise shares, government bonds and **investment funds**. Investment products, which you will learn about later in this chapter, are typically riskier than savings products. I also look at the importance of savings: why households save, and the different ways in which they can save.

Saving
The act of accumulating the part of income that is not spent on goods and services into savings or investment products.

Savings
The total value of all financial assets (including investments) that a household has at a particular point in time.

Investment fund
A financial product that invests in a broad range of different shares, bonds and/or other assets.

A key point about saving is that it *defers* (or puts off) consumption today for consumption at some time in the future. This future may be next month (such as a night out), next year (perhaps for a holiday), or many years ahead (a young person saving for retirement – see Chapter 8). Saving can even be for after death (some people save in order to leave money to their children).

Saving is the opposite of taking out debt, which, as you saw in Chapter 4, involves bringing forward consumption, by buying now and paying later.

debt advances consumption.

saving defers consumption.

2 How much do households save?

How much income a household saves is important both for the household in achieving its goals, and for the broader economy. In this section we'll look briefly at how saving habits may vary *between* countries at a given time, and *within* countries over time. We'll also consider why people save, and why saving matters.

2.1 The household saving ratio

The percentage of a household's annual disposable income that is saved, rather than spent, is known as the **household saving ratio**. Figure 5.1 shows that this ratio can vary significantly between countries, and over the period of just a few years.

Household saving ratio (also called saving rate)
Although measured in various ways, this is broadly the percentage of average annual household disposable income that is saved.

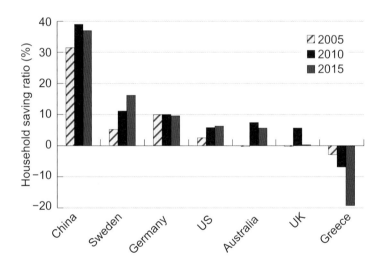

Figure 5.1 Household saving ratios in selected countries, 2005 to 2015 (data from OECD, 2018)

The most striking feature of Figure 5.1 is the large increase in the saving ratio between 2005 and 2010 for some countries. The likely reason for this is the financial crisis that occurred in 2008, which led to recession in many of the world's major economies. An economic downturn like this tends to make people anxious to pay off their debts and to try to safeguard their wealth. In the UK this spurt in saving was short-lived; households started to spend most of their income again by

2015, during a prolonged period of austerity policies and stagnating wages.

In Greece, the financial crisis affected incomes so much that households were unable to save at all. Figure 5.1 shows a negative saving ratio in Greece, which continually deteriorates over the period. On the other hand, China and Germany maintained stable ratios throughout the period, with Chinese households saving large proportions of their income compared to households in the other countries.

Activity 5.1 Calculating the saving ratio

Allow 5 minutes for this activity.

As you read at the start of this chapter, Charles Dickens' Mr Micawber felt that saving the equivalent of 2.5 pence out of an income of £20 would lead to happiness.

1 Calculate the saving ratio implied by his suggested saving habit.

2 How does it relate to the UK saving ratios shown in Figure 5.1 (and shown again here in Table 5.1)?

Table 5.1 UK saving ratios

2005	2010	2015
−0.21%	5.67%	0.16%

(Data from OECD, 2018)

3 How does it compare to your own household's saving ratio (over the last year)?

Comment

The answers to Activity 5.1 are given at the end of this chapter.

2.2 Why is household saving important?

Household saving can be beneficial not only for households themselves but also for the economy at large.

Benefits for households

As I mentioned in the introduction to this chapter, income that is not spent allows households to build up an asset: savings. Think of this asset as a vehicle for transferring spending power through time – deferring to consumption now – and saving enables a household to cope with both expected and unexpected expenses later. For example, the breakdown of a washing machine or a car could easily lead a household with no savings into debt, or force it to make cuts in other household expenditure, to pay for repairs or replacements.

Figure 5.2 (a), overleaf, shows how a monthly income of 2300 and regular expenditure of 2100 allow Janice to save 200 per month. This builds her stock of savings month after month (Figure 5.2 (b), overleaf). This means that in month eight, when her car breaks down and she faces a 1300 repair bill, Janice can use part of her savings to pay for it. As she has a regular 200 surplus each month (Figure 5.2 (a)) she needs to use an extra 1100 from her accumulated savings to pay for the repair, meaning her stock of assets falls from 1400 to 300. After the repair, she starts building her savings again as before.

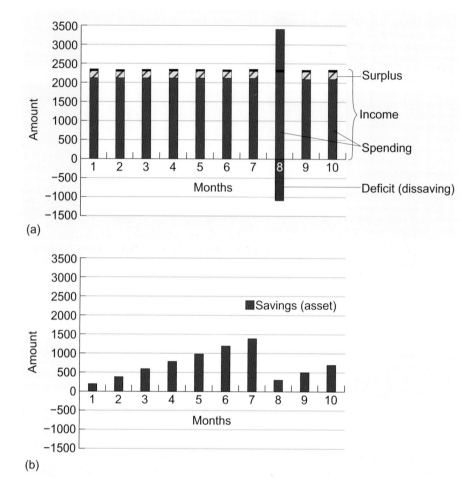

Figure 5.2 Janice's monthly saving and spending (a), and accumulated savings (b)

Benefits for corporations

As you first saw in Chapter 1, there is interdependence between the household sector and other sectors of the economy. As such, household saving has an impact on the corporate sector. For example, the amount that is deferred for later consumption (saved) means some of the goods and services produced by corporations are not bought. However, those savings are not usually sitting idle in a vault: they can be used by the household – often via financial intermediaries – to buy shares in firms, or to provide businesses with loans. This means that household savings are a potential source of funds for firms to expand and invest, to conceive new products and services that can then be purchased by households later on.

Benefits for governments

Governments often spend more than they receive from taxation, so have to borrow the difference – and they may borrow from the public. This is why they encourage people to save in government savings schemes (and so effectively lend the government money).

Sukanya Samriddhi Accounts

Interest payable, rates, periodicity etc.	Minimum amount for opening of account and maximum balance that can be retained
Rate of interest 8.1% per annum (with effect from 1-01-2018), calculated on yearly basis. Yearly compounded.	Minimum INR. 1000/- and Maximum INR. 1,50,000/- in a financial year. Subsequent deposit in multiple of INR 100/-. Deposits can be made in lump-sum. No limit on number of deposits either in a month or in a financial year.

Salient features including tax rebate

- A legal guardian/natural guardian can open an account in the name of a Girl Child.
- A guardian can open only one account in the name of one girl child and maximum two accounts in the name of two different girl children.
- Account can be opened up to age of 10 years only from the date of birth. For initial operations of Scheme, one year grace has been given. With the grace, girl child who is born between 2.12.2003 & 1.12.2004 can open account up to 1.12.2015.
- If minimum Rs 1000/- is not deposited in a financial year, account will become discontinued and can be revived with a penalty of Rs 50/- per year with minimum amount required for deposit for that year.
- Partial withdrawal, maximum of up to 50% of balance standing at the end of the preceding financial year, can be taken after account holder's attaining age of 18 years.
- Account can be closed after completion of 21 years.
- Normal premature closure will be allowed after completion of 18 years / provided that girl is married.

Figure 5.3 Features of a saving account for girls and young women in India (text taken from Department of Posts, Ministry of Communications, Government of India, www.indiapost.gov.in)

Governments also like households to save because robust saving habits make households more resilient, and less likely to fall back on state benefits. Household saving may also help governments achieve social objectives, such as increasing home ownership and improving human capital. More specific objectives can also be pursued – for example, aiming to achieve more economic independence for women, thereby reducing gender inequalities, by encouraging them to save more – as illustrated by Figure 5.3.

2.3 Saving inequality

Although saving is important for households and the economy, many households cannot afford to save because they barely have enough income to cover their expenditure. Many, as you saw in Chapter 4, have expenditure exceeding their income, and rely on borrowing from friends, family or financial providers to make ends meet.

Figure 5.1 showed differences in household saving between countries, but the data masked differences *within* countries: for example, between low-income and better-off households.

Table 5.2 shows the gradual increase (within countries) in the proportion of household income that is saved, as average household income increases. There are different patterns across countries.

Table 5.2 Households' median saving rate (% of disposable income), by income quintile group (selected EU countries, 2010)

	All households	Poorest 20%	Second poorest 20%	Middle 20%	Second richest 20%	Richest 20%
France	29.1	13.8	21.3	27.5	32.6	43.2
Poland	25.2	1.9	17.4	25.2	34.6	42.3
UK	23.2	−3.3	16.1	21.5	30.5	41.5
Sweden	20.7	−10.0	15.1	23.3	29.2	36.6
Spain	17.7	−15.8	4.3	16.0	26.3	37.2
Germany	13.6	−14.1	7.7	15.7	23.0	29.5
Romania	−5.0	−42.4	−18.7	−5.6	4.9	21.8
Greece	−9.5	−50.9	−10.0	−9.0	−0.4	1.2

Source: Eurostat (2017)

Activity 5.2 Comparing saving rates

Allow 10 minutes for this activity.

Using data from Table 5.2, make some notes that briefly describe two striking patterns of saving rate between countries and households in 2010.

Comment

The data are for 2010, with patterns likely to reflect the severe economic crisis that plagued many European countries after 2007. One of the most striking patterns is perhaps that – although the higher the income, the higher the saving rate – Spain, Romania and Greece had especially wide differences in saving rates between the least well-off and best-off households.

A second pattern is the difference between countries in the saving rate of low-income households: France and Poland differed from the other countries insofar as lower income households had positive saving rates, unlike in the other countries. In Greece, which was plagued with a severe economic crisis at the time these data was collected, even the higher-income households struggled to save any of their income, and most households had negative saving rates.

3 Why do households save?

In Section 2 of this chapter, I explained how saving defers consumption from the present to sometime in the future. Therefore, when thinking about the reasons why households save, we are really thinking about why households choose to defer consumption, rather than consuming now.

It is useful to consider the motives for saving under three main headings, because they have different implications for financial planning.

Saving as a precaution to provide a buffer against unexpected and unwanted events. Households are more resilient if they have built up some savings to cover loss of income resulting from accidents, serious illness or unemployment, or to meet unexpected expenses such as replacing domestic appliances. Determining the right level of saving is, however, difficult because of the unexpected nature of the events households want to protect against.

Saving for specific purposes such as a holiday, to start a business, help finance children's education, or to maintain a comfortable lifestyle in retirement. (Chapter 8 looks in detail at saving in pension funds.) This form of saving can be planned in advance with precise targets. However, with longer-term plans, there are increasing risks of not achieving the desired target.

Saving to accumulate wealth for which, at present, there may be no defined purpose, but there might be in future. This might include funds that provide a greater feeling of security or flexibility, or to provide inheritance for children.

3.1 Influences on the decision to save

Factors influencing the decision to save vary greatly between households, depending on their needs, preferences and constraints (Le Blanc et al., 2015). Among these are personal factors, including:

- income and wealth – the higher these are, the greater the saving propensity (as shown in Table 5.2 in the case of income)

- age and the life cycle – people have different motives, opportunities and needs at different stages of life

- the number of household members and the structure of the household (whether married, cohabiting, a single parent, etc.) – the presence of children is often linked to a greater need for saving but also to constraints on income and greater consumption

- employment status and education (associated with human capital) – this will influence the financial prospects of individuals and risks to their income (for example, precarious temporary employment versus a permanent contract).

External factors will also play a key role in determining the needs and opportunities for saving (Le Blanc et al., 2015). These fall under three categories:

- access to credit – the development of financial markets, and the relative ease with which people can access credit, influence the extent to which households can rely on borrowing (rather than building up a savings stock) if their expenditure exceeds their income

- friends and family – they can play a similar role to more formal corporate channels, helping with unexpected expenditure or lost income; the degree to which this can happen often depends on the culture and social norms of the community

- the welfare state – the generosity of the state in providing social security for its citizens will determine how much individuals need to save privately; generous unemployment benefits, income support and state pension will reduce a household's need to save for a rainy day or for retirement, while free education might reduce parental saving for their children.

The prevalence of different motives for saving varies considerably between countries. For example, Yao et al. (2011) found that Chinese households save a far greater proportion of their incomes than those in the US (also shown in Figure 5.1). The saving rate in China has been over 25% since the early 1990s, but the rate in the US has been under 10% during the same period (and has at times been negative). Chinese households were significantly more likely than US households to save for precautionary reasons, and to finance education, whereas there was little difference between the two countries in saving for retirement. Research for the eurozone countries also found that households primarily saved for precautionary motives and retirement (Le Blanc et al., 2015).

Yao et al. (2011) suggest that economic reforms in China in 1978, whereby the state no longer guaranteed jobs for life, led to uncertainty among Chinese households about future income, thus motivating them to save as a precaution. The reforms also shifted responsibility for financing education from the state to households. Fan et al. (1998, cited in Yao et al., 2011, p. 30) found that 'Chinese students were more likely to report abstract saving motives (e.g. "for better things in the future"), whereas American students were more likely to report concrete, goal-oriented saving motives (e.g. saving for purchasing durable goods)'.

Savings are an important buffer against unexpected bills

Activity 5.3 Your reasons for saving

Allow 15 minutes for this activity.

Write down your own reasons for saving (or wanting to save) at this moment in time. Have these reasons changed at different times in your life?

Comment

You may have mentioned precautionary motives, saving for specific purposes, or saving to accumulate wealth. Depending on your age, you may have considered how your motives for saving have become more numerous or complicated as you've got older; or that they involve more people than when you were younger, and your time horizons (the estimated time needed to achieve your plans or goals) may have changed. Of course, you may want to save but are not currently able to.

3.2 Saving and the life course

A household's overall level of saving is likely to vary a good deal over the life course. The cash flow model that has appeared in earlier chapters is based on the work of two economists. The 'life cycle hypothesis' (Modigliani and Brumberg, 1954) predicts that people typically start their adult life with expenditure exceeding their disposable income.

Franco Modigliani (1918–2003) was an Italian-born, naturalised American economist. He developed the life cycle hypothesis with his student Richard Brumberg in the 1950s.

For the majority of adult life, people are then modelled as accumulating savings until retirement (or near retirement), and then using their accumulated savings to provide their income in later life. So a key motivation for saving is believed to be saving for retirement. This is a broad generalisation though, and doesn't reveal anything about the detailed saving habits of individual households or the different patterns of saving in different countries, which will depend on all the other factors (personal and external) mentioned in Section 3.1, especially the level of generosity of the welfare state and employers in providing pension income.

There is a close link between the reasons for saving and the pattern of saving over the life cycle. For example, the findings of Fan et al. (1998, cited in Yao et al., 2011) about the different attitudes to saving of Chinese and American students, are likely to mean that Chinese students will show a higher and much more consistent rate of saving early in life than their American counterparts.

The example of Dan, that you have seen in Figure 4.5 of Chapter 4, illustrates the life-cycle model: Dan secures a consistent flow of saving over his working life that builds a growing stock of assets, which is then used in retirement. Figure 5.4 reproduces that figure.

Net saving
Disposable (net) household income minus household expenditure.

In graph (a) in Figure 5.4, the distance between any point on the solid income line and the point on the dotted expenditure line vertically below (or above) it represents **net saving** at that particular time in the life cycle. Positive net saving takes place when the income line lies above the expenditure line.

If at any time the expenditure line is above the income line, net saving at that time is negative (that person or household is in deficit). If the two lines are running over each other, so that neither is higher, net saving is zero.

Accumulated savings provide a household with assets, and graph (b) in Figure 5.4 shows how sustained positive net saving leads to a growing stock of assets during Dan's working life: a positive and growing net worth. Assets may increase not only through further saving but also through the income and capital returns that savings generate if these are reinvested.

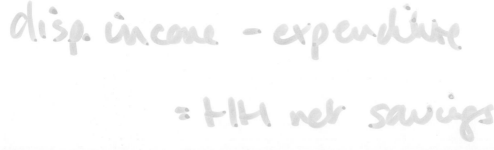

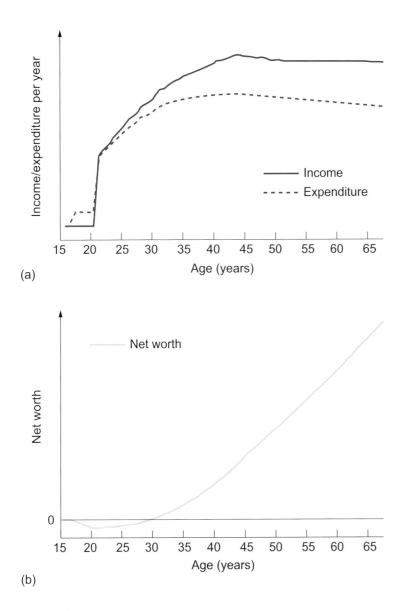

Figure 5.4 Dan's cash flow and resulting changes in net worth

Please note that Figure 5.4 (overleaf) only illustrates how positive net saving accumulates net worth over Dan's working life, with income exceeding expenditure. As a result, the net assets shown in graph (b) do not include all the resources that Dan could use in retirement that he might have accumulated in other ways – for example, any entitlement to a state pension.

Another omission from Figure 5.4 is the effect of mortgage debt. Some people may take out mortgages to purchase their home, while building up financial assets at the same time during their working life. Mortgage debt and housing assets are explored in Chapter 6.

3.3 Saving within the household

One of the themes of this book is the interrelationship between individuals and their households. In Chapter 3 you saw how the way in which money is managed by couples may influence control over household expenditure. This is also true of saving, as you need to have access to income to be able to save. Having individual savings, as well as joint savings, can provide more financial security for people in relationships. This can be linked back to the idea that independence is an important motivator for having savings, and is particularly important in terms of saving for retirement and if relationships break down. With a significant proportion of married couples divorcing, and a higher proportion of non-married couples separating, preparing for such an eventuality may be sensible.

Gender differences in saving habits

As the number of women in paid employment has increased, women increasingly save from their own income and make their own saving choices. However, as you read in Chapter 2, caring responsibilities are primarily borne by women, and affect their earnings as well as their expenditure (childcare costs). So a woman's ability to save may be more constrained compared to that of some men.

Several studies in both developed and developing countries have investigated gender differences in saving habits. Westaway and McKay (2007, cited in Lewis and Messy, 2012) found that women in the UK were as likely as men to save, but saved smaller sums and for shorter terms, and that women's savings were more likely than men's to be disrupted by events such as divorce or the birth of a child. The study also found that the impact of parenthood differed between men and women, with men tending to increase saving when they became fathers, and women tending to reduce saving when they became mothers. Further findings were that gender differences were much less marked for childless women, and that young women (16–24) saved more than young men.

It has been argued that women tend to be more risk-averse than men in their saving behaviour and that this may lead to a preference for cash (savings accounts) over stock market investments (Jianakoplos and Bernasek, 1998; Eckel and Grossman, 2008, cited in Lewis and Messy, 2012). These findings have been disputed though: others found no systematic difference when analysing populations as a whole rather than through experimental settings (Nelson, 2016). Moreover, feminist economists have argued that looking at financial risk aversion is missing the point, because this does not take into account the risks that women take overall, starting with the health risk associated with child birth, and continuing with the economic risks of taking on caring responsibilities, both during intact relationships and after separation, all of which have far-reaching financial implications.

Women in developing countries also have different saving behaviours and motives to men, as shown by a study from the World Bank in 20 countries (Floro and Seguino, 2002, cited in Lewis and Messy, 2012). The authors found that the type and level of income, as well as other sources of bargaining power within households, such as education and assets, influence household spending and saving decisions. Although women spend more of the money they control on their children than men do, especially for food, this could be seen as an investment, so that their children live to look after them in old age. Local culture also affects saving through the need to send remittances or to save for a dowry, or the norms regulating ownership of money.

Activity 5.4 Saving and managing money within households

Allow 10 minutes for this activity.

Look back at the different types of money management within households in Chapter 3 of this book. Which type of money management do you think would be associated with greater individual savings?

Comment

The answer to Activity 5.4 is given at the end of this chapter.

4 Making sense of savings products

Let's now turn to the different saving products available to households. In this section, I distinguish between savings and investment products as follows,

- Savings products pay interest, but the nominal value of the capital (the principal) stays the same.

- The value of the capital for investment products can go up and down.

This distinction between savings and investments is the one commonly used in personal finance (economics has a slightly different take on it, as you will discover if you go on to study more economics). I will return to this distinction in more detail in Section 5 of this chapter.

Note the term 'capital' in the savings or investment product description. This corresponds to the term 'principal' in a loan, which you explored in Chapter 4. Indeed in some markets – such as peer-to-peer lending or bonds (see Section 5 of this chapter) – the principal lent to a borrower is clearly the same sum that's set aside as capital by a saver (on the other side of the deal).

In many countries, savings products are protected by deposit insurance schemes, at least up to certain (fairly generous) amounts. This means that savers' money deposited with registered financial institutions will be safe even if these institutions are unable to repay it. This is not the case if money simply put under the mattress is lost.

There are thousands of different savings products available, offered by, for example, banks, building societies and government agencies, and the choice may seem daunting. Yet it is possible to make sense of the choice with reference to available interest rates, and the taxation of that interest. An understanding of these issues, as well as a clear idea about the reason for wanting to save, should provide enough background information for someone to make more informed decisions about savings products.

4.1 Interest rates on savings

Savings products can differ in the type of interest paid, the frequency of interest payments, and whether the interest rate is fixed or variable. But in all cases, as interest is a kind of reward for saving, we might expect that changes in the rate of interest would be a strong motivation for people to alter their saving habits.

The general principle that a rise in interest rates will encourage private saving has played an important part in economic theory over many years. Economist Alfred Marshall, in *Principles of Economics* said, '[a] strong balance of evidence seems to rest with the opinion that a rise in the rate of interest ... tends to increase the volume of saving' (Marshall, 1920, p. 306). He did, however, temper this statement by conceding that, 'saving in general is affected by many causes other than the rate of interest and ... the saving of many people is but little affected by the rate of interest' (p. 306).

Another very influential economist, John Maynard Keynes, was unimpressed by the theory that interest rates have a significant effect on saving habits, and instead focused on one of the many other causes affecting saving – namely, the level of income. In his words, 'The fundamental psychological law ... is that men are disposed, as a rule and on the average, to increase their consumption as their income increases but not by as much as the increase in the income' (Keynes, 1936, p. 96). The implication of this is that individuals and households tend to increase their saving when their income rises, and presumably, by the same token, to decrease it when their income falls.

While there is very scant recent evidence for the view that changes in interest rates over time are associated with corresponding changes in the volume of saving, there is certainly no doubt that a saver wishing to decide between alternative savings products will benefit from seeking out those that pay more interest.

Simple and compound interest

You learned about simple and compound interest on debt in Chapter 4 – the story is the same for savings as for debt. If you place £1000 in a savings account for five years and the account pays 5% interest per year, the amount you have in your account at the end of this period will depend on whether the account pays simple interest or compound interest. Compound interest is when the interest you earn on your money is reinvested and added to your stock of savings, increasing the capital on which the next interest is calculated; so your stock of asset at the end of the period will be greater than if it had only attracted simple interest.

Annual equivalent rate

In Chapter 4, you were introduced to the annual percentage rate (APR) on debt products, and saw how it differs from the headline interest rate on the debt. The corresponding rate for savings products is the **annual equivalent rate (AER)**. When interest on different savings products is paid at different periods, compounding effects produce different interest amounts at the end of the period (because of the difference in the frequency of interest calculations). The AER calculates comparable rates exactly as you have seen for APR (Chapter 4) in the case of borrowing.

Annual equivalent rate (AER)
The annual rate of interest on a savings product, calculated to take into account the frequency with which interest is added.

Activity 5.5 Same interest rate – different AER

Allow 5 minutes for this activity.

Three savings accounts offer the same annual interest rate of 5%, but with interest payable either weekly (Account a), monthly (Account b) or quarterly (Account c). Which account will have the highest AER?

Comment

The answer to Activity 5.5 is given at the end of this chapter.

Fixed and variable rates of interest

Savings accounts may pay fixed or variable rates of interest. **Term accounts** offer a fixed interest rate over a period of, say, three or five years, during which the capital cannot be withdrawn without penalty. An advantage of these fixed-interest products is that the interest rate paid does not fluctuate unpredictably. It is also likely to be higher than the rate paid on an instant-access savings account, as the financial institution providing it has a guarantee of retaining the saver's money for the specified time period. But an issue with savings products of this kind is the opportunity cost of 'locking into' a fixed interest rate. Indeed, variable interest rates on other products may rise during the

Term accounts
Savings products paying a fixed rate of interest over a period of years during which money cannot be withdrawn without penalty.

term over which the fixed-rate product is held, so you could end up earning less interest on your money when compared to other products.

Inflation and 'real' interest rates

Savers should of course be aware of the effect of inflation on the real interest rate they receive on their deposits. As you saw in Chapter 4, inflation reduces the real value of the principal and any interest paid, which generally makes inflation popular with borrowers and unpopular with savers. For example, if the rate of inflation is 3% and the nominal interest rate paid on a savings account or other product is only 2.5% (i.e. less than the rate of inflation), clearly the real rate of interest you are receiving is negative (about -0.5%) – your stock of savings is losing value.

4.2 Taxation of savings interest

Interest paid on savings is a type of income and, as such, may be subject to tax. Tax treatment of savings is often more complex than other forms of income such as earnings. Moreover, governments in many countries, including the UK, encourage household saving by allowing some savings products to be completely exempt from tax, or by affording specific tax allowances. A further consideration is whether income from savings is paid to the saver gross (before tax) or net (after tax has been deducted). For taxpayers, net payment is appropriate, but for non-taxpayers gross payment is more suitable.

5 Making sense of investment products

Financial investments are those products that come with the warning (often in small print): 'the value of your investment can go down as well as up'. They come in two main forms: bonds and shares. Both bonds and shares have a price which fluctuates, and both have the potential to earn an income for an investor.

Unfortunately not everyone reads the small print or understands all of the choices and all of the products' details before they invest: how many times have we read in the news stories about dismayed investors who have lost money on investment schemes, which were supposed to be the ultimate 'must buy' opportunity?

Also, despite the increased regulation of the finance industry in most countries in recent years, deliberate mis-selling of financial products still happens. Financial services are especially prone to scams, and 'if it sounds too good to be true', it probably is.

Always check the small print

Most personal investors invest in the world's stock markets through investment funds, because the funds allow them access to more investments with smaller sums than buying individual shares or bonds.

Indeed, the EU Commission explains investment funds as: 'investment products created with the sole purpose of gathering investors' capital, and investing that capital collectively through a portfolio of financial instruments such as stocks, bonds and other securities' (European Commission, 2017).

Investment funds use shares and bonds. Therefore, like all investment products, the original amount invested – the principal or capital – is usually at risk. If the price of the investment (the value of the capital) goes up, the investor benefits from a **capital gain**; if the price goes down, a **capital loss** is made. So for investments, it's not just any income generated that is relevant; it's the total return, which is made up of income and the change in the value of the capital.

5.1 Shares

Shares are also sometimes called equities. They are a form of investment that entitles the holder to a share, or part-ownership, in a company. Depending on the type of share, this may entitle the shareholder to vote on how the company is run.

There are two ways in which shares can generate financial gain:

- Shares usually entitle their owners to receive dividends, paid by the company out of the profit that it makes. The receipt of these dividends is, for the shareholder, income from their investment in the shares.

- The price at which a particular share can be bought and sold varies continuously, depending on the balance of investors who want to buy them, and existing shareholders who want to sell. If shareholders are able to sell their shares at a higher price than they originally paid, they make a capital gain (though this is reduced by dealing costs). On the other hand, if they sell for less, they make a capital loss.

Figure 5.5 shows how data on share prices, dividends, profits and the overall size of companies are typically presented. Information of this kind can be seen in some newspapers, notably the *Financial Times*, and via specialist broadcasters, such as Bloomberg.

Capital gain
A rise in the market value of an asset to more than the price originally paid.

Capital loss
A fall in the market value of an asset to less than the price originally paid.

Shares (or equities)
Type of investment that gives the investor part-ownership of a company.

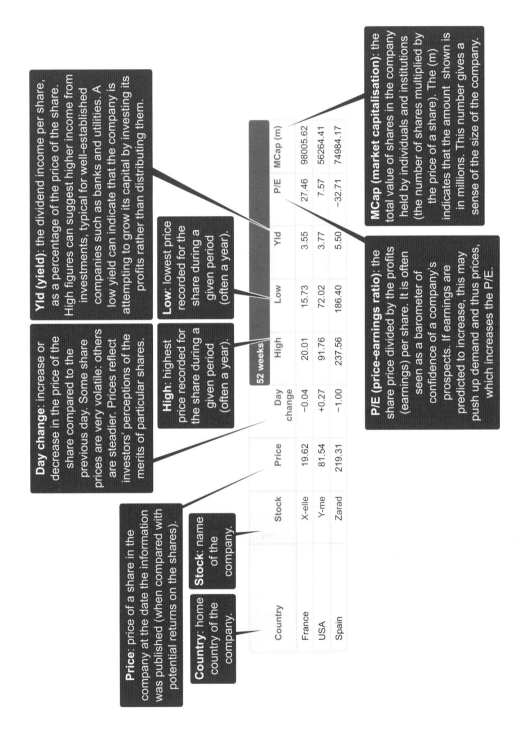

Day change: increase or decrease in the price of the share compared to the previous day. Some share prices are very volatile: others are steadier. Prices reflect investors' perceptions of the merits of particular shares.

Yld (yield): the dividend income per share, as a percentage of the price of the share. High figures can suggest higher income from investments, typical for well-established companies such as banks and utilities. A low yield can indicate that the company is attempting to grow its capital by investing its profits rather than distributing them.

Low: lowest price recorded for the share during a given period (often a year).

High: highest price recorded for the share during a given period (often a year).

Price: price of a share in the company at the date the information was published (when compared with potential returns on the shares).

Stock: name of the company.

Country: home country of the company.

P/E (price-earnings ratio): the share price divided by the profits (earnings) per share. It is often seen as a barometer of confidence of a company's prospects. If earnings are predicted to increase; this may push up demand and thus prices, which increases the P/E.

MCap (market capitalisation): the total value of shares in the company held by individuals and institutions (the number of shares multiplied by the price of a share). The (m) indicates that the amount shown is in millions. This number gives a sense of the size of the company.

Country	Stock	Price	Day change	52 weeks		Yld	P/E	MCap (m)
				High	Low			
France	X-elle	19.62	−0.04	20.01	15.73	3.55	27.46	98005.62
USA	Y-me	81.54	+0.27	91.76	72.02	3.77	7.57	56264.41
Spain	Zarad	219.31	−1.00	237.56	186.40	5.50	−32.71	74984.17

Figure 5.5 Share data for three hypothetical retail clothing companies

225

Activity 5.6 A negative P/E ratio?

Allow 5 minutes for this activity.

Look at the data in Figure 5.5 on the previous page. How would you explain the meaning of the negative P/E (price–earnings ratio) for shares in Zarad?

Comment

Since the P/E ratio is the share price divided by profits per share, the negative value must mean a loss (negative profit) has been made by the firm (since the share price cannot be negative). Note that profits per share are not the same thing as dividend income per share, as not all (and possibly none) of a company's profits are paid to shareholders as dividends. As well as being discouraged from buying shares in companies making losses, like Zarad, some investors looking for income rewards (rather than capital gains) may also be reluctant to buy shares in a company that does not pay large dividends.

How to buy and sell shares

These days, investors tend to buy and sell shares through an online 'share-dealing platform': a computer software program that is used to place orders with a financial intermediary (such as a stockbroker), rather than through the traditional route of contacting a stockbroker in person (the people shouting over their phone in movies).

Brokers in action

Investors pay for online broking through share-dealing platforms in various ways. Often, there is a quarterly fee, but the first few trades each month may be free of charge; for investors who do not trade, this quarterly fee will often be an inactivity fee.

5.2 Fixed-interest securities

Fixed-interest securities are commonly referred to as **bonds**. These can be issued by a company or a government wishing to borrow funds. Bonds resemble savings products in that they usually pay interest, but they are regarded as investments as they can be bought and sold before the end of the term, at whatever price the market dictates, in the same way as shares.

Bond
A certificate of debt issued by a government or corporation to raise money.

A bond generally represents a loan by a saver (the buyer) to a borrower (the company or the government selling the bond) of, broadly speaking, a given sum (the principal, called the 'nominal value') to be redeemed in full at the end of a fixed maturity period: the value repaid is called the redemption value and is equal to the principal or nominal value. A bond typically entails a promise (by the borrower) to pay regular interest (called the coupon) over a fixed term of years. The coupon is a fixed interest rate (as a percentage of the nominal value).

Figure 5.6 An example of payments received from a three-year bond

Figure 5.6 shows a fictional example of a three-year bond with a quarterly coupon of 5% on a principal (nominal) of 100 repaid at the end of the period.

Bonds tend to be less risky than shares because they have a promised interest rate, and because bondholders in a company have a prior financial claim over shareholders in the event of liquidation of the company – that is, bondholders will receive proceeds from the sale of remaining company assets before shareholders get a look in.

However, bonds are riskier than savings accounts. With savings products, typically the amount of capital you receive back is the amount you deposited. Bonds, unlike savings accounts, are financial products that can be bought and sold on financial markets, similarly to shares. As a result, the price of the bond fluctuates, so if you sell a bond before maturity you risk getting less than the promised nominal amount (although if the market price has risen you may get more). Even at the maturity date, when you receive the principal back as promised, if you bought the bond, either when first issued or from the market after it was issued, you may end up with a capital loss or a capital gain (depending on what price you purchased it at).

An additional risk of bonds is that the issuer may default. Bonds issued by governments are likely to be safer than those issued by private companies, as governments are in general less likely to default than private non-financial companies, or even retail banks.

Please note that not everyone means the same thing when they use the word 'bond'. This is why government stocks and corporate bonds are more commonly referred to as fixed-interest securities (they have a fixed interest rate and fixed repayment date). The term 'bond' is sometimes used for term accounts (a type of savings product) and for insurance products that are linked to shares.

5.3 Peer-to-peer lending

A major financial innovation, facilitated by the internet, is peer-to-peer lending, also known as 'social lending'. Online platforms bring together lenders (savers) directly with individuals and businesses who want to borrow, cutting out the banks as middlemen. This should result in interest rates that are somewhat lower for those wishing to borrow, but higher for people looking for a return on their savings.

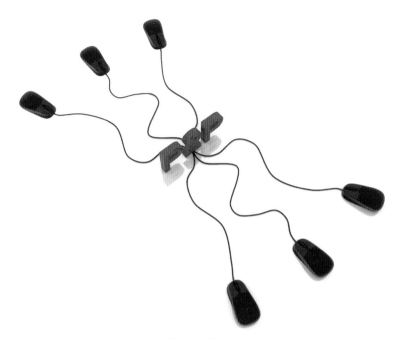

Peer-to-peer lending: online platforms directly connect savers and borrowers

Clearly, there are potential risks in this innovative approach – most obviously, not being repaid. Unlike depositing money in a bank, peer-to-peer investors cannot necessarily get their money back on demand and are not protected by any centralised compensation schemes (although some peer-to-peer platforms have their own small-scale compensation schemes). Peer-to-peer platforms use traditional credit-scoring techniques (like those you read about in Chapter 4) to give investors an idea of how much risk they may be taking on. Also, such platforms increasingly use all the different strands of digital information left by a user online – the so-called Big Data – to help with risk profiling. However, a low-interest period, such as the decade following the global financial crisis of 2008, which has benefited borrowers, may underplay the risks of investing this way. Only when interest rates rise is peer-to-peer investment likely to be put to a proper test.

Martin Lewis, founder of a popular personal finance website *MoneySavingExpert.com*, rather picturesquely places peer-to-peer lending in a kind of centre ground between savings and investments: '[it] looks like saving, tastes like saving, but as there's no savings' safety guarantee, it smells like an investment' (Lewis, 2017).

5.4 Taxation of investments

Income from investments (whether interest or dividends) is subject to income tax, but some countries, such as the UK, tax different types of income at different rates.

Capital gains, from the proceeds of selling investments, are usually subject to some form of tax (and it may be possible to claim tax relief on losses). And some countries have annual wealth taxes, which tax not the income or gains from selling, but the actual value of the assets at a given time (or average value over the year). Many countries also impose some sort of tax when wealth is passed on at death (inheritance/bequest tax). In addition to this, many countries levy taxes on transactions such as purchases of shares.

Some income or gains from investments may be tax-free, and there may be products, such as ISAs (Individual Savings Accounts) in the UK, that are tax-exempt up to a certain point. Governments may grant tax relief or exemption to encourage investment in new companies and social ventures, or to encourage household saving for specific purposes, such as retirement.

6 Planning savings and investments

Sections 4 and 5 of this chapter described the basic elements of savings and investment products that a household may choose to have. In this section we'll analyse these products together, as they share similar features that influence whether, and how, households save or invest.

6.1 Risk and return

The saying 'the safest way to double your money is to fold it in half' is a reminder that promises of high returns usually carry higher risks. On a risk–return spectrum, products with low risks tend to have lower returns, and those with higher risks have *potentially* higher returns (see Figure 5.7).

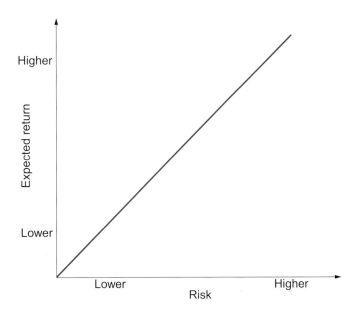

Figure 5.7 The risk–return spectrum

As you've read, bonds and shares are riskier than savings products: their prices can be volatile, going down, as well as up. And some bonds and shares are riskier than others. This trade-off between risk and return is crucial in making decisions about which financial products to choose, and the choice will, in part, be determined by a person's attitude towards risk (which is influenced by personality, how much risk they can afford, and also the purpose of the saving). If someone is risk-averse, they might need the promise of a greater potential return in order to take the same financial risk as someone who is more willing to take risks.

Of course, everyone would like high returns with no risk, but the reality is that low risk offers low returns, and alternatives must offer higher returns to induce savers or investors to take on the higher risks. Figure 5.8 (which looks rather like extreme alpine scenery) illustrates both the volatility of share prices and the tendency for an upward trend in the long term. It shows the trajectory of the FTSE All World Index from 3 January 1994 to 1 August 2017. The FTSE All World Index represents the performance of the larger equities from the FTSE Global Equity Index, which in turn covers around 7400 equities in 47 countries (FTSE Russell, 2017). It represents the average of a large number of monthly share prices from around the world. Like other indices you have met, such as the consumer price index (CPI) in Chapter 2, it has the value 100 in the base year (1994 in this case).

The volatility of prices, as seen in the peaks and troughs of Figure 5.8, represents the volatility of the prospective earnings and profits of companies, and investors' sentiment about them.

Despite significant volatility during the period covered, Figure 5.8 shows that on average the prices of shares in the companies more than tripled between 1994 and 2017.

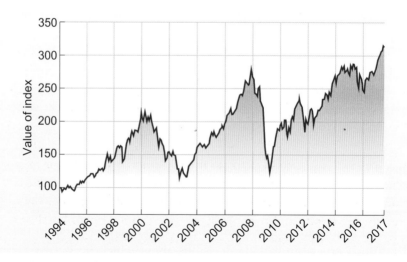

Figure 5.8 FTSE All World Index, 1994–2017, monthly (*Financial Times*, 2017)

Risk and length of investment

Attitude to risk also relates to the length of time of any investment. Normally, the longer someone intends to invest without needing to sell, the more risk can be tolerated.

If the investor needs money at short notice, investment products will generally be unsuitable. If a time horizon (to achieve a goal, etc.) is less than five years, it is not usually worth considering tying funds up in, for example, lots of company shares as their price fluctuates continually. On the other hand, if the time horizon is distant, more risk can be tolerated, and investment products are often a good bet, as in the long term capital gains on shares tend to outperform interest on savings. Indeed, prices of shares in companies spread over the entire economy simply reflect the performance of the economy, its GDP growth, which is often positive and above inflation over the long term.

Return and investment charges

Institutions that manage and broker savings and investments charge for their services, and these charges can adversely influence the returns on savings and investment products. When private investors buy and sell financial assets, transactions charges are levied. This may discourage households from undertaking frequent purchases and sales. If you invest directly in funds, this will attract management charges to reward the fund manager who deals with your **portfolio** on your behalf.

Portfolio
A set of financial assets held by an individual (or a bank or other financial institution).

6.2 Risk-reduction strategies

Although lengthening the time over which an investment is held can avoid day-to-day fluctuations of share prices, the main way in which to obtain superior returns from shares over savings products is to have a portfolio of many different shares. Indeed shares in individual companies are likely to be quite volatile, even over a long horizon. So to achieve the best financial results, **diversification** is needed. This means holding a portfolio with a variety of investment and savings products – preferably shares from companies based in a variety of countries and across different industries, and even a portfolio that mixes shares, bonds and cash savings. A diversified portfolio allows losses on some products to be compensated by gains on others.

Diversification
A strategy that aims to manage market risk by combining a variety of investments, such as shares and bonds, that are unlikely all to move in the same direction at the same time.

Your attitude to risk, together with your needs, time horizon, income constraints, and other factors explored in this chapter, will determine whether (and how much) you could invest in equities, bonds, and cash (or savings products).

If you are highly risk-averse, compared to someone else with exactly the same characteristics, preferences, needs and constraints, you would typically stick to savings products and bonds. If you are less risk-averse, then buying at least some shares might be attractive. But regardless of preferences or attitudes, people with greater means (income or wealth) can afford to take on more risk, as they may be able to weather negative outcomes without damaging their livelihood too much.

Managing risk: in the words of the old expression – 'don't put all your eggs in one basket'

Investment funds

Buying investment funds can lead to a more diversified portfolio. There are many different types of fund to choose from, with different mix of cash (savings), bonds and equities. Some funds look for capital growth; others emphasise income from dividends and interest. With a fund, managers create and adjust the portfolio for you, in exchange for management charges. Some specialise in a particular geographical market (such as the US), or a specific sector (for example, technology), while others offer widespread diversification across all asset classes, regions and sectors.

Different investment funds will do well or badly according to what assets they hold, and how 'good' (some would say lucky) the fund managers are. Potential investors can access data about different funds' performance, charges, risk ratings and other features via internet-based information providers, but it is still extremely hard to identify whether any are consistently better than others.

An alternative is for investors to buy what are known as 'tracker' funds, which are designed to mirror the performance of an index, such as the FTSE All Share Index. These funds are 'passively' managed, in contrast to 'actively' managed funds where the managers buy and sell to try to get their **market timing** right, or select only some shares — the performance of which they think are more promising compared to the market as a whole. Higher fees are charged for active management, and there is a good deal of controversy in the financial press and academia about whether the performance of these funds justifies the additional fees. Some argue that good managers today might not be equally good tomorrow because there is a significant amount of luck at play in a context of highly unpredictable market fluctuations.

Market timing
A technique of buying and selling shares in conjunction with the price fluctuations of the market.

Activity 5.7 Comparing risk and return

Allow 10 minutes for this activity.

Go back and look at the risk–return spectrum (Figure 5.7) again. Where on the straight line that represents the spectrum would you place the following financial products?

- Corporate bonds
- Shares in one company
- Tracker fund
- Savings account
- Current account
- Government bonds

Comment

The answer to Activity 5.7 is given at the end of this chapter.

Asset allocation
The division of a savings and investment portfolio across cash deposits, bonds and equities.

Cost averaging
Allocating a fixed sum for the regular purchase of particular investments. The fixed sum will buy more shares/units when prices fall although fewer when prices rise (so that the average price of shares/units bought is lower than the average price).

Asset allocation

How cash (meaning deposits, like savings products), bonds and equities are split across an investment portfolio is called the **asset allocation** decision, because each one (cash deposits, bonds and equities) is called an 'asset class'. If the portfolio is owned by an individual and their goal is a long-term one, an important factor when making decisions about the asset allocation is their age. Clearly, the asset allocation that may be appropriate when someone is relatively young may not be appropriate when close to retirement. This suggests that the pre-retirement years should perhaps be a time for adjusting risk. Indeed, the asset allocation should be regularly revised and reviewed over the life course.

Another investment strategy is to invest sums of money regularly (say, monthly, quarterly or yearly). This is called **cost averaging**. This technique removes the risk of getting market timing absolutely wrong (which would be buying at the highest point). Equally, however, regular purchases remove the chance of getting it absolutely right – buying at the lowest point. Furthermore, frequent trading incurs transactions charges.

Activity 5.8 Asset allocation and the life course

Allow 20 minutes for this activity.

Think about the risk and return of the various savings and investment products discussed in this chapter.

Task 1

Rank the asset allocation portfolios shown in Figure 5.9 (pie charts (a)–(f)) by order of risk.

Task 2

Match the investors and their goals (listed 1–5, opposite) with the appropriate portfolios (a)–(f).

You may have noticed that there are six portfolios and only five investors. This is because investors might be matched to more than one portfolio and a portfolio may suit different investor profiles.

Investors:

1 Sue, 34, single, setting aside savings for her newborn child to use on reaching 18.

2 Peter and Salma, in their early sixties, investing to provide essential income for the next 20 years.

3 Janet, in her mid-forties, saving for a holiday in two years' time.

4 Andrea, 29, saving for retirement in 40 years' time.

5 Lucy and Simon, in their mid-thirties, saving for a deposit to buy a house in four years' time.

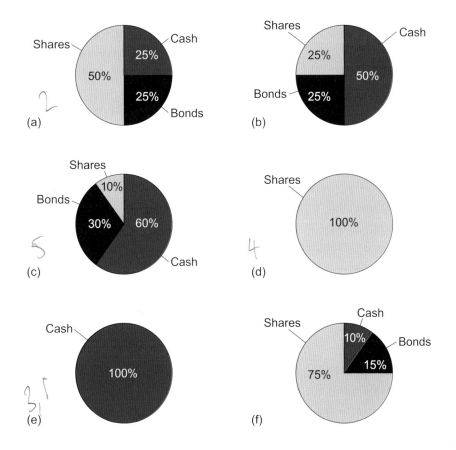

Figure 5.9 The proportion of three main asset classes (shares, cash and bonds) in six different portfolios

Comment

The answers to Activity 5.8 are given at the end of this chapter.

Note that there is no single right or wrong answer for Task 2.

6.3 Saving and investing in practice

You saw in Section 3.2 of this chapter how saving over the life course can be illustrated using the life cycle model. Reasons for saving vary both between households and within a household at different times, but it is important to plan at each stage, taking account of the current state of the household finances.

For many households, having a low income may prevent saving, but for others making relatively simple cuts in expenditure can lead to surplus income, as you saw in Chapter 3.

Personal finance experts often use the expression 'pay yourself first', meaning that saving should be allocated before other outgoings are budgeted for. In reality though, that is not possible for everyone. Moreover, even with some spare income to save, many low-income households would not have access to the kind of diverse portfolio necessary to reduce risk, as many funds often require minimum sums to invest (which are beyond the reach of these households). This effectively excludes (financially) these households from some products.

I mentioned earlier in this chapter that many people are both savers and borrowers at the same time. This may seem irrational, and indeed as borrowing costs tend to be higher than returns on savings, there is often a good case for using surplus income to pay off debt rather than to add to savings. There are exceptions, however. For example, there may be penalties for early repayment of a debt; or it may be possible to hold a debt, for example on a credit card, interest-free for a certain period of time while also putting aside money to add to savings.

Alternatively, it may be necessary to incur debt to purchase an expensive item such as a car if needed for immediate use. But this debt doesn't mean a household should halt a regular saving programme, as it may serve a different purpose, such as precautionary saving for a rainy day.

Ethical and socially responsible saving

In addition to striking a balance between saving and debt repayment, individuals and households need to decide what kinds of savings or investment products suit them. In Section 6.1, you explored the topic of risk and return, both of which play a large part in saving and investment decisions. But someone may also be concerned about *how* their money is used, and prefer to choose investments that they see as socially responsible or ethical, even if they perform financially less well, in terms of potential return for a given risk, than other products.

A company's profits may eventually be affected by its polluting behaviour

There are investment funds that seek out what they regard as socially responsible firms that 'make a positive contribution to society' through, for example, conservation of energy and natural resources, or maintaining a good equal opportunities record. These funds may also exclude those companies involved in what they see as harmful activities, such as environmentally damaging practices, or the manufacture of tobacco products and weaponry, from the portfolio (The Ethical Partnership Ltd, 2017).

In the narrow financial sense of risk–return trade-offs, ethical investments may seem to perform less well at first, with higher costs or lower returns and less diversified risk. However, even leaving aside the issue of ethical preferences over financial gains, an economic case can still be made for ethical or socially responsible investment. Indeed, analysing the wider implications of the activities of harmful companies may reveal that they are actually riskier and/or more costly than otherwise equivalent (but more socially responsible or ethical companies). For example, a textile company that makes huge profits (the shares of which are thus financially attractive) by employing cheap labour, in factories that emit extremely high levels of pollution (to reduce production costs), may in time find itself short of healthy workers, if those workers are affected by the pollution; and so it could be forced to close its production line entirely, so collapsing profits and thus share prices.

Sometimes, financial markets can take some of these aspects into account as well. For example, the Deepwater Horizon oil spill, which devastated the coasts of the Gulf of Mexico in 2010, caused the price of BP shares to tumble as investors anticipated that the cost of the resulting environmental clean-up would be borne by the company itself, thereby affecting its profit prospects worldwide.

7 Conclusion

While Chapter 4 looked at what happens when expenditure exceeds income, and borrowing takes place, this chapter has focused on the flip side of borrowing: when households defer consumption now by setting aside some of their income to be consumed later.

I started this chapter by examining the importance of savings and investments to both households and the broader economy (Sections 2 and 3), and the difficulty that some households have saving anything at all. I then explored, in Sections 4 and 5, the kinds of savings and investment products available in the marketplace, and the factors that influence household decisions on which product(s) to use. It is important to be aware of the variety of products available, so that you can tailor saving and investment plans to the specific circumstances you face at a given time.

In Section 6, we looked at the concepts of risk and return, and the central role they play in financial planning strategies: an individual's attitude to risk shapes their savings and investment decisions; the length of time they are prepared to wait to achieve their goals can influence how much risk they will take; and their financial situation will also determine how much they can afford to lose.

While diversification across a number of different asset classes typically allows to reduce risk without reducing expected return, other practical considerations, such as the horizon of investment will influence the composition of a portfolio. This includes attitudes towards ethical and socially responsible investments, the performance of which can be factored into a risk-and-return spectrum when their broader economic impact is taken into account.

Overall, this chapter has examined the process of building financial assets. However, for many households, savings can be achieved with an actual building: a more tangible, physical asset made of bricks and mortar. Those assets, homes, are the topic of the next chapter.

Answers to activities in Chapter 5

Answers to Activity 5.1

1   Saving 2.5 pence out of every £20 (2000 pence) implies a saving ratio of:

$$\frac{2.5}{2000} \times 100 = 0.125\%$$

2   Of the three sample years' ratios given, 0.125% is closest to that of 2015 (0.16%). I leave it to you to decide whether people in the UK were financially happy in 2015!

3   You may find that the proportion of your disposable income you saved over the last year is close to the average of your country (in the UK close to zero in recent years). But possibly not: remember this is an average ratio, that hides wide disparities between households in the opportunities and willingness to save in different situations (income, life cycle stage, household composition); it also doesn't reflect varying levels of saving over the years.

Answer to Activity 5.4

The type of money management certainly influences the amount of money members of a couple can get hold of and manage (although not always control). Individually managed systems, such as the whole wage system or independently managed incomes, may be more suitable for one person to make individual saving decisions. However, they would still need to have enough money to be able to save.

In pooled systems, building a joint-savings pot is more likely but it does not mean that the decisions required (how much to save, for what goal and how) are always made jointly or with individual interests and preferences of the couple equally represented.

In a housekeeping allowance system, the person who gives the allowance to the other partner is likely to have more control over how money is spent or saved, whereas the recipient is more likely to simply receive spending money for specific items. They could still set some money aside if there is a surplus but it is likely to be very small. This discussion highlights the fact that management of money and decision-making control are not the same thing.

Answer to Activity 5.5

The more frequent the payment, the more compounding of interest there will be. Therefore annual 5% interest paid weekly will have a higher AER than 5% paid monthly, which in turn will have a higher AER than 5% paid quarterly.

Answer to Activity 5.7

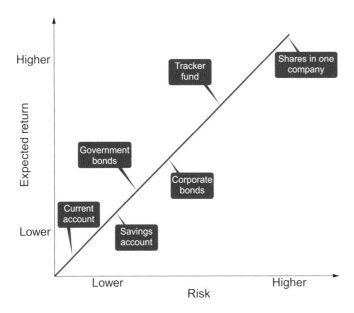

Figure 5.10 Financial assets placed on the risk–return spectrum

Answers to Activity 5.8

Task 1. The ranking of the portfolios, from lowest risk to highest risk is: (e), (c), (b), (a), (f), (d), as the proportion of riskier assets – shares – is growing (from no shares in portfolio (e) to 100% shares in (d)).

Task 2. Suggestions of pairings of the portfolios and investors are shown below, although you may have thought of other combinations.

1. Parents are often risk averse and so Sue – like many other parents – might be tempted by portfolio **(e)**, 100% cash. Rationally though, the most suitable portfolio is likely to be the polar opposite – **(d)**, 100% shares. This is a long-term (18-year) investment for a young person with no commitments. 100% shares at outset would normally be most suitable, perhaps gradually shifting to lower risk from around age 13 if the money is due to be spent at age 18.

2. Peter's and Salma's portfolio will need to provide them with income but also protect that income from inflation. They are likely to want a mix of shares, especially those of established companies paying relatively high dividends, and bonds. Rationally, they should resist the temptation to hold too much cash, since its buying power will be eroded by inflation, especially if they are drawing off the interest as income. Therefore, portfolio **(a)** is likely to be most suitable. And, if they have some secure retirement income from other sources, they might even consider taking a bit more risk with portfolio **(f)**. However, because many retired people are risk-averse, they often tend towards portfolios with more cash than they need, such as **(b)** or even **(c)**.

3. For Janet, who is in her mid-forties and saving for a holiday in two years' time, **(e)** seems the most appropriate portfolio, as the aim is to set aside some money so the capital needs to be safe (some two-year bonds might work, too, as the principal is guaranteed at maturity).

4. At age 29, Andrea has a very long timescale over which to save for retirement. Therefore, the most suitable portfolio is likely to be **(d)** – 100% in shares. When she gets within ten years or so of retirement, she may want to consider changing the mix, depending on how she plans to provide for her retirement income – you'll look at the main options in Chapter 8.

5. Lucy and Simon are saving over a short-term time horizon of just four years. They would be in trouble if they invested in the stock market and it happened to be in the doldrums at the time they were ready to buy their home. They should stick to 100% cash – portfolio **(e)**. In the UK, the government offers some tax-advantaged savings products specifically for would-be homebuyers like Lucy and Simon.

References

Dickens, C. (1850) *David Copperfield*, Oxford, Clarendon Press (this edition 1981).

The Ethical Partnership Ltd (2017) *What is Socially Responsible or Ethical Investment* [Online]. Available at www.the-ethical-partnership.co.uk/ethical-investment/WhatisEthicalInvestment.htm (Accessed 28 August 2017).

European Commission (2017) *Investment Funds: EU Laws and Initiatives Relating to Collective Investment funds* [Online]. Available at https://ec.europa.eu/info/business-economy-euro/growth-and-investment/investment-funds_en (Accessed 21 August 2017).

Eurostat (2017) 'Medium saving rate by income quintile, experimental statistics', *Eurostat Database* [Online] Available at http://ec.europa.eu/eurostat/data/database (Accessed 20 February 2018).

Financial Times (2017) 'Markets data: All-World Index' [Online]. Available at https://markets.ft.com/data/indices/tearsheet/charts?s=AW01:FSI (Accessed 25 August 2017).

FTSE Russell (2017) *FTSE Global Equity Index Series* (GEIS) [Online]. Available at www.ftse.com/products/indices/geis-series (Accessed 25 August 2017).

Keynes, J. M. (1936) *The General Theory of Employment, Interest and Money*, London, Macmillan and Co. (this edition 1967).

Le Blanc, J., Porpiglia, A., Teppa, F., Zhu, J. and Ziegelmeyer, M. (2015) *Household Saving Behaviour and Credit Constraints in the Euro Area*, working paper series, no. 1790, May, European Central Bank. Available at www.ecb.europa.eu/pub/pdf/scpwps/ecbwp1790.en.pdf (Accessed 21 February 2018).

Lewis, M. (2017) 'Peer-to-peer lending', *MoneySavingExpert.com* [Online]. Available at www.moneysavingexpert.com/savings/peer-to-peer-lending (Accessed 30 August 2017).

Lewis, S. and Messy, F. (2012) *Financial Education, Savings and Investments: An Overview*, OECD working papers on finance, insurance and private pensions, no. 22 [Online]. Available at http://dx.doi.org/10.1787/5k94gxrw760v-en (Accessed 23 August 2017.)

Marshall, A. (1920) *Principles of Economics*, 8th edn [Online], London, Macmillan and Co. Available at http://files.libertyfund.org/files/1676/Marshall_0197_EBk_v6.0.pdf (Accessed 30 August 2017).

Modigliani, F. and Brumberg, R. (1954) 'Utility analysis and the consumption function: an interpretation of cross-section data', in Kurihara, K. K. (ed.) *Post-Keynesian Economics*, New Brunswick, NJ, Rutgers University Press.

Nelson, J. (2016) 'Not-so-strong evidence for gender differences in risk taking', *Feminist Economics*, vol. 22, no. 2. pp. 114–42 [Online]. Available at www.tandfonline.com/doi/abs/10.1080/13545701.2015.1057609 (Accessed 22 February 2018).

OECD (2018) 'Household savings', *OECD Data* [Online]. Available at https://data.oecd.org/hha/household-savings.htm (Accessed 20 February 2018).

Yao, R., Wang, F., Weagley, R. O. and Liao, L. (2011) 'Household saving motives: comparing American and Chinese consumers', *Family & Consumer Sciences Research Journal*, vol. 40, no. 1, pp. 28–44 [Online]. Available at https://onlinelibrary.wiley.com/doi/full/10.1111/j.1552-3934.2011.02086.x (Accessed 20 August 2017).

To cite this chapter, use the following format in your reference list:

Stone, H. (2019) 'Savings and investments', in De Henau, J. and Lowe, J. (eds) *Personal Finance*, Milton Keynes, The Open University, pp. 197–247.

Chapter 6
Housing

Hedley Stone and Ian Fribbance

Contents

1 Introduction

Homes and choices about them come in all shapes and sizes

A house or an apartment is just a building, not a home. But it is a shell within which an individual, a family or a household can build a home to which they feel a sense of belonging. Decisions about where to live and how to pay for our accommodation are some of the biggest financial decisions we ever make. Therefore, housing is an important and often emotive subject.

In this chapter, you're going to explore some of the practical aspects relating to decisions about homes, tensions in society around homeownership, and an economist's view of what drives house prices.

In Section 2, we start by considering the advantages and disadvantages of the two main ways of occupying a home: renting and buying. While many people start their adult life by renting, you'll see that homeownership is an aspiration and popular choice in many countries. In addition, we look at how the prevalence of homeownership varies across countries, and the differences in homeownership between the generations. Section 3 delves further into renting, looking at different types of renting and the role governments may have in shaping the extent to which rental buildings can deliver secure and affordable homes.

Section 4 turns to buying a home. Most people have to borrow to buy, so we look at the types of mortgage available and some aspects of affordability. We then look at how the purchase of a home affects the household balance sheet that you have been building up since Chapter 4, and how the balance sheet ratios can tell us something about the financial risks homeowners may be exposed to. Section 5 deals with the nitty-gritty of the house-buying process.

Beneath much of the discussion about renting or buying is the idea that renting is somehow 'dead money' and buying a home is not simply buying a place to live but also an investment; and so, in Section 6, we turn the spotlight on this issue. Crucial to property as an investment is a belief that property prices will rise. So, last but not least, Section 7 explores the factors that cause house prices to move upwards – and downwards – over time. We'll do this by introducing you to a simple model, much favoured by economists, that provides a framework for analysing the impact of those factors.

2 Buy or rent?

The different ways of occupying a property are called **tenure**. The two most common types are buying and renting.

Living in a home that you own or are in the process of buying is known as **owner-occupation**. Few people have the resources to purchase a home outright, so most have to borrow, using a mortgage. (We will explore mortgages in Section 4 of this chapter.)

Living in a property owned by someone else, to whom you make regular payments for your accommodation, is called **renting**. Often, an individual or household rents a self-contained apartment or house. Alternatively, renters may share with other people – examples include sharing a flat with friends or a lodger renting a room in someone else's home. Other arrangements include a 'bedsit' – usually a room with its own front door, but often it involves sharing a kitchen and bathroom. A building containing several bedsits is known in the UK as a 'house in multiple occupation' (HMO).

Property may be rented from a private landlord (who might be an individual or a commercial company), or from a social landlord, such as a local council or housing association, in which case it is often referred to as 'social housing'.

There are also mixed-tenure schemes (usually available from social landlords) whereby people part-rent and part-buy the property they live in, typically called 'shared ownership'.

Tenure
The way in which a property is occupied, for example as an owner or as a tenant who is renting.

Owner-occupation
Form of tenure where the person living in a home owns it outright or is buying it with a mortgage.

Renting
Form of tenure where the person living in a home is a tenant or lodger, paying rent to a landlord, who owns the property.

2.1 Reasons for renting or buying

Most people have preferences about renting or buying, but they are not necessarily able to choose the type of tenure they would like best. In this section we'll look at a variety of advantages and disadvantages of renting and buying: you've probably thought of some already.

Activity 6.1 Reasons to rent or buy

Allow 10 minutes for this activity.

Write down as many reasons as you can think of as to why you are currently an owner-occupier or a renter and divide these reasons into financial and non-financial.

Comment

Keep your list handy as you read the rest of this section and add notes about any aspects or reasons that are new to you.

There are substantial financial considerations in deciding between renting and buying. Where rents are set by market forces, as is common in the UK, the monthly costs of renting may be higher as a proportion of household income than the monthly outlay borne by owner-occupiers. For example, in the UK in 2015–16, on average, those buying their home with a mortgage spent 18% of their household income on mortgage payments. By comparison, rent payments amounted to 35% of household income for private renters. For social renters, the figure was 28% (DCLG, 2017). In other countries, such as Germany and France, where the state exerts some degree of control over the level of rental charges, the discrepancy is much smaller.

For people who need to move home often, renting can be an attractive option

So the monthly outlay for buying may be lower, but generally people need to have saved up a substantial sum before they can buy a home.

They will also need to show that they have a stable income. For this reason, young people especially often have little choice but to start their adult lives renting their home.

However, renting has some advantages, both financial and non-financial. For example, moving home is quicker when renting because selling a property that you own can be a lengthy process. There are also hefty costs involved in selling and, in many countries, tax to pay when buying, and sometimes selling, a home. Consequently, when people need, or want, to move often – perhaps for employment reasons or as a young adult with no ties yet to a particular location – renting may be the more attractive option.

Another advantage to renting is that it may enable a person to live in a more desirable property than they could afford to buy. One way to keep housing costs down is to share a home with friends or other unrelated people. Legally this is simpler when renting than owning.

On the other hand, people in the UK often talk about paying rent as being 'dead money' compared with buying, since the latter can result in owning a substantial asset once the mortgage is paid off. It should be borne in mind, however, that owners still have to meet other ongoing costs, such as maintenance and repairs, and insuring their property.

While the acquisition of a valuable asset is an argument for buying, renting can improve financial flexibility. A lot of money is tied up in owning a property and there is an opportunity cost to this. (Recall from Chapter 1 that 'opportunity cost' means the loss of benefits that could have been had from alternative uses.) For example, households may decide not to spend money on holidays, going out, a nice car, and so on, for many years in order to save to buy a home. That money could have been invested, for example, in shares or bonds, as seen in Chapter 5, Savings and investments. These investments are typically more liquid than property, enabling goals and financial plans to be adjusted more easily in future.

Furthermore, while owners may bank on the value of their homes increasing, there is no guarantee that this will happen. Renters are not subject to the risks of financial loss from selling a house in a market where prices are falling.

Perhaps one of the strongest reasons for wanting to own a property is not financial; it is having the freedom to do as you like with it without the constraint of rules imposed by a landlord, and being able to create, maintain, style and decorate your home as you wish.

One last point is that many people, whatever their age or life stage, do not have a choice between renting and buying. As you saw in Chapter 4, in relation to financial exclusion and debt, choice is heavily constrained by household income.

2.2 International differences in housing tenure

A majority of people in the UK are owner-occupiers. Homeownership has traditionally been very much a part of British popular culture, captured by phrases such as 'home is where the heart is' and 'an Englishman's home is his castle'. The same is not true, however, of all European countries.

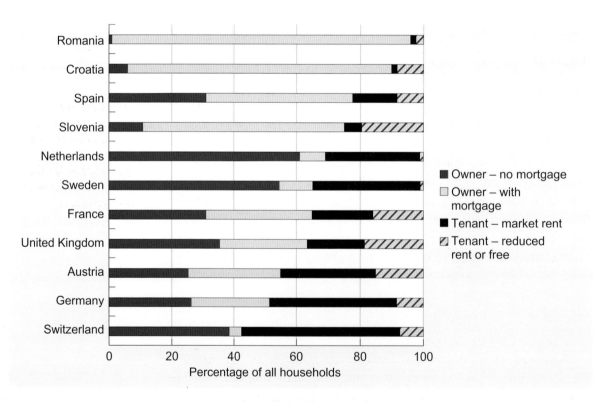

Figure 6.1 Distribution of population by tenure status, 2016 (Eurostat, 2017a)

Figure 6.1 gives a very mixed picture, with wide variation in rates of homeownership across the selection of countries shown. In 2016, Germany had a rate of owner-occupation of only 52%, while that of Romania was 96%. The UK rate was 63%. Even in Germany, the proportion of tenants did not exceed that of owner-occupiers. On the other hand, in Switzerland 58% of the population lived in rented accommodation (Eurostat 2017a).

It is important to be aware that there is also considerable variation in housing quality between countries. In the UK, homeownership is popularly associated with higher quality than renting. However, in Romania, where the rental market is tiny and the rate of owner-occupation is close to 100%, much owner-occupied property is of poor quality, having not been well constructed and the facilities being inadequate. Romania also recorded a high rate of overcrowding, at 48% (Eurostat, 2017b).

There are historical, political and social reasons for these international differences in tenure. For example, after the Second World War, both Germany and the UK had a severe housing shortage. The UK embarked on a programme of building social housing that largely resulted in the **crowding out** of private-sector landlords. Then, from the 1960s until 2000, UK governments of all political persuasions fostered owner-occupation through tax subsidies that reduced the cost of borrowing for the purchase of a home. On top of that, growing real incomes meant more people could afford to buy. Liberalisation of the financial services industry in the 1980s made getting a mortgage easier. The trend towards ownership was given a further boost by the sale of council homes to tenants at discounted prices during the Conservative government of Margaret Thatcher. Since the late 1990s, however, the trend has gone into reverse – a phenomenon we'll come back to in Section 2.3 of this chapter.

Crowding out
A squeezing out of consumption and/or investment opportunities for the private sector because of government spending.

Germany also embarked on a post-war expansion of social housing, but it gave equal encouragement to the development of the private rental sector, setting common standards and financial support for all. It did not introduce tax subsidies for homeownership (Voigtländer, 2009). Perhaps as a result, house prices have been more stable than in countries like the UK. The upshot is a market where there is an extensive good-quality rental sector and households are not in a hurry to 'get on the housing ladder' as early in life as they can with a view to trading up during the life course. Kofner (2014, p. 266) summarises the difference between the attitudes of British and German households:

> In Germany … households that could easily afford a home of their own often rent. Instead of the 'property ladder', in Germany, the motto is 'Once in a Lifetime': those who become homeowners do so late, but with full commitment.

The popular term the 'housing ladder' encapsulates the typically British aspiration for systematically upgrading their homeownership, while Germans aim for 'once in a lifetime'

The choice between renting and owning is not just important for households; it can also have a substantial influence on the economy and economic policy choices. This is another example of how the theme of the changing economic, political and social context (introduced in Chapter 1) involves interdependence, with the actions of households being capable of affecting the economy as a whole. For example, owner-occupation may make the UK economy somewhat more volatile compared to economies with lower homeownership levels. There is a strong tendency in the UK to regard a home not simply as a place to live but as a store of wealth. This means that changes in property prices, even if only 'on paper', affect the perceived wealth of many households, and this can influence their high-street spending. And, since mortgage payments account for such a large part of many households' monthly outgoings, changes in interest rates also affect household expenditure on other goods and services. Furthermore, taxes on home purchase and ownership – such as Stamp Duty Land Tax in England and Northern Ireland, and Council Tax in Britain (and equivalent taxes elsewhere) – can be important sources of revenue for a government.

2.3 Intergenerational differences in housing tenure

In the UK, despite the popularity of homeownership, there have been striking intergenerational differences in owner-occupation, as demonstrated in research by Cribb et al. (2016) – see Figure 6.2.

Each line in Figure 6.2 shows the changes (by percentage) in the homeownership rate for people born during a particular decade as their age increased. For example, the line labelled '1950s' traces the experience of people born in that decade. By age 30, around 65% of this group owned their own homes; by age 50 around 80% did so. The pattern is very similar for people born in the 1940s.

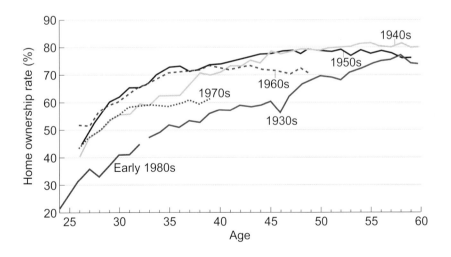

Figure 6.2 UK homeownership rate by age for people born in different decades (Cribb et al., 2016, fig. 7)

Activity 6.2 Intergenerational trends in homeownership in the UK

Allow 15 minutes for this activity.

1   Briefly describe the main trends of homeownership shown in Figure 6.2 for people born in the 1970s and early 1980s.

2   From your own experience or from news accounts, suggest what might be some of the reasons for the different patterns of ownership for people born in different decades.

Comment

1   In contrast with earlier generations, only about 55% of people born in the 1970s and 40% of people born in the early 1980s were homeowners by age 30. It is too early to say yet whether these groups are simply delaying buying their first home or whether more will be lifelong renters than for previous generations.

2   Various reasons have been suggested for the decline in UK homeownership among younger generations. These include, for example, house prices climbing to unaffordable levels, tighter conditions when applying for a mortgage, and the burden of student debt. You may have thought of other reasons.

3 Renting a property

Let's look in more detail at the mechanics of the rental sector. The two most important features of a rental contract are price (the rent) and security of tenure, in other words the tenant's right to remain in their home.

Private rentals take many forms, in terms of both type of accommodation and the legal basis on which the tenant lives in the property. The rights and responsibilities of a tenant and landlord of a property are generally determined by a tenancy agreement between the two parties. This agreement usually states, for example:

- the amount of rent payable

- the payment of an upfront deposit, which is generally returnable at the end of the tenancy less any amount deducted to pay for damages to the property or its fittings

- the minimum length of occupancy

- the amount of notice required from either side to end the tenancy agreement

- the division of responsibilities between the landlord and tenant in terms of the upkeep.

An important aspect of security of tenure is the length of the tenancy agreement. According to Oxley (2017), private rental contracts in England are typically for an initial period of no more than six months. After this, the tenancy may roll on but with the requirement of just two months' notice on either side. While contracts in the US and Australia also tend to be short term, ranging from six months to a year, private renters in France can expect contracts for three or six years, and in Germany tenancy lasts, in principle, indefinitely. Furthermore, in both France and Germany termination is allowed only in certain special circumstances.

In most parts of the world, some part of the housing stock is social housing. Either directly or indirectly, there is some kind of intervention by the state. In some countries, only housing rented from public or not-for-profit bodies is called 'social'; in others, affordability is the main requirement, with the emphasis on rents that are lower than private landlords would charge. (However, depending on how 'affordable' is defined, such subsidised rents may still be out of reach of many low-income households.)

In the UK, the terms of social renting are usually more favourable to the renter than those in the private sector. Typically, there is greater security of tenure with longer contracts, and there is often a right of surviving relatives of a deceased tenant to take over the tenancy, and so carry on living in the property.

In the UK, the proportion of social housing – which includes council housing and some housing association properties – has diminished significantly in recent decades, while the private rental sector has grown. Oxley (2017, cited in Social Market Foundation, 2017) has noted:

> Whilst private renting is advantageous to many occupants due to the flexibility of tenure, many households struggle with problems relating to tenure security due to short-term contracts, uncertainty about future rents and rogue landlords who do not guarantee the quality of accommodation.

Activity 6.3 Improving rental accommodation

Allow 5 minutes for this activity.

Suggest some ways in which the experience of renters might be improved, and possible drawbacks of the changes you suggest.

Comment

To increase the affordability of renting, one approach could be to build more social housing. Another could be to make tax subsidies available to private landlords who agree to lower rents, greater security of tenure and/or minimum quality standards. However, governments might be unwilling to bear the cost of these measures.

Governments could simply bring in new laws to cap private rents, increase security of tenure and require minimum quality standards. However, given that this would tend to cut landlords' profits, many might stop renting out properties and look for other ways to make money. This could lead to a shortage of housing for people who want to rent.

---

4 Buying a property

We now move on to examine the issues involved in buying a property. Note that there are variations in the legal arrangements across countries, both within and outside the UK, but there are some general principles with more or less universal application.

4.1 Freehold or leasehold

There are two modes of homeownership: freehold and leasehold. Essentially, freeholders own both the dwelling and the land (ground) it stands on. By contrast, a leaseholder owns only the dwelling. In this case the land is the property of a landlord to whom the whole land and property revert when the lease runs out. Having said that, some leases have a very long duration, for example 999 years, and traditionally, the rent due to the landlord (called 'ground rent') is very small. In that case, leasehold ownership is very similar to owning on a freehold basis.

However, some leases are shorter – say 99 years. Even if the ground rent is low, once the remaining term of the lease falls below about 80 years, it can be hard to find people willing to buy the home at anything like the price originally paid. Moreover, as described in Box 6.1, concerns about leasehold have gained prominence in recent years. There have been some high-profile examples of ground rents charged by housebuilding firms that increase over time and could be seen as extortionate.

It is usually possible for the leaseholder to purchase the freehold, although the expense of doing so may not make it worthwhile if the terms of the leasehold are favourable. Where the ground rent is high and/or escalating, the cost of buying the freehold may be prohibitive.

Activity 6.4 The importance of checking leasehold terms

Allow 30 minutes for this activity.

1 Read the extract from a *Guardian* article reproduced in Box 6.1 and summarise its main points in no more than 150 words.

2 The article says a typical starting ground rent for a house built by Taylor Wimpey was £295 per annum, which would double every ten years. Calculate what the ground rent would be after 10, 30 and 50 years.

Comment

The answers to Activity 6.4 are given at the end of this chapter.

Box 6.1 Taylor Wimpey to pay up to £130m to settle ground rent scandal

Housebuilder was criticised after some of its new-build leasehold properties were left near-worthless owing to spiralling charges

Taylor Wimpey is to pay out up to £130m to buyers of some of its new-build leasehold properties, which were rendered near-worthless after homeowners found themselves trapped in spiralling ground rent contracts. ...

An investigation by the *Guardian* last year in collaboration with campaign group Leasehold Knowledge Partnership uncovered how buyers of Taylor Wimpey homes, predominantly in the north-west, found them to be almost unsaleable because of the doubling ground rents.

One flat owner reported being trapped in a property that had been rendered virtually worthless just six years after being built. Others have been forced to pay £1000-plus fees to their freeholder for permission to build an extension, while attempts to buy out the leasehold have been met with demands of £35,000 or more, even though the lease has, in some cases, hundreds of years to run. ...

Ground rents that double every 10 years have become hugely attractive to specialist investors, because they imply an interest rate of 7% a year when the Bank of England base rate is just 0.25%.

> Many buyers were told that the 250- or even 999-year leases on their new-build homes were 'virtually freehold' because of the length of the lease. But the investors who have snapped up the leases, often for just a few thousand pounds, refuse to sell them to householders unless they pay £30,000 or more. In some cases they simply refuse to sell the freehold, and are not legally required to do so. ...
>
> Leasehold, once seen as a dying relic of the Victorian property market, has returned with a vengeance since the 1990s, according to the report. In 1996, just 22% of new builds in the UK were sold as leasehold, but this has doubled to 43% at present. In London, nine out of 10 new builds are now leasehold.
>
> (Collinson, 2017)

4.2 Borrowing to buy

Whether buying freehold or leasehold, the majority of house purchases are made using borrowed money, usually a mortgage. Under this arrangement, a financial institution (the lender) provides a secured loan to the house buyer (the borrower).

Mortgage repayment methods

There are two basic types of mortgage: repayment and interest-only.

With a **repayment mortgage**, the principal (the original sum borrowed, also called the 'capital') is paid off through regular monthly payments made throughout the life of the loan. The typical structure is a reducing balance loan. This is where payments are a set amount each month, initially based on the mortgage term but changing whenever there is a change to the mortgage interest rate. As you saw in Table 4.2 in Chapter 4, each payment is made up of both interest and repayment of a bit of the principal. Initially the payments are mainly interest. One consequence of this is that a borrower who wishes to repay in the early years might be surprised at how much of the principal remains. But the amount of principal repaid each month accelerates over the term of the mortgage.

Repayment mortgage
A mortgage where the periodic repayments relate to the sum of the interest due and an amount of the principal (the original sum borrowed).

An important feature of repayment mortgages is that, provided all the payments are made, the whole principal is paid off at the end of the mortgage term. The former 'borrower' now *owns* their home outright.

Interest-only mortgage
A mortgage where the periodic repayments relate solely to the interest due, and where the principal is paid off in full as a single lump sum at the end (or 'maturity') of the mortgage.

With an **interest-only mortgage**, the monthly payments during the term just pay the interest on the loan. There are no repayments of the principal sum during the life of the loan. The principal is paid off only at the end of the loan in a single lump sum. It's essential that the borrower then has the means to repay the principal. Failure to do so could result in the property being repossessed.

One way to plan for repayment of the principal is to pay money regularly throughout the life of the mortgage into a savings or investment scheme. To determine how much to save each month, the investment is projected to grow at an assumed rate in order to produce a lump sum large enough to repay the principal in full at the end of the mortgage term. Usually, there is no guarantee, so the homeowner runs the risk of having to adjust the amount they save each month, or having to find money from elsewhere to pay off the rump of the mortgage if the savings or investment plan falls short of the full amount needed.

Another option would be to plan to sell the property when the mortgage ends. That's suitable for someone who has bought a second home or a property they rent out, but would leave an owner-occupier with the problem of where to live.

Interest rate variations

There are many varieties of mortgage on offer. One way they vary – whether repayment or interest-only loans – is through the way the interest rate is set. The main variations are:

- **Standard variable-rate mortgage** – The rate of interest goes up and down broadly in line with movements of the official rate set by the country's central bank. Often this rate is quicker to go up than to come back down.

- **Tracker mortgage** – A type of variable-rate mortgage where the interest rate is guaranteed to be a specified amount above an official rate and will automatically adjust whenever that rate changes.

? more responsive

- **Fixed-rate mortgage** – The interest rate is fixed at a set amount for a period of years, regardless of what happens to the official interest rate. This gives the advantage to borrowers of knowing what their mortgage expenditure will be for several years ahead. Borrowers are protected from any interest rate rise. Equally, though, they are locked into an uncompetitive rate if interest rates fall, because fixed-rate mortgages typically have early redemption penalties – fees payable for repaying the mortgage early.

- **Capped-rate mortgage** – The interest rate is variable but cannot exceed a maximum level, so the borrower's maximum monthly mortgage payment is known in advance. Sometimes these mortgages also have a 'collar', a minimum below which the interest rate will not go even if competing rates fall further. These products are also likely to have early redemption penalties.

- **Discounted-rate mortgage** – Another type of variable-rate mortgage which offers a discount to the standard variable rate for an initial period. Another incentive from lenders is to offer a 'cashback' payment to the borrower. This could be used to help manage the mortgage repayments in the early years, if the household budget were tight – in effect, similar to having a discounted-rate mortgage.

early redemption penalties

With fixed-rate, capped and discounted rates, borrowers need to factor in whether they can afford a possible rise in monthly payments once the special-deal period ends. Borrowers commonly shop around for, and switch to, another mortgage at that point. However, redemption penalties sometimes extend beyond the special-deal period. Even if they don't, there will often be an upfront arrangement fee to pay for any new mortgage. Therefore, the costs of switching need to weighed up against the potential gains.

Other mortgage variations

There are some other types of mortgage that have advantages for some borrowers. These include:

- **Flexible mortgages** – A type of variable-rate repayment mortgage which may provide a number of repayment options, including a facility to overpay, underpay, reborrow amounts previously overpaid, or take payment holidays if needed. This type of mortgage can be especially useful for borrowers whose income tends to vary – for example, because they are self-employed.

- **Offset mortgages** – This may be a repayment mortgage or an interest-only mortgage. The key feature is that a cash balance in a current account or savings accounts with the same provider is deducted from (offset against) the outstanding mortgage debt before the monthly mortgage interest is worked out. No interest is paid on the current account or savings account, but offsetting reduces the amount of interest charged on the mortgage. In a variation on this scheme, with a family offset mortgage, family members – usually parents – open a savings account with the mortgage provider so that their savings can be offset against their son's or daughter's mortgage.

- **Shared-ownership mortgages** – The borrower buys just part of their home. The rest is owned by another party, usually a social landlord, to whom the householder pays rent. This means the amount of mortgage needed is smaller and the aim is that the sum of the mortgage payments and rent each month is lower than the mortgage payments would have been for buying the whole property. Often, over time, the householder can buy further chunks of the home, increasing the share they own – this is called 'staircasing'.

Equity
The market value of a property, less the outstanding mortgage debt secured against it.

Equity release scheme
A way of unlocking the wealth tied up in a home while continuing to live there, either by borrowing using a mortgage or selling part or all of the home to a specialist firm.

While mortgages are thought of mainly as a way to buy a home, they can be used in other circumstances, too. For example, a homeowner might take out a top-up loan. This is a further mortgage on top of the main loan, maybe to pay for home improvements or simply as a way to cash in some of the wealth – called **equity** – tied up in the home. On the other hand, people unfortunate enough to have debt problems might take out a further mortgage to pay off credit card debts and other debts incurred as a result of other expensive forms of borrowing they have had to resort to.

Homeowners who already own their home outright or have only a small mortgage left may consider taking out a 'lifetime mortgage', also called a 'reverse mortgage'. This is a type of **equity release scheme** and is used to extract wealth tied up in the home for other purposes without having to move house. Typically, there are no monthly repayments and the lender gets back both the principal and interest when the home is eventually sold (usually on the homeowner dying or moving into a care home).

> ## Box 6.2 Islamic home finance
>
> Home buying is also influenced by cultural differences. An important example of this is the development of Islamic home finance. This avoids the payment of interest, which is forbidden under sharia law. Al Rayan Bank is one of many offering an Islamic alternative to a conventional mortgage based upon the Islamic finance principles of a co-ownership (Diminishing Musharakah) and leasing (Ijara). At the outset, the bank and the buyer share ownership of the property. The bank typically starts by owning 60%, 70% or 80% of the property. The individual then makes a series of payments to the bank culminating in acquisition of full ownership by the buyer. The bank's website explains:
>
> 'Your monthly payment is made up of two elements, an acquisition payment which increases your share of the property and a rental payment for use of the portion that the Bank still owns. When all acquisition payments have been made and the finance has been settled, ownership of the property transfers to you.'
>
> (Al Rayan Bank, 2017)

4.3 Affordability

The biggest challenge facing a first-time homebuyer is usually affordability. There are three main aspects to this:

- **A deposit** – Commonly, mortgage lenders will not lend 100% of the cost of buying a property. The homebuyer will need to put in some money of their own, say 10% or more of the property's value. Moreover, the lender will base the amount they will lend on a professional valuation of what the property is worth. This may come out as less than the asking price for the home. The buyer may be able to negotiate a reduction in asking price but, if not, their deposit will also have to cover the difference between the asking price and the valuation.

- **Buying costs** – There will be a range of different fees and charges, such as the valuer's fees, legal costs, any transaction tax (such as Stamp Duty Land Tax in England and Northern Ireland (and equivalent taxes elsewhere)) and possibly a fee for securing the mortgage. Sellers typically pay estate agency fees.

- **Monthly mortgage payments** – In countries like the UK, lenders are obliged to check whether the borrower can afford the mortgage payments given their current income and spending commitments. This is the sort of budgeting exercise described in Section 4 of Chapter 3, Expenditure, that it would be wise for borrowers to carry out for themselves. It's important also to consider how to carry on managing the payments if, say, interest rates were to rise or income to fall.

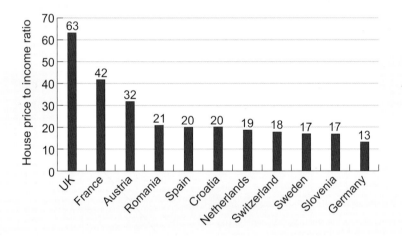

Figure 6.3 House-price-to-income ratio ((price per 100 square metres ÷ GDP per head) × 100) for selected countries (Global Property Guide, 2018)

While the affordability calculations above are personal to each household, it can be useful to look at the extent to which housing is affordable for the household sector as a whole. Probably the most widely used measure is the ratio of property prices to income, called the price-to-income ratio. Based on data about individual buyers, there are various methods of calculating the price–income ratio. Unfortunately they tend to vary from one country to another, which makes comparing affordability in different countries difficult.

However, Figure 6.3 illustrates an alternative approach. A price-to-income ratio has been calculated by measuring, in each country, the price of a standard unit of upscale housing (taken to be 100 square metres of reasonable quality housing) and dividing it by the country's GDP per head. You'll recall from Chapter 1 that GDP is the monetary value of everything produced within a country in a specified period, usually a year. If we divide it by the number of people living in the country, we get the value per person, which is a crude measure of average income. (It's crude because, as you discussed in Chapter 2, Income, the distribution of income is actually very unequal.) Figure 6.3 shows how this ratio varies across a selection of European countries.

[handwritten annotation: (housing price / GDP/head) no. of people in country]

Activity 6.5 Comparing affordability in different countries

Allow 5 minutes for this activity.

Based on the measure used in Figure 6.3, describe the affordability of housing in the UK compared with:

(a) Romania

(b) Germany.

Comment

Based on the measure in Figure 6.3, the UK has the least affordable housing, with a standard unit of upscale housing costing 63 times more than average income in the country.

(a) This is three times as much as the ratio for Romania (63 ÷ 21 = 3).

(b) This is nearly five times as much as the ratio for Germany (63 ÷ 13 = 4.8).

4.4 Housing and the household balance sheet

You first met the household balance sheet in Section 6 of Chapter 4. Figure 6.4 provides a quick reminder of the main elements you'll find in the balance sheet. The key balance sheet ratios are:

Net worth = Assets − Liabilities

Current asset ratio = Liquid assets ÷ Short-term liabilities

Leverage ratio = Liabilities ÷ Assets × 100

Purchasing a property adds to the balance sheet what for most households will be its biggest asset and (if it uses mortgage finance) its biggest liability. The information and ratios in the balance sheet can give helpful clues to how well a household may manage its mortgage if circumstances change.

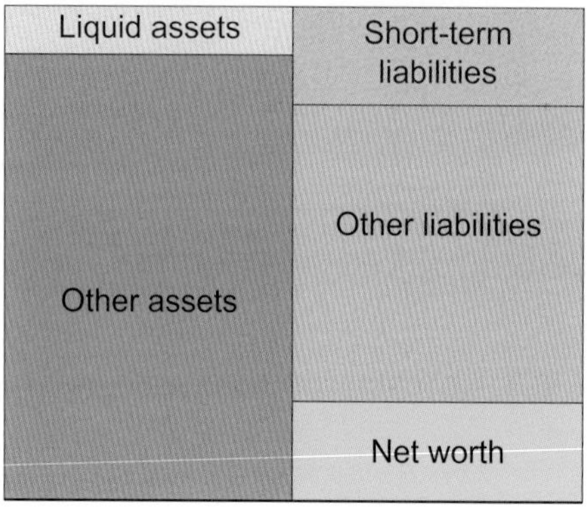

Figure 6.4 Main elements of the household balance sheet

Activity 6.6 The balance sheet as an aid to understanding risk

Allow 20 minutes for this activity.

1   Which elements of the balance sheet will be affected, and how, by the process of saving for a deposit?

2   Which elements of the balance sheet will be affected, and how, by the process of:

  o   paying the deposit

  o   taking out a mortgage

  o   purchasing a property?

3   In the light of your answers to Question 2, suggest how the current asset ratio and leverage ratio are likely to change as a result of purchasing a home and what this tells you about the household's financial situation.

Comment

1   The most likely effects of saving for the deposit are:

   o   an increase in liquid assets as the deposit is built up

   o   a consequent increase in total assets and net worth equal to the savings for the deposit.

2   The most likely effects of the home purchase are:

   o   a fall in liquid assets as the deposit is used for the purchase

   o   an increase in other assets when the value of the home is added

   o   a consequent increase in total assets when the home is bought, amounting to the value of the home minus the deposit paid

   o   an increase in other liabilities when the amount of the mortgage is added

   o   a consequent increase in total liabilities amounting to the value of mortgage

   o   no immediate change to net worth because the change in assets (value of the home less deposit) is exactly matched by the change in liabilities (the mortgage), if we ignore the costs of buying.

3   The most likely effects of the home purchase are:

   o   The current asset ratio will fall as the liquid assets (savings for the deposit) are swapped for other assets (the property). If the current asset ratio falls below 1, the household will no longer be able to pay off its short-term liabilities in a crisis.

   o   The leverage ratio will increase through the addition of the mortgage to liabilities. A high level of leverage indicates that servicing the debt could put a strain on cash flow, though this will also depend on the cost of the debt (in other words the interest rate). If interest rates are low, the household may easily service a large mortgage but could run into trouble if interest rates rise.

The balance sheet ratios tell us something about the household's exposure to risk. These risks include the possibility that, owing to sickness, unemployment, increases in interest rates or other unexpected events, mortgage repayments cannot be met. The lower the current asset ratio and the higher the leverage ratio, the more difficult it may be for the household to cut costs, draw on savings or run up temporary debt to tide it over a difficult patch. The lender will often allow a small number of missed payments, provided they are advised of what the borrower believes to be a temporary problem, but if payments are missed for a sustained period, the lender may take action, including possibly repossessing the property.

Unlike many assets, even when the mortgage is paid off, a house incurs some ongoing costs, such as maintenance. It also provides opportunities to generate an income, such as renting out a room. The existence of ongoing costs is more typical of liabilities than of assets. Nonetheless, acquisition of such an asset can increase future financial flexibility – for example, moving to a cheaper property or using equity release to extract some wealth, using the current property to create an income by taking in a lodger, or building up an inheritance.

The attractiveness of homeownership in certain respects depends on the direction of movement of property prices. The more they rise, the more powerful the argument about the acquisition of this asset becomes. On the other hand, because property ownership adds to wealth, rising values can lead to an increase in tax in countries where wealth or housing are part of the tax base.

There is no guarantee that house prices will rise in future. If prices fall, people who have bought homes may lose gains that had previously built up and will suffer a capital loss if price falls below the amount they paid for the home. Some owners may even suffer from **negative equity** – a situation where the value of the property falls below the outstanding mortgage debt. Negative equity need not be a problem, provided the owner does not need to sell the home. But, if they do have to sell, the proceeds will not be enough to pay off the mortgage in full, so money will need to be found from elsewhere to clear the debt.

Negative equity
A situation where the outstanding mortgage debt secured on a property exceeds the market value of the property.

↓ current asset ratio

&

↑ leverage

⇓

more risk of not covering needs

5 The purchasing process

Following careful consideration of affordability and choice of mortgage, the next step is the actual purchase. The process of purchasing varies not only between countries but also depends on the degree of competition among potential buyers.

A common way of commencing the buying process is by means of making a non-binding offer. This simply means that a potential buyer makes an offer, typically via an estate agent, based on the asking price of the property. This offer may well be below the asking price, and will be made 'subject to contract' and 'subject to survey'. An unfavourable survey may mean a reduced offer or even withdrawal of the offer. Even if the seller initially accepts the offer, they may legally accept a higher offer from someone else instead if the estate agent is still marketing the property. This destabilising practice is known as 'gazumping'.

Where there is keen competition to purchase a property, estate agents often invite 'sealed bids'. (For example, this is the system used in Scotland.) Potential buyers decide on their best offer, which will usually need to be above the asking price. They submit the bid, sometimes with a letter supporting it, in a sealed envelope. The seller decides which bid to accept (typically but not always the highest) and the person making this bid secures the property. A less formal version of the sealed-bid process is the 'best and final offer', whereby offers must be made by a specified date but can be made on the telephone or by letter, rather than by sealed envelope.

A property chain can be a major cause of stress when buying a home

An alternative to the use of a guide asking price and the invitation to make offers is the 'fixed price' system, under which the property is usually acquired by the first buyer to offer this fixed sum.

Some properties are sold by auction. This would not usually be the seller's first choice, as the price realised is likely to be less than might have been obtained through the conventional way of selling. It is, however, a quick way to sell. It may be appropriate for properties needing work, having undesirable features or where the owner needs to raise cash rapidly.

The point in the process of buying at which the buyer is legally committed to buy and the seller legally committed to sell varies from country to country. In the UK, this point is not reached till contracts (missives in Scotland) have been signed by both buyer and seller and 'exchanged'.

The exchange date is particularly important if the home is one of a number in a long chain that have to be sold, the purchase of each of which is dependent on the sale of those further down the chain. Usually buyers and sellers in a chain of housing transactions try to ensure that no one remains committed to buying a property without having secured a commitment to have their existing property bought. The longer the chain, the greater the risk of problems that will prevent completion of the individual transactions.

6 Property as an investment and as 'buy-to-let'

In the majority of developed countries, the historical trend has been for property prices to increase but, as was mentioned in relation to investments in Chapter 5, past performance is no guarantee of future market movements. When property prices do fall, or are flat or rising slowly, other investments can in theory make a better return. In practice, they seldom do because of the effect of leverage.

If an asset like a home is bought entirely for cash and its price rises, the owner makes a profit. For example, suppose a home is bought for £100,000 and over several years the price rises 25% to £125,000. If the owner sells, they will have made a profit of £25,000 (25%). Now suppose the same home was bought with a £75,000 mortgage, with the owners putting up just £25,000 of the purchase price. Now if the home is sold for £125,000, after paying off the mortgage, there will be £50,000. So the buyer paid £25,000 and has got back £50,000 which is a profit of 100%. So leverage magnifies gains and that is why, when house prices are on a rising trend, buying a home can be so profitable.

However, leverage also magnifies losses, so it is a risky strategy if prices are likely to fall. The smaller the deposit a buyer has to put up, the greater the impact of leverage, so the greater the chance of large profits or large losses.

If prices do look set to fall, there may be a financial gain from selling and then renting to obtain greater returns on the capital elsewhere. Such plans might entail only a temporary retreat from the property market: if prices did actually fall, it would then be possible to buy a better property than before. For many households, especially families, however, this process may be difficult in practice, because the future movement of house prices can only be guessed and there are substantial costs and disruption involved in selling and buying homes.

There are several other ways to increase the capital value of a home over and above what would be realised by any general rise in property prices. For example, homes can be bought either in an 'up and coming' area where property prices will rise more than the average, or perhaps at below the 'true' market value. Alternatively, someone can add value to a property by finding, for instance, a rundown home suitable for refurbishment and, when completed, sell at a profit.

People can sell their properties for different reasons

As mentioned in Section 4, another way to make money from a home is to rent out a spare room, effectively using the home as an income-producing asset. Some people may carry these ideas substantially further and rent out several rooms, or regularly buy, develop and then sell individual properties. Tax treatment of ventures of this kind varies from country to country.

Another way to invest in property is to 'buy-to-let'. This means buying a property specifically to rent out, rather than live in. Buy-to-let is a more attractive option in countries where governments offer tax subsidies for private landlords. While all property ownership carries a risk of capital loss, a buy-to-let landlord can still make a return in a falling market through the rents paid by tenants.

7 What makes property prices change?

As house prices are such a major influence on household finances, it is useful to have an understanding of how they are determined, so as to be able to make well-informed judgements about likely future fluctuations in price.

Trends in house price movements vary considerably between countries. Figure 6.5 shows real price movements for four industrialised economies during the period 1995 to 2016. The movements are shown in the form of indices based on 1995 prices. This means that the average price in 1995 is given the value 100. Changes are then shown in percentage terms; so, for example, we can see that in Sweden between 1995 and 2000 there was a 50% rise in average house prices (since the index rose from 100 to 150). By 2004, the index was 200, meaning that prices had doubled.

Demand
The quantity of a good or service that buyers wish to purchase over a specified period of time.

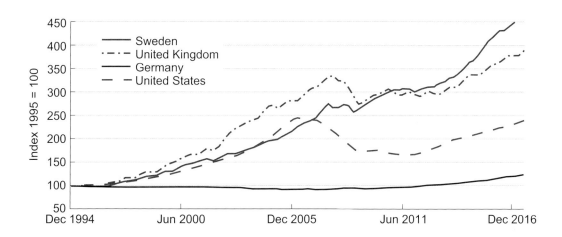

Figure 6.5 House price indices, 1994–2017 (based on data from BIS, 2018)

What brought about the changes in house prices we can see in Figure 6.5? The answer is largely to do with the forces of **demand** and **supply**.

The idea that high demand and restricted supply lead to price rises, while slack demand and over-supply lead to price falls, is a familiar and perhaps an intuitive one. It applies whether looking at houses, oil, coffee or any other type of good or service. Economists, however, develop this insight more formally and make use of what is known as

Supply
The quantity of a good or service that sellers wish to sell over a specified period of time.

the 'demand-and-supply model'. You'll recall from Chapter 1 that a model simplifies some aspect of the real world to help our understanding. Both natural scientists and social scientists, like economists, use modelling to help them to explain complex processes and make predictions about likely outcomes. A common example is forecasting the weather.

The remainder of this section develops the model of demand and supply in the context of the housing market.

7.1 The housing market

So what does the model of demand and supply represent and what simplifications does it make? The model pictures a market: a space where buyers and sellers come together. It simplifies this market by isolating the influence of price from the many other influences (such as changes in income, taste, and so on) on the quantities demanded and supplied. It does this in order to make the analysis of all the influences more manageable.

First, of course, it must be said that there is not really a single market for housing but rather a set of markets, some more or less separate. These include the housing market in different regions (say, London and Wales). Other markets that overlap include, say, the market for first-time buyers and buy-to-let landlords, where both may be interested in exactly the same properties. There are many other ways we could divide up the market – for example, by countries, type of dwelling, new-build or second-hand homes, and so on. For our present purposes, however, we shall lump all these segments together and treat the housing market for a single country as a single meeting place of buyers and sellers.

7.2 Demand for housing

To build the model, we shall start with the demand side of the market.

When house prices are relatively low, more people feel able and inclined to buy. Estate agents and home-buying websites become busier. At higher prices, some buyers are put off, either because they cannot afford to buy or because they think homes at that price are poor value. We can think of a spectrum of prices: the lower the average house price, the more accessible and attractive house purchase becomes. This means that more people, willing and able to buy, will enter the market during any given time period, raising the quantity demanded. We can show this relationship using a diagram.

Figure 6.6(a) plots the quantity of homes demanded on the horizontal axis and price on the vertical axis. There are no numbers on the axes because the diagram is simply going to show the direction of the relationship between price and quantity demanded, rather than exactly how strong or weak that relationship is. The diagram shows a line sloping downwards from left to right. This creates a picture of our argument above that the lower the price, the more demand (quantity) there is. This downward-sloping line is known as a **demand curve** – even if it is a straight line! (Straight lines keep the diagram simple.)

Figure 6.6(a) assumes that, for now, all other influences on quantity demanded are unchanged, so the model isolates the influence of price on quantity. It is very important to understand this assumption in order to understand how the model works. In reality, many influences are at work, but for now we are focusing on just one: price. Economists use a Latin phrase, *ceteris paribus*, which means 'with other things being equal', to signal this.

ceteris paribus
|||
all other things being equal

Demand curve
A line showing the quantity demanded of a good or service at each price, assuming that all other factors that influence demand are fixed.

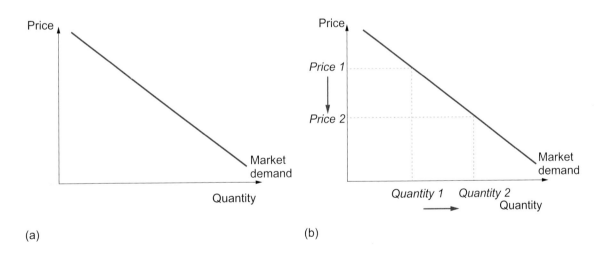

Figure 6.6 (a) A market demand curve and (b) a change in price

In Figure 6.6(b), you can see the effect that a change in house prices has on the quantity demanded. A change in price results in a movement along the demand curve. Figure 6.6(b) shows how a fall in price from Price 1 to Price 2 would result in a movement along the demand curve, so that the quantity of housing people want to buy increases from Quantity 1 to Quantity 2.

7.3 Supply of housing

Next, how does price relate to the quantity of homes supplied – that is, offered for sale – in a given period of time?

If prices are low, developers may be reluctant to build new homes, seeing little chance for profit. And people who already own their own homes who are thinking about moving may decide to put off selling at such low prices. Conversely, when house prices are high, developers may rush to build and sell lots of new homes and homeowners may decide this is a great time to sell and make a profit.

Supply curve
A line showing the quantity supplied of a good or service at each price, assuming that all other factors that influence supply are fixed.

It follows that the higher the price obtainable on the housing market, the more properties will be offered for sale. The upshot is that if we plot quantity supplied against price on a diagram similar to Figure 6.6(a), the result is a line that slopes upwards from left to right as in Figure 6.7(a). This is called a **supply curve** – even though, again, as presented here, it is a straight line.

As with demand, we make the *ceteris paribus* assumption – that is, we assume all other influences on quantity supplied are unchanged.

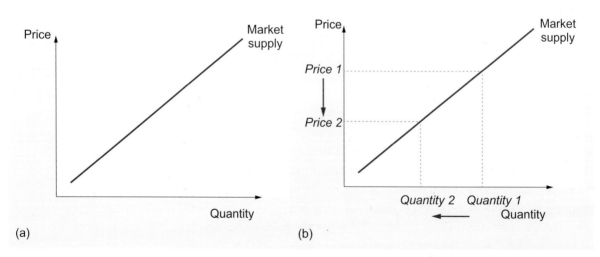

Figure 6.7 (a) A market supply curve and (b) a change in price

In Figure 6.7(b), you can see the effect that a change in house prices has on the quantity supplied. A change in price results in a movement along the supply curve. Figure 6.7(b) shows how a fall in price from Price 1 to Price 2 would result in a movement along the supply curve so that the quantity of housing people want to sell decreases from Quantity 1 to Quantity 2.

7.4 Price in the housing market

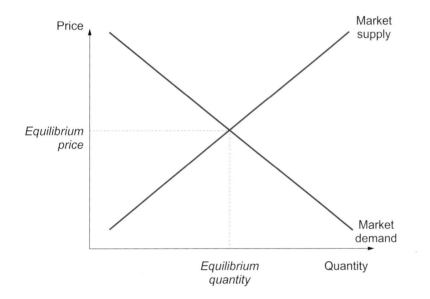

Figure 6.8 Market equilibrium

We can now bring demand and supply together on a single diagram. Figure 6.8 does this. We can use Figure 6.8 to bring out an important distinction. This is the distinction between planned and realised demand and between planned and realised supply. Any point on the demand curve shows the quantity buyers would be willing to buy at a given price (planned demand), and any point on the supply curve shows the quantity suppliers would be willing to supply at a given price (planned supply). But however willing the suppliers, they cannot sell more than buyers are willing to buy, and however willing the buyers, they cannot buy more than suppliers are willing to sell. This means that the quantity actually traded at any given price (realised demand and realised supply) will always be constrained either from the demand side or from the supply side, except when the exact price at which the quantity buyers are willing to buy is equal to the quantity suppliers are

Market equilibrium
A situation where the plans of both buyers and sellers are realised, so neither has an incentive to change their market behaviour.

Equilibrium price
The price at which the planned quantity demanded is equal to the planned quantity supplied.

willing to sell. At this price, the plans of both buyers and suppliers will be realised. This is a situation of **market equilibrium**. The price prevailing in this situation is called the **equilibrium price**.

To understand why the market converges on the equilibrium price and quantity, imagine what would happen if the price was 'too high' – in other words, above the equilibrium price. You can see in Figure 6.9 that sellers would plan to supply more than buyers want to buy. There would be an excess supply of housing. The plans of some sellers would be frustrated, because they would not be able to find buyers for their homes. They would have a choice: either drop their price or exit the market, leaving just those sellers who are prepared to accept a lower price. As the price comes down, new buyers will be attracted to the market and so gradually price and quantity both settle at their equilibrium levels.

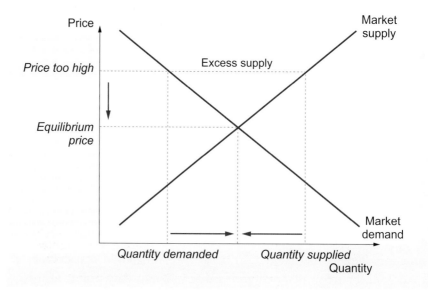

Figure 6.9 The effect of price being 'too high'

Activity 6.7 Price too low

Allow 15 minutes for this activity.

What would happen if the price were too low, in other words below the equilibrium price? Try to explain in words how sellers and buyers would react to a low house price and why this means price and quantity would tend to move towards the equilibrium level. If you would find it helpful, you could try drawing a diagram like the one in Figure 6.9 but starting with a price that's too low.

Comment

The answer to Activity 6.7 is given at the end of this chapter.

7.5 Non-price influences on demand and supply

Demand curves and supply curves show how quantity demanded or supplied varies with price. But there are other factors that can affect quantities demanded and supplied, even if prices do not change. For example, if incomes increase across the whole economy, more people will feel able to buy their own home and they are more likely to get a mortgage to do so. This would mean that at every possible level of house prices, there would be more willing buyers. This is depicted in Figure 6.10 by a shift in the whole demand curve to the right.

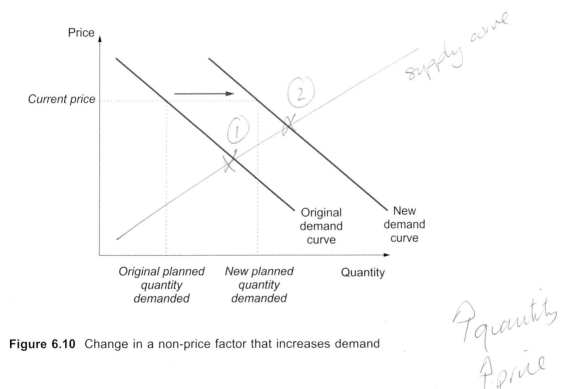

Figure 6.10 Change in a non-price factor that increases demand

---

Activity 6.8 Non-price influences on the demand for housing

Allow 15 minutes for this activity.

1 What influences other than price and income do you think might increase the overall quantity of housing demanded at every price level and so shift the demand curve to the right?

2 Using Figure 6.10 (or a copy if you prefer), draw in an upward sloping supply curve and describe the effect of the shift in the demand curve on the equilibrium price and the equilibrium quantity.

Comment

The answers to Activity 6.8 are given at the end of this chapter.

Of course, not all non-price factors increase demand. Some reduce demand, others may increase or reduce supply. Next time you read a story in the news about the housing market, you might have some fun trying to explain it using the demand-and-supply model!

8 Conclusion

In this chapter, you have seen that housing decisions have a major impact on a household's personal finances.

Whether renting or buying, housing costs will be a major item of expenditure. Homeownership is often an aspiration but may be unaffordable, especially in the earlier stages of the life course. Private renting can also be costly in some countries, and social housing, where available, is usually cheaper, while also offering better security of tenure. For homebuyers, there is a wide choice of mortgages, some of which can help the household to budget for housing costs with more certainty.

Renting may be convenient and the tenure of choice for some, but renters miss the chance to build a valuable asset into their balance sheet. Many households look on housing as an investment, rather than simply a place to live. This store of wealth can provide financial flexibility later in life. Rising house prices benefit existing homeowners, who see their housing wealth increase, but can make it harder for younger people to buy homes.

However, homeownership also exposes households to risks, especially the risk of being unable to keep up their mortgage payments due to unforeseen life events. Fortunately, it's possible to insure against some of those risks; insurance is the topic you will look at in the next chapter.

Answers to activities in Chapter 6

Answers to Activity 6.4

1 As an example, here is our summary:

> Leasehold is a form of tenure that used to seem old-fashioned but has become popular again, with 43% of newly-built homes in the UK now being sold this way. What has revived this type of tenure is a new approach to ground rents – the annual sum paid by leaseholders to the owners of the freehold, who are typically specialist investors.
>
> In the past, ground rents were trivial sums. Collinson (2017) explains that, with modern leaseholds, the starting amount may be just a few hundred pounds but can rise alarmingly over time – for example, doubling every ten years. Homeowners who want to escape this escalating bill by buying the freehold are told they must pay tens of thousands of pounds.
>
> The *Guardian*, MPs and others have campaigned against these leaseholds; property developer Taylor Wimpey is now set to pay £130 million in compensation to buyers of its leaseholds.
>
> [148 words]

2 Calculations for the ground rent at 10, 30 and 50 years are shown below.

After this many years:	The ground rent would be:
Start	£295
10 years	£590 (£295 × 2)
30 years	£2,360 (£590 × 2 × 2)
50 years	£9,440 (£2360 × 2 × 2)

Answer to Activity 6.7

Figure 6.11 (below) illustrates what would happen if the price was 'too low' – in other words, below the equilibrium price. You can see in Figure 6.11 that buyers would want to buy more than sellers would want to sell. The plans of some buyers would be frustrated, because they would not be able to find people willing to sell them homes. Some buyers would try to outbid each other to get one of the few homes available; other buyers would exit the market, leaving only those who are willing to pay more. This would tend to push up house prices. The rising price would also tempt some new sellers into the market. Gradually, price and quantity would both settle at their equilibrium levels.

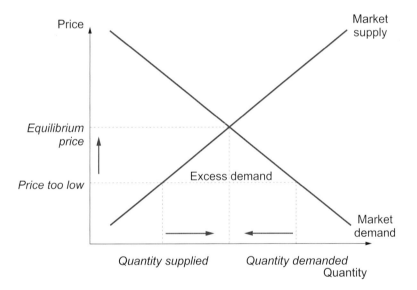

Figure 6.11 The effect of price being 'too low'

Answers to Activity 6.8

1 You might have suggested, say, a fall in mortgage rates, a reduction in the proportion of the asking price needed as a deposit, a cut in taxes on buying a home, or the introduction of government schemes aimed at helping first-time buyers.

2 Once you have added a supply curve, you can see that a change which shifts the demand curve to the right causes both the equilibrium price and the equilibrium quantity to increase, as shown in Figure 6.12.

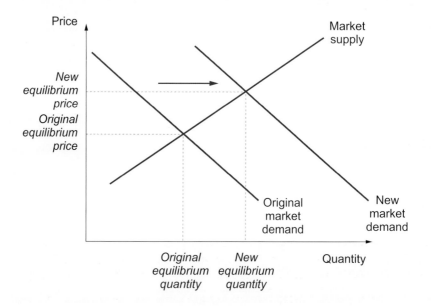

Figure 6.12 Effect on equilibrium price and quantity of a change in a non-price factor that increases demand

References

Al Rayan Bank (2017) *Home Purchase Plan* [Online]. Available at www.alrayanbank.co.uk/home-finance/home-purchase-plan/ (Accessed 6 June 2017).

Bank for International Settlements (BIS) (2018) *Long Series on Nominal Residential Property Prices* [Online]. Available at www.bis.org/statistics/pp_long.htm (Accessed 13 February 2018).

Collinson, P. (2017) 'Taylor Wimpey to pay up to £130m to settle ground rent scandal', *The Guardian*, 27 April [Online]. Available at www.theguardian.com/business/2017/apr/27/taylor-wimpey-ground-rent-scandal (Accessed 28 June 2017).

Cribb, A., Hood, J. and Joyce, R. (2016) *The Economic Circumstances of Different Generations: The Latest Picture*, Institute for Fiscal Studies briefing note, BN187 [Online]. Available at www.ifs.org.uk/uploads/publications/bns/bn187.pdf (Accessed 26 July 2017).

Department for Communities and Local Government (DCLG) (2017) *English Housing Survey Headline Report 2015–16* [Online]. Available at www.gov.uk/government/uploads/system/uploads/attachment_data/file/595785/201 5-16_EHS_Headline_Report.pdf (Accessed 26 July 2017).

Eurostat (2017a) *Distribution of Population by Tenure Status, Type of Household and Income Group – EU-SILC Survey*, EU Open Data Portal [Online]. Available at https://data.europa.eu/euodp/data/dataset/fAtiyJCKzLXUhNX3wZUw (Accessed 12 February 2018).

Eurostat (2017b) *Overcrowding Rate by Tenure Status – EU-SILC Survey*, EU Open Data Portal [Online] Available at https://data.europa.eu/euodp/data/dataset/SoA5tPlBI4yvq23IffL8g (Accessed 12 February 2018).

Global Property Guide (2018) *Europe: House Price to Income Ratio* [Online]. Available at www.globalpropertyguide.com/Europe/price-gdp-per-cap (Accessed 13 February 2018).

Kofner, S. (2014) 'The German housing system: fundamentally resilient?', *Journal of Housing and the Built Environment*, vol. 29, pp. 255–75 [Online]. Available at https://search-proquest-com.libezproxy.open.ac.uk/docview/1522856275?rfr_id=info%3Axri%2Fsid%3Aprimo (Accessed 27 July 2017).

Oxley, M. (2017) *Ask the Expert. The Private Rented housing Sector: The UK and Ideas from Other Countries*, PowerPoint presentation, 23 March [Online] Available at www.smf.co.uk/ask-expert-private-rented-housing-sector-uk-ideas-countries/?doing_wp_cron=1501087636.2844600677490234375000 (Accessed 15 May 2017).

Social Market Foundation (2017) *Ask the Expert. The Private Rented Housing Sector: The UK and Ideas from Other Countries*, 29 March [Online]. Available at www.smf.co.uk/ask-expert-private-rented-housing-sector-uk-ideas-countries/?doing_wp_cron=1501087636.28446006774902343750000 (Accessed 15 May 2017).

Voigtländer, M. (2009) 'Why is the German homeownership rate so low?', *Housing Studies*, vol. 24, no. 3, pp. 355–72.

To cite this chapter, use the following format in your reference list:

Stone, H. and Fribbance, I. (2019) 'Housing', in De Henau, J. and Lowe, J. (eds) *Personal Finance*, Milton Keynes, The Open University, pp. 249–294.

Chapter 7
Insurance and life events

Jonquil Lowe and Ian Fribbance

Contents

1 Introduction

When asked by a journalist what was most likely to blow a government off course, Harold Macmillan (UK Prime Minister, 1957–1963) allegedly said: 'events, dear boy, events'. The same could be said for households.

The cash flow model we have been building up through earlier chapters of *Personal Finance* is a useful aid for planning how to balance income, debt and assets to cover a household's current spending and achieve future goals. But reality is messy: plans can easily be upset by life events, whether good or bad. A crucial part of building a resilient financial plan is anticipating the sort of events that could happen, and building some protection into the plan. **Insurance** is an important way of doing this.

This chapter starts (in Section 2) by looking at the financial consequences of different types of life events, and Section 3 introduces you to some of the main types of insurance that households might use to prepare for these events taking place.

In Section 4, we dig down into the principles behind insurance, and look at some issues around consumer behaviour that insurers aim to tackle – which can make insurance policies a minefield of small print! Underlying these principles and problems for insurance is the assessment of risk which is founded on **probability**. In Section 5 we'll take a quick look at what we mean by 'probability' and ways of measuring it.

Section 6 shows how what you learn in this chapter can inform the decisions that individuals and households make, so that they are more financially resilient. But these decisions are not taken in isolation from the rest of the economy, so Section 6 also considers the political and social context that influences households' access to, and need for, insurance.

Insurance
A system by which individuals or households, in exchange for payment of a sum of money (called the 'premium'), are promised compensation for losses or costs incurred due to events specified in a contract.

Probability
A measure of the chance that an event will occur.

2 Life events and their financial consequences

There are two types of event that may occur over someone's life course: the expected and the unexpected.

The most obvious expected event that everyone shares is death, although the timing of each individual's death is, in almost all cases, uncertain. By contrast, unexpected events are things that *might* happen, even though many people never experience them.

Mostly, people are concerned about unexpected events that have bad outcomes, such as having their car stolen or becoming too ill to work. But there are also unexpected events that have good outcomes, such as winning a lottery. There are lots of life events that could be classified as unexpected but are so typical that it may make sense to anticipate and plan for them anyway. These could include moving in with a partner, having children, a relationship breaking down, and the need for care in old age. Most life events, whether expected or unexpected, have financial consequences.

Unexpected events have financial consequences

Activity 7.1 Impact of life events on your finances

Allow 15 minutes for this activity.

Think about one unexpected event that you or your household might face over the next few years, which may have a negative impact. Then answer Questions 1 and 2 below.

1   Would you be able to cope with the financial impact of this event by adjusting your income or spending?

2   Would this event have an impact on your balance sheet?

Comment

Some examples of unexpected events that can impact negatively on income include:

- being made redundant
- developing an illness that means you're off work for a long time
- suffering an injury that affects your ability to do your current work, meaning you could have to take a lower-paid job
- a close relative needing your care, so reducing the number of hours you can work
- the death of a partner whose earnings were an important part of the household income.

Unexpected events that can impact on spending include:

- finding dry rot in your home
- writing off your car in an accident
- an illness or injury that means you need to pay for a carer to look after yourself or a loved one
- starting to pay for care (say, childcare) because a partner who previously provided the care on an unpaid basis has died.

In many cases, it would be difficult or impossible to make sufficient adjustments to your income and spending to absorb the financial consequences of these and other events. This means they are likely to have an impact on your balance sheet, as you either use savings you've previously built up or borrow money to cover the fall in income and/or necessary increase in spending. Longer-term, unexpected events can adversely affect a person's financial planning and standard of living, and make attaining some or all of their future financial goals impossible.

2.1 The alternatives to buying insurance

It can be tempting to ignore the possibility of bad events happening. But being financially capable means anticipating what might happen and, if necessary, taking steps now to make your household financially shockproof.

As you saw in Chapter 5 of *Personal Finance*, one way to protect against unexpected events is to build up some savings for emergencies, to cover the cost of, say, a new washing machine or car repairs. An ideal emergency fund would be enough to cover three months' essential spending, providing protection against a temporary drop in income due to job loss or illness. But using saving as your shock absorber – a strategy called **self-insurance** – has its limitations: firstly, some financial shocks are just too big; and secondly shocks may happen at any time, even today, but it takes time to build up savings. By contrast, insurance can provide protection against shocks, big or small, with cover starting straight away.

Self-insurance
Deciding to meet the financial challenge of some or all life events out of savings, income or other resources (for example, help from family members) rather than buying insurance.

Using insurance does not necessarily mean households buying cover privately. As you saw in Chapter 2, governments may establish systems of social insurance whereby most individuals contribute by paying taxes and in return may receive state benefits when they are in need of financial help – for example, because of job loss or illness. Similarly, employers often provide some types of insurance and, in some cases, are required to by law. This might include sick pay for days taken off work due to illness; paid parental leave following the birth of a child; payment for hospital and dental treatment; and so on. The payouts from social insurance and employer-provided cover will not necessarily fully meet a household's needs but will reduce the level of private insurance it needs to buy.

3 Types of insurance

Private insurance is big business; it is often sold by large multinational firms and famously by Lloyd's of London, an internationally renowned, centuries-old insurance provider.

It's possible to buy private insurance against virtually anything that involves risk. For example, in 2006, footballer David Beckham's legs were insured for £100 million; UK house insurance in 1914 included cover against damage caused by suffragettes; and one story has it that 60,000 people have insured themselves against being turned into vampires or werewolves (Lloyd's, 2017)!

In the main, insurance is either for things (or using them) or people (their life and health).

Box 7.1 Insurance jargon explained

You may have taken out some insurance, and if so you'll know that insurance policies include a lot of jargon. Here are some of the most common terms that we'll be using in this section.

- **Policyholder** – the customer who has bought the insurance.

- **Premium** – the sum of money the policyholder pays to have insurance cover. This might be paid as a single lump sum or, more usually, annually or in monthly instalments.

- **Payout** – the sum of money the policyholder gets from the insurance if they make a successful claim.

3.1 Insuring things (general insurance)

General insurance mainly protects individuals and households from unexpected expenditure on replacing lost or damaged items, or compensating other people who have suffered as a result of the way the items have been used.

Whatever the type of insurance, it's important to read the policy to be sure about what is covered and not covered in each case. In addition to specific exclusions, policies may have an 'act of God' clause that excludes losses caused by what are deemed to be unpredictable natural events – such as a holiday being cancelled because of a volcanic eruption.

Home contents insurance covers possessions

Home insurance

Given how devastating it would be to lose the roof over your head, home insurance is one of the first types of insurance cover that households should take out. There are two types: buildings insurance, which covers the structure of the building; and contents insurance, which covers the things inside. Typically, buildings and contents insurances will pay out where a loss is caused by: 'fire, explosion, lightning, earthquake, storm, flood, subsidence, heave or landslip, theft or attempted theft, malicious damage, falling trees or branches, falling TV or satellite devices, riot and impact by aircraft, vehicle or animal' (ABI, 2016, p. 5).

Buildings insurance is only needed by homeowners and landlords. For those who rent their home, the building should be insured by their landlord – though the cost may be passed on to tenants (directly in some countries; in others, indirectly) through the amount of rent they pay.

Buildings and contents cover can often be combined. A combined policy may be cheaper and can make claims simpler if both a building's structure and the possessions inside are damaged or lost by, say, a fire, flood or break-in.

Activity 7.2 Keeping down the cost of home insurance

Allow 5 minutes for this activity.

Write down three things you think a policyholder could do to reduce their home insurance premiums.

Comment

The answers to Activity 7.2 are given at the end of this chapter.

Motor insurance

In most countries, anyone who uses a motor vehicle (such as a car, van or motorbike) on public roads needs, at a minimum, to have insurance called 'third-party cover', to ensure that compensation can be paid to anyone who is injured or whose property is damaged in connection with the policyholder's driving or their vehicle. These basic motor insurance policies also usually pay out to the policyholder if their vehicle becomes a **write-off** due to theft or fire damage. However, many people choose to take out 'comprehensive' insurance, which also covers damage to their vehicle in situations where their own or someone else's third-party, fire and theft cover would not pay out. While cover is mainly in relation to the policyholder's own car (or motorbike or other vehicle, as relevant), motor insurance also typically provides the policyholder with third-party cover while driving someone else's vehicle with their permission.

Write-off

In the context of insurance, a damaged car, motorbike or other vehicle that insurers decide to pay an agreed value for rather than paying for the cost of repairs.

Travel insurance

Travel insurance covers the risks of disruption to a holiday, loss or theft of baggage and belongings, injury or damage caused by the policyholder, and the cost of dealing with medical emergencies – or even death – while away. This may include, for example, the cost of ambulances and medical treatment, extra space on a plane if flown home with an injury and, in the event of death, repatriating the body. Traditionally these policies were taken out for each trip, and insurance cover might be bundled in with the price of the holiday. But it is common these days to take out annual policies that cover multiple holidays during the year.

The cost of cover varies according to:

- the holiday destination (for example, travel insurance for trips to the US is expensive, partly because claims for medical bills there can be very high)

- the traveller's age and health (sometimes people over 65 pay more because of an increased risk of medical claims)

- whether any risky activities, such as winter sports, are planned.

Other types of general insurance

General insurance is ubiquitous. Here are just a few examples of the other types of cover that are readily available:

- pet insurance covers owners against the cost of unexpected vet bills

- 'pluvius' (Latin for rain) insurance can be taken out against outdoor events being rained off

- you can even insure against the risk of having twins – a usually delightful but costly event – rather than a single baby.

3.2 Insuring people (life and health insurance)

While general insurance focuses mainly on protection from unexpected costs (the expenditure side of cash flow), life and health insurance is more about protecting income for either the policyholder or their survivors. However, some life and health policies do focus on expenditure, for example, some types of health insurance provide cover for unexpected medical bills; and life insurance may be used to pay off large debts like a mortgage, thus cutting survivors' outgoings.

Protection-only life insurance

Premature death, as well as being emotionally traumatic, can be a financial problem for those left behind if they were financially dependent on the person who died. Life insurance, which pays out on death, is typically used to replace the income of the person who has died, or to pay off a mortgage.

A single person with no dependants generally does not need life insurance. So the main people who should consider life cover are:

- earners who have dependants, such as a non-earning partner and/or children

- couples that are financially co-dependent, for example, both earning and sharing some bills

- a non-working partner who provides unpaid work (such as childcare) that would have to be paid for if they died.

While the financial consequences of a working-age person dying are usually severe, in developed countries, the probability of dying between, say, ages 16 and 65 is low. This means that the cost of life insurance designed to pay out only on death – often called 'protection-only' cover – is usually quite affordable. There are two types of protection-only life cover:

- **Lump-sum term insurance**. This pays out a large lump sum if death occurs within a specified time period (called the 'term'). If the insured person survives the term, the policy pays out nothing. For example, parents might take out insurance for a term that lasts until their youngest child reaches 18 or 21. Typically, survivors might invest any lump sum paid out, to provide the income they need.

- **Family-income-benefit insurance**. This is also taken out for a specified term but, if the insured person dies, it pays out a regular income from the date of death for the remainder of the term. This is generally cheaper than lump-sum term insurance, since a death later in the term means less money is paid out overall.

Life insurance cover is important for people doing unpaid work, too

Life insurance can be based on a single life (paying out if that person dies) or joint lives. A joint-life policy would commonly be taken out to cover a joint mortgage, with the whole mortgage being paid off if either person dies.

Usually, life cover is taken out by the person whose life is being insured. However, it is possible to take out a 'life-of-another' policy – for example, a parent receiving child maintenance payments from an ex-partner could take out insurance on the ex-partner's life (and without needing that person's consent to do so).

Income protection insurance

This is a type of health insurance designed to pay out a replacement income for someone who is prevented from working because of illness, injury or disability. It can also be taken out to pay a specified income if someone doing unpaid work develops health issues. The most comprehensive policies pay out until retirement or recovery, whichever happens first. However, cheaper policies pay out until recovery or the end of a fixed period, such as two or five years.

Unlike some other types of health insurance, income protection policies are usually 'individually underwritten', which means that the insurer asks for a large amount of information about the policyholder, about their health and that of their close family members, the type of work they do, the kind of hobbies they have, and so on. This helps the insurer measure, as accurately as possible, the risk of the policyholder making a claim and to set the cost of their premium accordingly. From the policyholder's viewpoint though, it makes the insurance seem complicated and harder to shop around for, since quotes have to be tailored.

Accident, sickness and unemployment (ASU) policy

This type of health insurance is similar to income protection but usually pays out for a year at most (occasionally two) and the payout is a fixed sum, rather than being linked to the income that the policyholder has lost. Another difference is that ASU policies are not individually underwritten; instead they rely on exclusions (events and circumstances that the contract stipulates are not covered) to screen out risks that the insurer does not want to take on. As a result, ASU policies seem simpler and easier to buy, but it's important that people are made aware of the exclusions before they buy an ASU policy, so that they can know whether it is suitable for them.

Box 7.2 Mis-selling of PPI

You may recall from Chapter 1 that a major mis-selling scandal in modern times has been the sale of payment protection insurance (PPI) in the UK.

PPI is a kind of ASU that from the 1990s onwards was heavily marketed to people taking out personal loans, credit cards and mortgages. The aim was that the PPI policy would take over the monthly loan repayments if the borrower was made redundant or could not work because of illness. However, since it is not individually underwritten, PPI typically has exclusions for claims that relate to any health condition the person already has at the time they start the policy (called a 'pre-existing condition'). It also often excludes claims from people who do not have a regular, full-time job, or who could be aware at the time the policy starts that they are likely to be made redundant.

With all types of insurance, it is essential that potential customers are warned about any significant exclusions before they buy. Otherwise they could end up with insurance on which it is very unlikely that they can ever claim given their particular circumstances. But during the 1990s and 2000s, typically PPI exclusions were not made clear. The mis-selling only came to light when policyholders tried to make a claim. Largely as a result of the policies being unsuitable, the proportion of successful PPI claims was shockingly low – just 14% compared with, say, 78% for motor insurance (Competition Commission, 2009). The sellers of PPI were ultimately required to pay back tens of billions of pounds to customers (FCA, 2017).

Activity 7.3 Protecting your human capital

Allow 10 minutes for this activity.

Life and health insurances can be thought of as ways to protect your ability to exploit your human capital (see Chapter 2 of *Personal Finance* if you need a reminder of what this is).

Can you think of any risks that could affect your ability to exploit your own human capital? Do you have any insurance as protection against those risks?

Comment

If you are of working age, the ability to turn your human capital into income is at risk if illness or disability would reduce or stop your earnings. Also if you have family or other dependants, they are at risk if they rely on your human capital to provide some or all of the income they need. Similarly, they are at risk if your human capital is the source of unpaid work (such as caring for children) that would have to be replaced if you could not do it.

You might have protection against some of these risks through insurance, either provided through your job or your own private insurance policies – for example, to pay off your mortgage in the event of your death.

Reasons for not taking out insurance vary. For example, you might think (rightly or wrongly) that your extended family or state benefits will protect you; that the risk of something bad happening is very low; or that the cost of cover is too high. Alternatively, you (and any dependants) might be reliant on sources of income (such as pensions or savings and investments) that do not depend on you working, in which case you might correctly conclude that no insurance is required.

Private medical insurance (PMI)

This type of insurance provides protection against bills for private medical treatment. In countries like the UK, which has a free-at-the-point-of-use National Health Service (NHS), private treatment may seem a luxury. However, as a condition of entry into the country, immigrants are often required to have private cover, so that they will not be a drain on state resources. And, as there are often long waiting lists for state-funded treatment, some employers provide private medical insurance to minimise the time that their employees are on sick leave.

In countries without a state-funded health service, private insurance is a necessity not a luxury. In some countries, the state legislates to ensure that citizens have access to at least the minimum medical insurance they need.

In the UK, PMI covers the cost of treatment for 'acute' medical conditions: in other words, ones that can be cured or where symptoms are largely relieved through treatment. This is in contrast to 'chronic' conditions which are persistent and cannot be cured; these are normally excluded from PMI. PMI tends to be expensive and the cost increases with age (because of the greater chance of health problems). Nevertheless it is chosen for various reasons: pleasanter, hotel-style surroundings; being treated at a time of the patient's choosing; and receiving treatment more quickly.

Private dental insurance is similar to PMI but pays for dental care. It is widespread even in the UK, where NHS dental provision exists but is limited.

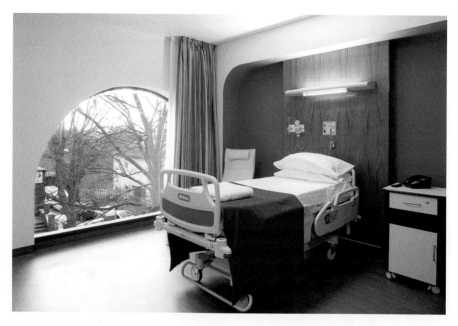

Medical insurance can cover treatment in a private hospital

4 How insurance works

Insurance is a way of transferring risk: individuals and households transfer the financial consequences of specified life events to the insurer. With private insurance, they do this by paying premiums to the insurer and in return receive a payout if an insured event happens. Insurers invest the premiums until required for payouts. This makes insurance companies some of the biggest investors in the world.

4.1 Insurance and risk

There are two fundamental requirements for private insurance:

- Risk – if an event is certain to happen, there is by definition no element of risk and it will be impossible to insure against it. An event will also be uninsurable if there is so little reliable data available that insurers cannot estimate the chance of it happening – in other words, there is too much **uncertainty**.

- Amount of loss – it must be possible to estimate reasonably well the maximum amount of loss, if the event were to happen.

Uncertainty
Where the chance of something happening cannot be measured or estimated.

Where these requirements are not met, a market for private insurance is unlikely to develop. An example is the difficulty of insuring privately against the costs of needing long-term care in later life. For example, a UK inquiry into funding long-term care noted that:

> The problem is that there is currently too much uncertainty involved for the private sector to take on the full risk. There is uncertainty over how long people will live, uncertainty over changing care and support needs, uncertainty over costs, and uncertainty over wider changes that could affect care (such as medical advances or changes to the economy). These uncertainties have meant that the sector has struggled to design affordable and attractive products that people want to buy. No country in the world relies solely on private insurance for funding the whole cost of social care.

> (Commission on Funding of Care and Support, 2011, p. 30)

Activity 7.4 Death and insurability

Allow 5 minutes for this activity.

As everyone must die one day, death is a certain-to-happen event. Why, then, are insurers still willing to offer life insurance?

Comment

The answer to Activity 7.4 is given at the end of this chapter.

4.2 The principles of insurance

The principles of insurance can be divided into two extremes: mutual insurance and commercial insurance (Mabbett, 2001). In practice, most insurance combines both elements.

Mutual insurance

Risk pooling

Spreading the cost of some individuals suffering a financial loss across a large number of people who all contribute towards that cost.

Under a mutual approach, all the people who take out a particular insurance contract are grouped together in what is often called a 'pool'. With **risk pooling**, in theory everyone in the pool could be charged the same premium (though in practice this is rare – you'll see why in Section 4.3). The money paid in (together with any return from investing it until it is needed) provides a fund from which claims are paid. There is a **cross-subsidy** from the people who don't make a claim to those who do. But everyone has the peace of mind that, if they are unlucky enough to suffer the insured event, they will get financial compensation.

Cross-subsidy

Using the money from goods or services bought by one group of customers to help pay for goods and services offered to other customers.

To take a very simple example, if there are 100 people in the pool and the risk is that 10% of them (10 people) will each claim £1000 in any year (total payouts of £10,000), then each person will need to pay a premium of £100 a year for the insurance fund to break even. If the probability of claiming rises (above 10%) or the average claim size increases (above £1000), then everyone's premium goes up.

Most mutual systems do not aim to make a profit (or any profit that is made is passed back to the policyholders as a bonus).

Commercial insurance

Commercial insurance can trace its origins to marine insurance, which goes back to Ancient Greek and Roman times, but started to formalise as an industry in the coffee shops (particularly Lloyd's) of seventeenth-century London (Birds and Hird, 2001).

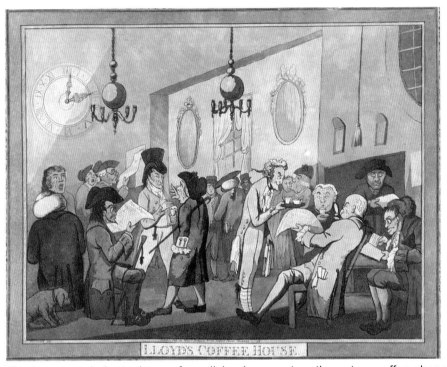

The insurance industry began formalising in seventeenth-century coffee shops

Then, backers (in essence, insurers) would agree to cover potential losses of a trading voyage should it be struck by pirates, bad weather or other disaster. Their decision was based on an estimation of the risks involved in a particular voyage given the information available, including details about the voyage, cargo and ship concerned, and about what had happened in the past to similar voyages. So, at the other extreme from mutual insurance, commercial insurance has no pooling of risk. However, there is still a pooling of information in order to estimate the individual risk as closely as possible. This is sometimes known as **risk-based pricing**.

Risk-based pricing
Charging consumers a higher amount if the likelihood of their claiming (in the case of insurance) or defaulting (in the case of loans) is higher.

For example, if there is a 10% chance of an individual claiming £1000 in any one year, the individual's annual premium needs to be set at £100 to break even. If the chance is 20%, the premium needs to be set higher at £200 a year to break even. Of course, the insurer will still be spreading its own risk across many different customers, only some of whom will claim in any particular year; but the key point is that, while mutual customers in the same pool may all pay the same price, with commercial insurance each customer may pay a different price.

Insurance in practice

The pure mutual principle was the basis, historically, of friendly societies and is most evident today in systems of social insurance. Friendly societies were originally mutual self-help groups formed by people who had some common link, such as working in the same industry. As you read in Chapter 1, members paid in and received support when ill or retired, or their families were helped if the member died. Although friendly societies still exist today, they now usually cater for any customer, not necessarily just people who have a common link.

As you learned in Chapter 2, social insurance is run by the state. Most people pay in and are then entitled to claim state benefits or services like healthcare when in need. Social insurance is mutual insurance in the sense that what people pay is not linked to their individual risk of claiming. However, it tends to be combined with a progressive tax or contribution system so that, rather than everyone paying in the same amount, those people who can afford to pay more are charged more.

Private insurance is often described as a system of risk-pooling, but it's argued that this is due more to historical circumstances than design:

> Historically, in the UK at least, almost all lines of insurance have subscribed to the principle that a customer pays a premium commensurate with the risk that they present. This has been the principle; the reality has been, inevitably, that the premium is commensurate with the insurer's best estimate of the risk presented ... So an oft-heard argument that 'sharing or pooling of risk has always been a principle of insurance' misses the point. The principle has been about pricing as accurately as possible given the techniques available at the time. This was the case in the 18th century when the price of ship insurance from Lloyd's would vary based on destination or cargo ... and it is the case in

the 21st century as highly sophisticated pricing models become widely used. But while a 'risk sharing' environment has never been a principle of insurance, it has been a historic norm created by a lack of granular risk information.

(Cullen, 2015, p. 40)

In other words, the underlying principle is that most private insurance uses risk-based pricing but, if there is not enough information from which to calculate the precise individual risk, insurers will put people with broadly similar risks into a pool. However, the pools will tend to get smaller and smaller as more detailed data becomes available, allowing people to be categorised into more precise risk groups. This process is sometimes referred to as increasing **risk segmentation**. This is clearly seen with, say, car insurance, where the premium a customer pays is based on detailed personal information, which is then matched to known risk factors; therefore premiums vary considerably between customers.

Risk segmentation
Dividing the pool of consumers for a particular type of insurance into smaller sub-pools on the basis of characteristics that are thought to predict their risk of claiming.

Activity 7.5 Risk and pricing

Allow 5 minutes for this activity.

If you were a travel insurance firm, would you offer the following customers a low insurance premium, a high insurance premium, or refuse to sell them cover? What are your reasons in each case?

1   A healthy 20-year-old travelling to Spain for a one-week beach holiday.

2   A 30-year-old, who has been in remission from cancer for the last three years, travelling to the US for a fortnight's holiday.

3   An 85-year-old, travelling to New Zealand to stay with relatives for a month.

Comment

The answers to Activity 7.5 are given at the end of this chapter.

4.3 Problems of insurance

Adverse selection
The tendency for people who have a greater than average chance of suffering an event to apply for insurance to a greater extent than other people.

The mutual approach to voluntary insurance is particularly prone to the problem of **adverse selection**. This occurs where the people who choose to take out the insurance are those at greatest risk of making a claim. For the pool as a whole, this pushes up the premiums charged. In turn, that makes the insurance look costly for people who think they have a low risk of claiming, and so more people choose not to buy the insurance. As a result, the pool shrinks and risk-spreading diminishes. In the extreme, the particular type of insurance may cease to exist, or the market for it may never get off the ground, making it impossible to insure against that event.

One solution to this is for the state to step in, using legislation or the benefits system to make insurance compulsory for all: the ultimate in risk-pooling.

For private insurers, a solution is to introduce or increase risk segmentation coupled with risk-based pricing. This means the insurer charges higher premiums to the people who pose the highest risk and lower premiums for those who pose the lowest risk. The need to address adverse selection through at least some degree of risk segmentation is one reason why pure mutual insurance, under which all members pay the same premium, is rare.

Asymmetric information
Where one party to an arrangement knows something that another does not and which, had it been known, would have affected the terms of the agreement.

Adverse selection does not just affect mutual insurance though; it is also a problem for commercial insurance because of **asymmetric information**. As soon as there is any element of risk-based pricing, information becomes key. Asymmetric information means one party to the insurance contract, in this case the person taking out the policy, has better information about the risk of their claiming than the insurer (whose starting point is evidence from groups of seemingly similar people). For example, someone working for a firm that is in financial difficulties might be more likely to take out redundancy insurance than the population as a whole, which is one reason why such cover is generally very limited, where available at all.

Insurance companies have two main strategies to try to address the problem of adverse selection caused by asymmetric information:

- **Improve the information through proposal forms, disclosure and Big Data**

  Proposal forms are sets of questions that insurers require answers to in order to assess the risk of a person making a claim, and so arrive at an appropriate premium for that person. If the person seeking insurance does not accurately and honestly disclose the information the insurer asks for, this is a breach of the insurance contract and any claims made might be turned down. These days, insurers may supplement this information from the consumer with Big Data (see Box 7.3).

- **Bypass the lack of information through exclusions**

  Instead of gathering information about potential risk factors, insurers may simply exclude certain risks from cover. The insurance contract sets out these exclusions. For example, health insurances commonly do not cover claims that arise because of pre-existing health conditions.

Box 7.3 Big Data and insurance

'Big Data' refers to very large sets of data from which computer analysis can reveal previously unmeasured associations, patterns, trends or behaviours. Sources of these data sets are commonly social media, the internet of things (like the telematics described below) and customers' account and transaction data held by firms.

One way that Big Data have an impact on insurance is through the use of telematics – devices that create data about the customer, which are passed to the insurer via the internet. For example, telematic 'black boxes' can be fitted to cars in order to gather information about time of travel, mileage, speed and braking. These data may be combined with global positioning system (GPS) information to identify where the policyholder drives and how they handle known blackspots. The data can be used to adjust car insurance premiums, check that terms and conditions of an insurance policy are being met, and even feed back to the policyholder to encourage them to drive more slowly or brake less sharply.

Young drivers, as a group, are statistically more likely to have road traffic accidents, and so usually pay much higher premiums than

---

older drivers. Telematics can help individual young drivers demonstrate that they are safer than their group as a whole, and so are eligible for lower premiums. Telematics, by shifting the focus from what a person owns to what they use and when, can also open up the market for buying car insurance for driving by the hour, rather than the usual approach of taking out an annual policy based on simply owning a car.

Similarly, telematics, in the form of wearable fitness devices, can lead to reduced health insurance premiums; they are also increasingly used in the home to generate data on, for example, whether doors and windows are closed and locked when a property is empty, which is useful for home insurers.

However, Big Data can also lead to financial exclusion if the data reveal someone to be a high risk; or, if people simply prefer not to be subject to continual data scrutiny, a lack of data may cause insurers to charge them higher premiums or refuse cover.

Moral hazard

Moral hazard
The tendency for an insured person to take on more risk because they are covered by insurance.

Another problem that can beset all types of insurance is **moral hazard**. This is the tendency of people to increase the risks they take when the cost of an event will be borne by others, such as the other people in an insurance pool or the insurer. For example, when a home's contents are insured, the inhabitants may be less prepared to spend on installing an alarm, and more carefree about leaving windows open when they are out, safe in the knowledge that any loss can be claimed on their insurance.

Insurance policies have features designed to combat moral hazard, including:

- **Terms and conditions**

  These may specify that insurance cover is valid only if the policyholder behaves in a certain way. For example, home insurance policyholders may be required to fit high-standard locks to their home's external doors and downstairs windows.

- **Exclusions**

  Some risks may simply be excluded. For example, travel insurance may exclude cover for winter sports or water sports (unless this additional cover is added and an extra premium paid).

Insurers face the problem of moral hazard

- **Excess**

    A policy excess is the first part of any loss that must be borne by policyholders themselves. Sharing the loss creates a financial incentive for the policyholder to be more careful and also deters them from making small claims (which saves the insurer administration costs). Policies often have a compulsory excess meaning that the policyholder has no choice but to accept they will share in any loss. With a voluntary excess, the policyholder chooses to have an excess (or a larger one) in return for a reduction in the premium.

- **No claims discount**

    This is a reduction in the premium, which increases for each year that the policyholder does not make a claim. If a claim is made, then some or all of the discount is lost, increasing the cost of the following year's premium. Like a policy excess, this is a financial incentive to encourage policyholders to behave in ways that reduce the likelihood of making a claim and to refrain from making small claims.

- **Big Data and telematics**

   As described in Box 7.3, with devices that we wear or that are implanted in the things that we use becoming increasingly ubiquitous, it is becoming easier for insurers to monitor and charge us for risky behaviour.

Activity 7.6 You and your insurance

Allow 5 minutes for this activity.

Think about any insurance policies you or your household currently have, or have had in the past.

1 Do they have any terms and conditions or exclusions that have caused you to make any changes to your way of life or how you look after your possessions?

2 Has an excess or no claims discount ever deterred you from claiming?

Comment

Everyone's experiences will be different, but here are some of Jonquil's (one of the Chapter 7 authors):

1 When I had to fit a new front-door lock, I made sure to buy one that met the standard specified in my home insurance policy. And on family holidays my dad used to take all our luggage into a hotel on an overnight stop, because the car insurance excluded claims for luggage left in the car overnight (even in a locked boot).

2 When I disturbed a burglar who'd broken a patio window trying to get into my home, I did make a claim, but with hindsight I wish I hadn't because on top of having to pay a £200 excess, I lost all of the no claims discount on the buildings section of my home insurance. This doubled the next year's premium and still affects the amount I'm paying.

---

5 Measuring risk

In Section 4 you saw that central to how insurance works is measuring how likely policyholders are to make a claim on their policies; in other words, estimating the risk involved, in order to calculate accurate premiums.

Risk is not the same as what will or will not be. The risk of something happening to you may be very low, but that does not mean it will not happen. By the same token, something can be quite probable and yet, by chance, never come to pass.

With some events, the probability of the event or a particular outcome occurring can be calculated by applying basic principles. But with other types of event, such as the chance of your car being stolen, there is no way to make that sort of definitive calculation. Nevertheless, by looking at past records for thefts of similar cars, in similar areas, in similar circumstances, the probability can be estimated.

While insurers use the second approach – using lots of data to estimate risk – it is easier to understand risk if we start with the sort of events where the probability can be precisely calculated. But first a word on how to express probabilities.

5.1 Expressing probabilities

Probability is a way of measuring the chance of a particular event occurring. There are various ways of expressing probabilities, but the most common is on a scale of 0 to 1. If an event has a probability of 0, there is no chance whatsoever of it happening. For example, the probability of pigs flying (unaided) is 0. If an event has a probability of 1, then it definitely will happen. As death is certain to happen at some point, it has a lifetime probability of 1.

Events that *might* happen have a probability between 0 and 1. The closer the probability of an event is to 1, the more likely it is to happen. The closer it is to 0, the smaller the chance of it happening.

There are other ways of expressing probabilities, which we often use in everyday speech:

- a one-in-ten chance is another way of saying 0.1 probability, or $\frac{1}{10}$th

- you have a 50–50 or 'evens' chance of getting heads with a single toss of a coin, which is the same as a probability of 0.5, 50%, or a half.

Figure 7.1 shows how to express some probabilities as decimals, or alternatively as percentages or fractions.

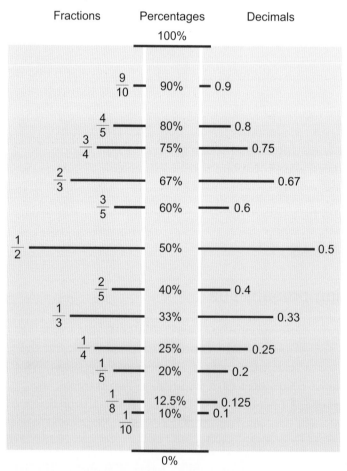

Figure 7.1 Alternative ways of expressing probabilities: fractions, percentages or decimals

If you want to compare the probabilities of several different events occurring, you first need to make sure all the probabilities are expressed in the same way (either as fractions, percentages or decimals).

This may mean you need to convert some probabilities:

- **From decimals to percentages**: multiply by 100. For example $0.5 \times 100 = 50\%$.

- **From percentages to decimals**: ignore the "%" symbol and divide by 100. For example $50\ (\%) \div 100 = 0.5$.

- **From decimals to fractions** $(\frac{1}{X})$: to calculate the value of X in the fraction, divide 1 by the decimal (it's often best to use a calculator for this).

  For example, to express a probability of 0.5 as a fraction: $1 \div 0.5 = 2$. As 2 is the X value in the fraction, a 0.5 probability is the same as $\frac{1}{2}$ (or a one-in-two chance).

- **From fractions to decimals**: divide the top number of the fraction by the bottom. For example, to express a probability of $\frac{1}{2}$ as a decimal, the calculation you need to do is $1 \div 2 = 0.5$.

Activity 7.7 Comparing probabilities

Allow 10 minutes for this activity.

In an extraordinarily crime-ridden town, House A has a $\frac{2}{9}$ chance of being burgled, House B, a 12% chance, and House C, a chance of 0.4.

Which house has the highest probability of being burgled?

Comment

The answer to Activity 7.7 is given at the end of this chapter.

5.2 Calculating probabilities from basic principles

In this section, we're going to use the example of dice, rather than life events, to demonstrate some basic principles when working with probabilities. The useful aspect of dice is that there is a known and limited set of possible 'events'. We'll assume the dice have not been loaded in any way, and that on every throw one side lands clearly face up.

With dice, exact probabilities can be calculated

Probability of a single event

If you have one dice that you roll once, there are six possible events: getting a 1, a 2, a 3, a 4, a 5, or a 6. You can be 100% sure (a probability of 1) that one of these events will occur. Since each of the six events is equally likely, the probability of any one event occurring is $\frac{1}{6}$ (a one-in-six chance), which, if you prefer, can be expressed as 0.167 or 16.7%.

Probability of either of two events

If you throw one dice once, the six possible events (throwing 1, 2, 3, 4, 5 or 6) are called **mutually exclusive** events because, if one event happens, the others cannot – your single dice cannot simultaneously land with both the 6 and the 2 face up.

If you want to know the probability that either of two (or more) mutually exclusive events will happen, just add together the probabilities of each event. For example, the probability of throwing a 6 or a 2 with one throw of one dice is: $\frac{1}{6} + \frac{1}{6} = \frac{2}{6}$ (which is the same as $\frac{1}{3}$).

But some events are not mutually exclusive (both can happen at the same time). So how do you work out the probability of either event happening in that case?

Suppose you have two dice and you want to work out the probability of either throwing a double or scoring ten.

- There are 36 possible events when you throw two dice; you might like to try listing them all on a sheet of paper if you're unsure about this.

- There are **three** ways to score ten:
  – throw a 4 with the first dice and a 6 with the second
  – throw a 5 with both dice
  – throw a 6 with the first dice and a 4 with the second.

  That means the probability of scoring ten is $\frac{3}{36}$.

- There are **six** ways to throw a double, so the probability is $\frac{6}{36}$.

Mutually exclusive
Describes two or more events that cannot occur together.

But to find the probability of scoring ten **or** throwing a double, you cannot simply add $\frac{3}{36}$ and $\frac{6}{36}$ together, because you'll have counted 'throwing double 5' twice – both as a double and one of the ways of scoring ten.

You need to correct the calculation by removing one of the double-counted events (so it is only counted once). In this example therefore, the answer would be:

$$\frac{3}{36} \text{ (probability of scoring 10)} + \frac{6}{36} \text{ (probability of throwing a double)}$$

minus

$$\frac{1}{36} \text{ (one of the 'double 5' events)}$$

$$=$$

$$\frac{8}{36}$$

Activity 7.8 Probability of either event

Allow 5 minutes for this activity.

Imagine you have taken out insurance to cover a community picnic in case it is called off because of bad weather. Suppose the probability of severe rain is $\frac{3}{10}$, the probability of high winds is $\frac{1}{5}$, and the probability of both is $\frac{3}{20}$, what is the probability of either rain or wind preventing the event going ahead?

Comment

The answer to Activity 7.8 is given at the end of this chapter.

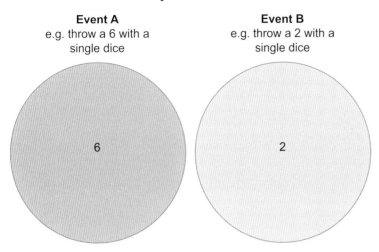

Mutually exclusive events

Event A
e.g. throw a 6 with a
single dice

Event B
e.g. throw a 2 with a
single dice

6

2

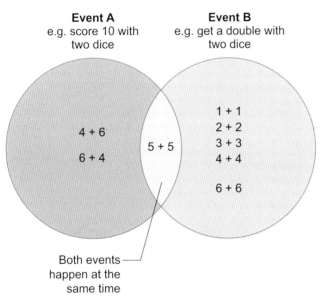

Not mutually exclusive events

Event A
e.g. score 10 with
two dice

Event B
e.g. get a double with
two dice

4 + 6

6 + 4

5 + 5

1 + 1
2 + 2
3 + 3
4 + 4

6 + 6

Both events
happen at the
same time

Figure 7.2 Events that cannot happen (mutually exclusive) and can happen
at the same time

Probability of two events both happening

Sometimes we want to know the probability of two (or more) events
occurring together. If the chance of one of these events happening is
not altered by the other one having happened, they are called
independent events. In that case, the probability of them both
happening is found by multiplying the probability of each event.

Independent events
Where one event
occurring does not
affect the probability
of the other(s)
occurring.

For example, suppose you have a pack of cards. A standard pack without jokers has 52 cards, comprising 13 cards of each suit: spades, hearts, diamonds and clubs. The chance of drawing a heart is therefore $\frac{13}{52}$. If you replace the card in the pack, you are back to the same situation as before and the chance of drawing a second heart is also $\frac{13}{52}$.

So the chance of drawing two hearts is: $\dfrac{13}{52} \times \dfrac{13}{52} = \dfrac{1}{16}$

But often events are not independent because the outcome of one event alters the chance of what happens next. To take an example that influences insurance premiums: when a home has been burgled once, the chance of it being burgled again increases – because the criminals know the layout of the property and are banking on stolen goods having been replaced with tempting new ones (Confused.com, 2014).

Non-independent scenarios can also be demonstrated using the pack of cards. As before, the chance of drawing a heart is $\frac{13}{52}$. But what is the chance of drawing a second heart if, in this case, the first card is not replaced? The second card is being drawn from a pack that now has only 51 cards and the chance of a second heart is $\frac{12}{51}$. The first event – being a heart – has altered the probability of the second event – the second heart – because there is one less heart and one less card in the remaining pack. The probability of drawing two hearts in succession is therefore:

$$\frac{13}{52} \times \frac{12}{51} = \frac{156}{2652} \text{ or } \frac{1}{17}$$

It has become less probable than when the card was replaced in the previous example ($\frac{1}{17}$ is smaller than $\frac{1}{16}$).

Non-independent events: drawing cards without replacing them

Activity 7.9 Independent events

Allow 5 minutes for this activity.

Which of the following 'events' are likely to be independent?

(a) Being six-feet tall and having a car accident.

(b) Working in a bank and having an accident at work.

(c) Having a lodger and being burgled.

Comment

The answers to Activity 7.9 are given at the end of this chapter.

5.3 Calculating statistical probabilities

You have seen in Activity 7.9 that principles of probability, such as independence, can apply to life events. However, the simple formulae of dice and cards do not, because in real-world situations there is usually no neatly defined set of possible events, so the probabilities will be complex, relying on a multitude of factors.

Think about a home being damaged by fire. The probability of this happening will vary depending on factors including: the materials the home is made from; the hazards inside, such as old wiring; and the habits of the residents, such as smoking. Moreover, outcomes might range from trivial (a small burn on a carpet) to major (a whole building being destroyed), so there may be questions about what even counts as an 'event'.

Actuaries
Professionals who analyse risk and its financial impact.

While the risk posed by the interaction of these many factors cannot be precisely calculated, it can be estimated through statistical analysis of data. This type of estimation is the work of specialists called **actuaries**.

Actuaries look at the probabilities of, say, dying at different ages, developing different types of ill health, losing property, causing injury to others, and even the likelihood of having twins or a local fête being rained off. When actuaries estimate the probability of events, they do so on the basis of sophisticated modelling. It's not just a case of extrapolating from the past into the future; they adapt their calculations to include new and emerging knowledge about how things may change in the future. For example, estimating the possible future impact of climate change is important to home insurers because it tends to increase the chance of claims due to, say, flooding and storm damage.

6 Decisions about insurance

Risk is part and parcel of life for all of us, so decisions about insurance are important both for individuals and households, and for society as a whole.

6.1 Decisions for individuals and households

In just a few areas of life, private insurance tends to be compulsory. For example, in most developed countries, anyone who drives on public roads is legally required to have at least 'third-party' insurance to pay out if the driver hurts other people or damages their property while driving. Employers must usually by law have insurance to compensate their employees if they suffer injury at work. In many countries, private medical insurance is compulsory. Also, as a contractual requirement, mortgage lenders will insist that the property against which the mortgage is secured is covered by buildings insurance.

In most other cases, it's up to each individual or household to decide whether to take out insurance. Rationally, an individual or household would be more likely to take out insurance:

- the higher the perceived probability of bad events happening

- the greater the maximum sum that might be lost

- the lower the cost of insurance cover

- the lower the availability and amount of other financial resources, such as extended family or savings, which they could fall back on instead.

However, insurance decisions are not always made in such a rational way. In general, people are affected by a variety of behavioural traits and some may make them more inclined to buy insurance than rational analysis would suggest is necessary.

Loss aversion
A tendency to give greater importance to avoiding losses than to making gains of the same size.

For example, **loss aversion** may cause some people to value avoiding potential future losses more highly than the saving on premiums by not buying insurance (even where the chance of an event occurring is low and the cost of insurance is high relative to the chance of it paying out). This can make them particularly susceptible to sales pressure and mis-selling, for example of PPI and extended warranties.

Another common behavioural trait is **availability bias**. This means we tend to overemphasise the importance of recent events (thinking them more likely to recur than is really the case) and underestimate other events. For example, Gallagher (2014) found that purchase of flood insurance in the US spiked in both flooded and non-flooded areas covered by the same TV region immediately after a serious flood, and then sales steadily declined back to their normal level.

Availability bias
The tendency to give greatest weight to examples and events that are most easily recalled.

On the other hand, other behavioural traits may deter people from taking out insurance when it would be useful. For example:

- **Over-confidence bias** – underestimating the likelihood of future adverse events occurring, such as falling ill, and so failing to take out insurance that would protect against a consequent loss of earnings.

- **Choice overload** – being deterred from making any decision because there are too many competing insurance products to choose from. This behavioural trait was demonstrated in a famous experiment involving jam (Iyengar and Leppar, 2000). They invited customers in a supermarket to sample jams and then use a money-off voucher to buy a pot. Of the customers invited to sample six jams, 30% made a purchase. But only 3% of the customers invited to sample 24 jams made a purchase.

Choice overload can deter people from making decisions

6.2 Choices for society

Buying insurance is a way to build resilience into financial planning, by protecting individuals and households from the financial impact of life events and the unexpected. However, in most cases, access to private insurance depends on being able to afford it. Households with low income or who are deemed high risk may be priced out of the market. In extreme cases, high-risk households may be denied cover altogether. Societies have a range of ways to address these issues:

* At one extreme, a rather brutal option is to accept that some groups will be denied access to the financial security that insurance can provide. Depending on their financial circumstances, these groups may be able to get help from family, friends, charitable organisations or other community groups, either in cash or kind when adverse events happen.

- In some countries, the cost of key insurances may be borne by employers. They may be required by law or simply by social norms to provide, say, sick pay and private medical insurance. Employees might pay for this indirectly, if employers are able to offset the cost of including such insurances in remuneration packages by paying lower wages. For individuals, a downside is that being self-employed, unemployed or doing unpaid work puts them outside this employer provision.

- The state can play a part in various ways. In this chapter, and earlier in Chapter 2, we considered cash support through contributory social insurance schemes and non-contributory means-tested benefits. Social insurance may be the only way to fill gaps left where private insurance is unprofitable or too uncertain, as in the example of care insurance (discussed in Section 4.1 of this chapter).

- Another option is for the state to provide public services that remove the need for insurance, as in the case of free-at-the-point-of-use health services (such as the UK's NHS). It may also use public spending and regulation to reduce the chance of adverse events – for example, by spending on flood defences or setting minimum fire-prevention standards.

- The state may support insurance cover in other ways – for example, by providing subsidies. These could be in the form of tax relief direct to policyholders to encourage take-up – in the UK, until the mid 1980s, life insurance was subsidised in this way. Alternatively, subsidies may be given to insurers, so that they reduce the price they charge for cover, or provide cover free to vulnerable groups – these features are common in the US medical insurance system.

7 Conclusion

In this chapter, you have looked at how individuals and households can take steps now to make their financial planning more resilient in the face of expected and unexpected future life events. This may involve using savings as a form of self-insurance, but more often relies on buying appropriate cover from insurance companies or mutual organisations. The cover required may be reduced if the state or employers provide some help.

You have seen that being able to measure risk underpins insurance products and, in a more intuitive way, informs individual and household decisions about taking out insurance. Wherever there is risk, insurance is likely to flourish. But policies can be complex. Insurers and consumers can sometimes seem to be in a wary dance with each other: consumers may be unsure what they are buying and vulnerable to mis-selling; meanwhile insurers are constantly striving to improve information about the risks they are taking on and to discourage policyholders from risky behaviour.

There is a tension between the two principles behind insurance: the mutual system and the commercial. Adverse selection and the growing availability of new data – for example, through telematics – are driving the commercial approach and increasing risk segmentation. This is good news for individuals and households who can demonstrate that they are low risk and eligible for reduced premiums, but may leave others with reduced access to private insurance. This may increase the need for state intervention to fill gaps and influence the way private insurance develops.

Answers to activities in Chapter 7

Answers to Activity 7.2

Here are some ways to keep down the cost of home insurance – you may have thought of others:

- fitting better door locks

- fitting a burglar alarm

- joining a neighbourhood watch scheme

- agreeing to a voluntary excess (which means policyholders agree to cover the first part of any claim themselves, reducing the amount their insurers pay out)

- building up a no claims discount (a reduction in next year's premium provided no claims have been made) by not claiming for small losses.

Answer to Activity 7.4

Insurers look at the probability of an event happening during a specified time period. While death is certain, the timing of death usually is not. For example, the risk of a healthy person dying before retirement is measurable and low, so insurers are happy to offer cover against this risk. As a person's age increases the cost of cover rises, and steeply for very old people.

Answers to Activity 7.5

An insurer would base its judgement on many more factors than have been provided here. However, on the information given, the likely answers are:

1 Low premium – because there is a low risk of a young, healthy person making a claim.

2 Refuse cover – this might mean selling them no travel insurance at all, or alternatively providing a policy that excludes cover for any cancer-related claims. The reasoning is that there is a high risk that this traveller will need healthcare while away, and potentially will make big claims because of the high cost of medical care in the US.

In the past, insurers have tended to pool together all people who have had cancer within the last ten years as too high risk to cover. However, this is an area where more, and better, information, especially in the light of improved cancer treatments, might enable insurers to more accurately measure a declining risk the longer someone has been in remission.

3 High premium – because of the greater risk that an elderly person will need medical treatment (or may even die) while away.

Answer to Activity 7.7

The probabilities need to be converted to the same format before they can be compared. It doesn't matter which format (decimals, percentages or fractions) – you choose what you prefer:

- **Decimals:** House A = 0.2222 (2 divided by 9); House B = 0.12 (12 (%) divided by 100); House C = 0.4. The decimal is highest for C, so House C has the highest probability of being burgled.

- **Percentages:** House A = 22.2% (2 divided by 9 and multiplied by 100); House B = 12%; House C = 40% (0.4 multiplied by 100). The percentage is highest for C, so House C has the highest probability of being burgled.

- **Fractions ('one in' format):** For House A the fraction currently has '2' on top, so divide the top and the bottom of the fraction by 2 to get the '$\frac{1}{X}$' format, giving:

House A = $\frac{1}{4.5}$

House B = $\frac{1}{8.333}$ (first divide 12 (%) by 100 to get 0.12; then divide 1 by 0.12).

House C = $\frac{1}{2.5}$ (divide 1 by 0.4).

The bottom of the fraction is smallest for House C, so House C has the highest probability of being burgled.

Answer to Activity 7.8

Rain does not prevent it being windy, or vice versa, so these events are not mutually exclusive. Therefore, to find the probability of either event happening, you need to add together the probability of each event ($\frac{3}{10} + \frac{1}{5}$) and then subtract the double-counting (the $\frac{3}{20}$ probability that it will be both rainy and windy).

The calculation is: $\dfrac{3}{10} + \dfrac{1}{5} - \dfrac{3}{20}$

Bear in mind that you need to convert these probabilities to fractions with the same denominator (the number on the bottom). A common factor is 20, so $\frac{3}{10}$ becomes $\frac{6}{20}$ and $\frac{1}{5}$ becomes $\frac{4}{20}$.

This means the answer is:

$$\frac{6 + 4 - 3}{20} = \frac{7}{20} \text{ (or 0.35)}$$

Answers to Activity 7.9

(a) Height (at least within a fairly 'normal' range) is unlikely to be associated with the risk of, say, having a car accident. So these 'events' are **likely to be independent**.

(b) Working in a bank – typically a desk-based job – is generally considered to be a low-risk occupation compared with, say, working on a building site. So working in a bank could reduce the chance of having an accident at work. Therefore these 'events' are **unlikely to be independent**. As a result, insurance companies will normally ask people taking out, say, income protection insurance what job they do.

(c) These 'events' are also **unlikely to be completely independent** – for example, the presence of the lodger might mean the property is occupied more of the time and so less likely to be broken into. Insurance companies may, therefore, reduce the premium if a lodger moves in.

References

Association of British Insurers (ABI) (2016) *Home insurance – what you need to know* [Online]. Available at www.abi.org.uk/globalassets/sitecore/files/documents/publications/public/2016/home-insurance/home-insurance-what-you-need-to-know.pdf (Accessed 17 April 2018).

Birds, J. and Hird, N.J. (2001) *Birds' Modern Insurance Law*, 5th edn, London, Sweet & Maxwell.

Commission on Funding of Care and Support (2011) *Fairer Care Funding* ('Dilnot Commission report') [Online]. Available at http://webarchive.nationalarchives.gov.uk/20130221121534/http://www.dilnotcommission.dh.gov.uk/our-report/ (Accessed 4 July 2017).

Competition Commission (2009) *Market Investigation into Payment Protection Insurance* [Online]. Available at http://webarchive.nationalarchives.gov.uk/20140403003432/http://www.competition-commission.org.uk/assets/competitioncommission/docs/pdf/non-inquiry/rep_pub/reports/2009/fulltext/542.pdf (Accessed 28 July 2017).

Confused.com (2014) *Burglars' code of conduct revealed* [Online]. Available at www.confused.com/press/releases/previous-years/burglars-code-of-conduct-revealed (Accessed 17 April 2018).

Cullen, M. (2015) 'Insurers, risk assessment and availability of insurance', in ABI, *A Brave New World* [Online]. Available at www.abi.org.uk/~/media/Files/Documents/Publications/Public/2015/A%20Brave%20New%20World/A%20Brave%20New%20World.pdf (Accessed 2 February 2016).

Financial Conduct Authority (FCA) (2017) *Monthly PPI refunds and compensation* [Online]. Available at www.fca.org.uk/consumers/payment-protection-insurance/monthly-ppi-refunds-and-compensation (Accessed 28 July 2017).

Gallagher, J. (2014) 'Learning about an infrequent event: evidence from flood insurance take-up in the US', *American Economic Journal: Applied Economics*, vol. 6, no. 3, pp. 206–33. Also available online at http://faculty.weatherhead.case.edu/jpg75/pdfs/flood_insurance_aeja.pdf (Accessed 24 July 2017).

Iyengar, S. S. and Leppar, M. R. (2000) 'When choice is demotivating. Can one desire too much of a good thing', *Journal of Personality & Social Psychology*, vol. 79, no. 6, pp. 995–1006 [Online]. DOI 10.1037//0022-3514.79.6.995. Available at https://faculty.washington.edu/jdb/345/345%20Articles/Iyengar%20%26%20Lepper%20(2000).pdf (Accessed 7 March 2018).

Lloyd's (2017) *Innovation and unusual risks* [Online]. Available at http://www.lloyds.com/lloyds/about-us/history/innovation-and-unusual-risks (Accessed 26 July 2017).

Mabbett, D. (2001). 'Mutuality in insurance and social security: retrospect and prospect', in Birchall, J. (ed.) *The New Mutualism in Public Policy*, London, Routledge. Also available online at www.bbk.ac.uk/politics/our-staff/academic/deborah-mabbett (Accessed 2 February 2016).

To cite this chapter, use the following format in your reference list:

Lowe, J. and Fribbance, I. (2019) 'Insurance and life events', in De Henau, J. and Lowe, J. (eds) *Personal Finance*, Milton Keynes, The Open University, pp. 295–342.

Chapter 8
Pensions

Jonquil Lowe

Contents

1 Introduction

In the news

'Brazilian Workers Protest Against Pension Changes: Workers across Brazil staged demonstrations over the government's plans to cap pension benefits and raise the retirement age.'

(Reeves, 2017)

'Pension poverty: millions face RUNNING OUT of money as they live to record old age.'

(O'Grady, 2016)

'Eight Largest Pensions Systems Will Have $400 Trillion Gap by 2050: World Economic Forum warns of "imperilling the incomes of future generations".'

(Katz, 2017)

Headlines like these have become increasingly familiar during the first quarter of the twenty-first century. Around the world, pundits are full of doom, predicting a future of impoverished pensioners and overburdened workers, often casting these issues as a conflict between the generations. Why is this the case, and are commentators right to be so gloomy and divisive? By the end of this chapter you will have an insight into the background to these sorts of claims and what they mean for individuals' and households' planning for financial security in later life.

I start by looking briefly, in Section 2, at the meaning of retirement, before moving on, in Section 3, to consider the role of **pension systems** and, in Section 4, how different types of pension schemes work. In Section 5 I turn to the pressure on pension systems as a result of ageing populations across the world – a phenomenon you considered in Chapter 1 on setting the context. In Section 6 I'll look at the way pension systems are being reformed because of this demographic shift. Against that backdrop, Section 7 explores the practical steps that individuals and households can take to improve their chances of achieving their retirement goals.

Pension systems
Arrangements designed to ensure that older people have some income to live on when they cease to have earnings from work.

2 What is retirement?

"I'm semi-retired."

CartoonStock.com

Retirement
Can mean the period of life after work ends, a life event that marks the end of working life, or a process of gradually withdrawing from work.

Pension
A regular payment that forms all or part of financial support in older age.

The meaning of 'retirement' has been changing

The term **retirement** is often loosely used to mean a period of later life after a person has stopped working – whether this is paid or unpaid work. In countries like the UK this used to be a cliff-edge event in the life course: a person would be working one week and retired the next. These days, retirement is often a process of more gradual withdrawal from work, with many people choosing or having to carry on working past the age at which they are able to draw a **pension**. So, retirement can be a period of life, an event or a process, and you will need to bear that shifting definition in mind as you explore the subject of pensions.

3 The role of pension systems

Pension systems are the main way of ensuring people have some income in retirement. Two key aims of pensions systems are smoothing consumption and alleviating poverty (Holzmann and Hinz, 2005).

Pension systems may be **state pension schemes** – in other words, public schemes provided by the government – or **private pension schemes** provided by employers or arranged directly by individuals themselves.

State pension scheme
A system of pensions provided by the government to everyone who qualifies.

Private pension scheme
Refers to any non-state pension scheme, typically provided through employers or arranged by individuals themselves.

Like many countries, Germany promotes saving through private pension schemes

3.1 Consumption smoothing

Most people would like to maintain broadly the same standard of living after retirement as they have achieved during their working lives. So, typically, they are willing to give up some consumption during their working years to support continuing consumption later on. This process is called consumption smoothing.

The need for income later on may be lower because retired households tend to be smaller, any children having grown up and left by then, and spending may be less, particularly on things like commuting and home ownership. Financial advisers often suggest that households aim for a gross retirement income that is, say, two-thirds or half their pre-retirement income. But this is just a rough rule of thumb. When setting a retirement income goal, it's usually better to start by estimating spending needs in retirement.

Activity 8.1 How might spending in retirement be different?

Allow 10 minutes for this activity.

If you're of working age, imagine how your spending might change when you reach retirement. If you've already retired, what changes did you make?

Comment

The answer to this activity is at the end of the chapter.

The main way to smooth consumption over the life course is to save and invest during the working years, then turn those savings into income during the period of retirement. This can be demonstrated using the cash flow diagram, as in Figure 8.1, for a fictional person, whom I'll call Callum.

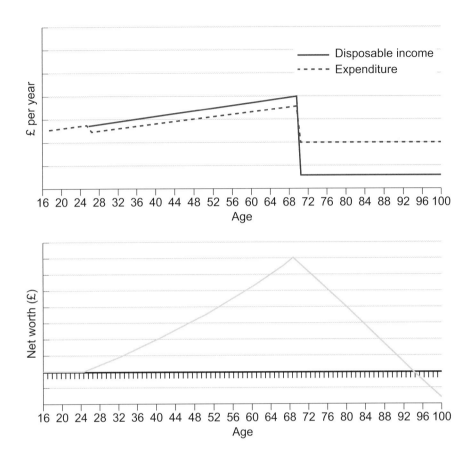

Figure 8.1 Cash flow and assets when planning for retirement

Callum has a very simple life course – no debts, no sudden life events. The only significant aspects of his cash flow are that he has steadily rising real disposable income during his working life and, from age 25, starts to save through a private pension scheme. This continues until age 70. In the lower chart you can see his net assets growing.

At 70, Callum retires. He has some steady income from a state pension that will be paid for as long as he lives: you can see that as the solid income line in the upper chart. The upper chart also shows that his spending in retirement is higher than his state pension income, so he draws out his savings to fund the gap. In the lower chart you can see his net worth falling as the savings are used up until they run out at age 94. (Callum might consider other options that mean his savings don't run out; I'll return to this in Section 7.2.)

3.2 Poverty alleviation

A fundamental problem with reliance on private pension systems is that they are little use to people who cannot afford to save. An important aspect of state pension schemes is that they can include features designed to overcome this problem.

Pension systems may aim to avoid pensioner poverty

State schemes can ensure that pensioners receive at least the minimum income they need to live on. This might be achieved through a means-tested pension (paid only to those whose income and savings are below a specified threshold). However, the availability of a means-tested pension could discourage people on modest incomes from saving privately for retirement. Activity 8.2 demonstrates how this happens.

Activity 8.2 Means-tested pensions

Allow 5 minutes for this activity.

Suppose a country guarantees its pensioners will have at least £150 a week to live on. If their income is less, a state means-tested pension tops up their income to that level.

1 Don has saved enough to provide himself with a private pension of £130 a week. How much means-tested pension can he get? What is his total income from these two pensions?

2 Haneen has saved enough to provide herself with a private pension of £145 a week. How much means-tested pension can she get? What is her total income from these two pensions? How does she fare compared to Don?

Comment

The answers to this activity are at the end of the chapter.

Governments can remove the disincentive to save by designing a means-tested system in such a way that claimants can keep at least some income resulting from their private saving. Alternatively, governments can design a system that does not use means-testing, such as a contribution-based system (where a pension is received by all who pay in).

The UK has a contribution-based state pension system. Workers and employers pay National Insurance contributions (NICs). A record is kept of the contributions paid. Provided a worker has a minimum number of years of contributions, they will qualify for the state pension when they reach a specified state pension age. Crucially for guarding against poverty in retirement, people of working age may be given National Insurance credits. These fill gaps in their contribution record during certain periods when they are unable to work – for example, because of caring responsibilities, illness or unemployment. These caring credits are particularly important in ensuring that women have an equal opportunity to men to build up a full state pension. In some countries (such as Belgium), university graduates too may claim credits, for their study years, but not in the UK.

Typically, state schemes provide a basic level of income that individuals and households are expected to top up through private saving if they want to enjoy a reasonably comfortable retirement.

3.3 Encouraging saving for retirement

A problem with relying on private pension systems to generate retirement income is the need for people to act rationally: in other words, choosing to make the necessary savings earlier in life to allow them to smooth their consumption as they shift into retirement. In reality, we are all subject to an array of behavioural traits that make us very bad at planning ahead in this way. Just a few of these traits are:

- **myopia (being short-sighted)** – a tendency to ignore the future and hope it will sort itself out somehow

- **present bias** – giving some thought to the future, but underestimating the value of benefits and costs that occur in the future compared with the value we place on them if experienced today

- **inertia (also called status quo bias)** – a tendency to stick with the current state of affairs rather than making changes, especially if changes would require a lot of mental or physical effort

- **over-confidence** – manifesting, in this case, as a tendency to assume all will go well in retirement and so underestimating the chance of, say, high spending on healthcare, or high inflation and poor investment returns reducing the income available.

Activity 8.3 Your own biases

Allow 5 minutes for this activity.

Can you think of an occasion when your actions or lack of action – not necessarily related to pensions – may have been influenced by these behavioural traits: myopia, present bias, inertia and over-confidence?

Comment

Here's my own admission! I have a private pension scheme where I choose how to invest my retirement savings. I'm quite good at choosing different investment funds when I pay new money in, but seldom switch my existing holdings. I think that's inertia at work.

Governments have a range of tools for trying to change people's saving behaviour, as represented by the scale in Figure 8.2.

Compulsory saving for retirement (state or private schemes)	Automatic enrolment into a pension scheme but with right to opt out	Matched saving from the state or employer	Tax relief from state on amount saved	Financial education to raise awaremess of outcomes if don't save

Compulsion   Persuasion

Figure 8.2 Policies to promote saving through private pension schemes

As Figure 8.2 shows, at one extreme is compulsion, forcing people to make provision for retirement – most commonly through a state pension scheme.

Automatic enrolment is one step down from compulsion. It goes with the grain of the behavioural traits, by altering the choice that individuals face. Instead of making a decision to save, the individual is put into a private pension scheme regardless, but can opt out. This means that inertia now works in favour of continuing to save. People might also be more inclined to stay in the scheme if that is what everyone else is doing, thus making a culture of saving the social norm.

Matched saving is where the state and/or employers add to the amount an individual pays into a pension scheme. It can be seen as a way of tackling present bias by reducing the cost today and boosting the value tomorrow. In the UK, from 2019, the automatic enrolment system requires a minimum 8% of salary to be paid into most people's workplace pensions, with half of this coming from the employer and the government combined.

With some pension arrangements, rather than directly matching part or all of what the individual pays, the government provides tax relief on that amount. This might also tackle present bias, but by definition only taxpayers benefit (and not those who have too little income to pay tax).

Finally, financial education might reduce myopia and present bias by heightening awareness of the consequences of not saving, and might reduce inertia if it makes the process of saving seem simpler.

There is little evidence on whether methods of persuasion work. A study by the National Audit Office (2014) found that the UK tax authority did not routinely monitor the effectiveness of tax reliefs. The fact that the UK introduced automatic enrolment from 2012 in response to inadequate pension saving suggests that the many previous decades of tax relief for pension saving had not been that successful. Some large-scale international studies of financial education (for example, Fernandes et al., 2014) have concluded that its effect on financial behaviour, although positive, is tiny.

4 How pension schemes work

To take your understanding of how to plan for retirement further, you need to know something about how different types of scheme work. Pension schemes can be described in several different ways:

- who provides or organises them

- the basis on which the pensions are calculated

- the way they are financed.

4.1 Who provides pension schemes?

You have already seen that there are two broad types of pension schemes:

- State pension schemes are provided by the government.

- Private schemes are provided by employers or arranged individually. Employers can include the state in its role as an employer of, for example, health workers, teachers and government officials.

Private pensions can be further divided into two types: **occupational pension schemes** and **personal pension schemes**. The three types of scheme are represented in Figure 8.3 – the availability and importance of each type varies from one country to another.

Occupational pension scheme
Scheme arranged by an employer to provide pensions for its workers and towards which the employer normally makes a substantial financial contribution.

Personal pension scheme
Saving scheme designed to provide retirement income for one particular individual. The scheme may be arranged by the individual or by their employer.

Provided by the state	Provided by employers	Provided by employers or arranged individually
State pension scheme	Occupational pension schemes	Personal pensions

Figure 8.3 Three main types of pension scheme by provider

With occupational pension schemes, an employer is normally obliged to pay into the scheme on behalf of their employees, though the scheme design usually requires workers to contribute something as well. These schemes may be provided by a single employer or be multi-employer schemes that cover workers from more than one employer.

Personal pension schemes are typically run by insurance companies or investment firms. Each person has their own separate plan. Personal pension schemes may be chosen and taken out by an individual or, alternatively, an employer may select the scheme and offer membership to workers through the workplace. Unless a country's legislation requires it (as in the case of workers within the scope of the UK's automatic enrolment laws), employers do not usually make contributions to an individual's personal pension scheme.

Defined benefit
Describes a pension scheme where the pension is worked out according to a formula, usually linked to pay (but sometimes just a fixed amount) and length of time in the scheme.

Defined contribution
Describes a pension scheme where the pension depends on the amount paid in, how the invested money grows and the amount of pension it can be converted to in retirement.

The term 'workplace pension' generally applies to any pension scheme available through work, which could be an occupational, multi-employer or personal scheme. In the UK, by law, employers must contribute to a workplace pension scheme for most of their employees.

4.2 How pensions are worked out

There are two main ways in which the amount of retirement income from a pension scheme is determined: on the basis of **defined benefit** or **defined contribution**.

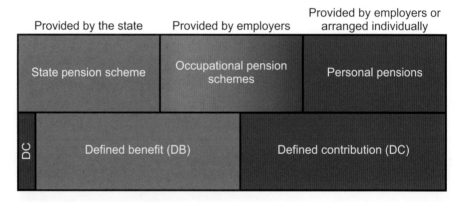

Figure 8.4 How pensions are worked out

Defined benefit schemes

In a defined benefit (DB) scheme, the members are promised a certain level of pension when they retire. Figure 8.4 illustrates which schemes tend to work on the basis of a defined benefit. To read the diagram, start at the top layer and look down to the next layer to see how the layers overlap:

- You can see that nearly all state pension schemes work on a defined benefit basis. They often pay the same rate of pension to all who qualify. Although most state schemes provide just a basic income, this does not have to be the case. State schemes can be designed to include quite generous earnings-related pensions which more closely address the issue of consumption smoothing. This was the case in the UK until 2016, and remains so in Sweden and many other continental European countries.

- You can also see that some occupational schemes work on a defined benefit basis. They usually promise pensions linked to pay while working. For example, the scheme may promise a pension worked out according to the following formula:

Yearly pension = Yearly earnings × Accrual rate × Years in scheme

The example below shows how this type of formula works. The accrual rate is a fraction, such as $\frac{1}{60}$th, $\frac{1}{80}$th, $\frac{1}{100}$th or some other proportion. In the past, yearly earnings often meant pay shortly before retirement, and these were called final salary schemes. A more common version these days links pay to salary averaged over all the years a person has belonged to the scheme – called a career average scheme. Because inflation means that pay many years ago will be worth little in today's money, the previous years' pay is usually increased in line with inflation before the average is worked out; these schemes are therefore called career average revalued earnings (CARE) schemes. In the UK, most public sector occupational schemes are CARE schemes.

Box 8.1 Example of a CARE scheme

Fran was in a job with a CARE pension scheme for five years and left six years before reaching the pension age for that scheme. She earned between £25,000 and £29,000 during those years. However, once these earnings are revalued in line with inflation, the real value of her pay was more than that. Her average revalued earnings over the years she was in the scheme comes to £31,783 at the time she reaches pension age. The scheme promises her a pension worked out according to the following formula:

Yearly pension = Yearly average revalued earnings × Accrual rate × Years in scheme

The accrual rate in this scheme is $\frac{1}{50}$th. Therefore, Fran's pension is £3178 a year (£31,783 × $\frac{1}{50}$ × 5).

Defined contribution schemes

In a defined contribution (DC) scheme (also called a money purchase scheme), there is no pension promise and no pension formula. Instead, each person builds up their own individual pot of savings. The size of this pot depends on the amounts paid in (contributions plus any matched saving or tax relief) and how well those amounts grow when invested. That means looking at the net return after deducting whatever is paid in charges to the firms involved in running the scheme. The pot of savings is then used to provide the retirement income, but how much that income will be is hard to predict. It depends, for example, on investment returns at, or during, retirement.

As Figure 8.4 suggests, all personal pensions and many occupational schemes work on a defined contribution basis. Very occasionally (for example, in Sweden), state pension schemes have a defined contribution element.

4.3 How pensions are financed

Finally, there are two main ways of financing pension schemes: on a **funded** or a **Pay-As-You-Go** (PAYG) basis. I have added these to the diagram, as shown in Figure 8.5.

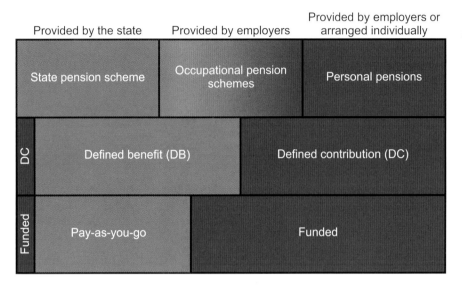

Figure 8.5 How pension schemes are financed

Funded
In the context of pensions, describes a pension scheme where an investment fund is built up from which to pay future pensions.

Pay-As-You-Go
In the context of pensions, a pension scheme where pensions paid out today are paid for out of contributions or tax revenues collected today.

Activity 8.4 How different schemes are financed

Allow 5 minutes for this activity.

Looking at Figure 8.5, which types of scheme – state, occupational or personal – are most likely to be funded schemes?

Comment

The answer to this activity is at the end of the chapter.

Funded schemes

With most occupational schemes and all personal pensions, money paid into the scheme is used to create a pension fund; these are therefore called funded schemes. The pension fund is a pool of investments that will be used to pay the pensions as they fall due – for example, out of the income earned by the investments and/or by selling some of the investments.

Pay-As-You-Go schemes

Most state pension schemes are not funded; instead they work on the PAYG basis. The pensions paid out today are paid out of the taxes being collected today (such as National Insurance in the UK). Sometimes, this is referred to as a 'contract between the generations' because today's taxpayers (in the UK, today's workers paying National Insurance) are paying for today's pensions on the understanding that, when they retire, their own pensions will be financed by the contributors of the future.

Some occupational pension schemes for public sector employees (in other words, where the state is their employer) also work on a PAYG basis, with retired workers' pensions being financed by the contributions paid by current workers and possibly general taxation, too.

Activity 8.5 Pension schemes you belong to

Allow 10 minutes for this activity.

Looking back over Section 4.3, what sort of pension schemes do you belong to? What sort of pensions can you expect them to provide?

Comment

Here's my own answer. Some of the pension schemes I belong to promise to pay me a certain level of pension when I retire (so they are defined benefit schemes). They are my state pension and an occupational pension scheme I belong to through my employer, The Open University. The state pension is a PAYG scheme, but the occupational scheme is funded. However, I've been self-employed for most of my working life, so I also have some personal pensions that I arranged for myself. They are funded schemes: each pension fund is my own personal pot of savings. I can only make an educated guess at how much pension I might get from them throughout my retirement, because they are defined contribution schemes.

4.4 Pensions and risk

To look at the risk involved in pension saving, I'm going to start by thinking about a defined benefit scheme that is funded. Let's say it's the pension fund of a fictitious firm called HappyDays PLC.

Risks for a funded defined benefit scheme

HappyDays sets up a scheme that promises to pay salary-related pensions at retirement. The employees have to pay something towards this pension – say, 5% of their pay – and HappyDays will pay in the rest.

HappyDays needs to know how much extra to contribute to the pension fund to ensure that the promised pensions can all be paid as they fall due. It's expecting to contribute something in the region of another 14% of salaries, but cannot be certain of the correct amount. This is because the eventual cost of the pensions will be subject to three important risks:

- **Investment risk** – As discussed in Chapter 5, when investing for the long term – and pension savings are very long term – stock market investments, like shares and bonds, are likely to be most suitable. It's impossible to know in advance how well these investments will perform. If HappyDays assumes they will perform well, that reduces the amount it needs to pay in. Yet if its assumption is wrong and the investments turn out badly, there will be too little in the fund to pay the promised pensions.

- **Inflation risk** – Chapter 2, on income, described how rising prices reduce purchasing power. HappyDays promises pensions that are salary-related, so they automatically rise if earnings go up. It also promises that it will increase pensions once they start to be paid in line with inflation: up to 2% a year, and more if funds allow. HappyDays needs to put extra money in the fund to pay for this protection, but can only estimate what the rate of inflation will be. If its estimate is too low, in real terms the pensions might have to be smaller than planned.

- **Longevity risk** – The longer the pensioners survive after retiring, the more years of pension will have to be paid out, and so the greater the total cost of the pension. HappyDays needs to make assumptions about how long its retired employees will live. If the assumption is wrong, either the money will run out before the pensioners die or more will have been paid into the scheme than originally planned.

In practice, the organisers of the HappyDays pension scheme will employ an actuary – the kind of specialist you read about in Chapter 7 when you looked at insurance – to try to forecast these risks and advise HappyDays on how much it needs to pay into the scheme.

As long as the actuary gets the sums right and HappyDays can afford to make the necessary payments, the members of the pension scheme don't need to worry about the risks. They will get their promised pensions, regardless.

Covenant risk
The risk that a promise or contractual agreement made by one person or organisation to another will be broken.

On the other hand, if the risks and costs of providing the pension scheme become too high, there is a risk – called **covenant risk** – that HappyDays might break the pension promise by changing the rules or even closing the scheme down. This can mean that future and even current pensions are lower than the members had been counting on, as starkly described in the extract in Box 8.2.

Covenant risk materialised for UK steelworkers

Box 8.2 Retired steelworkers face pension poverty, say campaigners

Older members of former Tata Steel UK retirement fund hit hard by restructuring

Campaigners are warning that thousands of elderly people who were steelworkers could be plunged into poverty unless changes are made to a deal to restructure a large pension scheme previously run by Tata Steel's UK business.

Tata Steel UK last month offloaded its £15bn pension scheme in return for keeping its lossmaking British plants open, but pensioners say they have a 'Hobson's choice' between two less generous alternative retirement funds. Tata's former scheme – which has 130,000 members and harks back to when the company's UK operations were part of British Steel – was handed to the Pension Protection Fund, an industry-backed lifeboat system focused on the defined benefit pension schemes of failed companies.

Members must choose between staying in the PPF-backed scheme or joining a new retirement fund sponsored by Tata Steel UK – neither of which offers benefits as generous as those previously available. They notably do not provide people with full protection against inflation … Most of those affected by these changes will be pensioners who were members of the old Tata retirement scheme, rather than workers. More than 88,000 members of the old scheme are pensioners.

Stefan Zaitschenko, a former Tata steelworker who helps run a Facebook group for members of the old scheme, said the failure to uprate pension benefits accrued before 1997 in line with inflation would leave thousands of elderly people – including widows – struggling to pay their bills. Explaining the predicament of one widow who was married to a scheme member, he added: 'We had one person asking how their 85-year-old mother could afford to stay in her nursing home when the fees go up next year if her pension did not. There are 120 members [aged] over 100. We are realistic and we accept that benefits are going to be reduced. I am 60 and can keep working. Older people can't.'

(Source: Bounds and Cumbo, 2017)

Risks and defined contribution schemes

The same three risks – investment risk, inflation risk and longevity risk – affect defined contribution schemes too, so in other words, all personal pensions and many occupational schemes. The big difference is that individuals themselves shoulder all the risks, not any employer.

The amount of pension an individual gets depends on the size of their pension pot by retirement and how much income that will provide. If investments perform badly, inflation is high or the person lives to a very old age, their pension will have to be smaller or may run out before they die.

That means different people saving the same amount can end up with very different pensions, and a person's pension can be markedly different depending on when they retire. It also makes it hard to estimate in advance how much pension they will get and how much they need to save.

With defined contribution schemes, individuals bear all the risks

Risks and PAYG defined benefit schemes

State schemes are financed on a PAYG basis, rather than funded. They are still subject to inflation and longevity risks, but not investment risk (as there is no investment fund). State schemes typically provide defined benefit pensions, so the state, not the individual, bears the risks.

If the cost of state pensions rises – for example, because people are living longer – the state can, in theory, simply raise more money by increasing taxes. In practice, this may be politically and socially unacceptable. So individuals face covenant risk: the risk that the state pension promises may be broken and benefits for future pensioners reduced. State pensions for existing pensioners could also be cut back, but this, too, may prove politically difficult.

Activity 8.6 Features of different types of pension scheme

Allow 5 minutes for this activity.

Test your knowledge of different types of pension scheme by answering the following questions.

1 Which one of the following types of pension scheme gives an individual some certainty about the amount of retirement income they will get?

(a) an occupational pension scheme

(b) a funded pension scheme

(c) a defined benefit pension scheme.

2 Which one of the following is a feature of a defined contribution pension scheme?

(a) The employer bears the investment risk, inflation risk and longevity risk.

(b) The individual bears the investment risk, inflation risk and longevity risk.

(c) They are available only through the workplace.

Comment

The answers to this activity are at the end of the chapter.

---

5 Pressure on pensions

Defined benefit pension schemes are sometimes thought of as the Rolls-Royce of pensions because they offer individuals and households some certainty about the level of pension they will get and shield them from the risks involved. But defined benefit pensions, whether provided by the state or employers, are being cut back in most countries. A major driver has been ageing populations.

5.1 Ageing populations

As you learned in Chapter 1, population ageing is due to falling birth rates and people living longer (Table 8.1). The reasons for lower birth rates are varied: women are choosing to have fewer children as their lifestyles change and birth control enables them to exercise that choice, while job insecurity, low earnings, lack of suitable housing and the cost of childcare act as constraints (OECD, 2015a; Buchanan and Rotkirch, 2013). A key reason for the longer survival of older people has been advances in medicine (particularly, in more recent years, the management of cardiovascular diseases), and changes in lifestyle, such as reduced smoking (WHO, 2014).

Table 8.1 Percentage of the population aged 65 and over in selected countries (data for 1950, 2015 and a forecast for 2050)

Country	1950	2015	2050	% change 1950 to 2050
Australia	8.2	20.4	22.5	174
Brazil	3.0	11.7	22.8	659
China	4.5	15.2	27.6	512
Germany	9.7	27.6	32.3	233
India	3.1	8.9	13.7	343
Japan	4.9	33.1	36.3	641
Russian Federation	4.8	20.0	20.9	336
South Africa	3.6	7.7	10.2	183
Sweden	10.2	25.5	23.8	133
UK	10.8	23.0	24.7	129
USA	8.3	20.7	22.2	168

Note: the % change is the change in the proportion of those aged 65 and over, not the % change in their number.

Source: United Nations (2015)

Activity 8.7 Ageing populations

Allow 10 minutes for this activity.

Using the data in Table 8.1, answer the following questions:

1   In 2050, which of the countries shown are forecast to have the largest and smallest proportion of their populations aged 65 and older?

2   Over the period 1950 to 2050, which two countries are expected to have experienced the largest rise in the proportion of their populations aged 65 and over?

Comment

The answers to this activity are at the end of the chapter.

5.2 Supporting older generations

Greater choice for women about their family–career balance and people living longer are surely causes for celebration, so the gloomy tone of discussions about ageing populations may seem surprising. Nonetheless, governments and employers argue that a consequent rise in pension costs is unaffordable. However, I'm going to invite you to step back and look at the bigger picture by thinking about supporting older generations as a set of choices about how a country's gross domestic product (GDP) is shared.

Sharing GDP

While the real world is certainly more complex, think of GDP for a moment as a large cake that you are going to cut into three slices: one for workers; another for retired people; and the third slice is for others who do not work, such as children (as in Figure 8.6). How much each group gets depends on the size of the cake (a bigger cake means everyone gets more) and the relative size of their slice (a bigger slice for one group means a smaller slice for one or both of the other groups).

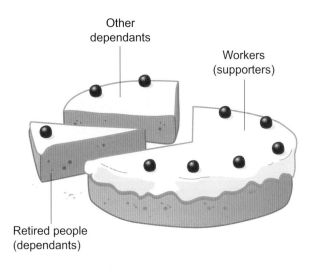

Figure 8.6 Sharing GDP

The workers can be thought of as a key ingredient in ensuring the cake is made, as they are the group currently most actively engaged in creating GDP, with the help of technology (to which I return later). I've called them the 'supporters' of the process. They get their share of GDP by selling their labour for wages, which they exchange for goods and services – either immediately or later on if they choose to save some of their pay.

The other two groups are also important to GDP: pensioners, because they are workers of the past who helped to make the cake what it is today, and children, because they are workers of the future. However, neither of these groups receive wages today, so they are classed as 'dependants' in Figure 8.6. They need to rely on some other mechanism for claiming their share of GDP. For older people, that is where pension systems step in.

Dependency ratio

Old-age dependency ratio
The number of older people in a country divided by the number of people of working age. An indicator of the number of pensioners to be supported by each worker.

Because workers are treated as key to making the GDP cake, changes in the number of people of working age relative to the number of older people are central to concerns about the affordability of pension systems. A way of measuring this relationship is the **old-age dependency ratio**, which is the number of people over a specified age chosen to loosely reflect the point when pensions start to be paid (say, 65) divided by the number of people of working age. For example, if there are 10 million pensioners and 30 million workers, this could be expressed as a dependency ratio of 0.333, or 33.3 per 100 workers (10 million divided by 30 million).

For selected countries, Figure 8.7 shows the old-age dependency ratio in 2015 and the level it is forecast to be by 2050. In 2015 the old-age dependency ratio in emerging countries, such as Brazil, China, India and South Africa, was much lower than in industrialised countries, such as the UK, the US and Japan. However, by 2050, all the countries are expected to see a substantial rise in the old-age dependency ratio, with Japan and Germany forecast to reach especially high levels.

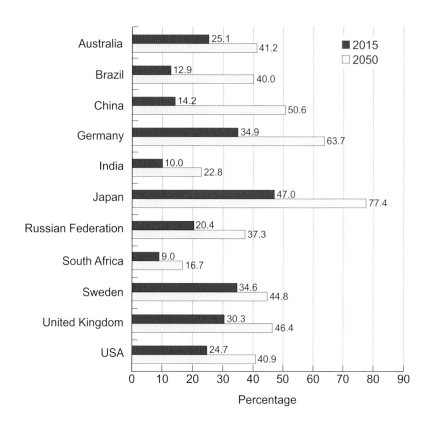

Figure 8.7 Old-age dependency ratios, 2015 (estimated) and 2050 (forecast). Note: the old-age dependency ratio used here is the number of individuals aged 65 and over for every 100 people of working age defined as aged 20 to 64 (Source: United Nations, 2015).

Activity 8.8 The impact of changing dependency ratios

Allow 10 minutes for this activity.

Explain how Figure 8.7 might support the argument that pension systems may become unaffordable in future.

Comment

Figure 8.7 shows that rising old-age dependency ratios is a worldwide phenomenon. With every 100 workers needing to create enough GDP to support not just themselves but a rising number of older people, it does on the face of it seem that paying pensions to all the extra older people could be impossibly expensive.

Interpreting the dependency ratio

There is a case for exercising caution in using the old-age dependency ratio as the best basis for determining a country's capacity to cope with an ageing population. Some reasons for this are:

- Forecasting the number of people of working age is tricky. It depends not only on the uncertainties of future birth rates and longevity but also the extent to which workers move around. Immigration of workers reduces a country's dependency ratio, while emigration increases it.

- Not everyone of working age is in productive work, because of, say, unemployment and illness. This means the dependency ratio may understate the true position.

Total dependency ratio
Children (aged 0 to, say, 19) and older people (aged, say, 65 and over) as a proportion of the working population (for example, those aged 20 to 64).

- Not everyone aged 65 and over has stopped productive work (including unpaid work, such as caring for grandchildren). Taking this into account would reduce the dependency ratio.

- Older people are not the only dependants. In particular, children and young adults still in education surely should also be included in a dependency ratio. If the proportion of children in the population is falling, the true dependency ratio (known as the **total dependency ratio**) may be rising less than the old-age dependency ratio suggests.

- The ratio assumes dependants are uniformly needy, but this may change over time. For example, if more pensioners choose to live alone, this might increase the resources that the average older person needs.

- The ratio implicitly assumes that average output of goods and services per worker is constant over time. But if **labour productivity** increases, fewer workers would be able to support more dependants.

Labour productivity
The amount of outputs (goods and services) produced by each unit of labour (for example, each hour worked).

A further potential problem is how dependency ratios are based on the idea that workers are the main drivers of GDP. However, digital innovation is bringing increasing automation – for example, driverless vehicles. Rather than simply changing the nature of work, such innovations could mean that economies of the future will not need as many workers to produce the same level of GDP (implying that the labour productivity of the remaining workers would increase, but also that unemployment could rise). In that scenario, a ratio based on the number of people of working age would no longer be a good indicator of the economy's capacity to support people who do not work. Everyone – of working age and pensioners – could in theory benefit from higher living standards, regardless of their having the opportunity or ability to work or movements in a crude dependency ratio. Looked at this way, it becomes clear that supporting non-workers, whatever their age, is crucially about the systems that societies choose to adopt in order to distribute GDP to their citizens. For centuries, the main distribution mechanism for most people has been to sell their labour for wages, but if an economy can produce ample goods and services with only minimal labour, different mechanisms may be needed. This is a topic you will return to in Chapter 10.

5.3 How ageing affects pension systems

Much is often made of the distinction between PAYG and funded pension systems. By cutting back state pension systems and encouraging private pension saving instead, governments often implicitly suggest that switching to funded schemes solves the problem of supporting ageing populations. However, this is a fallacy, as this section will demonstrate.

Ageing populations and PAYG systems

First, let's consider the argument that PAYG systems will not be able to cope. Remember that workers make contributions today which are used to pay the pensions of pensioners today.

Activity 8.9 PAYG under stress

Allow 15 minutes for this activity.

Imagine a small economy with 100 workers and 20 pensioners. This economy raises £200,000 through taxes paid by the workers and uses all this money to pay pensions to the pensioners through a PAYG system. (For simplicity, assume the pensioners pay no tax.) Answer the following questions:

1 How much tax does the average worker pay? *2,000*

2 How much pension does the average pensioner get? *10,000*

3 If the number of workers and the tax take stays the same, but the number of pensioners doubles to 40, how much pension would the average pensioner get? How might pensioners react? *5,000*

4 If the number of workers stays the same and the number of pensioners doubles to 40 but pensions are unchanged, how much tax would the average worker have to pay? How might workers react?

40,0000

4000

Comment

The answers to this activity are at the end of the chapter.

It is the unpalatable choice between the scenarios described in Questions 3 and 4 of Activity 8.9 that are often presented as creating a conflict between the generations. So, do funded systems provide the answer?

"Do let me know if I'm getting in the way, won't you?"

CartoonStock.com

Intergenerational conflict?

Ageing populations and funded systems

In a funded system, workers also make contributions today, but as you have seen these are used to buy investments. When they retire, these workers will want to turn their investments into income, either cashing them in or switching to income-producing assets. As a group, they will be mainly sellers of investments. The amount of retirement income they get depends on the price they can get for their investments. The main buyers are likely to be the next generation of workers who will be saving for their own retirement. But if ageing of the population means there are many pensioners relative to the number of workers, there will be more people trying to sell investments than people wanting to buy. You saw in Chapter 6, on housing, that if the supply of something exceeds demand, then the price will tend to fall. So pensioners may get less for their investments than they had expected, reducing their retirement incomes and so the share of GDP that they can claim.

PAYG versus funded systems

Thus, PAYG and funded systems both depend on the transfer of GDP, as summarised in Figure 8.8, and both are vulnerable to an ageing population. With both systems, what's important is that there is sufficient GDP at any point in time to meet citizens' needs. Whether or not GDP is sufficient, how it is shared out is always an ideological issue. Governments that are ideologically inclined towards a small government sector and reliance on market-based systems will tend towards funded pension systems as the mechanism for delivering a share of GDP to pensioners.

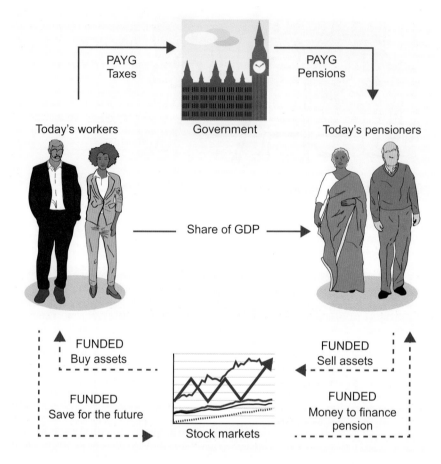

Figure 8.8 Pension systems as a way of passing GDP from workers to pensioners

6 Pension reform

Whether PAYG or funded pension systems are favoured, an increasing number of pensioners who are living longer does mean an increasing slice of GDP going to pensioners if nothing else changes. If society or the government deems this to be unacceptable, then there are three possible solutions, which can be mixed and matched:

- **Increase retirement ages** – This improves the dependency ratio in two ways: people stay in the workforce for longer, increasing the number of workers; and they spend fewer years in retirement, reducing the number of pensioners at any point in time and cutting the number of years for which the pension has to be paid. Some governments argue that raising state pension ages in line with increasing longevity is fair to all generations, as each will then spend a similar proportion of their adult lives in retirement.

- **Reduce the level of pensions** – In defined benefit schemes, cutting current pensions being paid to current pensioners is unlikely to be popular (because, as you saw in Box 8.2, this can tip pensioners into poverty). However, cutting future pensions to current pensioners by making inflation-linked increases less generous is a viable option. Even more common are cuts to the pensions that future pensioners will get through changes to the rules about how entitlements build up. More subtly, switching from defined benefit to defined contribution schemes can reduce future pensions indirectly if investment returns fall.

- **Increase the level of contributions workers pay** – Generally this is unpopular with voters in the case of the state pension scheme and only grudgingly accepted by members of workplace pension schemes, particularly if the same workers are being told that the pensions they eventually get will be less generous.

7 Financial planning for retirement

Despite the often uncertain outcomes of private saving for retirement, individuals and households must balance this against the near-certain alternative of retirement poverty or working for life in the absence of pension saving.

The GROW-ER financial planning tool introduced in Chapter 1 can be used to develop a plan for saving:

- **Goals** – The first step is to quantify the goal: how much income will be needed and when it should start.

- **Resources** – The next step is to see what resources are already available, for example in the form of expected state pension and private pensions already built up, and any other assets, including property.

- **Options and What's decided?** – The difference between the target retirement income (the goal) and the income that current resources can provide is the retirement income gap. The task is to choose between the various options and start saving enough to plug the gap. The options may include different financial products, but also changing the retirement income goal or deciding to retire later.

- **Evaluate and Review** – The calculations are reasonably straightforward in the case of pensions from defined benefit schemes because they promise amounts of pension income that can be predicted in advance – though even these are subject to covenant risk and so can change. However, with defined contribution schemes, there are two difficult questions to solve: what size lump sum is needed at the start of retirement to provide the desired income; and what level of saving is needed to build up that lump sum? Both can be answered only by making assumptions. As assumptions, by their nature, are unlikely to turn out to be exactly right, a crucial part of retirement planning is to review the plan regularly and adjust it as necessary to stay on track.

7.1 Building up assets

With defined contribution schemes, the amount of pension fund available at retirement depends on the following factors:

- **Amount paid in** – This is not necessarily the same as the cost to the individual because some of the money paid in may come from employer contributions (in the case of a workplace scheme) and/or tax relief from the state.

- **Amount taken in charges** – These tend to be many and varied, including, for example, administration charges paid to the organiser of the scheme, fund management charges paid to firms who provide the investments in the scheme, fees for any advice and for the safekeeping of the assets in the fund, and the costs of trading the investments in the fund.

- **Investment return** – The higher the assumed growth in value of the assets in the fund, the less needs to be paid in to reach the retirement income target. But the future rate of growth is unknown and can only be assumed when deciding on the amount to pay in. It's usually best to be cautious and assume a relatively low rate of growth.

- **Investment term** – The longer the term, the larger the eventual fund. This is for two reasons: first, there is time to pay in more; second, each amount paid in has longer to grow and benefits from greater compounding. (If you're unsure about the effect of compounding, look back to Chapter 5.) There are two ways to lengthen the term: start saving early and retire later.

Table 8.2 shows estimates of the total amount that would need to be paid in each month to produce each £100,000 of pension fund in today's money. (The next section discusses how much pension that might provide.)

Table 8.2 Examples of the monthly saving required to produce each £100,000 of pension fund*

Charges per annum	Investment term (years)				
	10	**20**	**30**	**40**	**50**
0.0%	£724	£310	£176	£111	£75
0.5%	£743	£327	£191	£125	£86
1.0%	£763	£345	£208	£140	£100
1.5%	£782	£364	£225	£156	£116
2.0%	£802	£383	£243	£174	£132

*All amounts in today's money. Assumes saving starts at this level and increases each year in line with price inflation and a real return (in other words, on top of inflation) on the invested contributions of 3% a year.

Source: author's calculations

Activity 8.10 Impact of charges and term

Allow 15 minutes for this activity.

Using Table 8.2, answer the following questions:

1   To build up £100,000 over a period of 30 years, what is the percentage increase in the amount a person needs to save if charges are 1.5% a year, rather than 0.5% a year?

2   To build up £100,000 by age 70 in a pension scheme with charges of 0.5% a year, what difference does it make to the amount saved each month if the person starts saving at age 20, rather than age 40?

3   For the two scenarios in Question 2, what in today's money would be the total amount paid in in each case? Comment on your answer.

Comment

The answers to this activity are at the end of the chapter.

7.2 Drawing an income

There are two ways of converting a defined contribution pension fund into retirement income. The first is to leave the fund invested and cash in slices of it as income is required – often called **drawdown**. The difficulty with this strategy is knowing how long the fund will need to last. It will also be necessary to make assumptions about how the drawdown fund is affected by the investment return and charges.

Table 8.3 shows the inflation-linked monthly income that a £100,000 pension fund would support, given different levels of charges and different number of years until death.

Drawdown
Taking retirement income direct from a fund of investments whose value may rise and fall.

Table 8.3 Examples of monthly income produced by each £100,000 of pension fund*

Charges per annum	Length of retirement (years)				
	10	**15**	**20**	**25**	**30**
0.0%	£967	£690	£553	£472	£419
0.5%	£945	£667	£529	£447	£393
1.0%	£923	£644	£505	£422	£368
1.5%	£901	£622	£482	£399	£344
2.0%	£880	£600	£460	£377	£321

*All amounts in today's money. Assumes income starts at this level and increases each year in line with price inflation, and assumes a real rate of return of 3% a year.

Source: author's calculations

Box 8.3 Case study: Dibyesh

Dibyesh earns £40,000 a year and thinks he could manage comfortably in retirement on an income of half that (£20,000 in today's money). He expects to receive around £14,636 a year from a state pension and a defined benefit scheme that he belongs to (both inflation-linked). This means he has a pension gap of £5364 in today's money. He thinks he might be retired for, say, 25 years and is confident that he can find a low-charging (0.5% a year) drawdown arrangement. Using Table 8.3, he finds that he might be able to draw £447 a month (£5364 a year) from a pension pot of £100,000. With 20 years until he plans to retire and again assuming a low-charging (0.5%) plan, Dibyesh sees, from

> Table 8.2, that he would need to start saving an extra £327 a month to stand a reasonable chance of retiring on the income he wants.

For an individual, normally there is no way to know when they will die (their longevity risk). The consequences of guessing wrongly are severe:

- if they draw down too much income too fast, they risk running out of money part way through retirement – recall Callum in Section 3.1 above, who would face financial problems if he lived beyond age 94

- if they are too cautious they may live an unnecessarily frugal existence.

Moreover, in real life, investments do not grow steadily year by year. Their value goes up and down (investment risk). Even if the trend is upwards, there may be years when the value of the investments in the drawdown fund falls sharply and the income being drawn out may need to be cut back.

Lifetime annuity
A type of insurance that guarantees a specified income payable for life in exchange for a lump sum payment.

As with any risk, a way to remove it is to take out insurance (if available). In the case of pensions, the insurance is called a **lifetime annuity**. In exchange for a lump sum (part or all of the pension pot), the individual is guaranteed an income for life, however long they live, thus removing both longevity risk and investment risk. By choosing an annuity that provides an income that increases each year (called an index-linked annuity), inflation risk can also be removed.

A sensible plan for retirement will often be to ensure that there is enough secure income to cover essential spending and then use drawdown to provide income on top of that. Sources of secure income are any defined benefit pensions, including the state pension, and any defined contribution pension that has been converted to an annuity.

7.3 Working in retirement

Individual decisions to continue working after pension age are the result of both constraints and preferences. A major constraint is having too little income to be able to afford a chosen lifestyle. State pensions, even when not particularly generous, are often essential, so increasing state pension ages are a key constraint leading to people working longer. A further constraint for couples may be a need to continue working until a partner is also ready to retire.

However, work is generally accepted to be about more than just selling your labour for money. Research into the impact of retiring (for example, Conroy et al., 2014) suggests that work may be an important source of identity, associated with self-esteem, social networks and support. Research by Celidoni et al. (2013) also suggests that taking early retirement is associated with a higher risk of dementia later on. However, some may find work physically or mentally stressful and feel it cannot end soon enough.

Box 8.4 Still flying at 65? In Japan, he might be a retiree

Shigekazu Miyazaki is spending what should have been his retirement 25,000 feet in the air.

Mr Miyazaki, a pilot with nearly four decades' experience at All Nippon Airways, Japan's largest airline, left the carrier last year at its mandatory retirement age of 65. But rather than take up golf or fishing, Mr Miyazaki since April has been piloting 39-seat propeller planes for Oriental Air Bridge, a tiny airline that connects the south-western city of Nagasaki to a group of remote islands. 'I never would have thought I'd still be flying at 65,' Mr Miyazaki, who is trim and has a deep voice and a full head of grey hair, said before a

---

recent flight. 'But I'm still healthy, and I love to fly, so why not do it as long as I can?'

A man in his seventh decade extending his commercial flying career still qualifies as a novelty in Japan – but maybe not for long. The ageing of Japan's workforce is prompting a rethinking of traditional career paths and government safety nets. The country has the world's longest life expectancy, little immigration and a dwindling population of young workers, the result of decades of low birth-rates. That makes older workers more crucial to the economy. More than half of Japanese men over 65 do some kind of paid work, according to government surveys, compared with a third of American men and as little as 10% in parts of Europe.

(Source: adapted from Soble, 2017)

A desire to work longer needs to be backed up with the opportunity to do so. With this end in mind, the OECD (2015b) has recommended that its member countries adopt three types of policies to:

- **strengthen incentives to work to later ages** – for example, by raising pension ages, through flexible retirement enabling the mixing of pension and work income, and restrictions on the availability of state-funded early retirement schemes.

- **encourage employers to retain and hire older workers** – for example, by outlawing age discrimination in the workplace, ensuring employment protection (concerning, say, redundancy) is not age related, and discouraging or eliminating mandatory retirement ages.

- **promote employability of workers throughout their working lives** – for example, through training adjusted to reflect experience and learning needs at different ages, setting the same job-search requirements and support systems for unemployment benefit recipients regardless of age, and enhancing job quality and work–life balance for workers across the whole age range.

7.4 Other retirement resources

As you saw in Section 3.3, employers and the government may help towards saving through pensions schemes, which makes them a popular option. But they are not the only way to plan for an income in later life. All that is required is something that can store wealth, so that consumption can be deferred from today until retirement.

One possibility is property, which you considered in Chapter 6 on housing. This could mean investing in a 'buy-to-let' property which can either be sold on reaching retirement or carry on providing an income through the rents paid by tenants. Alternatively, it could mean planning to sell a large family home on retirement and moving somewhere cheaper in order to release a cash lump sum (called downsizing). Chapter 6 also mentioned another option: an equity release scheme. This is a collective term for financial products that allow a homeowner to raise money from their property while still living in it. To be eligible, homeowners must have reached a minimum age (commonly, 65) and either own their home outright or have only a small mortgage left which can be paid off using part of the money raised from equity release. There are two types of product:

- a loan against the home, called a lifetime mortgage (or reverse mortgage), which is paid off only when the homeowner dies or moves into care

- a home reversion scheme, where part or all of the property is sold but the former owner can carry on living there as a tenant, either rent-free or for a token rent (say £1 a year), until they die or move into a care home.

8 Conclusion

This chapter has focused on pension systems as a way of supporting people financially in later life. Individuals and households are often encouraged to think of their future financial security as being in their own hands. However, you have seen that pension systems are mechanisms for transferring a share of GDP from workers to non-workers. You have also considered how these systems – whether organised on a PAYG basis or funded – are all vulnerable to population ageing, a phenomenon which is happening across the world.

Governments and employers have been reforming the pension schemes they provide in order to protect themselves from the increasing costs and risks of demographic change, for example by raising pension ages and reducing the benefits promised to future pensioners. This does not remove the pressure on pensions; rather, it shifts the pressure on to individuals. Those who can afford it may save extra through private pensions (usually on a defined contribution basis), and the state may employ a variety of policies – such as automatic enrolment and tax relief – to encourage this. However, there is no guarantee that funded defined contribution schemes will deliver the anticipated level of pensions, because this will depend on investment conditions at and during retirement, which in turn depends on the demographic and economic context at that time.

Answers to activities in Chapter 8

Answer to Activity 8.1

These are some of the ways in which spending might be different in retirement compared with your working-age years. You may have thought of others.

- If you are a homeowner, you may have finished paying off any mortgage, so spending on housing might have fallen.

- There could be savings on work-related costs, such as pension contributions and commuting.

- You might spend more on travel to see friends and relatives, but pensioners often qualify for reduced-rate or free travel, especially on public transport.

- You might spend more on holidays, especially in early retirement, but may save money by going away at off-peak times.

- You might spend more time at home, so bills for gas and electricity could rise.

- In later retirement, spending on health-related items such as help with personal care could rise.

- You might need less paid help, for example, with things like home maintenance and housework, if you now have time to do these tasks yourself. On the other hand, you might pay more if failing health means you can no longer do such tasks yourself.

Answers to Activity 8.2

1 Don would get £20 a week in means-tested pension, taking his total income up to the minimum £150 a week.

2 Haneen would get £5 means-tested pension, taking her total income to £150 a week.

Although Haneen has saved more, she is no better off than Don. In such a system, financially there is no incentive for a person to make private pension savings unless they can save enough to bring their retirement income well above the minimum level.

Answer to Activity 8.4

Very few state schemes are funded. The majority of occupational schemes, and all personal pension schemes, are funded. This is shown in Figure 8.9.

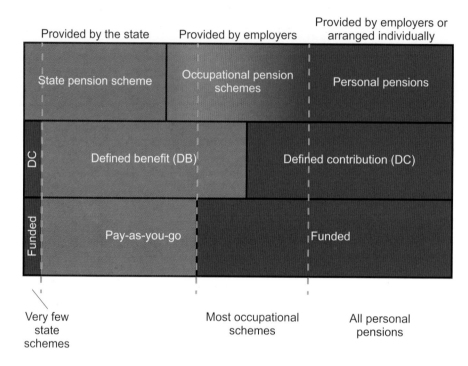

Figure 8.9 Which types of pension scheme are funded schemes?

Answers to Activity 8.6

1   The correct answer is (c). Defined benefit schemes promise a specified level of pension at retirement, making it easier to plan ahead – provided the pension promise is not broken. Nearly all state schemes and some occupational schemes work in this way.

2   The correct answer is (b). In defined contribution schemes, the individual bears all the risks. All personal pensions and many occupational schemes work in this way.

Answers to Activity 8.7

1   Of the countries shown in Table 8.1, the country forecast to have the largest proportion of older people (defined as being aged 65 and over) by 2050 is Japan: over a third of its population (36.3%). By contrast, South Africa is expected to have the smallest proportion of elderly people, at 10.2% (one person in ten), followed by India (13.7%).

2   Over the 100-year period, Japan and Brazil are both forecast to experience an increase of over 600% in their elderly populations. However, Brazil, starting from a low base of just 3% in 1950, will have a lower proportion of elderly people than Japan.

Answers to Activity 8.9

1   If £200,000 is raised from 100 workers, this means each worker on average pays £2000 tax.

2   Dividing £200,000 between 20 pensioners means that on average they get £10,000 each.

3   If everything else stays the same, but the number of pensioners increases to 40 (a doubling of the old-age dependency ratio), the amount each pensioner gets falls to £5000. It would be a brave government that halved the pensions of existing pensioners, even if the change were implemented gradually.

4   If the pension is kept at £10,000, the amount of tax each worker pays would need to rise to £4000. Again, a government might expect considerable resistance to such a steep rise in taxes.

Answers to Activity 8.10

1   Looking down the column for an investment term of 30 years, the amount that needs to be saved if charges are 0.5% a year is £191. If charges are 1.5% a year, this increases to £225, an extra £34 each month (£225 − £191). As a percentage, this is an increase in the monthly saving of 17.8% (£34 ÷ £191 × 100).

2   If the person starts saving at age 20, the investment term is 50 years, assuming retirement at age 70. With charges of 0.5%, this means saving £86 a month. Delaying the start of saving to age 40 reduces the term to 30 years and the saving required more than doubles to £191.

3 Saving £86 for 50 years makes a total of £51,600 (£86 × 50 × 12) in today's money. Saving £191 for 30 years results in a total of £68,760 (£191 × 30 × 12). Delaying the start of saving by 20 years has significantly increased the cost of building up a pension pot of £100,000. The clear message is that it pays to start saving early.

References

Bounds, A. and Cumbo, J. (2017) 'Retired steelworkers face pension poverty, say campaigners', *Financial Times*, 2 October [Online]. Available at www.ft.com/content/fb8c5bee-a5d5-11e7-93c5-648314d2c72c (Accessed 20 April 2018).

Buchanan, A. and Rotkirch, A. (2013) 'No time for children? The key questions', in Buchanan, A. and Rotkirch, A. (eds) *Fertility Rates and Population Decline. No Time for Children?*, Basingstoke, Palgrave Macmillan, pp. 3–21.

Celidoni, M., dal Bianco, C. and Weber, G. (2013) 'Early retirement and cognitive decline. A longitudinal analysis using SHARE data', *'Marco Fanno' Working Papers*, no. 0174, December, Dipartimento di Scienze Economiche 'Marco Fanno' [Online]. Available at http://econpapers.repec.org/paper/padwpaper/0174.htm (Accessed 28 May 2017).

Conroy, S., Franklin, D. and O'Leary-Kelly, A. M. (2014) 'Turmoil or opportunity? Retirement and identity-related coping', in Ford, J. K, Hollenbeck, J. R. and Ryan, A. M. (eds) *The Nature of Work: Advances in Psychological Theory, Methods and Practice*, Washington, DC, American Psychological Association, pp. 165–82.

Fernandes, D., Lynch, J. G. and Netemeyer, R. G. (2014) *Financial Literacy, Financial Education and Downstream Financial Behaviors* [Online]. Available at https://papers.ssrn.com/sol3/papers.cfm?abstract_id=2333898 (Accessed 20 September 2018).

Holzmann, R. and Hinz, R. (2005) *Old-Age Income Support in the 21st Century: An International Perspective on Pension Systems and Reform*, Washington, DC, World Bank.

Katz, M. (2017) 'Eight largest pension systems will have $400 trillion gap by 2050', *Chief Investment Officer*, 31 May [Online]. Available at www.ai-cio.com/news/eight-largest-pension-systems-will-400-trillion-gap-2050/ (Accessed 4 August 2017).

National Audit Office (NAO) (2014) *Tax Reliefs* [Online], London, National Audit Office. Available at https://www.nao.org.uk/wp-content/uploads/2014/03/Tax-reliefs.pdf (Accessed 20 September 2018).

O'Grady, S. (2016) 'Pension poverty: millions face running out of money as they live to record old age', *Express*, 27 January [Online]. Available at www.express.co.uk/news/uk/638286/working-Pension-poverty-millions-cancel-retirement (Accessed 4 August 2017).

Organisation for Economic Cooperation and Development (OECD) (2015a) *Pensions at a Glance 2015. OECD and G20 Indicators* [Online]. Available at https://www.oecd-ilibrary.org/docserver/pension_glance-2015-en.pdf? expires=1534838317&id=id&accname=guest&check-sum=B5482C57B06DDD665BE1B568565FF138 (Accessed 20 September 2018).

Organisation for Economic Cooperation and Development (OECD) (2015b) *Recommendation of the Council on Ageing and Employment Policies*, OECD/LEGAL/0419, adopted 14 December [Online]. Available at https://legalinstruments.oecd.org/public/doc/333/333.en.pdf (Accessed 21 August 2018).

Reeves, P. (2017) 'Brazilian workers protest against pension changes', *npr* (National Public Radio), 16 March [Online]. Available at www.npr.org/2017/03/16/520364008/brazilian-workers-protest-against-pension-changes (Accessed 4 August 2017).

Soble, J. (2017) 'Still flying at 65? In Japan, he might be a retiree', *The Hindu*, 29 July [Online]. Available at www.thehindu.com/news-service/still-flying-at-65-in-japan-he-might-be-a-retiree/article19385981.ece (Accessed 4 August 2017).

United Nations (2015) *World Population Prospects (2015 revision)* [Online], New York, United Nations, Department of Economic and Social Affairs. Available at https://esa.un.org/unpd/wpp/Publications/Files/Key_Findings_WPP_2015.pdf (Accessed 20 September 2018).

World Health Organisation (WHO) (2014) 'Life expectancy in the world in 2012' in *World Health Statistics 2014: Part II: Highlighted Topics* [Online]. Available at http://www.who.int/gho/publications/world_health_statistics/EN_WHS2014_Part2.pdf?ua=1 (Accessed 29 May 2017).

To cite this chapter, use the following format in your reference list:

Lowe, J. (2019) 'Pensions', in De Henau, J. and Lowe, J. (eds) *Personal Finance*, Milton Keynes, The Open University, pp. 343–392.

Chapter 9
Caring and sharing

Jerome De Henau and Susan Himmelweit

Contents

1 Introduction

Most of us have experienced living under the same roof with other people. And in many cases we, or others in the household, have needed looking after at some point: whether, for example, a child depending on parent(s); an adult with a disability; or a frail elderly relative who needs care.

As the composition of households changes over time, so do the people that need care within them. While we tend to concentrate on the emotional side of relationships within and between families, changes to households also have important financial implications that are often unanticipated. In telenovelas and 'soap operas' from around the world, many of the fictional events portrayed revolve around changes in living arrangements, and how children and older people are cared for.

Financial discussions concerning divorce, marriage and time spent **caring** for others often make for colourful dramas. Yet the personal financial implications of such events are often overlooked in public debates, relegated to the private sphere of the household.

This chapter examines such financial implications. It explains how decisions to set up or dissolve a household, and how caring for other household members, can both have important short-term and long-term financial effects. These effects are not always easy to get to grips with; this is because there are important opportunity costs that are often overlooked, particularly in the long term, in the decisions that people make about sharing their household with other people, and about caring for them.

Caring
Providing a personal service to help someone who is not capable of looking after their own personal needs, such as feeding or dressing them, helping them manage as independently as possible, and keeping them safe.

Caring and sharing drama is a core narrative of soap operas

The social and economic context in which sharing and caring decisions are being made is rapidly changing. Families and households in all parts of the world look quite different today from how they did a generation ago. Moreover, the social norms for caring and financial arrangements within households remain significantly different between countries.

We will tease out the most financially significant aspects of caring in this chapter. Section 2 looks at the issue of care in the context of household diversity across the world. Section 3 examines how households tend to organise caring for household members, and share paid and unpaid work between themselves. This leads into Section 4, which explores the short-term and long-term financial implications of reducing time in employment in order to care for someone. Section 5 then introduces the role of the state in influencing decisions for childcare provision, and Section 6 explores long-term care systems.

2 The issue of care within households

In Chapters 3, 5 and 8 of *Personal Finance* you saw how households make decisions about how to spend their income or save it for later consumption. Because of personal preferences, lack of supply, or when money is tight, they can also spend time producing the things they want to consume themselves, by doing **unpaid work**. One example, in more traditional settings but also in some households with environmental awareness, is self-production of agricultural goods, such as growing your own fruit and vegetables. Cooking at home, rather than eating out, is another example of self-production. These examples show that the relationship between buying goods and services, which are produced and sold on the market, and home production spans different activities.

Unpaid work
Unpaid activity that contributes to the well-being of people, and would otherwise have to be paid for. It includes looking after a household and caring for people, as well as voluntary work in the community.

Examples of self-production include: a family baking cookies, building a log cabin yourself and doing the laundry for the household

The same applies to looking after others who need care. Some of the resources accumulated through saving may be spent on care, for others or for yourself. In some cases that care can be sourced via the market by paying for services. Alternatively (or often, in addition), the family itself can provide such care, exchanging income (or leisure) for time to give to the task. This latter mechanism is a typical example of opportunity cost: for adults of working-age, the main opportunity cost is the earnings foregone by a household member who spends time caring instead of being in paid employment; for older carers no longer in employment, the opportunity cost may be their reduced leisure time or other unpaid work time. For many, it is all of these. Depending on the composition of the household and the cultural and institutional differences, these combinations of paid and unpaid care will vary greatly.

The trade-off between time and money is an important concept in personal finance and economics. However, it is not always considered fully in the financial decision-making process, owing to a series of behavioural traits. These are similar to the traits that put people off saving for a pension, often because the long-term implications are ignored or underestimated. We will come back to these behavioural traits as we progress through this chapter.

2.1 Different ways of providing care

Figure 9.1 illustrates the circular flow of income, which you first looked at in Chapter 1, but here time (understood as foregone income) involved in the process of delivering care to children and adults is included on the diagram.

Care can be provided informally by households themselves (core or extended family), or formally by the state or via the private sector (commercial providers or the voluntary sector).

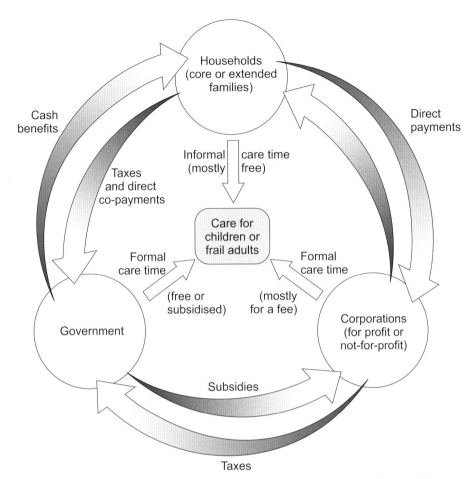

Figure 9.1 Flows of money and time spent caring for children and frail adults

Governments can enter the picture of care provision in different ways:

- organising and delivering care directly, free at the point of use via public services (or for a modest fee)

- subsidising private care providers (whether for-profit or not) in order to reduce the cost of care and thus fees for users

- supporting families financially via cash benefits or tax rebates to help with the cost of care.

The childcare system in France is a good example of all the arrows in Figure 9.1 at play (you may recognise some similarities with the UK's system too). Care for children in France is provided by a combination of state-subsidised private services, public services and family, as follows: the state subsidises private childcare centres and childminders so as to reduce the fee for families. It also provides free childcare directly, mainly for older pre-school children from the age of three (kindergartens), linked to the education system and funded by general taxation. Families then top up such provision with unpaid care by taking time off work or calling on informal care from grandparents. Families also receive financial help from the state via cash transfers and tax rebates to help them purchase care privately.

Activity 9.1 Care time and money flows

Allow 10 minutes for this activity.

Thinking about your own household, or the one you grew up in, identify one example of childcare or adult care within that household and locate on Figure 9.1 the way that you think that care was provided.

Comment

There are many different examples of care arrangements, which vary between countries but also depend on the type of household you live in and its income level.

As seen previously in Chapter 2, some cash benefits from the state may be means-tested (an example of a flow of income from Government to Households shown by the arrow in Figure 9.1). Some direct public services may be free at the point of use or provided at a nominal fee below market rates (shown by the arrow from Government to the Care box in Figure 9.1).

Within the Households box shown in Figure 9.1, you may rely on more unpaid care if the state doesn't provide sufficient support, especially if market provision (private care) is too expensive or non-existent. Indeed, your own parents may help significantly with the care of your children, or you might be a grandparent yourself, providing unpaid care to your grandchild(ren). Additionally, of course, you may also provide care to one or more of your household's adult members (or an adult in another household), sometimes in combination with childcare responsibilities.

2.2 Caring and sharing within changing households

In nearly all societies, families play an important role in the care of their members. Yet families vary across and within societies: in some there are households with extended families that include three or more generations. In such households, care for the young, the old and those with disabilities is often shared across the generations.

Multi-generation families can have many different 'caring and sharing' relationships

However, as you'll recall from Chapter 1, the size of households has fallen over the last few decades in many countries, owing to a combination of factors. This has had different implications for care provision within the family.

- Continuous decline in fertility rates has meant there are fewer children per family. This is happening even in developing countries, and has changed the nature of childcare debates from being about the quantity of children needing care to being about quality (how well the smaller number of children are looked after). But it has also meant fewer children are growing up to share in the care of their elderly parents if they are frail.

- The rise of educational enrolment, in particular for girls in developing countries, has also reduced the availability of informal carers to look after their younger siblings.

- The increase in female employment across the world, in part due to aspirations and women having greater autonomy in choosing whether, and if so, when, to have children, has meant the use of non-familial care for children and adults has grown.

- Economic growth and income increases have enabled more people to live on their own independently, and sometimes away from their relatives, thereby reducing the possibility for the provision of intra-family care.

- Increased migration possibilities have seen young adults look for better conditions elsewhere in the world, leaving their extended families behind. Often those that have migrated send money they earn back to their families, but there is still a care deficit if they are not physically with their families. The example of Filipino mothers, who leave their own young children behind in order to take paid jobs looking after the children of wealthy families in the Persian Gulf and the West, is telling (Santos, 2015).

2.3 Care costs, home production and living standards

Multi-person households can benefit from economies of scale in consumption. This also holds true for caring. Looking after three children doesn't take three times as much time as looking after one, for example. Broadly speaking, household members can decide whether to spend money on paying for non-familial care or provide the care themselves. However, the latter option is not without cost – it needs to account for who in the household will provide care and the opportunity costs of the earnings they will forego.

It is important to note that equivalised income – which you used in Chapter 3 to compare the standards of living of households that have different compositions and needs – only reflects different consumption costs. Common equivalence scales, such as the standard OECD scale, are not designed to consider opportunity costs, such as the foregone future income as a result of caring decisions today. Moreover, they also average consumption costs across all members of a certain age group and so are not equipped to account for additional needs of consumption in some households, such as special equipment for any disabled person, or childcare fees for younger children. These caveats do not invalidate the use of equivalence scales more generally but caution is necessary when using them for more specific purposes, such as comparing the living standard of families with different care needs.

Activity 9.2 Comparing equivalised incomes after childcare

Allow 15 minutes for this activity.

The Pearson family comprises two full-time employed adults and their two children aged under six. They have a net household income of 50,000 per year and spend 10,000 a year on childcare costs.

Their household equivalised net income is:

50,000 ÷ 2.1 (which is 1 + 0.5 + 0.3 + 0.3) = 23,810 (rounded)

40,000 ÷ 2.1

≈ 19,047

1   Calculate the equivalised income of another family – the Appledoughs – who are similar in all respects to the Pearsons, except that one of the parents reduces their working hours, and thus net annual earnings by 10,000, to provide childcare directly.

2   Assuming the 'amount' of childcare each family enjoys is the same, how do the two families' living standards compare:

(a) on the basis of their equivalised income?   *↓ ~ £4K*

(b) taking account of the childcare provision of each family?

↳ : better quality

Comment

The answers to Activity 9.2 are given at the end of this chapter.

There is also an alternative way to look at the issue of consumption and care costs. Some economists have suggested considering the self-production of childcare (or indeed, the value of any home production) as **imputed income** (Jenkins and O'Leary, 1996). This means adding the costs saved to actual income to construct a household's 'extended income', or 'total income'.

This relates to what you read in Chapter 2, about considering some public services delivered free at the point of use (such as school education) as benefits in kind, thereby increasing households' living standards. This is because, in the absence of public provision, these services would have to be paid for in the market out of actual income. For example, if you earn 20,000 but receive a free transport pass worth 1000, you could either say your income is 20,000 but your spending is reduced by 1000, or you could say your 'total' income is 21,000,

Imputed income
The value of a service or benefit in kind provided by an employer, the government, or self-produced by a household, which is equivalent to having extra income since it increases living standards.

because it is equivalent to the financial position of someone else who has to pay for transport but receives an actual salary of 21,000. Similar reasoning applies to home production.

Activity 9.3 Childcare production as imputed income

Allow 10 minutes for this activity.

Think about the two families we met in Activity 9.2. Now consider the childcare produced by the Appledoughs at home to be some kind of imputed income. On the basis of net total income only (imputed and actual), how would the Pearsons' and Appledoughs' living standards compare?

Comment

The 40,000 household income of the Appledoughs is now augmented by the 10,000 worth of home-produced childcare, so that their 'total' income (actual + imputed) is now equal to the actual net income of the Pearsons' of 50,000, and thus their living standard is similar.

So, in comparing the two households, you either deduct childcare costs as if they were a tax, or you add the value of unpaid childcare as imputed income. However, such a comparison is only looking at short-term effects on income. In the long term, the home production of childcare by the Appledoughs, in particular the fact that one of the partners has reduced their working hours and thus receives less in earnings, has different financial consequences than paying for childcare.

Accounting for opportunity costs is an important aspect of the decision-making process for a household looking into sharing responsibility for providing care and income. Opportunity costs can be short term (unpaid time versus paid time), as we have just explored, and long term (career prospects and pension income). In Section 3 of this chapter, we'll turn our attention to these aspects of sharing paid and unpaid work by examining the question of who bears the (opportunity) costs of caring.

3 Sharing paid and unpaid work

Looking after the household and caring for other members of the household is a form of unpaid work. In a multi-person household, some members may contribute more unpaid work than others, just as some members of the household may contribute more income. This means that members of a multi-person household have to make a variety of decisions about how to divide up paid and unpaid work between them, and share the resources and risks that this division entails. The household model of a male breadwinner and a female caregiver never applied to all families, but it used to be more common in the UK and many other countries than it is today (Lewis, 2001).

Overall, across the world, women still do more work than men when both paid and unpaid work are considered, as shown in Figure 9.2. For example, the information in Figure 9.2 suggests women in developing and emerging countries do 7 hours 10 minutes a day of work (on average), paid and unpaid, compared to 6 hours 20 minutes for men.

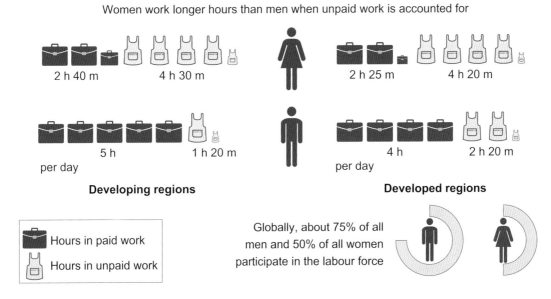

Figure 9.2 Time spent per day on paid and unpaid work for men and women (Source: United Nations, 2015)

Despite rapid changes in social norms with respect to the caring and earning roles of men and women, women are still considered the main caregivers in the vast majority of countries. This translates into lower employment rates for mothers than for fathers, and a gap between the two that is larger than that for childless men and women. Moreover, in some countries where the employment rate of mothers is relatively higher, or on par with those of childless women, it is often through part-time employment. As such, many couples with children adopt a so-called model of a 'one-and-a-half breadwinner', in which one partner earns full-time, and the other is doing part-time paid and part-time unpaid work (Grimshaw and Rubery, 2015).

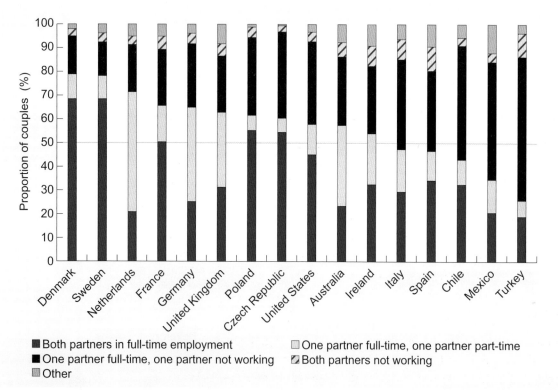

Figure 9.3 Distribution (%) of employment patterns in couples with at least one child aged 0–14 (circa 2014) (Source: OECD, 2018)

Activity 9.4 Comparing breadwinner models

Allow 10 minutes for this activity.

Using the data in Figure 9.3, identify the main differences across countries in employment patterns for couples with children.

Comment

Sweden and Denmark are by far the countries where a vast majority of couples are full-time dual earners. While both partners being in paid employment is the norm for a majority of couples in most countries, part-time employment for one partner dominates in the Netherlands, Germany and Australia (and is prominent in the UK too). Although Figure 9.3 does not show gender breakdowns, women take the largest share of part-time employment in all countries according to the same OECD (2018) database. Women also account for most of the partners not working. A male breadwinner model dominates in Chile, Mexico and, especially, Turkey.

A direct result of this unequal division of paid and unpaid work is that women earn on average much less than men, and mothers earn much less than fathers in all countries, even in the more gender-equal Scandinavian countries (World Bank, 2017).

While some women may prefer to be looking after their children and thus reduce their time in employment, a growing majority of women in many countries value paid employment, even when they have young children. However, many of them point to the lack of adequate institutional support – such as childcare services, flexible-working arrangements and more equal sharing of unpaid work with their partner – to explain the constraints they face in their career prospects, and why their working conditions are more precarious, and their work undervalued, compared with their male counterparts (Woodroffe, 2009; O'Reilly et al., 2014).

For a couple, decisions about who does the caring, and the balance of unpaid and paid work, need to be considered very carefully. If it is decided that the best way to meet the care needs of household members and relatives outside the household involves reducing time in employment, there is an issue of who should do this.

Is the full-time stay-at-home mother model of the late 1940s a thing of
the past?

Often, as you have seen, opposite-sex couples follow traditional gender
roles, but there is a slowly growing trend of couples who either divide
caring roles equally or where the man takes on the major share of
caring responsibilities, though the latter situation remains marginal
(Fondazione Giacomo Brodolini, 2011).

Although non-financial reasons may be decisive, there is some
economic incentive for the couple in having the lower-earning partner,
or the one with fewer career prospects, to cut down on paid

employment and do more unpaid work, because household income will fall less (with the higher earner possibly putting more time into paid work to make up the lost income). As you saw in Chapter 2, because women's wages are on average lower than men's, financial pressures will, in general, reinforce traditional gender roles. In turn, this may have long-lasting consequences for the person doing more unpaid work in relation to their earning prospects, and on their capacity to save and be more resilient in case of household breakdown (for whatever reason). Considering these risks is an important aspect of sound financial planning, to which we'll turn next.

4 Financial impact of taking 'time off'

Reducing time in employment has implications both in the short and long term, depending on the type of arrangement negotiated. Box 9.1 shows examples of different work–life balance arrangements that might be pursued.

Box 9.1 Different ways of reducing time in employment for care reasons

To allow more time for caring, someone in employment could:

- give up their current work and look for alternatives, with hours that fit better with their caring responsibilities

- give up their current work and look for other work only when they are ready to resume employment

- if they are an employee:

  - switch to working for themselves so that they can (theoretically at least) choose compatible working hours

  - take some statutory leave from their current job – this is a right in many countries, especially in the EU

  - negotiate with their employer to take some time out as a career break or sabbatical, or to reduce their hours in other ways, including by a 'job-share' arrangement.

The idea of human capital is useful when looking at the financial implications of work–life balance alternatives (Box 9.1). As you saw in Chapter 2, human capital is any accumulated education, training and work experience that make a person's work worth more to an employer than that of an unskilled new recruit, and so enables that person to earn more than a basic unskilled wage.

The effects on earnings of each of the ways of changing employment hours listed in Box 9.1 will depend on the types of skills required for a given job. However, in all cases when taking time off, especially for a prolonged period, there will be some loss of skills – including the more generic and transferable skills (as you saw in Chapter 2) – because skills need to be maintained through constant practice.

Moreover, specific skills related to a particular type of work may lose relevance if not updated regularly (think about a software developer or a pharmacist).

It is important at this stage to distinguish between two types of foregone earnings when reducing time in employment for caring reasons. One is the immediate loss of earnings when taking time off. In some cases, time off can be fully paid, either under statutory arrangement or because it is negotiated directly with (or offered by) the employer. A common example is paid holiday. Another example is maternity leave, although this is on full pay only in a few countries such as Germany, Spain and France (Blum et al., 2017). When time off is not fully paid, the immediate earning loss is easy to calculate before the decision to take time off is made, as information about payment is readily available from the employer, or nationally. We'll come back to these types of leave for looking after young children in Section 5 of this chapter.

The second type of foregone earnings is related to what happens when resuming employment after a break, especially on a part-time basis.

4.1 Part-time employment and earnings

When switching to part-time employment, pay conditions will not necessarily be pro rata to the previous full-time earnings, for the following reasons:

- There may be the possibility for the employee to reduce hours in their current job but not on the same level of hourly pay (although this is often seen as discriminatory and thus illegal).

- There may be no flexibility for an employee to reduce their hours, so they have to change jobs (even for a different job with the same employer) to one that may attract lower pay.

- A part-time job might only be found in a different industry or occupation, and often part-time jobs pay less well than full-time jobs precisely because they exist only in occupations that are less valued and demand 'lower' skills.

Research across OECD countries has consistently found that many carers trade-off more flexible and less stressful working time for lower wages, training and career prospects (OECD, 2010). This is called a **part-time pay penalty**. In the UK, for example, research has shown

Part-time pay penalty The difference between the hourly wage rate that a person would receive in full-time employment and what they receive in a part-time job.

413

that the gender gap in hourly wage rates between men and women was below 10% around the time of the birth of their first child, but grew gradually over the years to reach (and remain at) 30% by the time the child turned 12. Two thirds of that difference in hourly wages was due to women missing out on experience, and thus promotion prospects, through working part-time rather than full-time (Costa Dias et al., 2018).

Activity 9.5 Negotiating time off

Allow 10 minutes for this activity.

Not all workers do badly when changing to part-time work. Under what conditions would you expect the part-time pay penalty to be smaller?

Comment

Those who do best (financially) in part-time work are often those who negotiate working hours that enable them to stay with their current employer. Those in career jobs who negotiate taking a career break, reducing their hours or job-sharing, are much more likely to be able to retain their pay and promotion prospects.

Others who change employer but stay in the same occupation, where they can continue to use most of their skills, are subject to less of a pay penalty than those who change occupation, typically to less-skilled work.

Nevertheless, even those who stay in their current job do seem to suffer some long-term penalty for working part-time. Part-time workers tend to be offered fewer training opportunities and may not be as frequently promoted as full-time workers (Costa Dias et al., 2018; OECD, 2010). For the self-employed, it is important to consider how contracts can be honoured, so negotiating up front with clients about achievable goals and timelines might also help.

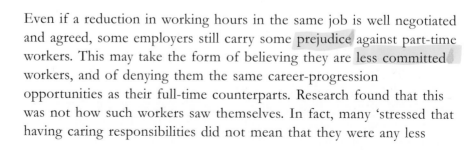

Even if a reduction in working hours in the same job is well negotiated and agreed, some employers still carry some prejudice against part-time workers. This may take the form of believing they are less committed workers, and of denying them the same career-progression opportunities as their full-time counterparts. Research found that this was not how such workers saw themselves. In fact, many 'stressed that having caring responsibilities did not mean that they were any less conscientious at work (although [many feared] … that that was how managers and colleagues would see them)' (Himmelweit and Sigala, 2004, p. 465).

Worries about how committed one is seen to be at work increase when unemployment is high because no one wants to be seen as dispensable. The law firm Leigh Day reported a rise in the number of calls during the 2008/09 recession from women facing maternity or pregnancy discrimination in the UK, and say there have been many examples of pregnant women being singled out for redundancy and of women returning from maternity leave to find their jobs have gone (Leigh Day, 2009).

Work–life balance is no game of scrabble

A 2014 survey in the UK by the firm Slater and Gordon found that:

> …three quarters of [women] polled reported their employer had been less interested in their career after they became a mother, while 63% said they felt their boss had a **negative perception of working mothers**. Nearly half said they were made to feel guilty for taking maternity leave and six in ten felt their career options were limited as soon as they announced they were pregnant.

4.2 Long-term considerations

Providing care by reducing time spent in employment has long-term implications through reducing earnings prospects. But paying for childcare has consequences too, in the form of foregone savings, especially in countries where childcare is expensive, such as the US, the UK and Ireland. However, if using non-familial childcare services allows everyone in the household to remain in employment with the same conditions, in the long term paying for childcare may be less damaging financially than undertaking unpaid care.

Persistence of lost income right through to retirement will also reduce the opportunity to build up pension wealth and pension rights (and the possibility of retiring early). More generally, caregivers – while accomplishing valuable and necessary unpaid work that is beneficial and enriching in many ways – may forego the opportunity to pursue all sorts of other life goals because of their reduced capacity to build up financial wealth. This in turn may affect their financial well-being in retirement, including the ability to pay for long-term care in old age, should it be needed.

Activity 9.6 considering short-term and long-term implications of caring

Allow 10 minutes for this activity.

If you were to have caring responsibilities now or in the future, how do you think you would consider the balance between immediate financial impacts and longer-term implications? What sort of behavioural traits might be at play in explaining the trade-offs?

Comment

There is no right or wrong answer to these questions, as many factors will be at play – including your preferences, your financial situation and your career prospects, as well as the system of state support and the type of services available in your country. Nevertheless, in the same way that saving and pension-planning decisions are affected by behavioural traits, so are caring decisions. Particularly relevant are a time preference for dealing with immediate issues (called myopia or present bias) and the difficulty of seeing the broader picture of how time and money are interrelated (thinking that caring decisions are different from financial decisions).

Of course these considerations implicitly assume that there are alternative choices and that behavioural biases influence these in a certain way. Another possibility, however, is someone being well aware of the future implications of having to care for a relative, but having no other option but to take time off work in the present.

4.3 A case study: Louise

The cash flow model that we have been building up throughout *Personal Finance* can be used to assess the long-term implications of caring decisions.

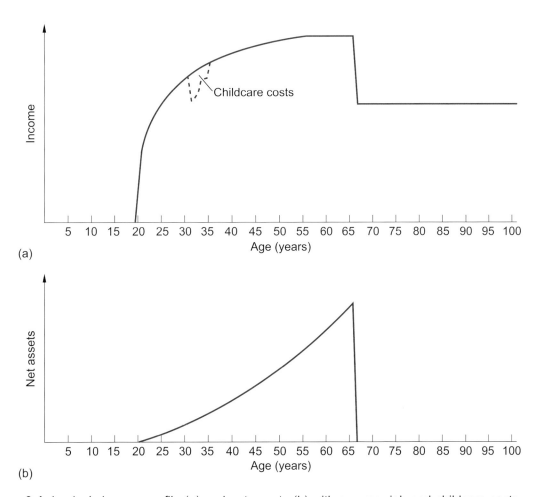

Figure 9.4 Louise's income profile (a) and net assets (b) with a career job and childcare costs

Consider, as an example for the UK, Louise, who has a career – a job in which she can expect her earnings to keep rising at least until her mid-fifties. When she is 30, she has her first child. Figure 9.4(a) on the previous page shows Louise's income profile if she carries on working after she has had the child, while paying for external childcare. Figure 9.4(b) (see previous page) shows her corresponding net assets building up until retirement, at which point she converts her pension fund into a lifetime annuity.

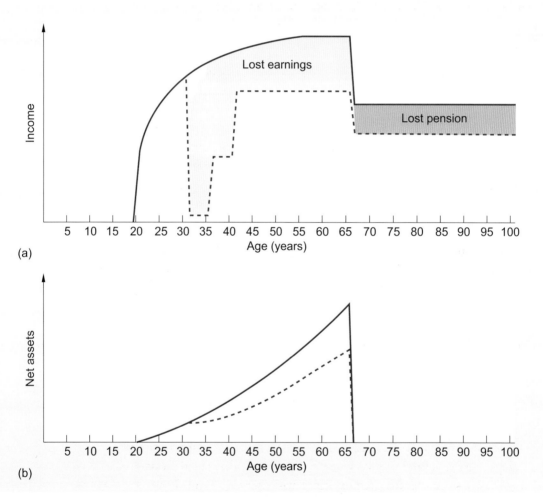

Figure 9.5 Louise's income profile (a) and net assets (b) with career breaks

By contrast, the stepped dashed line in Figure 9.5(a) shows what happens to Louise's income profile if she decides to give up employment to look after her child for five years, and then gets an unskilled job, because that is all that is available part-time. She then works part-time for the next five years, before moving back into full-time employment. As Figure 9.5(a) shows, her income drops significantly at age 30 (though she would still most likely receive some income from the state, including child benefit). When, five years later, she starts her part-time job (aged 35), her earnings are not even half as much as they would have been if she had stayed in her previous job (look back at Figure 9.4(a)) because she is not using her skills and is subject to the part-time pay penalty. At age 40, when Louise returns to full-time work, she escapes the part-time pay penalty and her earnings therefore more than double. Nonetheless, her earnings are still far below what they would have been had she stayed in employment, because she cannot get back onto her previous career ladder.

The shaded area between the two lines in Figure 9.5(a) gives a measure of the total earnings Louise has forgone throughout her working life. These forgone earnings mean a lower accumulation of net assets because of reduced contributions made to any workplace (and perhaps personal) pension scheme, both by herself and an employer, as shown by the dashed line in Figure 9.5(b). This in turn implies lower pension income from her annuity. Her state pension will be fully or partly protected by the protection the UK state pension scheme offers to carers (see Chapter 8).

We can use Louise's income profile to analyse her choice in terms of opportunity cost. For example, the opportunity cost of spending five years out of work and then five years in part-time work while looking after her child, is a loss of lifetime income (earnings plus pension) equal to the light and dark blue shaded areas in Figure 9.5(a): lost earnings plus lost pension, minus the cost to her of any extra childcare for which she would have had to pay if she had stayed in full-time employment. Another way to look at this is to say that the opportunity cost of Louise having the extra net income, is not having the time at home with her child.

There may be a way to reduce the opportunity costs of taking time out from employment. Think about what would have happened if Louise had negotiated some flexible arrangement with her employer. For example, instead of leaving her previous employment after a one-year break (maternity leave), she would remain in her previous job but on negotiated reduced hours (part-time) for nine years, paid at the same hourly rate as her previous full-time position. When she returns to her full-time position she accepts that her pay is to be a little lower than it would have been as a result of losing nine years' of full-time experience, but much higher than it would have been in a different part-time job, where she was unable to use her skills. This is shown by the dotted line in Figure 9.6(a).

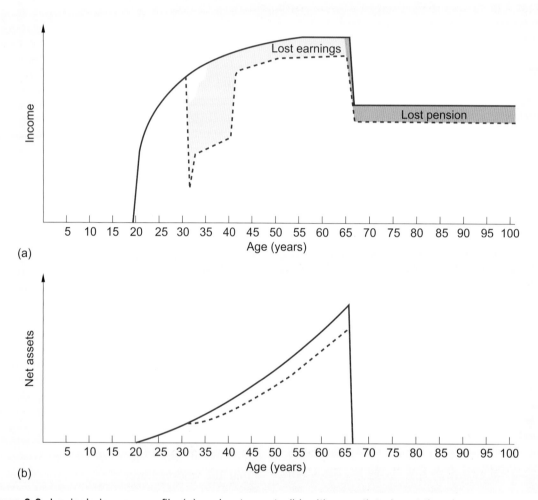

Figure 9.6 Louise's income profile (a) and net assets (b) with negotiated part-time hours

You can see the difference in Louise's lifetime earnings and pension income by looking at the shaded areas in Figure 9.6(a) and the dotted line showing net assets in Figure 9.6(b). Again, the full opportunity cost for Louise of this way of looking after her child is the difference in lifetime income minus any extra childcare costs that she would have incurred if she had stayed in full-time employment. In this latter example, for simplicity, Louise's childcare costs are assumed to be zero, which means it is assumed she found informal, free childcare from relatives.

Activity 9.7 Income profiles and caring

Allow 15 minutes for this activity.

Have a go at drawing income and net asset profiles (like those we have just analysed for Louise) for Jan, a mother who has a child at age 30 (the same age as Louise), and considers the same alternative patterns of employment as Louise. These are:

1 Carrying on working after a short period of paid maternity leave.
2 Caring for her child for five years, then working part-time for five years before returning to full-time employment.
3 After paid maternity leave of one year, working part-time until retirement.

Jan, unlike Louise, is not in a career job. She is in a job where she does not expect her earnings to rise after the age of 25.

Consider how this alters the opportunity costs of the different courses of action (1, 2 and 3 above) compared with Louise. (Assume that Jan receives a low flat minimum income from the state, as we did in Figure 9.5, and ignore childcare costs in all three scenarios.)

Comment

Suggested answers for this activity, showing income profiles for Jan and commentary about them, are provided at the end of this chapter.

The difference between Louise's and Jan's opportunity costs (outlined in the charts in this section and the suggested answers to Activity 9.7 at the end of this chapter) illustrates the choices mothers make in reality.

Mothers with high earnings from career jobs are far less likely to stop work when they have children than women who earn less or are not in career jobs. As a result, lower-earning women, who tend to give up work for long periods when they have children, end up paying higher opportunity costs (in foregone earnings) in the long run for having children than higher-earning women, who do not usually give up employment (Joshi and Davies, 2000). This is one of the reasons why the UK government (and governments in many other countries) subsidise childcare for mostly low-income households, especially lone parents. If Jan were eligible for such childcare subsidies, her financial position and choices would be different.

Another way to limit the long-term impact of time off to care for others is to retrain to obtain a new qualification or to enter a new career, including via courses provided by the Open University. However, even studying requires time, thus taking time away from caring, creating another trade-off.

The examples and discussion in this section have focused on childcare, but some people give up work or reduce their hours of employment in order to care for frail, disabled or elderly adults. The amount of time for which they will need these arrangements is generally less predictable than for children, and will often depend on the changing health of the person for whom they care. The effects on the income profile of a carer for an adult are thus much more difficult to predict, but in general the consequences on pension income may be important, even if the career break happens at a later age. Indeed, at a later age, the disruption may be more dramatic, with greater loss of earnings (greater opportunity cost), especially if the carer is on a career ladder. This is because earnings at the end of the career are typically larger than at the start. On the other hand, if the disruption occurs at a later stage in the career, the loss of compound return from reduced saving is comparatively lower.

The other main difference between childcare and long-term care for frail, disabled or elderly adults is how governments have organised and subsidised their formal provision, with a great variety of systems, which we will examine in turn in the next two sections of this chapter.

5 Government support for childcare

So far we have mainly considered how a couple decides on how to provide care for their family themselves, by reducing time in employment. This applies to both same-sex and opposite-sex couples, although the latter are more likely to operate along traditional gender role divisions. Single parents do not have to consider how to share paid and unpaid work within the household but they face similar trade-offs about work–life balance, while not being able to rely on a partner for income or care.

Parents (or carers more generally) may instead decide to increase their time in employment, in order to generate more income to pay for non-familial care. But often a combination of the two is at play, and as Figure 9.1 showed, the state also intervenes in many countries to support families financially and/or regulate the provision of care, including through care-related leave schemes (such as maternity or paternity leave).

When planning for immediate financial considerations of providing care, as well as the long-term financial implications, understanding the context in which these decisions need to be made is crucial, as countries differ widely in terms of their 'care regime', and they have also changed their priorities somewhat over the years.

In most countries, the material well-being of children and their social and cognitive development are seen as a matter of public concern and an investment in the future of society. Consequently, governments across the world have programmes to achieve these two objectives:

- **Material well-being** – programmes to counteract child poverty, with direct cash transfers for children, as well as helping parents to find decent employment and thus earnings (which requires adequate and affordable childcare).

- **Cognitive and social development** – accessible (often free) educational programmes and childcare subsidies.

You may also recall from Figure 9.1 that state intervention can occur via different channels of care provision. For childcare produced by parents (including by close relatives more generally), the following types of state intervention apply:

- Provision of paid parental leave (for the mother exclusively, for the father, or for both) and related career breaks, paid or unpaid but often with some degree of employment protection and non-discriminatory clauses.

- Regulation around flexible working and part-time work, with some protection on working conditions and pay, as well as setting a maximum working time over a given period, which could promote, among other things, more equal sharing of caring time between parents.

For non-familial care, typically two channels of care provision are promoted to varying degrees:

- Direct provision of childcare services and early education, free or with subsidised fees in public settings, or granting direct subsidies to private providers and capping their fees.

- Financial support for families to purchase childcare from the market, either via direct cash transfers or tax rebates, with or without means-testing.

Children at a learning centre in Brooklyn, US

5.1 Support for parental care

Typically countries offer some maternity leave that is well paid and protects mothers in their jobs, with some variation in pay level (and often there are some conditions about length of service before becoming pregnant). The UK is characterised by low-pay levels (low replacement rates) compared to its neighbours (Blum et al., 2017). The US is the only OECD country that didn't have statutory maternity leave at federal level at the time of writing (though some US states have legislated to provide for some paid leave).

The number of paid paternity leave days has increased over the years in most countries but remains well below that offered to mothers. Job-protected parental leave beyond the immediate period around birth is more diverse in Europe: some countries pay generous levels, such as Sweden, Iceland and Germany; others don't pay anything at all, like the UK and Ireland (Blum at al., 2017). The European Union has played an active role in developing a baseline minimum set of regulations to offer some employment-protected care-related leave, though member states could not agree on whether the leave should be paid or unpaid. In practice, member states differ in the extent to which they offer rights that are more generous than the minimum prescribed in EU regulations (Milotay, 2018).

Regulation of working time for individuals with caring responsibilities also varies greatly between countries. Some allow a statutory right to request a reduction in working hours (as in the UK, although it is not compulsory for the employer to agree to such a request); others allow part of the parental leave to be taken part-time over an extended period, as opposed to taking it all in a single block (Blum et al., 2017). However, these arrangements may still result in lower lifetime earnings owing to loss of human capital. By contrast, general regulation of the maximum length of the working week for all can help to level the playing field for people with caring responsibilities – and, at the same time, fostering improved gender equality – because it applies to all workers (De Henau and Himmelweit, 2013). Historically the length of the working week has been reduced in most countries. Some countries in Europe, such as Sweden, are even experimenting, at least in some industries, with six-hour working days, albeit with mixed results (Chapman, 2017).

Activity 9.8 General reduction of working time

Allow 5 minutes for this activity.

Why would a general reduction in working time for all be more effective in reducing gender inequalities, than offering flexible and job-protected leave arrangements for carers?

Comment

The idea behind such a move relies on the findings examined in the previous sections. In particular, carers are often penalised, relative to those continuing on a full-time basis, when reducing their working time individually. This happens even with protected jobs and conditions. But if everyone works less, it offers carers more time to look after their relatives (and more time for those without caring responsibilities to do other things) without needing special working arrangements. That means differentials in career prospects are less pronounced over time. Since fathers adjust their working pattern less than mothers on a voluntary basis, a blanket overall reduction of working time would mean all fathers would have more time to care for their children without suffering a penalty compared to childless colleagues, and thus in theory reduce gender inequalities in employment and pay.

Another form of support for parental care is for governments to provide direct cash benefits to stay-at-home carers. Doing so is similar to paid parental/maternity leave except that it is not related to employment, so carers who haven't been employed may still receive some payment in recognition of their caring work. Caring credits in the calculation of social security contributions – for example, towards a state pension, although not an actual cash transfer – are also a form of direct financial support. Some countries like the UK have even extended such protection to grandparents providing care, thereby recognising the significant contribution they make in allowing parents to combine paid work and caring responsibilities (Department for Work and Pensions, 2013).

Some countries also use the tax system to recognise the role of unpaid carers by allowing families to reduce their income tax bill when splitting income or sharing income between the partners. You will recall how Chapter 2 discussed the effect of individual versus household-based taxation systems. But although such cash benefits for stay-at-home care, and similar preferential tax treatment of full-time carers, may be seen as financial recognition of caring roles, they may also have long-term detrimental consequences on the financial position of the carer by entrenching their caring role and providing them with a disincentive to go back to (or to enter) the labour market (De Henau and Himmelweit, 2013).

Germany is a point in case as it used to have long, relatively low-paid parental leave (overwhelmingly taken up by mothers) and an equivalent home-care allowance for those mothers not in employment. This had the effect of trapping mothers either completely outside the labour market or, if they returned to work many years later, in low paid, low-career prospect (and often part-time) jobs (Geisler and Kreyenfeld, 2012). When the country switched to a shorter but earnings-related paid leave system, modelled on the more successful and more gender-equal Swedish system, mothers faced a lower penalty when returning to employment and had incentives to resume work earlier. This was, however, only possible through intervention in childcare provision, to cover care needs beyond the shorter parental leave period (Reimer et al., 2017).

5.2 Support for non-familial childcare

Non-familial care is often needed alongside parental care for several reasons:

- Not all parents can or want to spend all their time raising their children.

- Children benefit from contact with others, including other children from different families.

- Industrialised economies rely on more parents, especially mothers, working.

Despite initiatives by the EU and pressures from think tanks such as the OECD to increase good-quality, affordable provision of childcare, especially between the age of three and primary school, countries still differ widely by the degree to which the state subsidises childcare, and by the extent to which it does so via direct provision, subsidies for private provision, or cash transfers to families (OECD, 2018).

For children aged three and above, many countries have invested in direct provision of free or heavily subsidised provision (mostly in centres such as nurseries with some early educational elements). Provision for under-threes varies much more widely across countries, as Figure 9.7 shows.

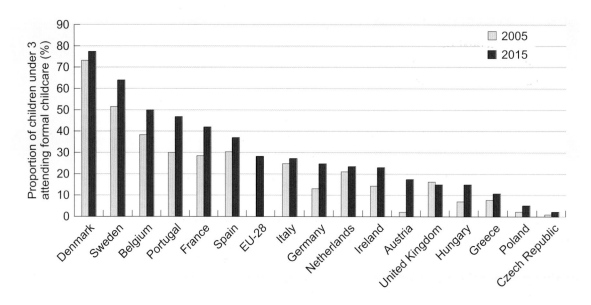

Figure 9.7 Proportion of children under the age of three attending formal childcare settings (for at least 30 hours per week), 2005 and 2015 (Source: EU-SILC survey (from the Eurostat Database), 2018)

Activity 9.9 Patterns of childcare enrolment for young children

Allow 5 minutes for this activity.

Looking at Figure 9.7, answer the following questions:

1 What is the main trend between 2005 and 2015 in terms of enrolment of young children in formal childcare services?

2 Do you recognise any regional pattern?

Comment

1 In all countries except the UK, enrolment rates have increased since 2005, especially in Austria and Germany.

2 Scandinavian countries such as Denmark and Sweden have much larger enrolment rates than eastern European countries, or English-speaking and German-speaking countries.

Only Scandinavian countries such as Sweden and Denmark have invested heavily in the provision of affordable childcare from a very early age of the child, followed closely by Belgium, Portugal and France. English-speaking countries have traditionally relied on private provision, mainly supported through cash transfers and tax relief to families, with unequal outcomes in terms of take-up and access (De Henau, 2017). In many eastern European countries, reliance on parental care for the first three years is still widespread, as state support for childcare collapsed after the fall of the Communist regimes in those countries, owing as much to resurgent traditional family values and renewed emphasis on the role of maternal care, as to persistent mistrust of institutionalised forms of care provision by the state (Thévenon and Solaz, 2013; Gauthier et al., 2016; Perek-Bialas and Raclaw, 2014).

When making decisions about childcare, parents often consider their employment and earnings prospects along with the cost of providing external care. They may consider the quality of care available, their own ability to provide equivalent care and their own assessment of how much parental care their children need (as well as how much time they would like to spend with their children). The resulting differences in childcare combinations that these constraints and preferences entail will have different financial and social implications for children, mothers and fathers, now and in the future.

While such decisions remain highly personal, a growing body of evidence has shown that high-quality, affordable formal childcare has long-lasting positive effects on a series of cognitive and social outcomes from an early age, especially for children from a more disadvantaged background (De Henau, 2017).

6 Planning for long-term care

Because of a disability, illness or frailty in old age, some adults need help from others to perform essential activities of daily living (ADL) such as getting dressed, washing, eating and going to the bathroom. They may also need help with activities that are necessary in order to achieve such essential daily living. These are often called instrumental activities of daily living (IADL) and include tasks such as cleaning the house, preparing meals, or dealing with finances (Bookman et al., 2007). The distinction is made between ADL and IADL because the latter can also be delegated to others by people who are not suffering from a loss of autonomy, but instead just don't have time or don't want to do them.

In most countries, those in need of long-term care (LTC) – often known in the UK as adult social care – rely heavily on informal help from partners and relatives. But the state also provides and organises some support, often prioritising those with more substantial needs (such as needing help for more than one ADL, without which their vital functions may be at risk), as well as those who cannot rely on informal help from relatives (including, sometimes, for IADL).

6.1 The process of assessing care needs and means

The issue of providing LTC differs to childcare in two main respects:

- First, long-term care needs are unpredictable – not all people will lose some autonomy and require help with activities of daily living. The intensity of the need also differs greatly.

- Second, often the condition that causes a loss of autonomy (mental impairment and/or physical disability) is permanent. So, with childcare, the state may see intervention and financial support as an investment in the productive capacity of the population, both current and future. This is less the case for long-term care. Therefore, state support for long-term care has traditionally been more neglected by governments and often considered as a burden. Sometimes it appears as a secondary objective behind solving issues in the health system (for example, having to intervene in the social care sector to reduce the pressure of hospital beds being clogged), or as an employment-creation policy, as the need for care workers keeps growing with an ageing population (De Henau et al., 2016).

The process of obtaining help from the state takes similar forms in many developed countries:

- The first stage is to assess someone's care needs. This is often done by a multidisciplinary team of health and social services professionals. It will include a health assessment but also assessment of the social situation of the person, including the role and availability that relatives can play, and whether care can be provided at home, or if it is better to move the person to a residential nursing home.

- The second stage is to determine the level and conditions of financial support to be provided. This is where systems differ most between countries, broadly along the following lines:

  (a) **universalism** – care is provided to all depending on their needs, not their means (as in the case of Denmark, with funding coming from general and local taxation)

  (b) **social insurance** – individuals make compulsory contributions to a social fund that will provide either the services they might need or financial support for the person to pay for care services on the market, including paid help from relatives (Germany is a typical case of this)

  (c) **social assistance** – individuals undergo a means-test on their income and/or assets that will determine how much financial support they can receive from the state; this support can take the form of a certain number of hours of services or a personal budget that they can freely spend on various ways of obtaining care (mainly in the UK and in France).

Financial support for carers of adults also exists in some cases, similar to that offered to child carers but often far less generous. Some countries, including Sweden, Germany and the UK, allow for caring time credits in the state pension entitlement calculations. They also offer direct cash benefits to help caregivers manage financially when caring full-time or having reduced their working hours. In Denmark, informal caregivers can be hired temporarily by the municipality to provide the care and receive a wage (MISSOC, 2018).

Governments can provide financial support for people who need care

6.2 Issues with care funded privately

Additional long-term caring needs not covered by the level of state support have to be self-funded or provided informally by relatives. There is a trade-off between depleting any potential inheritance through spending income and assets on care services, and relying on children and/or a partner to provide the care instead.

However, even informal care is not without cost. Caregivers need respite, and face opportunity costs themselves about combining work, leisure and care. And they may not be qualified for some types of complex needs, requiring professional assistance.

But spending on private professional services in the absence of state support is problematic too. Insuring privately for long-term care needs is also a difficult, if not impossible, endeavour owing to the unpredictability of the type and intensity of care needed. As Chapter 7 discussed, private insurers face too much uncertainty over risks to be able to develop attractive and affordable products that people may want to buy; as a result, adequate private long-term care coverage is almost non-existent without state support.

In Germany, private insurers exist but are subsidised by the state, and this is in addition to the country's compulsory social insurance scheme for long-term care. In the Netherlands, long-term care is provided solely through a compulsory social insurance scheme with no option to take out voluntary private insurance (MISSOC, 2018). Mayhew et al. (2017) explain that private long-term care insurance providers have disappeared in the UK, as people were reluctant to save for such protection. They note that adequate products would be far too expensive and people would be reluctant to buy them because they underestimate the risk of needing care in old age. Even in the US, a country prone to private market solutions, only about one in eight older Americans have long-term care insurance. Moreover, even for those who do, the cover is inadequate for most, with the daily payouts and the duration of payouts being limited. Most people have to rely on hands-on help from family and friends; or they pay for care as and when they need it, or, if they have insufficient income or assets, receive social assistance (Gleckman, 2015).

Activity 9.10 Issues with private long-term care insurance

Allow 10 minutes for this activity.

Recalling the principles of insurance that you explored in Chapter 7, why do you think private insurers would struggle to design suitable long-term care insurance products that people are willing to buy?

Comment

Several reasons can be suggested. First, the costs associated with long-term care can be huge (both on a day-to-day basis and over a prolonged period), affecting the premium, and at the same time it is difficult for the insurer to calculate the level of risk (about the length and intensity of care needs) if health information is not disclosed (such as, for example, predispositions to dementia). Second, on the demand side (that is, from a consumer perspective), many young and healthy people may not see the need to save or buy insurance products as the risk is perceived to affect only a minority of people in old age (even if long-term disability exists among working-age adults too). This is typical of behavioural biases such as myopia and present bias, as well as overconfidence.

Some insurers have developed care annuities, along the same lines as pension annuities: a lump sum is converted into a stream of guaranteed income, fixed or increasing over time by a predetermined amount, that helps pay for your care needs. However, because care needs are unpredictable, there is a high risk of the payouts being inadequate; for example, if a person's health condition(s) worsen(s), and requires additional time or spending on care. Also, the lump sum required to buy these annuities is substantial, and it's hard to know in advance how much to save, given that the amount and level of care required is uncertain.

Behavioural biases against saving for long-term care are also at play. As a result, care annuities are often not pre-planned, and available mainly to homeowners, as they have the capacity to release equity from their home (as you read about in Chapter 6) to buy a care annuity.

Because the costs associated with care can be very high, with assistance sometimes needed on a 24-hour basis, many people rely on informal care provided by relatives. A report by the US Congressional Budget Office (2013) found that long-term care delivered (at home or in institutions) through private insurance products constituted only 3% of the total spent on care provision in the US in 2011, compared to 30% by the government through its programmes for elderly (Medicare) and low-income people (Medicaid). 55% of the total was in fact delivered informally (with the time and effort doing care work valued at the price that would be charged if purchased on the market). As private commercial solutions are rare across the board, informal care tends to be more prevalent in countries with relatively little state investment in the sector. As Barczyk and Kredler (2018) document:

> In Northern countries with high public spending on LTC (Sweden, Denmark, Netherlands, Belgium) informal care accounts for only 28% of all care hours ... Southern European countries (Spain, Italy), in which the government spends least on LTC, have the highest percentage of informal care hours: 85%. The US, also a low public spender on LTC ... [has] an informal care share of 64%.
>
> (Barczyk and Kredler, 2018, p. 3)

Also paramount in many countries, especially in southern Europe, is the reliance on an informal (often migrant) care workforce to substitute for the lack of formal affordable solutions, and for when relatives are not able or willing to provide such care – either because they are themselves frail, live too far away, are already caring full-time for their children or other people, or in employment (van Hooren, 2014).

For those lacking both informal and formal support, long-term care needs are simply not met. A study of 12 European countries (excluding the UK) estimated that about 15% of adults aged 65 and over who had severe and critical need of care to perform essential daily activities did not receive any formal or informal help at all. It was more likely for these people to lack adequate help in central, southern and eastern Europe, where formal provision by government is less developed than in northern Europe; and the more materially and socially deprived their condition, the more likely they were to have unmet needs (Laferrere and Van den Bosch, 2015). In England alone in 2016, it was estimated that about 20% of men and 27% of women aged 65 and above had unmet care needs for at least one ADL. The proportion of those with unmet needs increased with age, especially for women, with 42% of those aged 80 or above reporting unmet needs for at least one ADL (NHS Digital, 2017).

7 Conclusion

This chapter has examined the financial implications of some of the most significant personal relationships people have: those that lead us to want to live with others and to care for them. It has also explained how changes over the life course that affect who we live with and the way in which we care for others, have significant and long-term effects on the financial situation of households and their individual members. Change over the life course and the interrelationship of individuals and their households are both key themes of *Personal Finance*.

Underlying these changes, we stressed how financial planning needs to take a life course perspective, assessing and adjusting plans as new information becomes available and implications of different decisions are compared, such as whether to stay in employment and pay for childcare, or negotiate career breaks.

In Sections 5 and 6, we looked at the extent and nature of government support towards childcare and long-term care respectively, highlighting different principles and traditions underpinning a wide range of systems across countries.

Knowing what the future holds is a luxury that not even very rich people have, and it is not only changes in relationships that can have financial implications. The changing context ultimately will determine the options faced by individuals when considering their long-term plans, including:

- demographic changes – such as an ageing population and the rise of single-person households

- technological changes, and the opportunities and challenges posed by automation with respect to the nature of caring relationships

- political and environmental changes, whereby nature and society are ultimately interdependent, and social reproduction – the possibility of a society to maintain and sustain itself – will only last if caring relationships and gender roles are considered central in discussions over sustainability (discussions which are often more geared towards the issues of climate change and natural resources).

All these key issues have fundamental implications for personal finance, and are explored in Chapter 10.

Answers to activities in Chapter 9

Answers to Activity 9.2

1 The Appledoughs' net income would be:

$50,000 - 10,000 = 40,000$

And their equivalised income would be 19,048.

2

(a) On the basis of equivalised income only, the Appledoughs seem to have a lower standard of living than the Pearsons.

(b) However, once childcare provision is considered, the standard of living of each family can be seen to be the same.

The Pearsons have a net income after childcare costs of 40,000, and thus their equivalised income after childcare is also 19,048. (You could think of the necessary spending on childcare by the Pearsons as a form of income tax: the income that a parent can earn from employment is reduced by the amount of childcare they have to pay in order to be able to work.)

This means that both families have an equivalised income of 19,048 combined with the benefit of the same amount of childcare. Of course, in choosing whether to buy in or self-produce childcare, non-financial considerations are at play, too – such as spending time with the children, the quality of the nursery, as well as longer term career prospects – which are looked at in Section 4 of this chapter.

Answers to Activity 9.7

Figure 9.8 shows Jan's income profile if she does not interrupt her employment when she has a child.

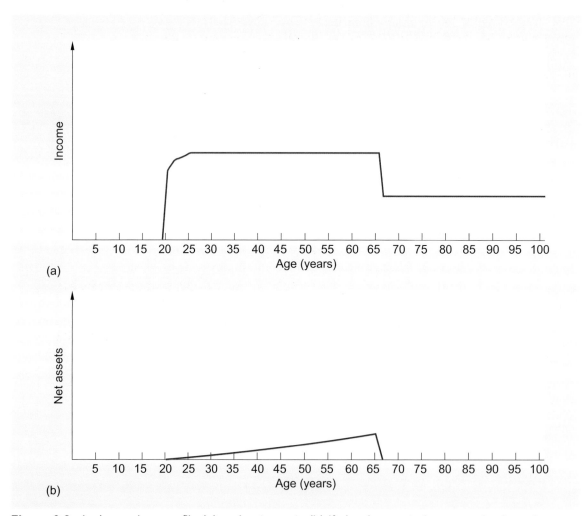

Figure 9.8 Jan's earnings profile (a) and net assets (b) if she does not give up work when she has a child

Figure 9.9 shows her income profile if she leaves her current job when she has a child, and then five years later gets a part-time job for five years, before returning to full-time employment. Her wage levels may remain a bit less than they would have if she had not left her original job, but Jan's total loss, including to her pension, is much less than it was for Louise following the same strategy. This is because Jan's earnings would not have kept rising had she stayed in employment, and her accumulated savings are so low that her pension income is mainly composed of a lump sum state pension.

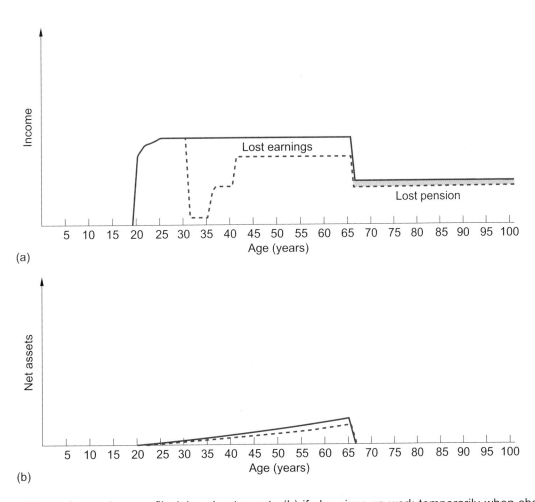

(a)

(b)

Figure 9.9 Jan's earnings profile (a) and net assets (b) if she gives up work temporarily when she has a child

Indeed, instead of a five-year break then a gradual return to full-time employment, if Jan takes a part-time job until she retires, as shown in Figure 9.10, she may lose relatively little in pension income despite losing more earnings overall, because of low savings accumulation and because she would get the same state pension.

Not surprisingly then, less educated women who are less likely to have career jobs, therefore have less to lose from taking time out of employment when they have children. They are therefore more likely to do so than more educated women.

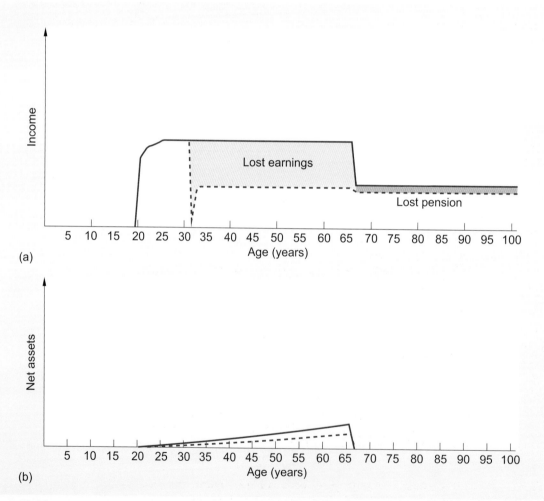

Figure 9.10 Jan's earnings profile (a) and net assets (b) if she works part-time for the rest of her life after maternity leave

References

Barczyk, D. and Kredler, M. (2018) 'Long-term care across Europe and the US: the role of informal and formal care', Department of Economics, University Carlos III de Madrid, January [Online]. Available at http://www.eco.uc3m.es/~mkredler/LTCEurope_Jan18.pdf (Accessed 3 May 2018).

Blum, S., Koslowski, A. and Moss, P. (2017) *13th International Review of Leave Policies and Related Research 2017*, International Network on Leave Policies and Research, June [Online]. Available at http://www.population-europe.eu/books-and-reports/13th-international-review-leave-policies-and-related-research-2017 (Accessed 5 October 2018).

Bookman, A., Harrington, M., Pass, L. and Reisner, E. (2007) *Family Caregiver Handbook: Finding Elder Care Resources in Massachusetts*, Cambridge, MA, Massachusetts Institute of Technology [Online]. Available at http://web.mit.edu/workplacecenter/hndbk/ (Accessed 3 May 2018).

Chapman, B. (2017) 'Sweden's six-hour working day is "too expensive" and could be scrapped', *The Independent,* 4 January [Online]. Available at http://www.independent.co.uk/news/business/news/sweden-six-hour-working-day-too-expensive-scrapped-experiment-cothenburg-pilot-scheme-a7508581.html (Accessed 13 February 2018).

Congressional Budget Office (2013) *Rising Demand for Long-Term Services and Supports for Elderly People*, Washington, DC, June [Online] Available at http://www.cbo.gov/sites/default/files/cbofiles/attachments/44363-LTC.pdf (Accessed 3 May 2018).

Costa Dias, M., Joyce, R. and Parodi, F. (2018) *Wage Progression and the Gender Wage Gap: The Causal Impact of Hours of Work*, Institute for Fiscal Studies, briefing note, no. BN223, London, IFS.

De Henau, J. and Himmelweit, S. (2013) 'Examining public policy from a gendered intra-household perspective: changes in family-related policies in the UK, Australia and Germany since the mid-nineties', *Oñati Socio-Legal Series*, vol. 3, no. 7, pp. 1222–48 [Online]. Available at http://ssrn.com/abstract=2296683 (Accessed 20 April 2014).

De Henau, J., Himmelweit, S., Lapniewska, Z. and Perrons, D. (2016) *Investing in the Care Economy. A gender analysis of employment stimulus in seven OECD countries*, Women's Budget Group, report to the International Trade Union Confederation, Brussels, March [Online]. Available at http://www.ituc-csi.org/IMG/pdf/care_economy_en.pdf (Accessed 20 May 2017).

De Henau, J. (2017) 'Costing a feminist plan for a caring economy: the case of free universal childcare in the UK', in Bargawi, H., Cozzi, G. and Himmelweit, S. (eds) *Lives After Austerity: Gendered Impacts and Sustainable Alternatives for Europe*, London, Routledge, pp. 169–88.

Department for Work and Pensions (2013) 'Looking after the grandchildren? Make sure it counts towards your state pension', press release [Online]. Available at http://www.gov.uk/government/news/looking-after-the-grandchildren-make-sure-it-counts-towards-your-state-pension (Accessed 20 September 2017).

Eurostat (2018) Database [Online]. Available at http://ec.europa.eu/eurostat/data/database (Accessed 10 April 2018).

Fondazione Giacomo Brodolini (2011) 'Gender equality in caring responsibilities over the lifecycle', conference background note, *Equality Between Women and Men*, European Commission (DG Justice), 19–20 September, Brussels [Online]. Available at http://www.bollettinoadapt.it/old/files/document/14955dg_justice_III_2.pdf (Accessed 20 September 2017).

Gauthier, A., Emery, T. and Bartovac, A. (2016) 'The labour market intentions and behaviour of stay-at-home mothers in Western and Eastern Europe', *Advances in Life Course Research*, vol. 30, December, pp. 1–15 [Online]. Available at http://www.sciencedirect.com/science/article/pii/S1040260815300010#bib0010 (Accessed 23 October 2017).

Geisler, E. and Kreyenfeld, M. (2012) *How Policy Matters: Germany's Parental Leave Benefit Reform and Fathers' Behavior 1999–2009*, MPIDR working paper, no. WP 2012-021, July, Rostock, Max Planck Institute for Demographic Research [Online]. Available at http://www.demogr.mpg.de/papers/working/wp-2012-021.pdf (Accessed 30 October 2017).

Gleckman, H. (2015) 'Steps on the path to public/private long-term care financing', *Forbes*, 24 June [Online]. Available at http://www.forbes.com/sites/howardgleckman/2015/06/24/steps-on-the-path-to-publicprivate-long-term-care-financing/#6c0f4e83314f (Accessed 20 April 2018).

Grimshaw, D. and Rubery, J. (2015) *The Motherhood Pay Gap: A Review of the Issues, Theory and International Evidence*, ILO working paper, no. 1, Geneva [Online]. Available at http://eige.europa.eu/resources/wcms_371804.pdf (Accessed 4 April 2018).

Himmelweit, S. and Sigala, M. (2004) 'Choice and the relationship between identities and behaviour for mothers with pre-school children: some implications for policy from a UK study', *Journal of Social Policy*, vol. 33, no. 3, July, pp. 455–78.

Jenkins, S. and O'Leary, N. (1996) 'Household income plus household production: the distribution of extended income in the UK', *Review of Income and Wealth*, vol. 42, no. 4, pp. 401–19.

Joshi, H. and Davies, H. (2000) 'The price of parenthood and the value of children', in Fraser, N. and Hills, J. (eds) *Public Policy for the 21st Century: Social and Economic Essays in Memory of Henry Neuberger*, Bristol, Policy Press.

Laferrere and Van den Bosch (2015) 'Unmet need for long-term care and social exclusion', in Börsch-Supan, A., Kneip, T., Litwin, H., Myck, M. and Weber, G. (eds) *Ageing in Europe – Supporting Policies for an Inclusive Society*, Berlin, De Gruyter, pp. 331–42.

Leigh Day (2009) 'Campaign against pregnancy discrimination launched', 21 May [Online]. Available at http://www.leighday.co.uk/News/2009/May-2009/Campaign-against-pregnancy-discrimination-launched (Accessed 20 February 2018).

Lewis, J. (2001) 'The decline of the male breadwinner model: the implications for work and care', *Social Politics*, vol. 8, no. 2, pp. 152–70.

Mayhew, L., Rickayzen, B. and Smith, D. (2017) 'Flexible and affordable methods of paying for long term care insurance', *International Longevity Centre – UK*, January, London [Online]. Available at http://www.ilcuk.org.uk/index.php/publications/publication_details/flexible_and_affordable_methods_of_paying_for_long_term_care_insurance (Accessed 6 April 2018).

Milotay, N. (2018) *A New Directive on Work-Life Balance*, briefing paper, European Parliamentary Research Service, Brussels [Online]. Available at http://www.europarl.europa.eu/RegData/etudes/BRIE/2018/614708/EPRS_BRI(2018)614708_EN.pdf (Accessed 2 May 2018).

Mutual Information System on Social Protection (MISSOC) (2018) 'Comparative tables', database [Online]. Available at http://www.missoc.org/missoc-database/comparative-tables/ (Accessed 20 April 2018).

NHS Digital (2017) *Health Survey for England, 2016*, 13 December [Online]. Available at https://digital.nhs.uk/data-and-information/publications/statistical/health-survey-for-england/health-survey-for-england-2016 (Accessed 12 February 2018).

O'Reilly, J., Nazio, T. and Roche, J. M. (2014) 'Compromising conventions: attitudes of dissonance and indifference towards full-time maternal employment in Denmark, Spain, Poland and the UK', *Work, Employment and Society*, vol. 28, no. 2, pp. 168–88.

Organisation for Economic Co-operation and Development (OECD) (2010) 'Chapter 4: How good is part-time work, *OECD Employment Outlook 2010 – Moving Beyond the Jobs Crisis* [Online] Paris, OECD, pp. 216–62. Available at http://www.oecd.org/employment/emp/48806797.pdf (Accessed 20 February 2018).

Organisation for Economic Co-operation and Development (OECD) (2018) 'OECD family database' [Online]. Available at http://www.oecd.org/els/family/　ibase.htm (Accessed 3 May 2018).

Perek-Bialas, J. and Raclaw, M. (2014) 'Transformation of elderly care in Poland', in Leon, M. (ed.) *The Transformation of Care in European Societies* [Online], Basingstoke, Palgrave MacMillan, pp. 256–75. Available at https://link.springer.com/content/pdf/10.1057%2F9781137326515.pdf (Accessed 3 May 2018).

Reimer, T., Erler, D. and Blum, S. (2017) 'Germany country note', in Blum, S., Koslowski, A., and Moss, P. (eds.) *International Review of Leave Policies and Research 2017* [Online]. Available at: http://www.leavenetwork.org/lp_and_r_reports/ (Accessed 12 March 2018).

Santos, A. (2015) 'Philippines: missing their parents', *Gulf News*, 27 July [Online]. Available at https://pulitzercenter.org/reporting/philippines-missing-their-parents (Accessed 3 December 2017).

Slater and Gordon (2014) *Working Mothers' Careers 'Derailed' after Becoming Pregnant*, press release, 12 August [Online]. Available at http://www.slatergordon.co.uk/media-centre/press-releases/2014/08/working-mothers-careers-derailed-after-becoming-pregnant/ (Accessed 20 October 2017).

Thévenon, O. and Solaz, A. (2013) 'Labour market effects of parental leave policies in OECD countries', *OECD Social, Employment and Migration Working Papers*, no. 141 [Online]. Available at http://www.oecd-ilibrary.org/social-issues-migration-health/oecd-social-employment-and-migration-working-papers_1815199x (Accessed 5 October 2018).

United Nations (2015) *The World's Women 2015, Trends and Statistics*, United Nations Statistics Division [Online]. Available at https://unstats.un.org/unsd/gender/worldswomen.html (Accessed 24 August 2017).

van Hooren, F. (2014) 'Migrant care work in Europe: variety and institutional determinants', in Leon, M. (ed.) *The Transformation of Care in European Societies*, Basingstoke, Palgrave MacMillan, pp. 62–82. Available at https://link.springer.com/content/pdf/10.1057%2F9781137326515.pdf (Accessed 3 May 2018).

Woodroffe, J. (2009) *Not Having It All: How Motherhood Reduces Women's Pay and Employment Prospects*, London, Fawcett Society [Online]. Available at http://www.equality-ne.co.uk/downloads/445_NotHavingItAll.pdf (Accessed 20 September 2017).

World Bank (2017) 'Gender Data Portal' [Online]. Available at http://datatopics.worldbank.org/gender/ (Accessed 20 September 2017).

To cite this chapter, use the following format in your reference list:

De Henau, J and Himmelweit, S. (2019) 'Caring and sharing', in De Henau, J. and Lowe, J. (eds) *Personal Finance*, Milton Keynes, The Open University, pp. 393–444.

Chapter 10
Personal finance in context

Rajiv Prabhakar

Contents

1 Introduction

[We] need new forms of regulation, social protection and redistribution appropriate for the global market system … The primary problem is systematic uncertainty, epitomised by a rising probability of economic volatility, insecurity and widening … income inequality. Citizens suffer stress and loss of well-being as a result, and consumption and investment are erratic and hypersensitive.

(Standing, 2011, p. 18)

Personal Finance has introduced and explored the decisions that individuals and households make about financial matters, such as expenditure, investment, debt, insurance and care. As the themes running through the chapters have reminded you, all these decisions are made within a particular context, taking account of specific relationships within households and reflecting different life stages. The aim of this chapter is to conclude and critically consider how financial decisions are shaped by a context that not only differs between countries, but that is also constantly changing and can be shaped by individual and collective actions.

Section 2 of this chapter offers a recap of how goals of personal finance are addressed. As achieving personal finance goals generally contributes to financial well-being, it is important to reflect on what is meant by 'financial well-being', which is the subject of Section 3.

Section 4 highlights how financial capability – which is one of the key factors that impacts on financial well-being – applies in different contexts. It introduces an influential taxonomy that is used to analyse different systems of social protection and thus different approaches to financial capability. Section 4 also examines how each system offers different roles for the family, the market and the state to provide financial security, and discusses their relative advantages and limitations.

Universal basic income
A regular payment made to all citizens or residents of a country, irrespective of their financial, employment or family situation.

Section 5 considers extensions of current aspects of social protection that have been proposed over many years, such as the idea of a **universal basic income**, which means that everyone receives a regular income payment from government. The section explores alternatives to basic income approaches to social protection, and how private and public ownership of resources can be remodelled to address technological, environmental, demographic and political challenges.

Juggling between the multiple aspects of personal finance decisions

2 Personal financial goals – a recap

Personal finance is understood in this book to mean the decisions, methods and products that individuals or households make or use regarding their money. Although money is central to this understanding of personal finance, the chapters have also examined decisions that do not directly involve monetary exchanges, such as spending time caring for a family member, but which nevertheless have financial implications.

Beyond the communities that we are part of and with which we meet regularly face to face, money is a way of keeping tally of who owes what to whom – whether this is in the form of debts, savings, insurance, taxes or benefits – and this is the bedrock of personal finance. Financial capability is, then (as you have seen), the ability to navigate successfully this type of monetised system. Households make decisions about helping each member, financially and otherwise. These decisions depend on the context of how employers, communities, the market and the state interact in a particular country, which will shape the type of financial capabilities required to achieve personal financial goals to varying degrees. As you have seen in the preceding chapters, there are a wide range of possible goals that people aim for, and these can differ between different people and households.

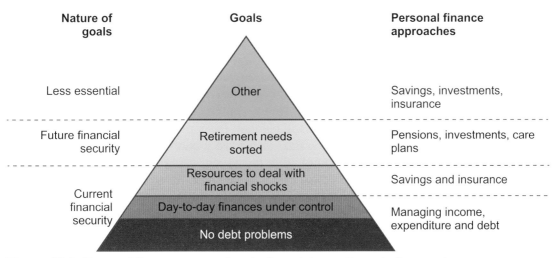

Figure 10.1 Personal finance approaches to financial security and other goals

Of course, goals need not fit into a neat pattern of addressing first current financial security, then future financial security, and finally less essential goals. Often we pursue a mix of different goals at any one time, and place different priorities on different goals. Because of behavioural traits, less essential goals may sometimes become a priority – such as treating oneself to an expensive holiday, while dismissing future financial consequences of maxing the credit card to achieve it – though most of the time these 'nice to do' or 'nice to have' treats will sit far behind other priorities. But this does not mean such goals are only possible if there is any money left over: planning for them can be achieved through investment and insurance too (saving for a holiday, insuring smaller risks, etc.).

Activity 10.1 Achieving your financial goals

Allow 20 minutes for this activity.

Think about some of the personal financial decisions that you have taken since you started reading this book.

1   Have your decisions followed a neat order of priority that resembles Figure 10.1 (on the previous page) or were they more intricate?
2   To what extent have contextual factors played a role in those decisions and influenced your goals?

Comment

Examples abound depending on your circumstances and preferences, such as: starting a budget, revising your pension options, clearing debts, saving for a house deposit, and preparing caring plans for a child. Because these decisions build on your unique personal financial situation, they might not look like they are following a neat pyramid. You may well be in a position where you can think of less essential goals because you have already planned for current and future financial security. However, you may also have thought that everything had been well planned, but then had to review decisions to achieve both current and future financial well-being because of, for example, a change in the context (such as a change in employment, a change in the law, or an unexpected family event). What you have learned so far about personal finance may also have improved your financial capability, changing the way you deal with financial decisions.

---

3 Financial well-being

Achieving financial security now and in the future, as well as achieving less essential goals, contributes to financial well-being, which allows you to attain a certain living standard – for example, being well fed, warm and sheltered. As such, financial well-being contributes to overall well-being, a multidimensional concept of quality of life, which includes having leisure time, maintaining physical and mental health, engaging in social interactions, experiencing new adventures, improving your knowledge and discovering the world, helping and caring for others, and so on. Often, financial well-being is needed to achieve other aspects of well-being, especially in more monetised societies. However, there may also be trade-offs between financial well-being and other parts of overall well-being; for example, if people have to give up leisure time to work to increase their income, and if achieving a certain living standard comes at the expense of their mental health (e.g. burnout from working too many hours).

Financial well-being contributes to the concept of general well-being

3.1 Is financial well-being subjective?

The concept of financial well-being has attracted growing interest among academics and policymakers. Based on a review of the existing literature, Brüggen et al. (2017) have defined financial well-being as the 'perception of being able to sustain current and anticipated desired living standards and financial freedom' (p. 229). They highlight four dimensions to their definition of financial well-being:

- First, they take a subjective approach (as the definition refers to how people perceive their own financial situation). This definition implies that people can only assess personally whether or not they themselves have financial well-being. The definition does not refer to any objective measures of their financial situation, such as how much wealth they own for a given set of needs. It is possible that two individuals have exactly the same financial situation (e.g. the same income and wealth) and the same household composition, yet one person might be more satisfied or optimistic about their situation, while the other might be pessimistic or unhappy about it.

- The second dimension refers to time, as the definition discusses both current and future living standards. Financial well-being does not focus simply on the present but also on how it can be achieved in the future (in line with the goals outlined in Figure 10.1).

- The third dimension points to a desired living standard. Not only do individuals subjectively assess their financial situation, but also what they want to achieve – well-being can be achieved for very different goals. Two individuals may find themselves living perfectly comfortably and feeling financially secure and complete, while living differently because of their different desires and values. One could be satisfied with growing their own crop and living in a shed surrounded by a loving and vibrant community, while another may prefer travelling around the world without a fixed home, and then there is the person who loves luxury items. So different goals may also mean different financial requirements. This subjective conceptualisation has been implicit throughout *Personal Finance* when looking at personal goals to achieve (rather than objective levels of income or wealth).

- Finally, the definition mentions financial freedom, capturing the idea that people should not feel stressed or constrained about making financial choices; for example, that they have sufficient resources available to splurge once in a while and be able to afford treats without it affecting their financial security. At the extreme it could mean being independent from an employment income, and living on the income generated by sufficient assets.

Activity 10.2 The Fox and the Grapes

Allow 10 minutes for this activity.

Aesop's fable *The Fox and the Grapes* tells the story of a fox who wants to eat some grapes but the grapes are too high on the vine for it to reach. Instead of admitting defeat, the fox declares that the grapes are undesirable as they are sour.

Write down some notes about the way in which this fable might be thought to undermine a view that financial well-being should be associated with self-perceptions.

Comment

Self-perceptions are subject to personality traits (optimistic, cheerful, cynical, etc.), adaptation (as in the fox's case) and comparison with others, which shape expectations. This means that self-perceptions may not always be a reliable guide to a more objective measure of living standards.

In the fable, when it is clear that the grapes are out of reach, the fox decides they are sour. So the fox adapts its desired objective to cope with the constraints that it faces, although it might starve as a result. In the same way, people might change their preferences to suit their situation, even if they are faced with a less desirable situation.

Illustration of Aesop's fable of *The Fox and the Grapes*

Chapter 3 of *Personal Finance* discussed how marketing pressures can shape individual preferences, and relying on self-perceptions alone creates the possibility that people might be manipulated into making financial decisions that can be harmful to their future financial security (e.g. taking on too much debt). Assessing our own financial situation may often require an outside benchmark, and this may involve using objective measures alongside our self-perceptions. Objective measures might include a minimum level of income or owning sufficient assets.

On the other hand, governments that ignore completely the existence of individuals' self-perceptions when designing policy interventions may fail to achieve the desired policy goals. For example, trying to incentivise people to save more by offering tax relief or attractive interest rates may not achieve the desired result in relation to people who are perfectly satisfied with their low levels of saving, because they want to live life to the full, even if this might go against their future financial security.

This tension has implicitly been explored throughout *Personal Finance*, and improving financial capability intends to offer some convergence between subjective and objective financial well-being (present and future).

3.2 Financial capability and well-being

Financial well-being, then, might be better seen as a blend of self-perceptions, as well as objective measures – such as whether or not people fall below a minimum level of income.

Brüggen et al. (2017) highlight four different factors that shape financial well-being, namely:

- interventions
- contextual factors
- personal factors
- financial behaviour.

'Interventions' (often by government) try to change the underlying conditions or structures that can shape decision-making. For example, automatic enrolment into a workplace pension is an example of a policy that seeks to shape the underlying environment. Tax relief on savings products is another example. Interventions might also aim to increase the knowledge, and change the perceptions, of individuals through education, advice, marketing or communication (Beshears et al., 2015).

'Contextual factors' refer to broad economic factors, such as levels of employment, interest rates, inflation and trade opportunities.

'Personal factors' – such as age, gender, socio-economic status or ethnicity – impact on financial well-being in different ways, as you have seen throughout this book. For example, in Chapters 5 and 9 you saw that men and women not only have different attitudes to risk but also face different financial risks, owing to different caring responsibilities.

Brüggen et al. (2017) put 'financial behaviour' as the central part of their model of financial well-being, which broadly covers the concept of financial capability examined in Chapter 1. Indeed, the set of skills, attitudes and behaviours that people display when making financial decisions will impact on their financial well-being, bearing in mind the contextual factors and the resources available to them.

Figure 10.2 outlines a model for interpreting and representing the main parts of financial capability as it is applied in the UK and similar industrialised countries. In the figure, financial capability is only one of the influences on financial well-being; two other factors – financial means and financial pressures – are also picked out as relevant.

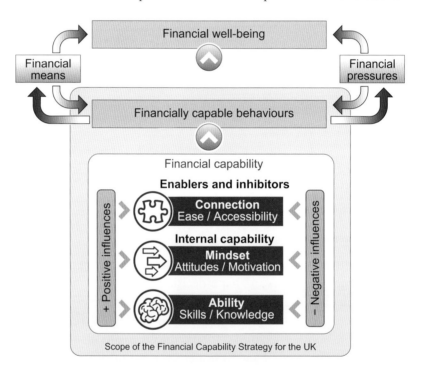

Figure 10.2 A model of the determinants of financial capability and financial well-being (Source: The Money Advice Service, 2015)

Importantly, Figure 10.2 also shows the different factors contributing to financial capability itself. 'Internal capability' highlights that if people are to make financial decisions, then they must be both able and willing to make decisions. Within that, 'mindset' refers to the disposition of people to make decisions, their motivations and attitudes. The prospect of financial gain or reward might give people a direct incentive or motive to make a decision. Previous chapters have introduced the importance of behavioural biases for individual financial decisions and how these can be exploited to achieve desirable goals by governments. For example, Chapter 8 examined pensions and how automatic enrolment in pension schemes has exploited the role played by inertia (being slow or reluctant to change behaviour).

'Connection' in Figure 10.2 refers to the extent to which people have access to the financial system. People or households may have all the knowledge and skills to make financial decisions but may be financially excluded because they don't have access to financial products. This may occur for different reasons: financial institutions can place direct barriers such as credit ratings, or exclude people more indirectly by designing products unsuitable for some households (such as requiring a minimum lump-sum to open a savings account, or providing online-only products). People can also self-exclude if they do not trust financial institutions for whatever reason.

4 Revisiting the context of financial capability

As examined throughout this book, the social and economic context influences not only the resources, pressures and constraints that we all face, but also our financial capability to achieve our financial goals. This context essentially relates to the interplay between interventions by the market (financial and non-financial corporations), government, and the household sector (core and extended families). Note that the household sector also generally includes the community of our friends, neighbours and charities providing 'free' services. This interplay determines the degree of financial security we can aspire to, and the extent to which our financial goals can be realised and needs satisfied. Individual and collective **agency** can be exerted to shape this social and economic context – through consumer choices, political action and social movements – and has indeed contributed to multiple changes over the years.

Agency
Attempts to respond to, and influence, circumstances and the broader social and economic context.

4.1 Three worlds of 'welfare capitalism'

To provide financial security, industrialised countries have traditionally relied variously on three main types of institutions – market, state and family – which broadly correspond to the sectors (corporations, government and households) identified in the circular flow of income in Chapter 1. This has led to the emergence of different types of welfare regimes. You have already explored some of these issues in previous chapters when looking at particular elements of social protection such as pensions (Chapter 8), care (Chapter 9) and social security benefits for working-age people (Chapters 2 and 7).

The Danish sociologist Gøsta Esping-Andersen (1990) wrote a book called *The Three Worlds of Welfare Capitalism* that has been hailed as a classic within comparative social policy research. Esping-Andersen developed a typology that became very influential in analysing different welfare regimes in economies based on **capitalism**, which make up the majority of the world's countries. Although looking only at some OECD countries, he identifies three broad types of social protection system, which are distinguished in Table 10.1. Systems differ by the extent to which they rely on market solutions, rather than state provision of social security, and by the extent to which entitlements are

Capitalism
An economic and political system in which the factors necessary for the production and sale of goods and services (such as land, machines and patents) are controlled by private owners seeking profit, rather than by the state or the community.

linked to employment status or are more universal. He classified systems conceptually, according to the degree to which people depended on selling their labour in order to survive and gain financial security (through which an income would provide for their needs), versus systems that enacted social rights for all citizens, not just those who are, or have been, employed.

Table 10.1 Different welfare regimes

	Liberal	Conservative	Social democratic
Country that exemplifies this system	US	Germany	Sweden
Other countries include	UK, Australia, Canada, New Zealand, and many from central and eastern Europe	Japan, Korea, Austria, France, Belgium, Italy, Spain, Greece	Denmark, Norway, Netherlands
Key institution	Market	Family (and type of employer)	State
Extent of social security benefits	Means-tested	Benefits linked to occupational status	Universal
Role of the market	Prominent	Moderate	Limited
Role of the family (and women as carers)	Limited: women encouraged to participate in the labour market	Important: married women encouraged to perform caring responsibilities within the family	Limited: strong support for female independence and autonomy of citizens, including children

Source: adapted from Esping-Andersen, 1990, 1999; Sainsbury, 1994

In a later publication, Esping-Andersen (1999) responded to feminist criticism of the lack of gender analysis in his original classification, which ignored how the family (and thus women as primary caregivers) was also being given a role of providing social protection, separate from interventions by the market and the state (Lewis, 1992; Sainsbury, 1994). In welfare regimes where this was more the case, women would gain less economic independence as there would be more expectation on them to provide for their family by doing unpaid work. The main features of this model of welfare systems are outlined in Table 10.1 on the previous page.

He named the three regimes the 'liberal', 'conservative' and 'social democratic' worlds of welfare capitalism. Using data from the 1980s for 18 OECD countries, he identified the following countries as typical examples of each regime: the US is the prime example of a liberal system, Germany of a conservative system, and Sweden of a social-democratic system.

Liberal

In a liberal system, the market is the main way of organising economic and social life. The role of the state is mainly to regulate the smooth operation of the market, but it also intervenes as a safety net to help those falling below a certain threshold (of income or health). These welfare regimes are also called 'residual' for this reason (residual role of the state). Benefits are means-tested and aimed at the poorest in society, while public services partly operate with private, for-profit mechanisms. Women have no choice but to take an active role within the labour market in order to provide for family needs, because no specific protection is given to homemakers and carers. However, countries that have this type of welfare regime differ in the extent to which they provide help for caring responsibilities. In some countries, rather than limiting its intervention, the state could, for example, provide childcare support to ensure all parents can work and so achieve economic security through their earnings.

Conservative

Under a conservative welfare regime, a single breadwinner model is seen as a bedrock of the social protection system. Conservative systems prioritise transfers within the family, with one earner being granted protection through their employment status that can be extended to dependent members of the family, while at the same time the other partner is encouraged to provide care at home. The system establishes rules of familial support and facilitates transfers of wealth from parents to children through inheritance. It institutionalises caring responsibilities performed by women at home, sometimes with financial rewards in the form of cash benefits (as explored in Chapter 9).

Social democratic

The role of the state is much more important within social-democratic systems, and it is often aimed at ensuring equality and economic independence of all citizens, including children, by granting them social rights. This means an emphasis is placed on the redistribution of wealth and income throughout society and on making sure individuals do not depend on selling their labour to survive.

Activity 10.3 Applying the three worlds of welfare capitalism

Allow 15 minutes for this activity.

Think about a welfare regime that you know well – perhaps the system that exists where you are currently living. To what extent does the welfare system slot neatly into the threefold typology summarised in Table 10.1? Is it more accurate to say that the welfare system is a blend of the different types, depending on which policy is looked at and when?

Comment

In principle, the three welfare regimes can be applied to a large variety of different countries. However, the three different systems described are 'ideal types' – that is, where a particular system exists in a 'pure' form. The reality is usually much more complex and messy than the typology. Welfare systems have evolved over time and in response to a wide variety of factors. They do not fit easily within a single category.

For example, in the UK:

- The National Health Service (NHS) is universal and free at the point of delivery. This falls within a social-democratic regime.

- Some married couples (and civil partners) have particular benefits in the tax system to operate transfers between spouses. These tax breaks might be considered part of a conservative approach to welfare.

- Means-tested benefits are payable, conditional on strict requirements to seek employment, which belong to a liberal model.

The UK therefore has a mix of the three different welfare regimes, even if on balance it could be seen as relying on market solutions more often than not.

Even Germany, which used to slot neatly into the conservative system, has evolved towards a more Scandinavian, social-democratic model, with more generous state intervention to support working parents with childcare.

The different worlds of welfare capitalism typology has sparked a huge amount of academic literature by both supporters and critics discussing the framework, the principles, the countries used, and the conclusions, but broadly agreeing about the interplay between the respective roles of the market, the state and the family (as reviewed by Arts and Gelissen, 2002; Emmenegger et al., 2015).

Esping-Andersen (1999) accepted that his typology, even revised, remains a simplification of reality. However, typologies can be useful as models for analysis and synthesis of complex relationships in the real world.

Welfare regimes have also evolved over time in response to changes in political philosophies, such as the fall of communist regimes in Europe and central Asia.

Demographic pressures of an ageing population and pressures to move away from a traditional gendered division of roles have also influenced policy changes. And changing social norms with respect to traditional gender roles have increasingly seen countries offer more public support to help with childcare responsibilities and enable women to gain more economic independence from their partners.

At the same time, economies with an ageing population have seen many governments transfer back more and more risk from the state on to individuals, while also promoting employment for all (as a source of financial security). As a result most countries today could be classified as 'hybrid', with a mixture of family, market and state roles providing social protection and financial security (as represented in Figure 10.3). Let's look again at the main advantages and disadvantages of each of these in turn.

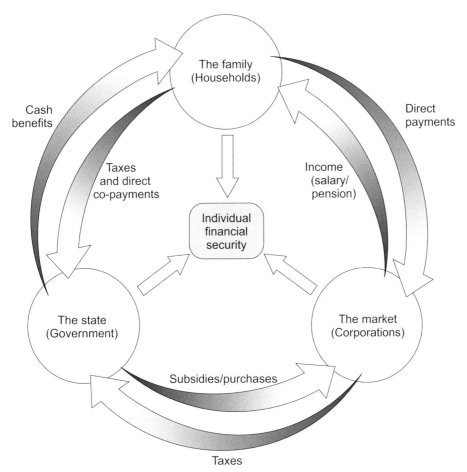

Figure 10.3 Three institutions providing social protection

4.2 The role of the family

The family – core or extended, including the local community – could meet caring needs, provide financial help or create economies of scale for household tasks. Using the family to achieve welfare needs has a number of possible advantages:

- no money exchange is usually involved in household tasks (although parents might reward children with pocket money for certain household jobs)

- there is good mutual knowledge within the family, and trust and shared values may be important

465

- money as a transaction instrument can be replaced by mutual obligations, enforced by norms and customs, so that a system of credits and debts can still apply to such relations – for example: 'I help you today so that you will help me tomorrow'; 'I provide food in the expectation that you will provide care'.

However, there are important disadvantages of relying on the family to provide all forms of social protection, such as:

- families may be quite small and cannot be used as an efficient or effective form of risk pooling to protect people against certain events such as natural disasters (flooding or contagious diseases)

- families may break down (death or separation), which disrupts the reliance on specific roles to provide harmonious mutual social protection

- as we have seen, specialised roles imposed by social norms can be disputed as being less beneficial to some family members, in particular women

- a possible limited capacity for different members of the family to develop skills to meet future challenges.

As a result, the market and the state may be needed to address the limitations of familial social protection.

4.3 The role of the market

A market-based approach to social protection stresses the role of transactions as a solution to nearly all welfare challenges. People satisfy their preferences and needs by making choices within markets.

Chapter 6 taught the demand and supply model in the context of a housing market. In that context, a price emerges that allows for the sale of a property. This means that there is a buyer who is willing to purchase a particular property at a particular price, and also a seller who is willing to sell at that price. This market transaction is described as being in equilibrium.

This general idea of demand and supply applies to all types of markets. For example, you can buy chocolate, insurance and a holiday in the retail market. You can sell your skills and experience (your human capital) on the labour market in exchange for income (as explained in Chapter 2). Even illegal transactions (such as loans that charge interest in sharia law countries; or the purchase of some medications in countries where they are unauthorised) often take place on the grey market if there is a buyer and seller that find interest in the transaction, notwithstanding the risks of being caught.

Markets have a number of possible advantages (over the family or the state) to provide some social protection. One is that, under the right conditions, they lead to 'an efficient allocation of resources'. This is typical economic jargon that essentially means that everyone finds or provides what they want at the price they are happy with: in other words, buyers and sellers reach equilibrium in all types of markets.

In market-based systems, choice for the consumer is essential. Therefore another advantage of markets is that they may provide strong incentives for innovation if, for example, there is a lot of competition between many players to provide the best product or service and attract more customers.

In market-based systems, people exchange money for goods and services to achieve their goals

However, these two advantages of allocative efficiency and choice of innovative products can only exist if:

- everyone has access to complete and full information about the products or services available in the market

- there are a very large number of suppliers competing with one another.

Deviations from these two conditions can introduce inefficiencies and frictions. For example, Chapter 7 studied the problem of adverse selection in insurance markets owing to asymmetric information between the buyers and the sellers of insurance. This creates inefficiency because sellers of insurance find it difficult to set premiums based on actual risk types, and so low-risk individuals face the prospect of higher premiums than they would otherwise pay if there was complete and full information available.

Another disadvantage of market mechanisms is determining whether or not people get access to goods and services based on their ability to pay for them. Having access to money (income or debt) as a prerequisite to achieve financial security means that markets are exclusionary to those without the ability to pay. Consumers also need to be financially capable if they are to make effective choices within markets.

Consumers bear much of the risk for outcomes within markets, as you have seen, for example, with defined contribution pensions in Chapter 8. Critics argue that the fact that consumers have to bear so much risk highlights some of the main flaws with a market-based system for achieving financial security. In particular, you might possess financial capability and plan ahead for retirement and all the care that may be needed in later life, but the outcome might be shaped ultimately by factors entirely out of your control. Standing (2011) says that precisely this situation occurred around the time of the global financial crisis of 2007–08. He argues that financial institutions were mainly responsible for the crisis, and this had a direct effect on pensioners because it depleted the size of their final pension pots after the crisis. He writes:

> Savers have done nothing wrong, except to follow the urgings of successive governments [and international institutions] over two decades [which] had all eulogised 'private savings accounts' and defined contribution private pensions. Now those who took their advice were penalised.

> (Standing, 2011, p. 13)

Activity 10.4 The financial capability model in market-based systems

Allow 15 minutes for this activity.

Apply the model of financial capability outlined in Figure 10.2 (which you encountered earlier in this chapter) to highlight the likely features of financial capability within a market-based system.

Comment

Financial capability is particularly important within a market-based system, where people have the main responsibility for meeting their own welfare needs.

Figure 10.2 can be used to give a broad outline of the nature of financial capability within a market-based system. In such a system, people have to rely mainly on their own financial means: their income and wealth. People might also have to borrow to pay for certain things, so they need to be able to make decisions about the appropriate level of borrowing given their repayment capacity.

People also need full access ('connection') to the financial system as the main provider of social protection (e.g. insurance and pension products) – and there may be a role for government here in tackling and reducing financial exclusion. Also, individuals need to have specific skills such as the ability to choose between different products and keep track of their finances, as well as household budgeting. They also need to have skills in planning ahead, as they are required to make their own provisions for their retirement and care plans.

Box 10.1 Personal finance and the global financial crisis

Financial capability has attracted increasing attention among policymakers following the 2007–08 global financial crisis. O'Donnell and Keeney (2010) write that the financial crisis 'only serves to highlight the importance of finance capability. It can be argued that the sub-prime crisis in the US, which had such global ramifications, was a manifestation of poor levels of financial capability there' (p. 362).

A key concern is that shortfalls in financial capability is thought to have contributed directly to the crisis. In particular, in places such as the US and UK, it is claimed that people made poor decisions about secured borrowing.

The 'sub-prime' housing market refers to housing aimed at those on low incomes. Financial institutions such as Freddie Mac targeted low-income consumers, and encouraged them to borrow heavily to purchase a home. With such seemingly attractive loans, demand for housing increased rapidly, so that house prices inflated into a bubble. Once this bubble burst, many low-income households faced negative equity and/or problems in meeting their mortgage repayments.

The sub-prime crisis had its origins in the US, but the global nature of financial markets meant that it spread quickly to places such as Iceland and the UK. Policy-makers argue that higher levels of financial capability would have allowed borrowers to make more informed choices about levels of personal borrowing, and could avert a future crisis.

Critics of this view suggest that the focus on financial capability ignores the critical role played by financial institutions and governments in creating the crisis. Financial institutions aggressively targeted low-income consumers, and the complexity of financial products created difficulties for regulators. Furthermore, governments encouraged consumers to spend money on housing by relaxing credit constraints on secured borrowing. Sceptics suggest that the focus of reform should, accordingly, be on governments and financial institutions, rather than consumers (Crouch, 2008; 2009).

4.4 The role of the state

State interventions in providing social protection can either be as a complement or an alternative to family and market solutions. When social protection is deemed to be ensured by the state, it is often understood as covering all citizens (nationals), or sometimes all residents, in a country, based on principles of universalism and social rights. This is in contrast to systems in which social protection for individuals depends on them belonging to a family, a firm (as an employee), and/or selling their labour for an income, or owning assets and thus being able to 'afford' financial security.

In general, the state has been tasked (by social pressures and public opinion in favour of guaranteeing some social and human rights) with intervening in domains where the market or the family do not provide adequate services (for reasons linked to inefficiencies, as discussed in the previous sections). For example, in most industrialised countries, health protection is more adequately delivered by collective (state) systems that include everyone. Because of asymmetric information on needs and costs, state systems are the only way to guarantee that nobody is excluded from accessing healthcare, in principle (as seen in Chapter 7). A collective system of 'social insurance' is based on a larger pool of people than families or those who can buy protection from the market, and so can spread risk more effectively and equitably than families and markets can.

The state can regulate markets to try to avoid issues such as mis-selling of products or services. It can also make long-term decisions about the environment, training and qualifications for the future, and basic scientific research. These long-term decisions will sometimes only bear fruit in the distant future (or not at all) and therefore may not be undertaken easily by families or corporations that have more immediate preoccupations.

Social protection services and cash payments (benefits) in a state system do not operate by following price mechanisms of demand and supply. Instead, taxation levied on corporations and households is used to redistribute resources in the country according to needs. Although not all public services are free at the point of use, they are often subsidised and cheaper than services (such as transport, healthcare in some countries, childcare, etc.) provided by the market. In redistributing resources through progressive taxation, cash benefits and services (benefits in kind), the state also performs a fundamental role in helping people enjoy a minimum standard of living. At the same time, redistributing resources fosters social cohesion and mutual trust by reducing inequalities, which is not only a matter of human rights but also an important factor for sustainable economic activity.

Changing the welfare state is a political risk

However, state intervention also has significant disadvantages. For example, long-term strategies implemented by governments may be jeopardised by short-term considerations: as political consensus is needed and votes are sought, short-term priorities can sometimes lead to large breaks in policy and undermine stability (e.g. Donald Trump's U-turn on some environmental-protection rules). Politicians and bureaucrats might also be more interested in pursuing their own specific interests, rather than responding always to the needs of citizens or consumers. Under some (extreme) conditions, some politicians might be prone to certain types of corruption, for example by flouting rules on procurement to benefit their own friends and political allies.

State-funded services have also been criticised for stifling creativity and competition because, being the only provider in place, they restrict options for users and can sometimes lead to inefficient provision, or services costing too much. This tension has played a big role in the gradual (and sometimes radical) introduction of market mechanisms in public services and state-owned industries over the last 40 years, as examined in Chapter 1, through privatisation and deregulation. Fierce debates in economic and political circles have essentially gravitated around the questions of what 'costing too much' means and for whom (including opportunity costs), and how much choice should there be for consumers, when information on products and services is not complete.

Activity 10.5 Financial capability in a universal welfare state

Allow 15 minutes for this activity.

Consider a social-democratic welfare regime (with generous state intervention in providing public services and universal cash benefits, based on needs rather than income), as summarised in Table 10.1. Apply the model of financial capability described earlier in this chapter (Figure 10.2) to such a system, to outline its main implications for your personal finance decisions and planning.

Comment

A generous, social democratic-style welfare state might guarantee people a minimum standard of living, and provide universal and generously funded benefits paid for through collective taxation. In terms of the elements of the model in Figure 10.2, this would then provide households with a minimum level of financial means and relieve financial pressures on many (to cope with sickness, loss of job, care needs, etc.).

Widely accessible provision of public services would limit the extent to which you need to make your own provision for essential goods and services. This means that some domains of financial capability may be less important than in a market-based system. For example, the accessibility you may have to the financial system (i.e. 'connection' in Figure 10.2) may not be a priority, given that these goods and services might be provided by the state (such as a generous pension). However, you would still need financial capability, because you would still have to make decisions about how to spend any benefit you may receive, and also to make choices about employment given the prevailing tax regime. For example, if you were retired, you would need to have appropriate skills or knowledge of household budgeting, even if you had a generous state pension.

Although universal state provision of many aspects of financial security may reduce the need for knowledge and understanding of specific financial products, citizens would still need to be financially capable to be able to scrutinise policy choices and hold policymakers to account for their spending priorities. In particular, they would need to understand tensions between long-term and short-term interests (and the influence of behavioural biases on these), in order to avoid derailing political commitments based on long-term strategies, which might appear costly for the taxpayer of today (for example, tackling climate change by taxing uses of fossil fuels more heavily).

Some of the economic principles, such as trade-offs and opportunity costs, examined earlier in *Personal Finance* are useful to think about here. For example, levying a tax on the current adult population to fund vast programmes of childcare – even on those with grown-up children or who won't have any children – may seem a burden now, for many people. However, as discussed in Chapter 9, it yields larger benefits for all in the future, because, in general, well-cared-for children will turn out to be more productive contributors to society, and that contribution may include looking after those who paid the tax in the first place, if or when they become elderly. Similar reasoning applies to investing in protecting the natural environment.

5 Beyond the welfare state: robots, work and universal income

Funding welfare states still relies heavily on taxes levied on income and consumption, and in most countries of the world income (and thus consumption) arise mainly from paid employment (rather than from property and financial wealth). Market-based solutions to social protection also rely on people's income from employment. Therefore, the spectre of the 'end of work' due to technological change – such as the spread of artificial intelligence and computing connectedness – is looming ominously in many contemporary debates.

Artificial intelligence concerns the extent to which it may be possible for computers to 'think' like humans and replicate human thought processes. This has a wide set of possible applications. More sophisticated generations of robots might be able to perform a greater range of human activities, making more human workers 'redundant'. Although, on the other hand, they could help take on the burden of many tasks (such as the heavy lifting of patients, surgery performed remotely, processing administrative tasks, carrying out the night watch of premises – you name it!).

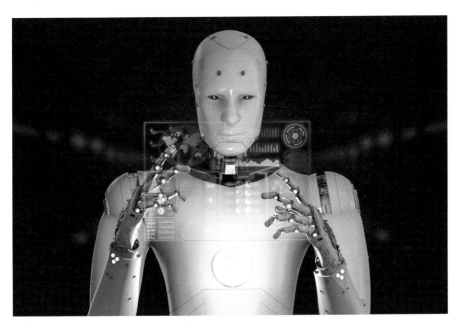

It may be possible for robots to take on complex human tasks

Some argue that as a result of technological changes making more jobs obsolete, a form of permanent universal social protection is needed. As people navigate from one type of activity to another more quickly than in the past (training, paid job, caring, career breaks), a form of safety net to fall back on could offer a better solution than the current complex mix of contributory and means-tested benefits. The rise of the robots has also sparked debate about who would benefit from the fruits of their activity, if they replaced human employees (as robots would not need an income) – this raises an old issue about private versus public ownership of natural (and now artificial) resources. In this modern context, the ideas of universal basic income, universal basic assets and universal basic services, albeit not new, have resurfaced with renewed popular traction.

5.1 A universal basic income

The general idea of a basic income is fairly simple. Under a universal basic income (UBI) each citizen receives a regular income payment from government, regardless of their financial, employment or family situation. UBI is usually tied to citizenship of a country, but could also extend to regular residents. Different versions of this idea vary according to the size of the income payment, as well as the regularity of the payment (Van Parijs, 1997; White, 2003; Standing, 2011; Olin Wright, 2015).

Supporters of a UBI argue that it provides a guaranteed minimum income and so a basic safety net for all individuals. It would be a spur to entrepreneurship too, they argue, as a regular and stable income would allow people to take entrepreneurial risks knowing that they have some income to fall back on. It would also be simple to administer and might be used to streamline the provision of other benefits. As the basic income is universal, recipients may not experience the stigma that may be provoked by having to apply for means-tested benefits.

Despite a renewed attention in current debates, the UBI idea is quite old and can be traced back to writings of the eighteenth-century radical Thomas Paine, in his pamphlet *Agrarian Justice* (Paine, 1795). Paine's ideas are based on a theory of natural justice about how to share resources provided by nature (and some human intervention in the form of exploitation of land and mineral extraction). He argues that the earth in its original state, before the development of modern civilisation, was the property of all, and that private property emerged as a way to ensure the cultivation of the earth from its natural state to the modern world. In a nutshell, people would only be incentivised to cultivate natural resources if there was a possibility to benefit from it privately – to 'claim' the profit for themselves. This is the essence of capitalist systems. However, the downside of this is that private ownership excludes those who lack property from claiming any natural resources, and so deprives them of their natural inheritance. Paine argues that justice demands that those who don't have property should be compensated for the loss of their natural inheritance.

Thomas Paine conceived the idea of a universal basic income in the eighteenth century

Paine (1795) concludes that a tax should be placed on natural resources and this should be used to provide all adults a capital grant (a lump sum) and a regular income. He proposes that everyone should receive (in eighteenth-century money) £15 once they reach 21 years of age. Furthermore, he says that people should have an annual income of £10 on reaching 50 years of age. These amounts correspond to about £1920 and £1280 in today's money, respectively (Morley, 2018). This would be three times lower than the current minimum Income Support offered in the UK, perhaps reflecting different conceptions of minimum incomes at the time. In modern times, the rise in income and wealth inequality, tensions between the role of the state and markets, and technological changes, have fuelled renewed debates about introducing some form of universal income, as the extract in Box 10.2 argues.

Box 10.2 Technology, wealth and a basic income

Change is always disruptive but the upheaval likely as a result of the next wave of automation will be especially marked. Driverless cars, for instance, are possible because intelligent machines can sense and have conversations with each other. They can do things – or will eventually be able to do things – that were once the exclusive preserve of humans. That means higher growth but also the risk that the owners of the machines get richer and richer while those displaced get angrier and angrier ...

But there are going to be middle-class casualties too: machines can replace radiologists, lawyers and journalists just as they have already replaced bank cashiers and will soon be replacing lorry drivers ...

New models of ownership are needed to ensure that the dividends of automation are broadly shared. One [suggestion] is a citizens' wealth fund that would own a broad portfolio of assets on behalf of the public and would pay out a universal capital dividend. This could be financed either from the proceeds of asset sales or by companies paying corporation tax in the form of shares that would become more valuable due to the higher profits generated by automation.

But the dislocation will be considerable, and comes at a time when social fabrics are already frayed. To ensure that, as in the past, technological change leads to a net increase in jobs, the benefits will have to be spread around and the concept of what constitutes work rethought ... the case for a universal basic income, an idea that has its critics on both left and right, but whose time may well have come.

(Elliott, 2018)

In the extract in Box 10.2, Larry Elliott claims that technological change will affect all types of jobs. The effect of robots will not simply be on low- or semi-skilled jobs, but will also affect professions such as lawyers and journalists. He claims that automation will result in higher growth, but that the proceeds of that growth will have to be shared out more equally, to protect those jobs and employment opportunities that are displaced by automation, for example in the form of a UBI. Elliott also mentions a universal capital dividend – an idea explored further in Section 5.3 of this chapter.

Activity 10.6 Automation and jobs

Allow 10 minutes for this activity.

Think about what you have just read in Box 10.2. Do you think that automation will necessarily displace jobs or replace the need for humans to work altogether? Jot down a few thoughts both for and against this particular claim.

Comment

One argument against this claim might draw up examples from economic history. Technological change is not a new thing and has arguably always been a part of human society. For example, since the eighteenth century, there have been a range of technological changes that have included the invention of the steam engine, weaving looms in textile mills, and the introduction of the modern computer. All of these have been disruptive technologies, displacing jobs. There have also been fears that technology would undermine work. The Luddites, during the nineteenth century, took to smashing machinery as they feared it would take their jobs. However, although the world of work was transformed by these changes, and jobs now require different skills, it has not disappeared. So the present wave of automation is not different to what has happened in the past. There may well be strong reasons for a UBI, but these do not necessarily have to be linked to technological change affecting work (Van Parijs, 1997; White, 2003). What would be needed though, is a way to reduce the immediate effects of disruption when people need to retrain in the face of new technology, so a UBI could be one way of smoothing that disruption.

The basic income idea attracts criticism as well as support. The following extract from a letter to *The Guardian* newspaper in 2016 highlights some of these concerns. In it, Professor Ian Gough comments on recent plans for a UBI in the UK:

> The underlying belief or dream is that basic income will provide a mobilising theme to bring about radical change ... Similar proposals have been made every few years for the last 50 years and they have got nowhere. The problem is that it combines a radical vision with a naive or insouciant view of politics ... I fear that this latest plan will drain the energies of the left in social policy and will divert attention from so many other worthwhile policy alternatives: the living wage, boosting trade unionism, free childcare, radical changes in housing policy, policies to reduce working time to limit turbo-consumption, green investment and so on.

> (Gough, 2016)

Activity 10.7 Criticisms of a basic income

Allow 10 minutes for this activity.

What are the different criticisms made in Gough's letter about a UBI?

Comment

One criticism is pragmatic. Gough observes that similar proposals have been made for about 50 years with little sign of success, highlighting a naive view of politics in the minds of supporters of UBI. The second piece of criticism is more fundamental: even if a UBI was feasible, it might not be desirable. This highlights the view that economics is concerned with how best to allocate scarce resources to meet a potentially limitless set of competing demands. This criticism refers to the idea of the opportunity cost of this policy, although the opportunity cost here applies at the national level. Gough claims that any public money spent on a UBI may be better spent on other uses, such as free childcare and housing provision.

5.2 From basic income to universal services

Like any cash benefit from the state – and UBI is essentially another form of cash benefit – there are trade-offs that cannot be avoided. The main disadvantage of providing a decent level of basic income is its huge cost, the financing of which would require much higher levels of taxation. As you may recall from Chapter 2, if social security benefits are not generous enough, they won't be able to meet the needs of many people if they cannot find suitable employment, thereby creating poverty traps. However, if the level is raised to provide for a decent standard of living, the cost to the state may be prohibitive, and if the amount is sufficient to live on, it can also reduce the incentive for people to work (Martinelli, 2017).

Another issue for critics of a UBI is that people have different needs and so need different levels of support, for example to cope with a disability. Therefore these critics argue that UBI should not replace all types of cash benefits.

More fundamentally, money may not be the best way of helping people: some needs may only be satisfied if adequate services are provided, and these might not exist in sufficient quantity or quality for different reasons, as we have seen in the previous chapters on insurance and care. Therefore direct provision of services might be a more effective way of delivering financial security for a series of aspects of life.

Universal basic services already exist in many countries, chiefly with respect to school education, which is often free at the point of use, and tax-funded in most countries. Some countries like the UK have universal public healthcare services free at the point of use (and most European countries have variants of a universal public healthcare service). Access to justice and policing are also forms of universal services developed in most countries to guarantee personal safety, although the former is not always 'free'.

These services could be extended to other essential aspects of life, such as transport, food and shelter, but also communications. For example, the Social Prosperity Network (2017), based at University College London (UCL), argues that such services would allow people not only to be safe (physically, mentally and financially), but also to participate actively in society and face a level playing field in fulfilling their opportunities in life.

Free bus transport everywhere, for everyone?

Others have argued that perhaps the most pressing need to extend universal provision is for childcare and long-term care services, as discussed in Chapter 9, as they are a major part of the public services currently inadequately provided in most countries (De Henau et al., 2016; Lansley et al., 2018). Similarly, cases for universal energy provision could be made, not just for those benefiting from social housing, as in the UCL proposal.

Ultimately it becomes a discussion about achieving an adequate balance between private and public ownership and operation of services for the population, with tensions between criteria such as:

- choice (individual preferences differ)

- accessibility (ability to pay and equal opportunities to participate)

- quality (attractiveness of the service and delivering adequate outcomes)

- sustainability (enough resources to keep the service going, without depleting other domains, including the environment).

5.3 Capitalism under public ownership: sovereign wealth funds

Perhaps the most compelling argument in favour of universal services or income, as alluded to in the extract in Box 10.2, and directly based on the ideas of Paine (1795), is about sharing the legitimate ownership of resources. For Paine, natural resources belong to everyone, as we all live on the same planet. In a more modern argument, as technological advances have been obtained by the cumulative effort and discoveries of a multitude of agents (building on each other's knowledge), no one can really claim full ownership of artificial intelligence technology – even if they do in practice. After all, even Google – the epitome of current technological innovations – has a motto for its search engine of academic journal articles (Google Scholar) that reads 'Stand on the shoulders of giants', after Isaac Newton's famous quote: 'If I have seen further it is by standing on the shoulders of giants' (Newton, 1676).

Universal income and services could be seen as a form of economic justice. If robots can be used to produce economic growth with a much reduced workforce, then it is important for the proceeds of such growth to be shared around, otherwise there will be sharp divides between those who own the machines and those who don't. This echoes a distinction made by some political economists, such as Karl Marx and John Maynard Keynes, that key differences in the economy are between those who do or do not own wealth. This raises the question of ownership of the fruits of human activity and natural-resource exploitation.

Taxation is a form of redistribution of the proceeds of growth, and thus sharing of ownership, via state intervention. Profits made by companies (which are the source of income for their shareholders) are taxed and redistributed to the population according to needs and political priorities. Income from employment (of those able to contribute to the production of goods and services) is taxed too, redistributing resources between those who can work and those who can't (as discussed in Chapter 8). So, in this sense, the state offers a form of redistribution of ownership.

A more direct form of ownership, inspired by the ideas of Paine, was mentioned in the extract in Box 10.2: the idea of a capital dividend offered to everyone out of the proceeds of a 'citizen's wealth fund'. This essentially is the same as building a pot of savings that generates future income, exactly as you examined in Chapter 5 of *Personal Finance*. However, in this case, instead of building it privately and individually, it would be achieved at the national level, and owned by all citizens.

Sovereign wealth fund

A portfolio of investments derived from a country's reserves generated by budget and trade surpluses, including exports of natural resources, typically to benefit the country's economy and citizens now and in the future.

Many oil-rich countries (but not only them) have created **sovereign wealth funds** that reinvest the revenue generated by the exploitation of their mineral resources into a series of assets across the globe: a mixture of equities, bonds, property and cash (in the same way as individuals invest in portfolios, as described in Chapter 5). The government owns the assets on behalf of its citizens, although critics have argued that many states operate under opaque investment rules, as many are not democracies (such as the oil-rich Gulf states) and the benefits to the citizens are not well-known (apart from investing in infrastructure locally) (Lansley et al., 2018).

Norway's sovereign wealth fund is an example of a more transparent fund held by the government, in trust for perpetuity, on behalf of its citizens. In 2018 it held assets in about 9000 companies across 72 different countries (Norges Bank Investment Management, 2018). It is also the largest sovereign wealth fund in value, of the 50-plus countries who have created one, followed by those of China, Abu Dhabi, Kuwait and Saudi Arabia (Sovereign Wealth Fund Institute, 2018).

Norway's oil-rich resources are reinvested for future generations

Part of the income generated by a sovereign wealth fund can in turn be used as a regular dividend income (such as the Alaska Permanent Fund), or for building a country's reserves to pay future income to its population. Norway's fund is built out of revenue from the country's oil reserves, to guarantee future revenue for public spending (for when oil resources are depleted, or if oil as a source of energy is made obsolete by new technologies).

Sovereign wealth funds could also be used to complement tax-funded services. For example, Lansley et al. (2018) have suggested a UK-based Social Wealth Fund made up of a 'Citizen's Dividend Fund' that would redistribute a universal income (similar to that of Alaska), a 'Social Care Trust Fund' that would provide free universal adult social care, and a series of 'Urban Land Trust Funds' aimed at developing local land for building social housing (Lansley et al., 2018).

The idea of a sovereign wealth fund is said to be an intermediate form of wealth ownership within a capitalist system. It sits between a model of state-owned industries, typical of the post-war era before the 1980s, and a model of private ownership, typical of the nineteenth century capitalism or the post-1970s liberalisation decades, which led to huge wealth inequalities and reduced economic performance (Lansley et al., 2018; OECD, 2015). Although still subject to similar risks that individuals face with their own investments, the sheer scale of sovereign wealth funds and their well-diversified portfolios not only reduces risk more effectively on behalf of all citizens, but also in effect provides every citizen access to wealth ownership and thus 'a say', equally afforded, in the running of private companies (even though they would have a very indirect 'say').

Activity 10.8 Financial capability of the future

Allow 15 minutes for this activity.

Thinking about yourself, but also about future generations and the system in place in your country, to what extent do you think any of these solutions and systems to provide social protection and financial security could gain traction, and why?

Comment

Well, this is a tough question to finish this book with! It is a bit rhetorical, but hopefully it will spark some interesting discussions between you and your friends and relatives.

Personal Finance started with the premise that financial risk has shifted from the state to the individual, and most chapters have looked at methods, tools and principles concerned with dealing with your personal finances in this context. Yet, in this chapter, we have opened up the possibility for rethinking the scope of personal finance by changing the context to different models of social protection and financial ownership.

It has probably occurred to you that political traction will depend on the degree to which interests of the population are best served by one system or another, and this will itself depend on whether people look for immediate benefits or consider longer-term implications too. For example, throughout the chapters we have seen that behavioural traits explain a lot of discrepancies between what would be an ideal route to follow and what is favoured in reality.

As you can see from this and the previous sections, different strategies have been deployed in different countries over different periods to try and address how to best deliver social protection, both now and for the future. Most social protection systems adopt a mix of cash transfers, public services, market provision, family support and obligations. They find funding through revenue generated by taxation or by investments in private companies through sovereign wealth funds. All of these aspects have different implications for personal finance and for the type of financial capabilities individuals require to secure their living standards. Economic principles can be used to examine the trade-offs between them.

6 Conclusion

This chapter has looked at the wider context in which personal financial decisions are made. It suggests that people and households make financial decisions essentially to achieve financial well-being – a part of overall well-being.

Financial capability is important for helping people make financial decisions. It can be shaped by different social and economic contexts, and this chapter has looked at particular systems of providing financial security via the family, the market and the state, and their extension in the form of universal income and universal services.

This chapter has concluded with discussions at the core of economics – how to allocate scarce resources within a society. For example, the discussion of Thomas Paine's (1795) ideas about a basic income and basic capital are based on a theory of natural justice. This theory touches upon key issues that are important for financial decisions and financial well-being; namely, if people and households are to accumulate material resources to satisfy goals now and in the future, where do such resources come from? Is anyone entitled to own resources or should these be restricted to some citizens or residents? And who can be seen as the deserving beneficiary of wealth creation? This leads into a discussion of private property and its more collective alternatives. Paine invokes an idea of common ownership of the earth to justify paying people a capital grant and a basic income, raising the question of the extent of the role of collective or social forms of ownership, as well as private.

These questions all have direct implications for personal finance, including your own, and will hopefully spark interesting discussions. Additionally, the economics and politics explaining the mechanisms behind these issues map out further areas for study or research.

Indeed, we very much hope that reading *Personal Finance* has offered you as many answers – which contribute to improving your skills and knowledge for managing your own personal finances (including its economic underpinnings) – as it has provoked new and exciting questions for you to explore.

References

Arts, W. and Gelissen, J. (2002) 'Three worlds of welfare capitalism or more? A state-of-the-art report', *Journal of European Social Policy*, vol. 20, no. 2, pp. 137–58.

Beshears, J., Choi, J. J., Laibson, D., Madrian, B. C. and Milkman, K. L. (2015) 'The effect of providing peer information on retirement savings behavior', *Journal of Finance*, vol. 70, no. 3, pp. 1161–1201.

Brüggen, E. C., Hogreve, J., Holmlund, M., Kabadayi, S. and Löfgren, M. (2017) 'Financial well-being: a conceptualization and research agenda', *Journal of Business Research*, vol. 79, pp. 228–37.

Crouch, C. (2008) 'What will follow the demise of privatised Keynesianism?', *Political Quarterly*, vol. 79, no. 4, pp. 476–87.

Crouch, C. (2009) 'Privatised Keynesianism: an unacknowledged policy regime', *British Journal of Politics and International Relations*, vol. 11, no. 3, pp. 382–99.

De Henau, J., Himmelweit, S., Lapniewska, Z. and Perrons, D. (2016) 'Investing in the Care Economy. A gender analysis of employment stimulus in seven OECD countries', *Women's Budget Group Report to the International Trade Union Confederation*, Brussels, March [Online]. Available at http://www.ituc-csi.org/IMG/pdf/care_economy_en.pdf (Accessed 20 May 2018).

Elliott, L. (2018) 'Robots will take our jobs. We'd better plan now, before it's too late', *The Guardian*, 1 February [Online]. Available at https://www.theguardian.com/commentisfree/2018/feb/01/robots-take-our-jobs-amazon-go-seattle (Accessed 2 February 2018).

Emmenegger, P., Kvist, J., Marx, P. and Petersen, K. (2015) 'Three Worlds of Welfare Capitalism: the making of a classic', *Journal of European Social Policy*, vol. 25, no. 1, pp. 3–13.

Esping-Andersen, G. (1990) *The Three Worlds of Welfare Capitalism*, Oxford, Polity.

Esping-Andersen, G. (1999) *Social Foundations of Postindustrial Economies*, Oxford, Oxford University Press.

Gough, I. (2016) 'Potential benefits and pitfalls of a universal basic income', *The Guardian*, 10 June [Online]. Available at http://www.theguardian.com/politics/2016/jun/10/potential-benefits-and-pitfalls-of-a-universal-basic-income (Accessed 22 January 2018).

Lansley, S., McCann, D. and Schifferes, S. (2018) *Remodelling Capitalism. How Social Wealth Funds Could Transform Britain*, May, Friends Provident Foundation, York [Online]. Available at http://www.friendsprovidentfoundation.org/wp-content/uploads/2018/05/Remodelling-Capitalism-Report-How-Social-Wealth-Funds-could-transform-Britain.pdf (Accessed 2 June 2018).

Lewis, J. (1992) 'Gender and the development of welfare regimes', *Journal of European Social Policy*, vol. 2, no. 3, pp. 159–73.

Martinelli, L. (2017) *The Fiscal and Distributional Implications of Alternative Universal Basic Income Schemes in the UK*, working paper, Institute for Policy Research, Bath [Online]. Available at http://www.bath.ac.uk/publications/the-fiscal-and-distributional-implications-of-alternative-universal-basic-income-schemes-in-the-uk/attachments/Basic_Income_Working_Paper.pdf (Accessed 3 May 2018).

The Money Advice Service (2015) *Financial Capability in the UK 2015. Initial Results from the 2015 UK Financial Capability Survey*, November, The Money Advice Service, London [Online]. Available at https://prismic-io.s3.amazonaws.com/fincap-two%2Fd08746d1-e667-4c9e-84ad-8539ce5c62e0_mas_fincap_uk_survey_2015_aw.pdf (Accessed 11 January 2018).

Morley, K. (2018) *Historical UK inflation rates and calculator* [Online]. Available at http://inflation.iamkate.com/ (Accessed 31 May 2018).

Newton, I. (1676) Letter from Sir Isaac Newton to Robert Hooke, Historical Society of Pennsylvania. The letter is dated 5 February, which is 15 February in the Gregorian calendar.

Norges Bank Investment Management (2018) 'Government Pension Fund Global' [Online]. Available at http://www.nbim.no/en/the-fund/ (Accessed 1 June 2018).

O'Donnell, N. and Keeney, M. (2010) 'Financial capability in Ireland and a comparison with the UK', *Public Money and Management*, vol. 30, no. 6, pp. 355–62.

OECD (2015) *In It Together: Why Less Inequality Benefits All*, OECD, Paris [Online]. Available at http://www.oecd.org/els/in-it-together-why-less-inequality-benefits-all-9789264235120-en.htm (Accessed 2 February 2018).

Olin Wright, E. (2015) 'Eroding Capitalism: a comment on Stuart White's "Basic Capital in the Egalitarian Toolkit"', *Journal of Applied Philosophy*, vol. 32, no. 4, pp. 432–39.

Paine, T. (1795) 'Agrarian justice', in Foot, M. and Kramnick, I. (eds) *The Thomas Paine Reader* (1987), London, Penguin.

Sainsbury, D. (ed.) (1994) *Gendering Welfare States*, London, Sage.

Social Prosperity Network (2017) *Social Prosperity for the Future: A Proposal for Universal Basic Services*, Institute for Global Prosperity, University College London, London [Online]. Available at http://www.ucl.ac.uk/bartlett/igp/sites/bartlett/files/universal_basic_services_-_the_institute_for_global_prosperity_.pdf (Accessed 22 January 2018).

Sovereign Wealth Fund Institute (2018) *Sovereign Wealth Fund Rankings* [Online]. Available at http://www.swfinstitute.org/sovereign-wealth-fund-rankings/ (Accessed 1 June 2018).

Standing, G. (2011) 'Responding to the crisis: economic stabilisation grants', *Policy and Politics*, vol. 39, no. 1, pp. 9–25.

Van Parijs, P. (1997) *Real Freedom for All: What (if anything) can justify capitalism?*, Oxford, Clarendon Press.

White, S. (2003) *The Civic Minimum: On the Rights and Obligations of Economic Citizenship*, Oxford, Oxford University Press.

To cite this chapter, use the following format in your reference list:

Prabhakar, R. (2019) 'Personal finance in context', in De Henau, J. and Lowe, J. (eds) *Personal Finance*, Milton Keynes, The Open University, pp. 445–490.

Glossary

Actuaries

Professionals who analyse risk and its financial impact.

Adverse selection

The tendency for people who have a greater than average chance of suffering an event to apply for insurance to a greater extent than other people.

Agency

Attempts to respond to, and influence, circumstances and the broader social and economic context.

Annual equivalent rate (AER)

The annual rate of interest on a savings product, calculated to take into account the frequency with which interest is added.

Annual percentage rate (APR)

A summary figure for comparing the cost of different debt products which reflects interest and other compulsory charges, as well as when and the frequency with which they are paid.

Asset allocation

The division of a savings and investment portfolio across cash deposits, bonds and equities.

Asymmetric information

Where one party to an arrangement knows something that another does not and which, had it been known, would have affected the terms of the agreement.

At-risk-of monetary poverty rate

Measure of the risk of falling into poverty when having too low an income. It is the proportion of households with an income below a threshold (called the poverty line), usually 60% of the median income of the population.

Availability bias

The tendency to give greatest weight to examples and events that are most easily recalled.

Average tax rate

Amount of tax due divided by taxable income, expressed as a percentage.

Balance sheet

A record at a particular point in time of what a household (or business) owns or has use of, and what it owes.

Basic bank account (BBA)

A bank account with reduced features.

Behavioural nudges

Indirect suggestions designed to change or influence a person's behaviour.

Behavioural trait

Psychological features that influence the way an individual processes information and makes a decision, and that reflect their bounded rationality.

Big Data

Very large sets of data, often sourced from online interactions and transactions, on which statistical analysis can reveal previously unmeasured associations, patterns, trends or behaviours.

Bond

A certificate of debt issued by a government or corporation to raise money.

Bounded rationality

Capacity for reasoned decision that is constrained by lack of time and the ability to process information.

Budgeting

The process of using a detailed plan of future income and expenditure to manage personal finances, and work towards achieving goals.

Capital gain

A rise in the market value of an asset to more than the price originally paid.

Capital loss

A fall in the market value of an asset to less than the price originally paid.

Capitalism

An economic and political system in which the factors necessary for the production and sale of goods and services (such as land, machines and patents) are controlled by private owners seeking profit, rather than by the state or the community.

Caring

Providing a personal service to help someone who is not capable of looking after their own personal needs, such as feeding or dressing them, helping them manage as independently as possible, and keeping them safe.

Cash flow statement

A record of income and spending over a certain past period of time.

Circular flow of income

A simple economic model illustrating the exchange of goods, services and money within the economy.

Classical economics

A school of economic thought developed in the late eighteenth to nineteenth centuries.

Compounding

The process by which interest is added to the original amount borrowed or saved, increasing the outstanding balance and so causing the next sum of interest to be higher.

Conspicuous consumption

The ostentatious display of wealth in order to gain recognition by others of one's assumed or actual high status.

Consumer society

A society in which people place a high value on possessions and are continually encouraged to buy more.

Consumer sovereignty

An assumption that consumers have the power to dictate the types, quality and quantity of the goods and services provided in a market place.

Consumption smoothing

Keeping expenditure relatively constant when there are variations in income, typically by use of borrowing, savings and/or insurance.

Cost averaging

Allocating a fixed sum for the regular purchase of particular investments. The fixed sum will buy more shares/units when prices fall although fewer when prices rise (so that the average price of shares/units bought is lower than the average price).

Covenant risk

The risk that a promise or contractual agreement made by one person or organisation to another will be broken.

Credit

An arrangement to receive cash, goods or services now and to pay for them in the future.

Credit reference agency

A business that specialises in gathering and selling to lenders data used to assess individuals' creditworthiness on the basis of their circumstances and past borrowing record.

Credit score

A rating based on financial information about an individual used to assess their creditworthiness, which affects how much they can borrow and on what terms.

Creditworthiness

A borrower's capacity to repay a loan or other credit.

Cross-subsidy

Using the money from goods or services bought by one group of customers to help pay for goods and services offered to other customers.

Crowding out

A squeezing out of consumption and/or investment opportunities for the private sector because of government spending.

Current account

A bank account that allows money to be deposited and paid out immediately by cash, card or electronically.

Current asset ratio

Total liquid assets as a proportion of short-term liabilities, giving an indication of liquidity.

Debt-to-income (DTI) ratio

The proportion of gross income that is absorbed by debt repayments.

Default option

Situation or option someone is left in/with, if they do not act to change it.

Defined benefit

Describes a pension scheme where the pension is worked out according to a formula, usually linked to pay (but sometimes just a fixed amount) and length of time in the scheme.

Defined contribution

Describes a pension scheme where the pension depends on the amount paid in, how the invested money grows and the amount of pension it can be converted to in retirement.

Deflation

A continual decrease in the general level of prices.

Demand

The quantity of a good or service that buyers wish to purchase over a specified period of time.

Demand curve

A line showing the quantity demanded of a good or service at each price, assuming that all other factors that influence demand are fixed.

Demography

The structure of a country's population taking account of factors such as age, sex and ethnicity.

Deposit insurance

A compulsory scheme that refunds depositors (up to a maximum amount) if their bank becomes unable to return their money.

Deregulation

Removal of state regulation, usually aimed at promoting competition, innovation and new entry.

Direct taxes

Taxes on income or profits payable by the person or organisation receiving them (in contrast to indirect taxes, which apply to spending).

Disposable income

Also called 'net income'. Income after income tax and social security contributions have been deducted from gross income.

Diversification

A strategy that aims to manage market risk by combining a variety of investments, such as shares and bonds, that are unlikely all to move in the same direction at the same time.

Drawdown

Taking retirement income direct from a fund of investments whose value may rise and fall.

Economies of scale in consumption

A decrease in the cost per person of maintaining a given (material) standard of living, as the size of a household increases.

Emerging countries (or economies)

Countries that are getting richer by emerging from economic isolation and/or newly industrialising (also called 'developing countries').

Equilibrium price

The price at which the planned quantity demanded is equal to the planned quantity supplied.

Equity

The market value of a property, less the outstanding mortgage debt secured against it.

Equity release scheme

A way of unlocking the wealth tied up in a home while continuing to live there, either by borrowing using a mortgage or selling part or all of the home to a specialist firm.

Equivalised household income

A household's actual (usually disposable) income adjusted to take account of household size and composition, to enable comparison of different households' (material) standards of living.

Fertility rate

The average number of children (live births) per woman.

Financial capability

The knowledge, skills, attitudes and behaviours that mean people manage money well, both day-to-day and through significant life events, and can handle periods of financial difficulty.

Financial exclusion

Inability to obtain necessary products and services from financial providers in an appropriate form or at an affordable price.

Financial resilience

The ability to cope financially with life events or quickly return to the pre-event financial situation.

Financial services

The part of the economy that delivers financial products, including banking and insurance.

Friendly societies

Membership organisations where, in return for regular small payments, members could claim financial support if unable to work due to, say, illness or old age. Some still exist today.

Funded

In the context of pensions, describes a pension scheme where an investment fund is built up from which to pay future pensions.

Global financial crisis

An event that started in the US mortgage market and rapidly brought the international banking sector to the brink of collapse, averted only by governments spending billions on 'bailing out' the banks.

Great Depression

A period of falling or stagnant economic activity and high unemployment in the US and many other countries during the 1930s.

Gross domestic product (GDP)

The monetary value of everything produced within a country, in a specified period (usually a year).

Gross income

Original income from employment and investments plus cash transfers (benefits) from the state, but before any deduction in the form of income tax and social security contributions.

Heuristics

Mental short cuts used to guide someone in the direction of probable solutions to a problem, while minimising mental effort.

Household consumption

A term used by economists to describe total spending on goods and services by all the households living in a particular country or economy (as distinct from spending by an individual household).

Household equivalence scale

An adjustment to the incomes of households of different size and composition, so that their (material) standards of living can be compared.

Household saving ratio

Although measured in various ways, this is broadly the percentage of average annual household disposable income that is saved.

Human capital

The value of your skills, experience and education that allows you to sell a service as labour in exchange for earnings.

Imputed income

The value of a service or benefit in kind provided by an employer, the government, or self-produced by a household, which is equivalent to having extra income since it increases living standards.

Income

Money *flows* received over a specified period of time.

Independent events

Where one event occurring does not affect the probability of the other(s) occurring.

Industrialised countries (or economies)

Countries with relatively high incomes per inhabitant and mature industrial structures (also called 'developed countries').

Inflation

A continual increase in the level of prices.

Insurance

A system by which individuals or households, in exchange for payment of a sum of money (called the 'premium'), are promised compensation for losses or costs incurred due to events specified in a contract.

Interest

The charge a borrower pays for the use of someone else's money; also the reward a saver gets for allowing their money to be used by someone else.

Interest-only loan

A loan whereby each regular payment pays the interest but the principal is left to be paid off in a single lump sum at the end of the term.

Interest-only mortgage

A mortgage where the periodic repayments relate solely to the interest due, and where the principal is paid off in full as a single lump sum at the end (or 'maturity') of the mortgage.

Investment fund

A financial product that invests in a broad range of different shares, bonds and/or other assets.

Labour market

The arena in which employers (who need labour) come together with employees (who supply their labour in exchange for pay) to decide on activities to perform (working hours and tasks) and rewards (pay).

Labour productivity

The amount of outputs (goods and services) produced by each unit of labour (for example, each hour worked).

Leverage

The act of borrowing to buy an asset. Also a measure of the total liabilities as a percentage of total assets, giving an indication of solvency.

Liability

An amount of money owed at a particular point in time.

Lifetime annuity

A type of insurance that guarantees a specified income payable for life in exchange for a lump sum payment.

Liquid assets

Those assets that can be quickly converted into a reliable, predictable sum of cash.

Liquidity

The ability to turn assets into ready money to finance immediate debt repayments and other expenditure.

Longevity

The length of an individual's life (usually measured in years).

Loss aversion

A tendency to give greater importance to avoiding losses than to making gains of the same size.

Marginal tax rate

Percentage of tax due on the last (highest or top) unit of income (e.g. last pound or euro).

Market equilibrium

A situation where the plans of both buyers and sellers are realised, so neither has an incentive to change their market behaviour.

Market timing

A technique of buying and selling shares in conjunction with the price fluctuations of the market.

Mean

The average of a set of values measured as the sum of all the observations divided by the number of observations.

Means-tested

Payments that are made only to those who are assessed to have a certain level of income or less, and in some cases a certain level of assets or less.

Median

The average of a set of values measured as the middle value when the set is arranged in order.

Mis-selling

Selling a product or service that is unnecessary or inappropriate for the buyer, and/or not fully explained to them.

Moral hazard

The tendency for an insured person to take on more risk because they are covered by insurance.

Mortgage

A loan secured against property or land.

Mutually exclusive

Describes two or more events that cannot occur together.

National Insurance contributions

A UK tax paid by both workers and employers that forms the basis for entitlement to a range of state benefits, including a state pension.

Negative equity

A situation where the outstanding mortgage debt secured on a property exceeds the market value of the property.

Net saving

Disposable (net) household income minus household expenditure.

Net worth

The difference between total assets and total liabilities.

Nominal value

The monetary or cash value of an item as it stands.

Non-dependent children

Children (or a child) who have reached a specified minimum age, are not in full-time education, and have no known partner or children.

Occupational pension scheme

Scheme arranged by an employer to provide pensions for its workers and towards which the employer normally makes a substantial financial contribution.

Old-age dependency ratio

The number of older people in a country divided by the number of people of working age. An indicator of the number of pensioners to be supported by each worker.

Ombudsman scheme

An alternative to going to court, for resolving disputes between consumers and firms. Typically free for consumers to use.

Opportunity cost

The cost of having (or doing) something, measured in terms of the best alternative that could have been had (or done) instead.

Original income

Also sometimes called 'market income'. Income from employment, savings and investment prior to any government intervention.

Other things being equal

From the Latin *ceteris paribus*, this term is used by economists and others to indicate that while changing one factor, other factors remain unchanged.

Owner-occupation

Form of tenure where the person living in a home owns it outright or is buying it with a mortgage.

Part-time pay penalty

The difference between the hourly wage rate that a person would receive in full-time employment and what they receive in a part-time job.

Pay As You Earn (PAYE)

A system that a UK employer or a pension provider uses to deduct income tax and National Insurance contributions before they pay the wages of employees or the pension of the beneficiaries.

Pay-As-You-Go (PAYG)

In the context of pensions, a pension scheme where pensions paid out today are paid for out of contributions or tax revenues collected today.

Pension

A regular payment that forms all or part of financial support in older age.

Pension systems

Arrangements designed to ensure that older people have some income to live on when they cease to have earnings from work.

Percentile

The value at any one of the points that divides a set of values into 100 equal parts when the set is arranged in order.

Personal pension scheme

Saving scheme designed to provide retirement income for one particular individual. The scheme may be arranged by the individual or by their employer.

Portfolio

A set of financial assets held by an individual (or a bank or other financial institution).

Poverty trap

A situation in which workless people cannot find a job that pays decent enough income, while the income that they receive from the state remains too low to escape the risk of poverty.

Price discrimination

Charging different people or groups a different price for the same, or similar, goods or services.

Principal

Also called 'capital'. The original amount of debt taken out; also the sum put into savings or an investment.

Private pension scheme

Refers to any non-state pension scheme, typically provided through employers or arranged by individuals themselves.

Probability

A measure of the chance that an event will occur.

Progressive tax system

A system of taxation that is characterised by an average tax rate that increases with taxable income. In other words, the higher a person's income, the greater the proportion taken away in tax.

Public good

A good or service that can be consumed simultaneously by different people, and from which each person can benefit, and cannot be excluded.

Real interest rate

An interest rate adjusted for inflation – lower than the nominal interest rate if prices are rising.

Real value

The nominal value adjusted for inflation to reflect the purchasing power of an item.

Reducing-balance loan (also called a repayment loan)

A loan whereby each regular repayment pays the interest and part of the principal. This reduces the amount owed and interest for each period is calculated on that reduced amount.

Renting

Form of tenure where the person living in a home is a tenant or lodger, paying rent to a landlord, who owns the property.

Repayment mortgage

A mortgage where the periodic repayments relate to the sum of the interest due and an amount of the principal (the original sum borrowed).

Retirement

Can mean the period of life after work ends, a life event that marks the end of working life or a process of gradually withdrawing from work.

Return

The actual or expected reward from saving or making an investment, which may comprise a flow of income and/or a profit or loss due to a change in the value of the investment.

Risk

Where the chance of something happening can be measured or estimated.

Risk-based pricing

Charging consumers a higher amount if the likelihood of their claiming (in the case of insurance) or defaulting (in the case of loans) is higher.

Risk pooling

Spreading the cost of some individuals suffering a financial loss across a large number of people who all contribute towards that cost.

Risk segmentation

Dividing the pool of consumers for a particular type of insurance into smaller sub-pools on the basis of characteristics that are thought to predict their risk of claiming.

Saving

The act of accumulating the part of income that is not spent on goods and services into savings or investment products.

Savings

The total value of all financial assets (including investments) that a household has at a particular point in time.

Secured debt

Type of borrowing, backed by an asset, such as a home, which the lender may seize if the debt is not repaid.

Self-insurance

Deciding to meet the financial challenge of some or all life events out of savings, income or other resources (for example, help from family members) rather than buying insurance.

Shares (or equities)

Type of investment that gives the investor part-ownership of a company.

Social class

An informal ranking of people in a society based on their income, occupation, education and other factors.

Social norms

Informal understandings and rules that govern the appropriate behaviour of members of a society or a group.

Social security contributions

Regular (mostly compulsory) payments made by people of working age to a social fund, used to provide them with certain cash benefits in case of accidental or planned loss of income (unemployment, illness, retirement).

Social status

A position within society, or the honour or prestige that a particular individual or group is accorded by other members of society.

Socio-demographic groups

Categories in which individuals may be placed, based on a range of social, demographic and economic factors, such as age, gender, family type, income, occupation and ethnicity.

Solvency

The ability to repay all debts, typically shown by assets exceeding liabilities.

Sovereign wealth fund

Portfolio of investments derived from a country's reserves generated by budget and trade surpluses, including exports of natural resources, typically to benefit the country's economy and citizens now and in the future.

Standard of living

The material, mental, physical and social quality of life enjoyed by an individual or household, depending on factors such as income, housing conditions, the environment and public services such as health and education.

State pension scheme

A system of pensions provided by the government to everyone who qualifies.

Status symbol

Something that indicates the social standing of its owner. Usually a mark of high or superior standing.

Subsidy

Money paid to reduce the purchase price of a product or service.

Supply

The quantity of a good or service that sellers wish to sell over a specified period of time.

Supply curve

A line showing the quantity supplied of a good or service at each price, assuming that all other factors that influence supply are fixed.

Symbolic consumption

Consuming products or lifestyles for the social meanings attached to them, and for others to see.

Tenure

The way in which a property is occupied, for example as an owner or as a tenant who is renting.

Term

The period of time over which a debt is to be repaid; also the period of time over which money is saved or invested.

Term accounts

Savings products paying a fixed rate of interest over a period of years during which money cannot be withdrawn without penalty.

Third-party products

Items sold or distributed by one company but supplied by another (the third party).

Total dependency ratio

Children (aged 0 to, say, 19) and older people (aged, say, 65 and over) as a proportion of the working population (for example, those aged 20 to 64).

Trade-off

A sacrifice of something in order to have (more of) something else.

Uncertainty

Where the chance of something happening cannot be measured or estimated.

Unemployment trap

A situation in which people looking for jobs cannot find any that pay better income than that they get when unemployed.

Universal basic income

A regular payment made to all citizens or residents of a country, irrespective of their financial, employment or family situation.

Unsecured debt

Type of borrowing not backed by any asset.

Unpaid work

Unpaid activity that contributes to the well-being of people, and would otherwise have to be paid for. It includes looking after a household and caring for people, as well as voluntary work in the community.

Wealth, or assets

The *stock* of everything that a person owns at a given point in time that has a monetary value (for example, property, investments and cash).

Welfare state

A system where the state funds or provides public services and redistributes income and wealth to provide social protection to its citizens.

Working age

The age range within which people are assumed to be available for work.

Write-off

In the context of insurance, a damaged car, motorbike or other vehicle that insurers decide to pay an agreed value for rather than paying for the cost of repairs.

Acknowledgements

Every effort has been made to contact copyright holders. If any have been inadvertently overlooked the publishers will be pleased to make the necessary arrangements at the first opportunity.

Grateful acknowledgement is made to the following sources:

Cover image
© The Open University/Nic Morris with permission of the Bank of England.

Chapter 1

Photographs, figures and cartoons:

Image (Section 2.2) © Spencer Grant/Getty Images; Image (Section 2.4) © curraheeshutter/iStock/Getty Images Plus; Image (Section 2.5) © Jose Luis Pelaez Inc/iStock/Getty Images Plus; Images (Section 3.1), clockwise, left to right: © DGLimages/iStock/Getty Images Plus; © Dan Gair/Getty Images; © Caron Badkin/Shutterstock.com; © piranka/iStock/Getty Images Plus; Image (Section 4.2) © Janet Kimber/Getty Images; Image (Section 5.1) © Raquel Maria Carbonell Pagola/Getty Images.

Text:

Activity 1.3 questions: OECD (2017), *G20/OECD INFE report on adult financial literacy in G20 countries*, http://www.oecd.org/daf/fin/financial-education/G20-OECD-INFE-report-adult-financial-literacy-in-G20-countries.pdf

Chapter 2

Photographs, figures and cartoons:

Images in Section 2: (a) AF archive/Alamy Stock Photo, (b) Hoxton/Chris Ryan/iStock/Getty Images Plus, (c) Aaron Hawkins. This file is licensed under the Creative Commons Attribution-No Derivatives Licence http://creativecommons.org/licenses/by-nd/2.0/, (d) adventtr/iStock/Getty Images Plus; Figure 2.1: adapted from 'Global Wage Report 2014-15', International Labour Office. Copyright © International Labour Organization 2015; Figure 2.2: taken from Annual Survey of Hours and Earnings (2016, provisional – ONS).

Chapter 4

Photographs, figures and cartoons:

Image (young man with computer): Norma Jean Gargasz/Alamy Stock Photo; Image (credit cards): Slim Plantagenate/Alamy Stock Photo; Image (photo of cars): Justin Kase zsixz/Alamy Stock Photo; Image (three gold balls): Peter Atkinson/Alamy Stock Photo; Image (man with music system): 81a/Photolibrary/Getty Images; Figure 4.2: Adapted from Bernanke, B. S. (2015), 'Why are interest rates so low?', 30th March 2015, Brookings, Copyright © 2018 The Brookings Institution.

Chapter 5

Photographs, figures and cartoons:

Figure 5.3: taken from Department of Posts, Ministry of Communications, Government of India, www.indiapost.gov.in; Image in Figure 5.3: Tim Gainey/Alamy Stock Photo; Image (Franco Modigliani): Bachrach/Contributor/Getty Images; Image (brokers in action): © Dragonimages | Dreamstime.com; Image (peer-to-peer lending): age fotostock/Alamy Stock Photo; Image (polluted water): Dennis Cox/Alamy Stock Photo.

Chapter 6

Photographs, figures and cartoons:

Images of houses, clockwise, left to right: © Tyler Lowmiller; David Burrows/Shutterstock; Volodymyr Kyrylyuk/Shutterstock; James Clarke/Shutterstock; Image (moving house) Caiaimage/Paul Bradbury/Getty Images; Figure 6.1: data taken from 'Distribution of population by tenure status, type of household and income group – EU-SILC survey'. Copyright © Eurostat Database 2017; Image (properties for sale): Chris Ratcliffe/Bloomberg/Getty Images; Figure 6.2: adapted from Cribb, J. et al (2016), 'The Economic Circumstances of Different Generations: The Latest Picture', The Institute for Fiscal Studies. Copyright © 2016 Institute for Fiscal Studies.

Text:

Box 6.1: Collinson, P. (2017) 'Taylor Wimpey to pay up to £130m to settle ground rent scandal', *The Guardian,* 27 April 2017. Guardian News & Media Ltd.

Chapter 7

Photographs, figures and cartoons:

Image (Section 2): barmixmaster/iStock/Getty Images Plus; Image (Section 3.1): Copyright © Nick Keppol. This image is licensed under the Creative Commons Attribution Licence http://creativecommons. org/licenses/by/2.0/; Image (Section 3.5, subsection: Protection-only life insurance): Tyler Olson/123 Royalty Free; Image (Section 3.5, subsection: Private medical insurance): © Richard Chivers-VIEW/ Alamy Stock Photo; Illustration (Section 4.2): © National Trust Images/John Hammond; Image (Section 5.2): bernie_photo/iStock/ Getty Images Plus; Image (Section 5.2, subsection: Probability of two events both happening): Yvan Duube/iStock/Getty Images Plus; Image (Section 6.1): © NikomMaelao Production/Shutterstock.

Chapter 8

Photographs, figures and cartoons:

Cartoon (Section 2): Tim Cordell/www.CartoonStock.com; Image (Section 3): Agencja Fotograficzna Caro/Alamy Stock Photo; Image (Section 3.2): © Clynt Garnham/Alamy Stock Photo; Image (Section 4.4, subsection: Risks for a funded defined benefit scheme): © Cultura Creative (RF)/Alamy Stock Photo; Cartoon (Section 5.3, subsection: Ageing populations and PAYG systems): Tim Cordell/ Cartoonstock; Figure 8.8 (Section 5.3, subsection: PAYG versus funded systems): Kazuhiro Yokozeki.

Chapter 9

Photographs, figures and cartoons:

Images (Section 1, Introduction): left image: © Lalo de Almeida/ New York Times, right image: Nik Wheeler/Alamy Stock Photo; Images (Section 2, examples of self-production): top left image: BlueOrange Studio/Shutterstock, top right image: Anna Anisimova/ Shutterstock, bottom image: Michele Burgess/Alamy Stock Photo;

Images (Section 2.2): left image: Alena Ozerova/Shutterstock, right image: Monkey Business Images/Shutterstock; Figure 9.2 (Section 3): Adapted from United Nations, (2015), 'The World's Women 2015'. Copyright © United Nations; Image (Section 3, black and white photograph): ClassicStock/Alamy Stock Photo; Image (Section 4.1): artsilense/Alamy Stock Photo; Image (Section 5): David Grossman/Alamy Stock Photo; Image (Section 6.1): lemonade/Alamy Stock Photo.

Chapter 10

Photographs, figures and cartoons:

Image (Section 1, Introduction): Rawpixel.com/Shutterstock; Image (Section 3): Richard Thomas/123RF; Illustration (Section 3.1): Morphart Creation/Shutterstock; Figure 10.2 (Section 3.2): Adapted from 'Financial Capability in the UK 2015', November 2015, Money Advice Service. Copyright © 2015 Money Advice Service; Image (Section 4.3): Peter Bernik/123RF; Image (Section 4.4): theodore liasi/Alamy Stock Photo; Image (Section 5): Phonlamai Photo/Shutterstock; Image (Section 5.1): Philip Bird LRPS CPAGB/Shutterstock; Image (Section 5.2): John Morrison/Alamy Stock Photo; Image (Section 5.3): BuzzB/Alamy Stock Photo.

Text:

Box 10.2 (Section 5.1): Elliott, L. (2018), 'Robots will take our jobs. We'd better plan now before it's too late', *The Guardian*, 1 February 2018. Copyright © 2018 Guardian News & Media Ltd; Extract from Professor Ian Gough article (Section 5.1): Gough, I. (2016), 'Potential benefits and pitfalls of a universal basic income', *The Guardian* [online]. Copyright Guardian News & Media Ltd, 2018.

Index

size of households, equivalence scales 141, 142
skills
    and financial capability 458, 469
    loss of and part-time work 412–13
    and pay differentials 79–80, 81
Slater and Gordon, maternity/pregnancy
  discrimination in the workplace 415
Slovenia
    house-price-to-income ratio 272
    housing tenure 258
social assistance, long-term care systems 431
social care 77, 93
social change 11
social cohesion, and income inequality 68
social democratic welfare regimes 461, 462, 463,
  464
social exclusion 133
social housing 256, 259, 263–5
social influences on consumption 118–26
social insurance 16, 302, 316, 336, 471
    long-term care systems 431, 433
social media
    advertising 125–6
    and Big Data 166
social movements, and financial capability 460
social norms
    and household money management system 145
    on spending patterns 133
social (peer-to-peer) lending 21, 219, 228–9
Social Prosperity Network 481–2
social protection 450, 486
    expenditure on 115
    and income tax 89–99
    role of the family in 465–6
    role of the market in 465,
      466–70, 475
    role of the state in 465, 471–4
    three models of welfare capitalism 460–5
    see also state benefits; universal basic
      income (UBI)
social relationships, and well-being 69
social rights, and the state 471
social security benefits *see* state benefits
social security contributions 87
    and benefits 98
    in different countries 88–9
    and disposable income 72

social status 118–19
    displays of 119–20
socially responsible saving 238–40
solar energy 23
Solomon, M. R. 136
solvency problems 185–8
    current asset ratio 186–7
    leverage 187
    technical insolvency 186
South Africa
    ageing population data 368, 371
    fertility rates 14
southern Europe, long-term care provision 434–5
sovereign wealth funds 483–5
Spain
    childcare provision 428
    employment patterns for couples with children
      408
    house-price-to-income ratio 272
    household saving rates 208, 209
    housing tenure 258
    income tax 90
    long-term care provision 434
    maternity leave 413
    welfare regime 461
staircasing 270
standard of living *see* living standards
standard variable-rate mortgages 268
Standing, G. 449, 468–9
state agencies 32
state benefits 59, 93–7
    cash payments 87, 93
    child benefit 419
    and childcare 401
    contributory 96
    in different welfare regimes 461
    and employers 94–5
    for families 143
    financing 15–16
    flat-rate payments 94, 95–6
    importance to personal finance 88
    income from 63, 64
      in cash flow statements 98
    and income inequalities 74
    income-related payments 95–6
    and insurance 311, 336
    in kind 93
    means-tested 96–7, 336, 402, 461, 462, 463